TRADITION & TRANSITION

Studies in
Anabaptist and Mennonite History
No. 31

TRADITION & TRANSITION

Amish Mennonites and Old Order Amish
1800-1900

Paton Yoder

Studies in Anabaptist and Mennonite History

Edited by Cornelius J. Dyck, Leonard Gross, Leland Harder, Albert N. Keim, Walter Klaassen, John S. Oyer, Editor-in-Chief Theron F. Schlabach, and John H. Yoder.

Published by Herald Press, Scottdale, Pennsylvania, and Waterloo, Ontario, in cooperation with Mennonite Historical Society, Goshen, Indiana. The Society is primarily responsible for the content of studies, and Herald Press for their publication.

°*Out of print but available in microfilm or photocopies.*

TRADITION & TRANSITION

Amish Mennonites and Old Order Amish
1800-1900

Paton Yoder

Foreword by Donald B. Kraybill

Wipf and Stock Publishers
150 West Broadway • Eugene OR 97401
2001

Tradition and Transition

By Yoder, Paton
Copyright©1991 by Herald Press
ISBN: 1-57910-468-1

Reprinted by *Wipf and Stock Publishers*
150 West Broadway • Eugene OR 97401

Previously published by Herald Press, 1991.

To Jill and Alev
Gary and Erin
Karla and Karen
Karl and Ben
Michael and Shaunti
Tammy and Jessica
Lesley
Who call me Grandpa

Contents

Foreword

The ability of the Amish to preserve traditional ways in the face of modernization has given them a special place in American religious history. Indeed, the rapid growth of an Old Order culture in the midst of a modern, industrial twentieth century has been surprising.

Many treatments of the Old Order Amish abound. Most of them, however, briefly describe the European origins of the Amish, skip the nineteenth century, and then focus on the twentieth century. Paton Yoder has filled this gap by providing a carefully researched history of the Amish in the nineteenth century. By uncovering new primary source materials and collating them with known ones, Yoder has compiled a narrative history which takes us into the nineteenth-century world of the Amish. This era is typically overlooked by many Amish scholars, but it was a foundational one. It forged the identity and character of the Amish church in ways that have reached far into the twentieth century.

Yoder's work is organized into four basic areas. After an introductory overview, he describes the consolidation and gelling of Amish church life in the first half of the nineteenth century. Second, he outlines the polity, beliefs, and discipline—the ecclesiastical milieu—of the Amish at midcentury. He explains the evolution of the various titles and functions of ordained offices, as well as the practice of shunning and the practical implications of separation from the world. This is particularly significant because many of the congregational practices taking shape at this time became normative for the twentieth century.

Third and perhaps most important, Yoder describes the development of the Great Schism of 1865 that fractured the Amish community and led to an increasing division. The progressives eventually formed the Amish Mennonite church and merged with the Mennonite Church in the early twentieth century. Using newly discovered primary source documents, Yoder describes in considerable detail the sixteen annual Amish ministers' meetings that wrestled with the progressive–traditional tensions rupturing the Amish church at midcentury. The minutes of these meetings and their subsequent controversy provide moderns with a unique glimpse inside the Amish world and the Amish mind as it struggled with the early waves of modernity.

Finally, Yoder traces the subsequent journey of the two factions —the progressives or Amish Mennonites—as well as their conservative counterparts, who eventually became known as the Old Order Amish. An Old Order Mennonite historian has noted that a schism often gives license to both parties to move more quickly in their preferred directions. The progressives, unfettered by conservative forces, liberalize quickly. And the conservatives, no longer prodded by the liberals, dig their roots ever deeper into traditional bedrock. And so it was in the Great Schism described by Yoder.

The Amish Mennonites, no longer obstructed by conservative forces, moved rapidly toward mainstream Mennonites in the last quarter of the nineteenth century and eventually joined them. The conservatives—freed from the troublesome liberals—eventually became Old Order Amish. They clung more tenaciously than ever to traditional practices and by all means steered clear of the incipient worldliness emanating from the progressive Amish Mennonites.

The Great Schism, as Yoder calls it, had at least two major consequences. It crystallized the identity and character of the Old Order Amish in ways that would govern their cultural responses to modernity in the twentieth century. Moreover, it spurred a cultural migration of progressives toward the Mennonite Church. Indeed, Yoder contends that as many as half the members of the Mennonite Church can trace their roots back to the Amish. The book will be of interest to a wide variety of persons and especially to those interested in Amish studies. Modern Mennonites who, like Yoder, find their family trees leading back to the Amish, will find the story intriguing.

We are indebted to Yoder for opening a window into the Amish world of the nineteenth century. A window that allows us to see with new clarity and greater perspective the essentials of Anabaptist practice as they were taking shape in the new world. But more dramatically, *Tradition and Transition* allows us to listen in on the debate as a traditional religious minority enters its first round in a long struggle with the focus of modernity—a struggle that would intensify in the twentieth century.

The Great Schism was a crucial turning point. The great-grandchildren of those who said no to the overtures of modernity today read by lantern light, farm with horses, and shun high school. The great-grandchildren of the progressives have for many practical purposes merged with the mainstream of American life. The Great Schism, which Yoder so carefully describes, did make a difference!

—Donald B. Kraybill
Elizabethtown, Pennsylvania

Author's Preface

One day in June 1916 Noah Long, a trustee in the Clinton Frame Amish Mennonite church, went to the church house five miles east of Goshen, Indiana, with a ladder and some white paint. He climbed above the entrance to the sign, CLINTON FRAME AMISH MENNONITE CHURCH, and expunged the word *Amish.* A day or two before, the Indiana-Michigan Amish Mennonite Conference had decided to merge with the Indiana-Michigan Mennonite Conference. Noah had lost no time making the appropriate change in the name of the congregation. Most of Noah's fellow members in the congregation were agreeable to dropping *Amish* from the name of their church, although some of them murmured that he need not have acted with so much haste. The Western District and then the Eastern District of Amish Mennonites soon followed the lead of the Indiana-Michigan Amish Mennonites, joining with the Mennonites in organization and name.

In dropping *Amish* from their name, the Amish Mennonites had undoubtedly facilitated the merger, but at a price. Although constituting more than half of the union, the Amish Mennonites had unwittingly covered their tracks. So now I, and all other Mennonites with Amish Mennonite roots, find it necessary to uncover these tracks if we are to discover—or rediscover—our Amish and Amish Mennonite origins.

The Amish Mennonite church, the church from which so many Mennonites have come, had its origins in the nineteenth century as the progressive or change-minded branch of the Amish church. The conservative branch in that division eventually came to be called Old Order Amish. Unlike the Amish Mennonites, the identity of these Old Order Amish has never been obscured. The principal purpose of this account is to tell the story of this division (I call it the Great Schism) and of the subsequent histories of the two branches to 1900. Hopefully, I will alert many Mennonites to their Amish roots—persons named Beiler, Detweiler, Hershberger, Hostetler, Hertzler, Kauffman, Kurtz, Lapp, Plank, Stutzman, Smucker, Stoltzfus, Yoder, Zook, and others. For the Old Order Amish, whose name and lifestyle tie them—in contrast to those Mennonites with Amish Mennonite roots—much more clearly to the Amish of the nineteenth century, I have tried to tell their story fairly and dispassionately.

This volume is basically in the form of a narrative, with occasional pauses for analyses of events and movements. For those who prefer a more analytical approach, perhaps this account will provide some of the raw material for a further critical examination of the Amish church in the nineteenth century.

To tell any story with the scope of this volume without bias is impossible, as the comments of those who have read my manuscript have made clear to me. The criticisms, corrections, and suggestions of these readers have been invaluable, not only in baring my biases to the light of truth, but in many other ways as well. Some have gone beyond the usual contributions and have called to my attention documents which I had not discovered. They alerted me to pieces of the Amish story which I had overlooked.

Of these latter I must name Steven Estes of Hopedale, Illinois, author of several Illinois Mennonite congregational histories; David Luthy of the Heritage Historical Library, Aylmer, Ontario; Joseph Stoll, editor of *Family Life*, Aylmer, Ontario; Bennie C. Yoder, Amish historian of Springs, Pennsylvania; Joseph F. Beiler, Editor of *The Diary*, Gordonville, Pennsylvania; and the late Amos L. Fisher, Amish genealogist of Ronks, Pennsylvania. Others who have read my manuscript carefully enough to make valuable suggestions and save me from embarrassing mistakes are Eli Gingerich, Middlebury, Indiana; Leonard Gross, Director of the Archives of the Mennonite Church, Goshen, Indiana; Trennis King, Belleville, Pennsylvania; Ivan J. Miller, Grantsville, Maryland; Tilman Smith, Goshen, Indiana; and John C. Wenger, Goshen, Indiana.

As good editors always do, Albert N. Keim (for the Mennonite Historical Society) and S. David Garber (for Herald Press) have made the largest investment of all in time and energy, and the biggest contribution likewise, to the publication of this volume. In raising questions about several of my interpretations, Keim has saved me from overstatements, and at other points has encouraged me to be less tentative in my pronouncements. His suggestions for improvement in style have been beneficial, yet he has generously acceded to my preferences when I have felt constrained to tell it my way. David Garber, in his careful and minute scrutiny of the text, identified some technical and substantive mistakes which have been corrected before they could reach the public eye. The errors which remain should be charged to the author.

The personnel of five ·historical libraries must be named. Lena Lehman, Nelson Springer, and Joe Springer of the Mennonite Historical Library, Goshen College, Goshen, Indiana, have provided unending service with unlimited patience in the course of my research. Rachel Shenk, J. Kevin Miller, and Leonard Gross of the Mennonite Archives were equally proficient and cooperative, as were Carolyn C. Wenger and Gladys S. Graybill of the Lancaster Mennonite Historical Society Library. David Luthy, of the Heritage Historical Library, not only provided consultant services, as already mentioned, but also uncovered significant documents for me, as has Abner F. Beiler of the Pequea Bruderschaft Library, Gordonville, Pennsylvania. For the services of these librarians, which reached beyond normal expectations, I am most grateful.

Of those who have helped financially in the publication of this volume, I wish to thank especially Ora M. and Grace Yoder, Samuel L. and Lillian Yoder, Tilman and Luella Smith, and contributors to a freewill offering taken in Kansas.

—*Paton Yoder*
Goshen, Indiana

Introducing the
Amish in America

1
The Amish in America: An Overview

To 1800

On September 23, 1752, Christian Schmucker and family arrived at Philadelphia on the ship *St. Andrew*. The family may have sojourned briefly with Christian's Amish brethren in Berks County. But not long after he landed in this country, he was living in eastern Lancaster County, Pennsylvania, where he remained until his death in 1782.[1] Another Amish immigrant family, that of Nicholas Stoltzfus, arrived at the same port in the next decade—on October 18, 1766.[2]

When the Smucker family came to America a small but steady stream of Mennonites had been flowing into England's colonies—primarily Pennsylvania—on the American continent for more than half a century. It was only in the 1730s, however, that a few Amish immigrants also found their way into the colony. Among them were the natural and spiritual kin of the aforementioned Schmuckers and Stoltzfuses: the Beilers, Detweilers, Hertzlers, Kauffmans, Kurtzes, Lapps, Planks or Blanks, Stutzmans, Yoders, Zooks, and others. By the time the Stoltzfuses had arrived that first small surge of Amish immigration had all but ended, not to be resumed until well after the turn of the century.[3]

Recent research has put the number of Amish families migrating to America before 1800 at 102, and the number of persons at 500.[4] For the Amish of Pennsylvania, however, there was another source of population growth. John, son of Christian Schmucker, married Barbara, daughter of Nicholas Stoltzfus, and the Zooks and the Lapps and all the other families intermarried likewise. The result was a natural increase not attributable to immigration. Of that increase, however, a large proportion did not remain in the Amish church.[5] In 1800 the Amish population in America probably numbered less than 1,000 persons.

The principal concentration of Amish population before 1800 was in counties of Pennsylvania: Berks and Chester and the eastern parts of Lancaster and Lebanon. Well before that date, enterprising Amish from this eastern base, along with some newly arrived immigrants from Europe, moved westward. They got caught up in that general movement of the American people which continued until the early decades of the twentieth century. In migrating westward the Amish as a group, like the Mennonites, were never quite ready to expose themselves at the cutting edge of the frontier. They usually waited until the Indians' resistance to the white man's encroachment had abated, but sometimes scarcely a day longer.[6] As early as the 1760s some Amish families found their way to Somerset County, Pennsylvania, with more following thereafter. In the 1790s others chose to go to the northwest rather than to the southwest, settling in Mifflin County, Pennsylvania.[7]

The Amish branch of the Anabaptists had separated from the main body of Swiss Brethren and Mennonites in Europe in the 1690s. Jacob Ammann, their leader, had become very concerned about keeping the church pure. He felt that preserving the purity of the church required strict discipline, including the use of the instruments of excommunication and shunning. Shunning, that supreme disciplinary device, required the social ostracism—but not the physical isolation—of the offender, to be observed even by members of his own family, including his spouse.[8]

Jacob Ammann could be very specific. Those who spoke falsehoods were to be excommunicated. The Lord's Supper should be observed twice a year, rather than only once, and accompanied with the ordinance of foot washing. Garments were to be fastened with hooks and eyes, and the beard should not be trimmed. Although the leadership of the Amish church following the time of Jacob Ammann manifested a softer disposition,[9] yet Ammann's original reforms, as he thought them to be, were not appreciably modified.

Ammann had strong support for his position on the use of the ban and the shunning of backsliders in the writings of Menno Simons and of Dirk or Dietrich Philips, and in the 16th and 17th articles of the Dordrecht Confession of Faith. The latter document, drawn up in 1632, had been the result of a sustained and concerted effort among the Anabaptists of Europe to restore the unity of the denomination.

Clearly, to use the terminology of recent decades, Jacob Ammann and those who followed him in later generations believed in radical discipleship. They were to follow in "the path of Jesus"—as they understood it—who was "the way-shower" (terms appearing frequently in Amish literature) not only in principle, but in every detail of life. The Amish called this careful ordering of lifestyle the *Ordnung*. It was expressed in the rules and regulations of the church and the established patterns of congregational life. As an Amish minister has recently asserted, such regulation "gives freedom of heart, peace of mind, and a clear conscience."[10]

In those early years in America before 1800, church control was rather weak. Families were scattered, making congregational organization and discipline difficult. Traveling bishops were able to do little more than perform marriages, administer communion, and officiate at baptisms. With the virtual cessation of immigration in the late 1760s, these immigrant families were left to fend for themselves; the very identity of the group may have been in some danger.

They succeeded in this effort at self-preservation, but barely.[11] According to Amish historian Joseph F. Beiler,

> most of our initial ancestor families in America have not raised more than one son to remain in the old faith. Some have not kept any sons in the church, some have kept a few, but not one record do we have that kept the whole family within before the revolution. It is evident that many sons who came to this land of freedom were overwhelmed with this air of freedom in America.[12]

Such conditions may account for the eventual disintegration of several of the earlier congregational districts in eastern Pennsylvania.[13] Incidentally, similar demographic circumstances may be responsible in some measure for the complete disintegration in the twentieth century of the Amish church in Europe.[14]

From 1800 to 1850

With the coming of the 3000-strong second wave of Amish immigrants, 1816-60, the proliferation of Amish settlements continued unabated. Usually the new communities followed the westward movement of population in general, but occasionally new colonies were planted to the north or to the south of these east-west lines. By 1850 the western frontier of Amish settlements had reached southeastern Iowa. Sometimes the new immigrants settled among their native American Amish brethren. Much more frequently they established new communities, often geographically contingent to, but separate from, the latter.

The first half of the nineteenth century is marked also by the strengthening of the authority of the Amish church. The church sought to use this increased power to sharpen its sense of identity. The rules and regulations of the individual congregations were enlarged and made more specific. In addition, regional ministers' meetings were held occasionally; they furthered the ascendancy of the church over the family and the individual Amish community.

After 1850

The last half of the nineteenth century in the Amish church was marred by the Great Schism. Some would describe it as a sequence of schisms related to each other like the ripples in a pond after a stone has been thrown into the water. Many forces from within and without the denomination were calling for change. Some Amish leaders were inclined to respond to these influences with overall resistance. Others were persuaded in their hearts that some—perhaps a very few— changes in the Ordnung of the church were needed. Still others, scarcely more than a handful but including certain influential leaders, were prepared to adopt immediately more substantive innovations. But they often differed among themselves as to what these changes should be.

Alarmed by these divisive forces and by ruptures already in progress in certain areas of the country, some Amish leaders devised a plan for annual churchwide ministers' meetings. They hoped that this addition to the polity of the church could prevent further schism and restore already-broken relations. The annual *Diener Versammlungen* (ministers' meetings) of 1862-78 were the result of this effort. For several reasons these conferences were not successful in restoring unity to the Amish church.

The more conservative Amish leaders, failing to find sufficient support for their position, virtually boycotted the meetings after 1865. From the beginning they had been uneasy about the direction which the conferences might take. However, even after 1865 and the withdrawal of the conservatives, those more change-minded leaders who had dominated the meetings from the first were not able to hold their own group together without the travail of some additional divisions.

The Old Order Amish and the Amish Mennonites

The ministers' meetings of the 1860s and 1870s failed to restore the unity of the Amish church. Yet they are credited with shaping and giving identity to that body which came to be called the Amish Mennonite church. Even the change-minded ministers who dominated these conferences felt it necessary to build and maintain some ecclesiastical fences. Those fences excluded a few of the more liberal brethren, such as Joseph Stuckey and Benjamin Eicher, and gave identity to those who found it proper, comfortable, or convenient to remain inside the fences.

The conservatives wanted to retain the "old order" of church practices. They were eventually dubbed "Old Order Amish." In fact, the Great Schism may have caused some polarization between the change-minded faction and the conservatives. For example, at this time the latter gained more vigor to resist technological change, labor-saving devices, and modern conveniences.

On the other hand, the Amish Mennonites, who early on had proposed only a few carefully selected changes, welcomed and embraced the new technology. The few carefully selected changes—such as baptism in a stream, the use of meetinghouses, the substitution of buttons for hooks and eyes, and the adoption of four-part singing—were virtually overwhelmed by the flood of additional innovations. Carefully designed retaining walls or fences of church discipline, particularly in the area of dress, quickly broke down. The century closed on the Amish Mennonites as they and the (Old) Mennonites were moving slowly and methodically toward merger.

2

Era of Consolidation, 1800-50

The Golden Years?

Writing in 1862 the aged David Beiler (1786-1871), bishop in the Upper Pequea Amish congregation in Lancaster County, Pennsylvania, reminisced about conditions in his church in the early years of the century. "At that time," he said, "Christian simplicity was practiced much more, and much more submission was shown toward the ministers, especially toward the old bishops."[1]

That same year Deacon John Stoltzfus (1805-87) in the nearby Lower Pequea congregation wrote an account of church practices of earlier decades. Speaking of the same condition of tranquillity in the church which Beiler had described, Stoltzfus declared that in the two Lancaster congregations of those earlier decades he knew of no "withholding of the kiss of peace among the old people so long as I knew them" and "much less did they consider withholding fellowship with each other."[2]

The reminiscence of layman Daniel D. Miller (1829-1911), a native of Somerset County, Pennsylvania, is even more nostalgic. He wrote,

> At the time when I joined the church [1846] the people were all united together in one mindedness. The Amish and the Mennonites were both satisfied to live a lowly humble life. They were well contented with the possessions they had. There was very little trouble among them, and if any trouble existed, it was soon arbitrated in peace. So that God's blessing might rest upon the Churches, pride and all disorder was punished. The Church order in dress fashion was of lowly estate and all alike. . . . Now this good time of fifty years ago has vanished away.[3]

Such are the recollections of a bishop in his mid-seventies, a deacon in his late fifties, and a sixty-four-year-old layman. Laced with nostalgia, they must be taken with some reservation. They do coincide to a considerable extent, however, with the findings of anthropologist-historian John A. Hostetler. He observed that "with the growth of settlements, the Amish ordained resident bishops, and thus church control began to be exercised over family and kinship rule."[4]

That only three isolated instances of division occurred in this "golden age"—each case involving only one congregation—likewise gives some support to the claims of Beiler, Stoltzfus, and Miller.[5] Certainly this record stands out in stark contrast to that of the latter part of the century. Then schism seemed to become almost the order of the day, especially among the various factions of change-minded Amish Mennonites.

Strengthening the Authority of the Church

The Amish never surrendered the principle of congregational supremacy in matters relating to church government. But in spite of this limiting factor, efforts to strengthen the authority of the church over the Amish community continued throughout this era of consolidation. In times of crisis they were ready to resort to ad hoc local or regional ministers' meetings to resolve current disputes. The findings or rulings coming out of these meetings clearly indicate a consistent effort to strengthen and extend the controls of the church.

The first such ministers' meeting in America on record—quite certainly the first of the nineteenth century—took place in October 1809. It presumably was held somewhere in the Berks-Chester-Lancaster County settlement. The "Discipline of 1809," drawn up at this meeting, dealt with matters relating to shunning, the swearing of oaths, personal adornment, serving on juries, and participation in congregational council meetings.[6] Most of these concerns emerge again and again in the annals of the Amish church in the 1800s. If Bishop David Beiler's interpretation is correct, this meeting or conference, along with its rulings, represents one of the earlier efforts of the church to assert more clearly and to extend further the authority of the church over the individual. Said Beiler:

> So it was among our ancestors that through paternal love parents were influenced to wink at their children's behavior even though they knew they were not in the order of the church. They even in part supported them. For this reason the ministers . . . drew up a set of resolutions and a

majority subscribed to them. But some of them seem to have agreed to them [merely] . . . because he [*sic*] did not wish to disagree. Afterward, however, some of them regretted their action. Through this disunity arose and it did more harm than good.[7]

Beiler had not participated in the conference of 1809 (he dated it "1806 or 1807"). He was only twenty-three years old at that time. Nevertheless, his analysis is extremely significant. Here was an early attempt to strengthen the authority of the church over the family by resort to a regional—perhaps virtually churchwide—meeting of Amish ministers. Although Beiler was in sympathy with the purpose of the meeting, he indicates that he was not certain that the means used was effective.

Of the nine articles in the Discipline of 1809, two of them affirmed shunning as an instrument of church discipline and set up procedures to strengthen its use by the members of the congregation. Article 5 of this discipline ruled that

anyone who transgresses the rule of shunning in weakness or ignorance can be reconciled by confession to the church that he has erred; whoever transgresses intentionally but is not stubborn about it when admonished, can be reconciled by a "full" confession but whoever stubbornly refuses to hearken to the admonition shall be excommunicated from the church.

The first article of that same discipline declared that "all those of our members who leave us to join other churches shall be treated as apostate persons . . . and shall be separated and be recognized as subjects for the ban." However, the practice of shunning defectors did not have unanimous support. It was challenged already in 1826 in an Amish ministers' conference in Ohio, probably in Wayne County. Some ministers proposed that if a member who has been put in the ban "is then taken in by the Mennonites or Dunkards," then shunning should be lifted. However, the conservatives controlled this conference and rejected this manifestation of a "liberal spirit."[8]

The increased use of the ban and shunning to strengthen the authority of the congregation is strikingly illustrated by a ruling made in a conference held in 1837 in Somerset County, Pennsylvania. Here the ministers

decided that those who marry outside are no longer to be received again so lightly into fellowship, unless they bring their marriage partners with them into Christian discipline, and are received after true repentance and change of heart has been shown.[9]

The meeting of 1837 went further. Not only were the regulations extended, but excommunication and shunning themselves were to be used unsparingly to enforce such regulations. The first provision of the eleven-article discipline adopted at that meeting observed that the application of the God-given ordinance "of the ban is greatly neglected." It should be applied "toward all disobedient ones without regard of person, whether man or woman."

Rebaptizing Mennonites and Dunkards

What C. Z. Mast has called "The First Church Controversy Among the Amish in America,"[10] took place in the 1820s. It was clearly resolved in a manner which strengthened the authority of the congregation and particularly the ministry. In 1820 or soon thereafter immigrant John Burkholder (1799-1876), a Mennonite, arrived in Mifflin County, Pennsylvania. Finding himself among Amish he applied for membership in that denomination. He was told that he would need to be rebaptized before he could be admitted into the Amish congregation at that place. To have complied would have violated his conscience, so he refused.

A few (perhaps two or three) years later, Burkholder moved to Wayne County, Ohio. Here David Zook (1780-1863), bishop of what came to be called the Oak Grove Amish Mennonite church, received him into the church without rebaptism. The leveling influence of the frontier may have reached into the workings of that Amish congregation.

The ministers of Mifflin County heard of the indulgent action of the Wayne County congregation and sent it a letter of protest. When Bishop Zook came to Mifflin County to set matters right, he was refused the hand of fellowship. Five or more years and at least two ministers' meetings later, the issue was finally resolved (October 1830) at a meeting of "between 30 and 35 ministers and elders from many congregations" held at the Glades in Somerset County, Pennsylvania. Mennonite and Dunkard applicants for membership in an Amish congregation, it was decreed, must be rebaptized by an Amish bishop. If the local bishop could not in good conscience do so, he must call in another bishop, one who would be willing to rebaptize the applicant for membership in the setting of an Amish congregation.

The rationale given for this ruling seems long and labored. Since Mennonite ministers were not qualified to come into an Amish service and administer baptism, neither could baptism administered by such leaders in a Mennonite service be accepted as valid. Acts 6:2,

Ephesians 4:6, and 1 Corinthians 12:15 were quoted, Scriptures which signified to them not only the unity but also the uniformity of the church of Christ. The 1830 ministers' meeting asserted that "a minister who administers baptism must be chosen in the church where he is known as a disciple or brother and he must be at peace with the church and the church with him so that they break bread and wash feet with one another."

In a follow-up meeting in Wayne County, Ohio, on May 25, 1831, this principle was expressed more forcefully in the form of a prohibition. "The functions of the Holy Trinity in the church of the Lord," it was declared, "are not fittingly administered by a stranger, who is stained with some spots of unbelief," so that "the ministry of baptism is not more fitting" to be administered by such stranger "than the ministry of the Lord's Supper."[11] Although this ruling and the justification for it are couched in biblical terms, it seems clear that here again the authority of the congregation and of the ministers in particular was reinforced.

Imposing New Restrictions and Reinforcing the Old

In this era of consolidation, controversies increasingly related to details of lifestyle. In settling them, the Amish church tended to strengthen the old restraints and sometimes impose new ones. As a result, says John A. Hostetler, "a new identity began to emerge as Amish were distinguished from non-Amish." But a serious side effect of these restrictive practices, he adds, was that "both religious and secular controversies began to plague the Amish people."[12]

Considerable disputation occurred in the council meetings of Amish congregations and in the several ad hoc ministers' meetings held in this period. A delineation of Amish controversies in this era of consolidation will illustrate the flavor of the struggles. Questions concerning the use of shunning and the rebaptism of Mennonites were resolved relatively successfully. Matters relating to lifestyle were more difficult. Rulings were made with less success against bundling, the marriage of couples whose blood relationship was closer than that of second cousins, certain expressions of affluence which conflicted with the Amish emphasis on simplicity, and the indiscriminate acceptance of technological change.

Bundling was a common practice among the working classes of both Europe and America in this era. It was a dating custom in which young couples went to bed together fully clothed. In considerable part it must have been an adaptation to the chilly temperatures in the primitive homes of that period. Tradition maintains, however, that the Amish in Europe had quite largely abstained from this practice. When Minister Jacob Swartzendruber (1800-68) arrived in the United States in 1833 and observed the widespread custom of bundling among the Amish, he was distressed.[13] Evidently bundling had become accepted in the Amish church in America during the colonial period. By the time Swartzendruber arrived, bundling "was no longer viewed as a worldly custom; it became an old practice (*alter Gebrauch*)." Accordingly, "the more conservative segments" of the Amish church "sought to maintain these practices."[14]

When Swartzendruber arrived in America he was not alone in his opposition to bundling. Three years before his arrival, the ministers assembled at the Glades in Somerset County in 1830 had spoken out against the custom. This concern was reiterated in the aforementioned 1837 conference confined to the ministers of the three Somerset County congregations. The pertinent article states:

> With regard to the excesses practiced among the youth, namely that the youth take the liberty to sleep or lie together without any fear or shame, such things shall not be tolerated at all. And when it takes place with the knowledge of the parents and something bad happens on account of it, the parents shall not go unpunished.[15]

Ruling against bundling was easier than enforcing the rule. One and one-half years after the 1830 meeting in Wayne County, Bishop John Stoltzfus (1776-1857) of Lancaster County, son of immigrant Christian Stoltzfus, wrote to his fellow ministers in Mifflin County: "It looks as if nothing that was voted on [at the 1830 meeting] is to stand for they tell me that the young people go to bed together [just] as they did before and that neither is it observed among you. . . ."

Stoltzfus was disturbed. "What can be done about the matter," he continued, "shall we let it go on this way or shall we begin once more to forbid it? I think it is real immorality."[16] Bundling, however, had reached the status of an *alter Gebrauch* and was not to be eradicated so easily. Apparently part of Swartzendruber's reason for moving to Iowa in 1851 was because he wanted to serve his church in a community where this custom was not so deeply entrenched. From that state he continued to cry out against the practice.[17]

Another arrangement which had crept into the church was the marriage of first cousins and of first cousins-once-removed. Marriages of such close relatives were more common among the European Amish than among those in America.[18] Accordingly, as the second wave (1816-

60) of Amish immigration reached the United States and Canada, this practice became more common also in America.

Other circumstances may account in part for the increase in the marriages of close relatives. The Amish families in that first wave of immigration numbered only slightly more than one hundred. Scarcely a generation or two of intermarriage would have been required to bring about a situation in which a large proportion of the young people would live in Amish communities composed largely of first and second cousins. Moreover, in this period the children of a marriage often numbered ten or fifteen or even more. Thus groups of first cousins each numbering over one hundred could not have been uncommon. This reduced almost automatically the familiarity commonly obtaining between close relatives.

With such a social climate, situations obviously arose in which two young people more closely related to each other than second cousins might be attracted to each other. The Amish church based its opposition to such marriages on Old Testament passages forbidding the union of close relatives. The biological consequences of the marriage of close relatives were not then known.

The marriage of first cousins never had the acceptance—or, perhaps more accurately, the tolerance—of the Amish community which evidently was accorded to bundling. Quite possibly the issue arose only occasionally when first cousins became enamored of each other or perhaps when parents or grandparents wanted to consolidate their family landholdings. In contrast to bundling, which took place privately and under cover of night, control over marriages, which were initiated by a public ceremony, was relatively easy.

Concern over the marriage of closely related persons was expressed in the ministers' meeting in Wayne County in 1826. It was decided that "none should marry in closer blood relationship than if on both sides they are one generation farther removed than children of brothers or sisters (*Geschwisterenkel*)."[19] According to Bishop David Beiler's reminiscences, this ruling was soon challenged by some ministers or laymen or both, which "caused considerable discord and dissatisfaction." But it stood until about 1858, when it was reviewed following a fresh violation by a couple in the Amish congregation in Buffalo Valley, Union County, Pennsylvania.[20]

Amish Simplicity and the New Affluence

In 1837 Jacob Yoder (b. 1762) died, leaving a considerable estate of real and personal property in Wayne County, Ohio. He had moved there in 1818 with nine of his eleven children. Prosperity had opened the way for Jacob and family to depart from the standards of simplicity which had prevailed in the Amish church up to that time. Material blessings had a similar effect on many other Amish families of that day and was to have a mighty impact on the Amish church in general.

Although a pioneer, Jacob was not the typical indigent frontiersman of his day. Neither was he altogether a typical Amishman, with a high regard for traditional Amish simplicity. The list of his personal property offered at auction after his death indicates that he had not hesitated to use his relative affluence to practice a bit of "conspicuous consumption." Sold were hundreds of items, including six pairs of shoes; a pair of "specks" (spectacles); a shaving box with razor, strap, and mirror; all kinds of pants, including one pair of velvet trousers and two pairs of cotton twilled pants; three silk handkerchiefs; one silk pocket kerchief; one neckerchief; an "alpaca" coat; a silver watch; five smoke pipes and a "paper of cigars"; eight "stem glasses" and a set of "cups and sasers." Other items listed in Jacob's estate papers were only slightly less indicative of the lifestyle of Jacob and his family. In 1840, only three years after Jacob's death, his son Samuel emulated the pattern of his affluent father by building a large modern barn and soon thereafter replacing his log cabin with a large house.[21]

Jacob and his family were probably not fully aware of the extent to which they were charting a new course. The right to own land, freedom from harassment and persecution, and the prospect of prosperity had not been the lot of most Amish families back in Europe. When the new conditions became a reality for second- and third-generation Amish families in America they may have accepted the benefits of the new economic and political freedom without giving much thought to the effect of these changes on Amish patterns of living.

Jacob Yoder and his kind may have been aware of all these changes, but not concerned about them overmuch. However, many Amish bishops and other leaders took a more sober view of the situation. Interestingly but certainly not entirely coincidentally, in the same year that Jacob Yoder's silk pocket and neckerchiefs were sold at auction, the ministers' conference that was held in Somerset County noted that "there is awful pride in clothing, namely with respect to silken neck-cloths . . . so that mothers tie silken neck-cloths on their children, and make high collars on their children's shirts. . . ."[22]

This same Discipline of 1837 decreed "that there shall be no display in houses" and that such should not be "painted with various colors, or filled with showy furniture, namely with wooden, porcelain, or glass utensils (dishes), and having cupboards and mirrors hung on the wall, and such things." Furniture was not to be decorated "with such loud or checkered (*scheckich*) colors." Tailors were forbidden "to make new or worldly styles of clothing for members of the church" but were rather "to follow the old style and such as is indicated by the ministers and older people of the church." In a ruling that was probably directed to young people it was decreed that "excessive driving of sleighs or other vehicles is not to be, and also that vehicles are not to be painted with two colors, as has already occurred too much."

The earlier Discipline of 1809 contained a few restrictions relating to the outward trappings of Amish lifestyle: "the cutting of the hair and of the beard" and the wearing of "proud dresses, proud trousers, hats, and combs in the hair." The Discipline of 1837 was much more specific and detailed in these matters. Still later, in 1865, in a position paper drawn up in Holmes County, Ohio, some of the more conservative Amish ministers from across the denomination were to enumerate such restrictions once again—and greatly enlarge the list.

The aged Bishop David Beiler must have been referring to people such as Jacob and Samuel Yoder when he described the material prosperity which had come to the succeeding generations of Amish in America. Said he, "It was a good time according to material things. . . . The old people became rich in natural goods, but, it is to be feared, poor in heavenly riches. . . . And the young people tried to carry on high and to imitate the fashions of the world more and more. . . ."

Beiler was concerned about "strange colored fine store clothes" and commercially produced fabrics, the "splendid houses and barns," fancy harness and saddles and bridles for the horses, and painted wagons. House furnishings had likewise become more elaborate. "Spotted and flowered dishes" had come into the homes, along with "sofas and writing desks and bureaus" and "rag carpets." Meals had become more sumptuous, with coffee, preserves, and similar supplements to such basics as "soup and mush." Children were going "to school every winter for months at a time," which was more than was required to learn to read and write.[23]

The Westward Movement of the Amish and the New Immigration, 1816-60

The Amish were not immune to the lure of the West. Starting in 1808 Amish families from Somerset County, Pennsylvania, had found their way to Tuscarawas and Holmes counties in Ohio. A similar movement took place from Mifflin County, Pennsylvania, to Wayne County, Ohio. The Richville settlement in Stark County, Ohio, sometimes identified as the Canton congregation, originated in about 1810, with Amish arriving from different places in Pennsylvania. In the 1840s settlers from Mifflin County moved to Logan and Champaign counties, Ohio, south and west of Wayne County. In some instances the Amish followed directly on the heels of Mennonite settlers, as in Fairfield County, Ohio, and Waterloo County, Ontario (then Upper Canada but soon to become Canada West).[24]

The Ohio settlements in turn supplied many of the Amish families which were to establish communities still further west. Holmes County became the base from which many Amish settlers took off for Lagrange and Elkhart counties in Indiana. The Johnson County, Iowa, settlement, however, was founded by migrants coming directly from Somerset County, Pennsylvania.[25] The Amish community in Butler County, Ohio, originally settled by families directly from Alsace, became the way station for many immigrants moving farther west. It was somewhat disturbed in 1833 by the arrival of about one hundred immigrant Hessian Amish.[26]

These Amish from the principality of Hesse were a tiny part of the second wave of Amish immigration to America, stretching from about 1816 to 1860. The first wave, a small one, had dissipated by 1770. By 1816 conditions in western Europe, coupled with the prosperity and the religious liberty which the Amish were experiencing in the New World, were again conducive to migration to America.

Most frequently mentioned as a motive for leaving Europe at this time was the anticipated conscription of the young male members of the family who were about to reach military age. More than twenty-five years of intermittent warfare in western Europe, sometimes reaching to eastern Europe, had produced unstable conditions and universal military conscription. This subjected the Amish to various forms of property despoilation and caused considerable social dislocation.[27]

Although attracted to America by their Amish brethren, these newcomers for the most part did not fuse unobtrusively with the former. Frequently, however, they settled in communities near American Amish districts. Philadelphia, and also Baltimore, continued to be the port of entry for many of these immigrants. Like other German-speaking immigrants of the nineteenth century, they mostly settled in Ohio and states even farther west. The greater availability of land in the west, along with lower land prices, probably accounts for their bypassing the eastern states.

Many of those who swelled the new settlements in Illinois entered the States by way of New Orleans. New communities were formed in Butler, Stark, and Fulton counties in Ohio; in Adams and Allen counties in Indiana; in several counties in central Illinois; in Lewis County, New York; and in Waterloo County, Ontario. The Indiana settlement centering in the Nappanee area, including the corners of Marshall, Kosciusko, and Elkhart counties, began in 1839. It was composed largely of recent immigrants, although many had sojourned briefly either in Wayne or in Stark County, Ohio.[28] While somewhat less than comprehensive, this enumeration serves as confirmation of the fact that Amish immigrants of the 1816-60 period commonly established new communities rather than joining older Amish settlements.

While the older families and the new Amish immigrants generally did not fuse freely, neither did they ignore each other. And melding did occur occasionally. In Somerset County, Pennsylvania, the Brennemans, the Gingeriches, the Orendorfs, the Beitzels, the Kinsingers, and the Benders "were warmly welcomed and assisted" by the native-born Amish of that region[29] In Davis County, Iowa, immigrants and native Amish mingled similarly.[30]

When small groups or individual families found themselves located in an established Amish community, they did not hesitate to affiliate with the local congregation. Thus in Wayne County, Ohio, Valentine and Jacobina Nafziger, immigrants of 1824, affiliated with what later was to become the Oak Grove congregation, composed of settlers from Pennsylvania. Their daughter Catharine married Samuel Yoder of that same congregation, a native American by three generations whose forebears probably landed in 1742.[31] The Nafzigers' son Peter (1809-77), however, chose to move on to Fulton County, Ohio, where he associated with the new Amish community and later served as bishop of the congregation.

In central Illinois the mixing of the old and the new followed a different pattern. Here the immigrants were first on the scene, arriving already in the 1830s, while few American Amish from the East arrived until the late 1840s. Although in the minority in the larger Amish community in central Illinois, the number of easterners was not inconsequential. At the time of its organization as a separate congregation in 1851, twenty of the members of the Rock Creek church, including its bishop, had come there from Pennsylvania. Only sixteen members were of the new immigration.[32] That same year Bishop Isaac Schmucker, a native of Pennsylvania, moved from Elkhart County, Indiana, to the Rock Creek area. He was received as a bishop by that congregation, although as an understudy to the older bishop, Jonathan Yoder. Ill health in the family induced Schmucker to return to northern Indiana a year later. In the meantime he is credited by some with providing the impetus for building the first Amish meetinghouse at Rock Creek, the first in the state of Illinois.[33]

Well after the close (1850) of this era of consolidation, congregations of native American Amish continued to maintain "fellowship" with congregations composed primarily of new immigrants. This relationship (maintaining fellowship) was said to exist between congregations when close cooperation was observed between them in all congregational activities. This especially applied to sharing ministers in baptismal and communion services, and providing help in administering discipline.

There was one exception, however, to the analysis made above. A small segment of the new immigration, the Hessian Amish from the German principality of Hesse, was not so well received by the established congregations. These immigrants of 1833 and following years wore buttons, played musical instruments, and had made other adaptations to the culture of their contemporaries. Settling first in Butler County, Ohio, some soon made their way from that area to McLean County, Illinois. Already in 1835 in Butler County, the Hessians had found it necessary to form a separate congregation because of the above practices. Much later (1859) in Illinois, they were squeezed out of the Rock Creek congregation, although the main body of Illinois Amish continued to treat them with a considerable measure of toleration.[34] Smaller settlements of Hessians were made elsewhere, both in Illinois and in other states.

Although welcomed in the formal sense, the newcomers were received with varying degrees of acceptance and enthusiasm. It has been repeatedly asserted that the new immigrants were somewhat less tradition-minded. This is probably true for the majority,[35] although much depended on the circumstances obtaining in the particular European congregation from which such migrants came. It is not surprising, therefore, that the highly tradition-minded Bishop David Beiler of the Upper Pequea congregation of Lancaster County later spoke of the recent Amish immigrants as having "strange manners and customs" which had led to "differences of opinion."[36]

On the other hand "Tennessee" John Stoltzfus of the neighboring congregation of Lower Pequea, at that time only slightly less tradition-minded than Beiler, was prepared to receive the newcomers and welcome them to the land of liberty with open arms. "The brethren and sisters received each other with joy always," he asserted in his Family History, "and if they came from Germany with a letter [of membership] they were gladly received with hand[shake] and kiss, and all worked together with glad and charitable spirit."[37]

This half century (1800-50) then, was not really as golden as it was thought to be by those who later were experiencing the trauma of a division in the church. At its beginning the authority of the Amish church was weak and whole families were being lost. A struggling for survival was evident. In the course of the half century many of the seeds were sown for the Great Schism which was to sweep across the church in the next quarter century. As the era ended, the controversial issue of whether baptism should be administered in a stream or in a house was beginning to disturb congregations from Elkhart County, Indiana, to Mifflin County, Pennsylvania.

Amish Church Polity, Beliefs, and Discipline

3

The Amish Congregation and the Structure of the Ministry

To grasp the complexities and travail associated with Amish church affairs in the latter half of the nineteenth century, three aspects of Amish faith and practice need to be examined. The first facet relates to church polity and particularly the structure of the ministry (this chapter). The second is concerned with Amish theology expressed in sermons, in correspondence, and in published documents (chapters 4–5). The third examines the Amish concept and practice of discipline (chapter 6).

Though differences arose in the third quarter of the century which were to produce several divisions in the Amish church, these differences did not relate to Amish polity or theology. On these the traditionalists and the several change-minded Amish groups were in essential agreement. Only in the last two decades of the century did the change-minded groups come to adopt the revivalist patterns of the major Protestant denominations, along with the theology which underlay this revivalism. This happened some years after most of the divisions had occurred.

Congregational Government

After the close of the regular morning services on Sunday, June 21, 1863, Bishop Abraham Peachey (1799-1884) of the Amish congregation in the Upper district of the Kishacoquillas Valley of Mifflin County, Pennsylvania, called a meeting of the members of the congregation. Uniform practice throughout the Amish church required the exclusion of children and unbaptized young people from such counsel meetings.

Peachey announced to the congregation that a churchwide Amish ministers' meeting had recently asked him to attempt a reconciliation between himself and Bishop Solomon Beiler (1798-1888) of the neighboring Middle district. The request had specified the procedure to be observed. Peachey, seeking the support of his own congregation and recognizing that custom required that he "take the counsel of the congregation" on such matters, proposed that he and the congregation disregard the counsel or the ruling of that body of ministers. He had never really been in favor of submitting his problem to that churchwide ministerial meeting. In any case, he had a better idea; he would attempt reconciliation by a different route.

There followed a discussion in which two of Peachey's ministers opposed his proposal. Thereupon he declared a divided counsel (no agreement) and dismissed the meeting.[1] Eventually, however, after excluding the two dissenting ministers from the communion table, he evidently got the consent of the congregation to try his "better" idea.[2] The specific nature of the controversy will come to light in chapter 8. This incomplete account illustrates how congregational government in the Amish church often functioned.

Following traditional Anabaptist church polity, governance in the Amish church was congregational throughout the nineteenth century. This statement applies to the several branches of that church which were born in the course of the century through schism, as well as to the parent church which preceded them. Each congregation was to make its own rules and live by them, select its own ministers, determine who should be admitted into membership in the congregation and who should be excommunicated and shunned, and exercise various other options in the application of church discipline.

In those congregational counsel meetings there was a considerable measure of democracy, with women having the same rights as men in expressing opinions, in nominating persons for the ministry, and in the informal voting common to such meetings. Quite likely the women exercised these rights less aggressively than did the men.

As illustrated forthrightly above, the congregation owned no authority in church affairs above its own, not even that of a churchwide ministers' meeting. Peachey, however, may have overstepped the traditional role of a bishop at that meeting and especially later in excluding two of his ministers from the communion table without the counsel of the congregation. Bishop John Esh (1807-79) of Juniata County, Pennsylvania, could say that "the ministers are the builders; the members are the stones in the building."[3] Yet the role of lay members in Amish congregational life was never as passive as this metaphor suggests. It was accepted—indeed expected—that ministers and bishops, as those who "blow the trumpets on the walls of Zion," should guard the church against all impurity, even when opposed by members of their own congregations. Nevertheless, to actually thwart the will of the congregation, as Peachey may have been doing in the above situation, was not the bishop's traditional prerogative.

Such congregational counsel meetings, much like the old New England town meetings, were sometimes fraught with considerable strife. The correspondence of Christian Stoltzfus (1803-83), deacon of the Buffalo Valley congregation in Union County, Pennsylvania, reads like a broken record. There always seemed to be someone who was violating the rules and regulations of the church. Others were not coming to the Lord's Supper in protest against such indications of disobedience. The Riehls stole from the Stoltzfuses the agency granted by the Halliday Company for constructing windmills. A young woman wrote a frivolous letter to herself but let the congregation think that the writer was some young man from the congregation. A Stoltzfus girl married her first cousin-once-removed. And so the list grows.[4]

By 1860-61 a permanent division of the congregation in Buffalo Valley threatened, and only the gentle perseverance of Deacon Christian Stoltzfus in family visitation prevented it. In one of his lengthy letters he suggests that the problems of his congregation were not related to substantive issues. Instead, they were centered around personalities and petty concerns laced with large doses of misunderstanding, gossip, and deliberate untruth.

"Where strife and disunity are generated," he wrote in 1860 to his fellow deacon and paternal brother, John Stoltzfus,

> there it produces hard words. Then it's the enemy's turn. Harsh words are blurted out more ugly than they are intended to be. Then the enemy seeks to make a confusion. The words become stretched, perhaps intentionally misconstrued. Then the command of Matt. 18 [about confronting one's brother] comes into neglect and instead of making a brotherly address they tell others that so-and-so had told him or done it and add perhaps still more to it. . . . Then it goes from one to another and becomes always bigger until finally the matter is completely altered from what the meaning was in the beginning. Finally the matter comes before the congregation or before the spiritual rulers [the ministry]. Then the enemy is not idle. Then he uses the opportunity to have the matter handled in passion and quarrelsomeness. . . . Then it comes to disorder. This is what pleases the enemy. And after this it goes from slander to talking behind the back. Love grows cold and if one is overtaken in a fault, the opposition party tries, if possible, to tumble him down further, instead of helping him back.

In this fragmentation the enemy [Satan] is always victorious. Now one comes to believe that we can no longer go forward with one another.[5]

In a final crescendo of that anguish-filled letter, Christian blurted out: "Oh my hand and heart are badly twisted" at the prospect of a division of the congregation. From 1873 to 1880 dissension was so great in the Buffalo Valley congregation that the Lord's Supper, normally a twice-a-year event, could be observed only once.[6] A few years later, in the early 1880s, this congregation experienced almost total disintegration.

For much of the same decade (1871-77) and under similar circumstances, no communion services were held in the Lower Pequea congregation in Lancaster County. In this instance the strife resulted in a permanent division of the congregation. Although the experiences of the Buffalo Valley and the Lower Pequea congregations are not entirely typical, it is clear that the council meetings of many congregations left much to be desired.

Congregations engulfed in controversy were not under any mandate to seek outside help. No permanent agency of the church was on the ready to attempt to put out these congregational brush fires. Yet resources were available to such congregations which could be called upon, impromptu fashion, if given sufficient time. Ministers and especially bishops of congregations experiencing a crisis frequently wrote letters to their fellow ministers in other congregations, sometimes quite distant, requesting advice. No doubt counsel was also solicited in person if the ministers of the respective congregations lived within commuting distance of each other.

There was a standard procedure in critical situations requiring decisive action, however. The local ministers might invite certain of their co-workers in other congregations to come in and give their counsel to the problems at hand. Commonly the task of choosing such outside advisers was shared between the congregation and the ministry, resulting sometimes in a stalemate when the two parties disagreed.

In some instances these visiting brethren, usually bishops, were merely to provide advice. But not infrequently they were to come to a conclusion, a *Beschluss,* the acceptance of which the congregation had committed itself to in advance. Sometimes the use of such ad hoc ministers' meetings worked well, but with no continuing agency to supervise the execution of the ruling it failed more often than not. The weaknesses of this kind of improvisation will be forcefully illustrated in chapter 7.

Forces in Support of Denominational Unity

The formal structure of the Amish church was congregational. But a familial and ethnic infrastructure—to use a term borrowed from other disciplines—mostly invisible but quite potent, much wider than the congregation, contributed greatly to denominational unity. Family and ethnic ties reached from the congregations in Lancaster County to Mifflin and Somerset counties, and much farther—from Pennsylvania to Iowa.

In 1868 the ministry of the Lancaster County congregations decided to break off relations with all churches west of the Susquehanna River. The above-mentioned Christian Stoltzfus, who lived in Union County, immediately west of that natural dividing line, wrote a forceful protest to his deacon brother John in Lancaster County. He asked how his brethren in Lancaster County could do such a thing so lightly to the Union County brethren, especially since many of the latter were "blood relatives" as well as spiritual brothers of the former.[7]

Blood relationships affected church affairs elsewhere. Almost a decade later, in 1877, the Conestoga congregation on the Lancaster-Berks County line was in the process of rejecting the authority of the conservative bishop Christian Ummel (1809-96). Henry and Fannie Fisher wrote a gracious letter to Fannie's brother and his wife (Henry U. and Malinda Stoltzfus) pleading earnestly that they and their congregation should not persist in their present course of action.[8] Neither of the letters prevented division, but they reveal a force which must have been conducive to unity.

These letters illustrate another kind of denominational tie. Mail and intercommunity visitation were significant elements in the infrastructure of the Amish church. Letters between relatives were often concerned primarily with mundane and earthly affairs, ranging from weather conditions to the prices of farm products, family health, and deaths of friends and relatives. But even such correspondence surely helped denominational unity. More clearly helpful in holding the denomination together were the letters between church leaders. Large numbers of letters found in the Lydia Mast Collection, the Christian Z. Mast Papers, and the "Long" Christian Zug Papers prove emphatically that such correspondence was useful in resolving church problems.[9] Occasional uncharitable comments could and did produce opposite results.

Intercommunity visiting likewise served to promote understanding and peace within the Amish church. Even those virtually institutionalized treks taken by young men in search of a wife were beneficial. Such trips sometimes extended from Pennsylvania to Iowa or from Iowa to Pennsylvania.[10] Railway transportation, which became generally available by 1860 or before, greatly facilitated such visiting. Amish families—commonly only husbands and wives—who had become relatively prosperous, promptly used that means to visit friends and relatives in distant localities and states.[11] This practice also strengthened denominational ties as well as those of kinship.

Most impressive of all such visiting are the trips which Amish ministers took in pursuit of denominational peace and harmony. Early in the century such travel was by horseback. One of the most notable of such was the journey undertaken in about 1826 by Bishop David Zook and a fellow minister of Wayne County, Ohio, to Mifflin County, Pennsylvania, and then on to Lancaster County. They were trying to end the controversy concerning the rebaptism of Mennonites who sought membership in an Amish congregation.

When Zook's efforts failed, Bishop Christian Yoder, Senior (1758-1838), of Somerset County, Pennsylvania, made two trips to Wayne County in a further attempt to bring about a solution to the rebaptism controversy. But Yoder was no more successful than Zook,[12] although the endeavors of these two men probably laid the groundwork for the ultimate resolution of the controversy. On this matter it took the more formal structure of several specially called ministers' meetings to arrive at a solution.[13]

When rail transportation became widely available, travel by ministers and bishops in the interests of the church multiplied dramatically. In the third quarter of the century the Amish church suffered one division after another. Exchange of preaching privileges between ministers across the entire church was constantly encouraged as a principal means of stemming the epidemic of schisms. This practice was not very effective. But it may have contributed appreciably to the organization of a majority of the change-oriented Amish congregations into that body which came to be called Amish Mennonite.

Spiritual kinship was also powerful. The strong religious beliefs and practices of the Amish were interlaced by generations of common observance. These were reinforced by persecution and by the almost sacred respect given to the *Ausbund* and the *Martyrs Mirror*, with their accounts of martyrdom. Such elements all helped to keep the unity of the faith and resist schism.

In addition to these informal forces in support of denominational unity, Amish church polity provided two structured procedures for maintaining that harmony. These procedures were used in cases where whole congregations were aligned against each other, or the congregations of one region against another region. In such events a meeting or meetings of the ministers of the congregations involved, often including some ministers from neutral congregations, might be called. Most of the ministers' meetings mentioned in chapter 2—in the first half of the century—served in a general way to keep the unity of the faith.

Noteworthy are the several meetings held between 1826 and 1831 in Wayne County, Ohio, and Somerset County, Pennsylvania, in particular—called to reconcile sharp differences between the two regions. The rulings coming out of these meetings of 1826-31 were accepted only reluctantly by the Wayne County congregation. Nevertheless they served to reduce the differences between the two regions for a considerable period of time.[14] A conference attended by ministers from Illinois and Iowa as well as from Holmes and Wayne counties, heretofore not mentioned, was held in 1849 at Berlin in Holmes County, Ohio. The controversy addressed by the conference related to the new issue—that of baptizing converts while kneeling in a stream of water.[15]

After 1850 ad hoc regional meetings became quite common. Some correspondence among the Lancaster County ministers leads one to believe that in the 1860s the latter were meeting at regular intervals.[16] As will be seen in chapters 8 and 9, the biggest innovation in the governance of the Amish church after 1850 was the introduction of annual churchwide ministers' meetings (Mennonites would have called them conferences).

Reference was made above to the Lancaster County congregations breaking off relations with some of the western congregations. This was a second kind of device—a sanction in effect—which could be used to discourage congregational deviation from established norms of Amish faith and practice. It meant the termination of various forms of cooperation and of the sharing of responsibilities between the ministers east of the Susquehanna River with those west of that line. Ministerial duties in view included administering baptism and communion, preaching, or giving an admonition at a regular Sunday morning service. In Amish religious parlance, the Lancaster ministers would no longer serve (*dienen; diena* in the vernacular) with their western brethren.

A formal signal was available, if needed, to indicate this breaking of fellowship between congregations. If ministers from an offending congregation attended services at an offended congregation, the ministers of the latter would openly withhold the customary kiss of peace from the former. Sometimes this was done without prior notice, to the dismay and humiliation of the ministers so snubbed. An offending congregation could be thus isolated and shown the united disapproval of all other congregations. On occasion this kind of ostracism or the threat of it may well have been effective. However, when the Lancaster congregations tried to use it against a large number of western churches, its effect was divisive rather than unifying.

The Structure of the Amish Ministry

The Amish of the nineteenth century—and the Mennonites as well—had a common name for their several categories of ordained men. They called them *Diener*, the literal translation for which is *servant*, although the common translation, *minister*, having a similar root meaning, is quite appropriate. The Amish never completely lost sight of the literal meaning of this word, and their leadership continued to maintain a low profile. Yet clearly this title had come to denote a considerable degree of distinction, prestige, and even power, although the expressions of such were subdued. Evidences of this trend become visible as one follows the changes in the several ministerial offices of the Amish church in the course of the nineteenth century.

For most of the century the Amish church had four categories of ordained men. The names attached to each of these classifications varied greatly, but back of those variations was a common image. For the office of deacon the Amish usually used the German terms *Diacon* or *Armendiener* (minister to the poor), although in the latter part of the century *Almosenpfleger* (alms administrator) came into common use. They called their ministers or preachers *Diener zum Buch* or *Diener des Worts* (minister to the Book or minister of the Word) or *Lehrer* (teacher or preacher).

A faithful deacon might be advanced to full deacon (*völliger Armendiener* or *bestätigten Diacon*). Still other terms were available to indicate this office. Finally, a faithful minister might in due time be advanced to full minister or elder (*völliger Diener* or *Ältester*). In the 1860s the Amish began occasionally to call them *bishops* (*Bischöfe*).

Little concern can be detected as to which of the several terms for each office should be used.[17] On the other hand, however, there was an unyielding insistence that an ordained official at any level must carry out the duties of his office. There was equal insistence that he carry out only those duties and not infringe on the assignments of other officers.[18]

To avoid confusion and following precedent in writing about Amish, the terms *deacon, minister,* and *bishop* are regularly used in this account, even for the earlier period, before *bishop* appears in the records. Whatever the label, the leaders were accountable to God and the congregation for fulfilling their delegated responsibilities.

The Office of Deacon

The office of deacon was imported full-blown from Europe and remained essentially unchanged throughout the nineteenth century. The several ministers' manuals of the late eighteenth and nineteenth centuries are in essential agreement as to the duties assigned to this office. The deacon was "to care for widows and orphans and receive alms and give them out with the counsel of the church," participate in the procedures required for the proper ordering of marriages, "read the Scriptures for the ministers when it is requested and . . . serve with water in the baptismal ceremony if . . . requested to do so."[19]

An older document, written by a European bishop in 1781 and widely circulated and respected in America, adds to these duties of deacons. They were to assist the elders "in matters of the government and discipline of the church or in dealings with the government."[20] This responsibility of assisting the elder or bishop in adjusting church difficulties was clearly one of the deacon's duties in the Amish church in America as well as in Europe. The best example is Deacon Christian Stoltzfus, whose principal churchly activity for forty-four years was that of maintaining the ecclesiastical fences and dealing with strife within the congregation.

Custom also gave the deacon a specific duty at baptismal services. He was to prepare and stand by with a pitcher of water. When the elder held out his cupped hands over the head of the applicant, the deacon poured in some water. The elder then released the water on the head. When some congregations began to baptize in a stream, the elder or bishop would dip the water directly from the stream. In such circumstances this function assigned to the deacon's office became obsolete.

The Office of Full Deacon or Confirmed Deacon

The Amish included in their categories of ministerial offices that of full deacon or confirmed deacon. The several German terms for this office numbered at least six (with variations of each). These were *völliger Armendiener, bestätigten Armendiener, völliger Almosenpfleger, bestätigten Almosenpfleger, bestätigten Diacon,* and *Ältester Armen-diener!*

This office of full deacon was clearly not one established in New Testament times. Neither is it found in any other Anabaptist groups in any era. It was imported from Europe. Full deacon is listed as one of the four standard offices in a fully organized Amish congregation in all minister's manuals originating in Europe and in all their revisions in nineteenth-century America.

A deacon could be promoted or raised (*erhöhet*) to full deacon after a period of probationary service, sometimes indicated as eight years but often stated in less precise language.[21] In studying the minister's manuals, one is drawn toward the conclusion that promotion to full deacon was intended to be virtually automatic, provided a deacon proved satisfactory and faithful during his trial period. Always, however, such advancement required the formality of approval by the congregation.

Sometimes the several German terms for full deacon are translated *deacon bishop,* a less-than-literal translation but nevertheless descriptive of the office. As the term implies, the responsibilities assigned to this office infringed appreciably on those of the other three offices. This fact distressed both the ministry and the laity who wanted such matters to be carefully delineated.

To begin with, a full deacon retained all the duties which had been his as ordinary deacon. Now in addition he was also to serve as designated critic of the sermon or sermons of the Sunday morning services. He had a "special responsibility for seeing that the Word" was "taught in its purity." He usually did this when called upon to give his testimony each Sunday by saying: "So far as I have heard and understood I believe that we have heard God's Word preached today,"[22] or words to that effect.

A full deacon also had greater responsibility for dealing with personal and family conflicts within the congregation and in the administration of church discipline. He was "to have oversight over the regulations of the church and to be responsible for their enforcement," a duty which often made him quite unpopular.[23] It seems that he was expected to be the buffer between the congregation and the elder or bishop, taking the brunt of any "ill feelings against the elder."[24]

One function of a full deacon which led to considerable trouble was that of preaching. He was not to take a regular turn with the ministers of the Word. However, he was to preach if "requested to do so." He could not even open the service unless requested by a minister of the Word or the bishop, or possibly in the latter's absence.[25] Later, in the third quarter of the century, the frequent preaching of a few fluent full deacons was to cause extreme ill will in their respective communities.

One further responsibility of a full deacon was that of acting in the capacity of a bishop when such was not available. This duty is not found in any extant minister's manual but is strongly confirmed by tradition and custom. The historical origin of such authorization probably dates back to eighteenth-century Europe, when the bishop was sometimes in prison or in hiding.[26] It was this function which led Full Deacon John C. Yoder (d. 1906) of Lagrange County, Indiana, to say that his office was a "difficult" one, for such "official must be ready at a moment's notice to perform any of the rites of the church" although "he might seldom or never be called upon to do so."[27]

Ambiguities surrounded the duties of a full deacon. It is not surprising that one full deacon might function quite differently from another, depending on his own personality and the attitude of the Amish community which he served. Michael Schwartz (1804-85) was silenced in 1861 for reasons unknown while serving in Lancaster County but restored to his office in 1869 after moving to the Buffalo Valley community. He seemed never to have the full respect of the latter congregation and was overshadowed by ordinary Deacon Christian Stoltzfus, who had served the congregation since 1839.

At the other extreme Samuel Yoder (1824-84) of Mifflin County, and John P. King (1827-87) of West Liberty, Ohio, functioned virtually as regularly ordained bishops, but incurred severe criticism in doing so. Yoder was then moved directly from full deacon to full minister or bishop—a highly irregular procedure—in an effort to avoid further disapproval. Full deacons Eli S. Miller (1821-1917), first of Holmes County, Ohio, but later of the Clinton Frame congregation in Elkhart County, Indiana[28]; Jacob Graber of Daviess County, Indiana; and Frederick Swartzendruber (1825-95) of Johnson County, Iowa, all served practically as full ministers or bishops to the end of their active ministries. In the case of Swartzendruber a muffled undercurrent of criticism persisted. As a full deacon, he was performing all the duties of a bishop, and that on a permanent basis.[29]

The case of John Stoltzfus (1805-87), illustrates the more traditional role of a full deacon. Ordained an ordinary deacon in Lancaster County in 1844, he led a small contingent of Amish settlers to Knox County, Tennessee, in 1871-72. When a congregation was organized there in 1874 he was advanced to full deacon.[30] There, in the absence of a resident bishop and far removed from other Amish communities, he could and did perform the duties of a bishop without violating or stretching the traditional patterns of church governance.

Earlier research, notably that by John S. Umble, had indicated that in nineteenth-century America a deacon was rarely and almost inadvertently advanced to full deacon. Umble viewed the office itself as an anomaly. He stated that deacons were raised to the stature of full deacon only in those few instances in which they were put in the lot, along with ministers of the congregation, for bishop. Under such circumstances, if the lot then fell on the deacon, the ordination procedure had, in a sense, miscarried. A deacon, it was thought, was not really eligible for ordination as a bishop. Nevertheless, in some regions of the church he could arrive at that office after being chosen and serving for a time as a minister of the Word. As a way out of this dilemma, said Umble, such deacons would then be ordained to the office of full deacon. After all, was not a full deacon a sort of assistant bishop?[31] This misinformation may have come to Umble from those church leaders who were active during the twilight of this office. They wanted to be rid of it and were perhaps ill-informed as to its earlier role in the affairs of an Amish congregation.

In spite of the entrenched position which this office occupied in Amish tradition, new ordinations of full deacons all but ceased by the 1880s. The practice was retained only by the Swiss Amish of Adams and Allen counties in Indiana. Already in the 1860s, questions relating to that office were creating serious dissension in the church.

Those several full deacons who could preach well and were doing so frequently came under severe criticism. Then too, the conditions for advancement from deacon to full deacon, including the length of the probationary period, were not clear. What probably disturbed these Amish leaders most was the fact that the duties of this office overlapped so extensively with those of the other three ministerial offices.[32] It therefore was fitting that, in the last decades of the nineteenth century, the office of full deacon was gradually laid to rest by both the Old Order Amish and the change-minded Amish Mennonites.

The Office of Minister or Preacher

The principal but not the only duty of the minister of the Word or the minister of the Book was to preach, or to "expound the Word." In the Sunday morning service he might open the service (make the *Anfang*), although this could be done by the deacon or full deacon. He took his turn in preaching the principal sermon of the morning. If he did none of these on a particular Sunday, quite certainly he would be expected to state his response, his *Zeugnis*, to what his fellow minister had said.

In addition to admonishing "the people with the Word of the Lord," he was to "conduct prayers, visit the widows and orphans, care for and comfort [them], watch over the congregation according to the discipline, [and] assist the elders in the work of the Lord."[33] Other than preaching and praying, most of the other duties here listed were obviously to be carried out in cooperation with either the deacon or the elder, depending on the nature of the responsibility. The role of the minister remained essentially unchanged throughout the nineteenth century.

The term *Lehrer* (literally *teacher*, but more descriptively *preacher*) was sometimes applied to any ordained person who admonished or "instructed in the Word," whether he was deacon, minister, or bishop. More commonly *Lehrer* referred specifically to the minister. *Lehrer* appears in Anabaptist church literature intermittently from the early years of the movement through and beyond the nineteenth century.

Another term, *Prediger* (preacher), was used by the Amish at Montbéliard in Alsace already in the 1750s.[34] The first appearance of that term among the Amish in America thus far discovered is in the writings of immigrant Christian Erismann, Illinois schoolteacher. In the latter 1860s, he referred to the *Prediger* repeatedly in his *Tagebuch*. Abram Mast, minister at Walnut Creek in Holmes County, Ohio, for the last four decades of the nineteenth century, used this term both in private correspondence and in his congregational record book.[35] Use of *Prediger* among the conservative or Old Order Amish in this period has not been discovered. However, in informal conversation today the Old Order Amish talk freely about the *Prediger*, the more traditional terms being used primarily at ordination services. Quite possibly this layman's use of *Prediger* in informal conversation reaches back into the nineteenth century.

The Office of Elder or Full Minister

The senior ministerial office in an Amish congregation, in Europe and later in America, was that of *Ältester* (elder) or *völliger Diener* (full minister). In spite of assertions by researchers in Amish church history to the contrary,[36] these terms and minor variations of the same always referred to the senior ministerial office in the congregation. Throughout most of the nineteenth century, *Ältester* (elder) was the most common term used for this office. Full minister was used much less frequently. The term *Bischof* (bishop), introduced in the 1860s, comes in for a weak third.

Some of the confusion revolving around the ministerial offices is attributable to the practice in the Mennonite Church of using *elder* for the one who performed the duties of a deacon. The Amish used *elder* for a full minister. This confusion found its way into the pages of the *Herald of Truth* and the *Herold der Wahrheit* in 1865 and was shared by both the readers and the editorial staff.[37]

Just as a deacon could be advanced to the office of full or confirmed deacon, so a minister might be raised to the office of full or confirmed minister, or elder. Such advancement was almost routine for a deacon until early in the nineteenth century. The same cannot be asserted with finality for a minister, although the evidence suggests such to be the case.

This theory is supported by an overview of the several minister's manuals of the eighteenth and nineteenth centuries, along with some churchly letters and other literature. These sources imply—or suggest—that it was intended that the lower level of officers, the ordinary or "designated" deacons and ministers, be retained in these respective offices for only a limited or probationary period. Advancement was apparently dependent only, or largely, upon faithful performance of duties during the trial period.

That congregational record book, the *Gemeinde Buch*, of the congregation at Montbéliard for the years 1750-1896, is clear on this point. The sole criterion for the advancement of a minister to the office of elder in that region was the faithful completion of a term of service in his original office.[38] The minister's manual of 1781, drawn up by the European bishop, Hans Nafziger, likewise calls for a probationary interval before a minister may be advanced to full minister. No other qualification is mentioned nor reference made to any other circumstance calling for such ordination—such as a vacancy in the office of elder. It therefore seems that here again faithfulness in the trial period was the sole requirement for such advancement.[39] Under such arrangements several elders might serve together in the same congregation, a not uncommon circumstance in a nineteenth-century Amish congregation.

However, the documents show a shift in the Amish ministerial structure during the first half or more of the nineteenth century in the direction of a ministerial hierarchy. By 1862 Deacon John Stoltzfus was saying in his "Short Account" that the choice of full minister was to be made from among the several ministers of the congregation. The remaining ministers clearly retained the lesser status.

Shortly after Stoltzfus made this observation, a new title was introduced into Amish nomenclature, that of *Bischof.* Use of this term as a synonym for full minister or elder appears abruptly in 1864. It may be found at several points in the minutes of the annual churchwide meeting of Amish ministers held in June 1864. In that same year the term was used repeatedly in a ministerial letter composed by Bishop Christian Ummel and several of his fellow ministers in Lancaster County.

This new title was also used in that anonymous document which appears to be the unfinished minutes of a meeting of Pennsylvania ministers on April 20, 1864, at Pequea, Lancaster County, Pennsylvania. It mentions the *Altesten [sic] Diener oder Bischof* (the elder-minister or bishop).[40] After 1864, but sparingly at first, the Amish used *bishop* interchangeably with elder and full minister.

The term *bishop,* appropriated by the Amish in the mid-1860s, may have been the result of Mennonite influence. If so, it had substantive significance. Among the Mennonites a bishop was clearly an administrative officer (and not one of several) who had oversight of a congregation or of a cluster of congregations. The earlier and perhaps more biblical procedure was to advance a minister on the basis of faithful service rather than because of the need for an administrative head. One is drawn toward the conclusion that the older pattern was gradually, perhaps almost imperceptibly, losing ground to a more hierarchical arrangement for the ministers of a congregation.

Whether a particular congregation had only one, or more than one, elder or full minister, the duties of these officers were arduous. As chief administrator the elder presided over congregational counsel meetings in which a wide range of matters could arise. The wearing of a single button alongside the customary hooks and eyes, gross immorality, or the silencing of a minister might be under consideration.[41] Thereafter it was his duty, at least for the more important decisions, to carry out the mandate of the congregation.

Only an elder (or, if such were not available, a full deacon) could baptize, preside at the observance of the Lord's Supper or at ordination services, or officiate at weddings. Serious infractions of the rules and regulations of the church were handled by him. Administering the congregational rite of excommunication was his awesome duty, as was the more happy one of restoring the disobedient on evidence of their repentance. Similarly it was his duty to formally silence a disqualified minister and likewise to preside over his reinstatement if it was decided that he should be restored.[42]

The Awesome Charge of Amish Ministry

In 1866, near the close of his life, Bishop Jacob Swartzendruber (1800-68) wrote disconsolately of his life as a minister and bishop. "God knows everything," he said,

> I have often stood before the church in fear and in a troubled spirit and in tears have warned the congregation . . . and what is my reward for the fifteen years in Iowa? God knows that often I did not feel myself worthy to stand before the church, but my calling compelled it.
> I have been in the ministry . . . for forty years, and thirty-three years in America. I was there [in the Grantsville, Maryland, area] before Benedict Miller died, an upright man, and I also was with Jonas Bitsch [Beachy] and saw that all of these men were criticized by ungrateful members of the church and so it has gone with nearly all ministers that I can recall. It does not surprise me that the same thing happens to me in my weakness. . . .
> Written by me the distressed, depressed human being Jacob Swartzendruber. . . . It seems that I must live my short life in trouble, and if I were not in the ministry I could be in peace with almost all men, according to the teachings of Paul.[43]

Ordained a minister in Europe in about 1826, Swartzendruber had moved to America with his family in 1833. After serving at two locations in the area of Somerset County, Pennsylvania, and Grantsville, Maryland, he had moved to Johnson County, Iowa, in 1851. There two years later he was ordained a full minister.[44]

Some of Swartzendruber's troubles may be attributed to the rough edges of his personality. Nevertheless, his kind of experience was shared by many of his "fellow workers in the vineyard of the Lord." Much of what he and other ministers experienced was virtually built into the structure and theology of the Amish ministry. According to early Anabaptist tradition, a *Diener* was truly to be a servant. He must keep a low profile, for the Amish insistence on humility was binding on the ministry as well as the laity.

Bishop Isaac Schmucker (1810-93), of the Haw Patch congregation in Lagrange County, Indiana, may have combined humility with faithfulness in pastoral responsibilities more satisfactorily than did Bishop Swartzendruber. J. S. Hartzler served under Schmucker in the early years of his (Hartzler's) ministry. He said that sometimes Schmucker would become involved personally in some of the troubles of the congregation, but he had one redeeming feature. He was a splendid confessor. When he saw his mistakes, no one needed to ask him to make a confession. He would do that without being asked, and oftentimes before any one had the opportunity to ask it of him. He usually wanted the congregation to give expression in his absence as to whether he was forgiven or not. It would be a wretchedly hard-hearted brother that would hold anything against a man like that.[45]

The Amish expected a minister to keep a low profile. Yet, by going to the Old Testament, they had developed a view of the ministry—including all ordained men—which bordered on the sacerdotal. The calling of ministers sometimes was compared to the ceremonial ordination and purification of priests.[46] Also from the Old Testament came the comparison of ministers to the "watchmen on the walls of Zion" who were to be "on guard and on the watch" for the enemy and to blow the trumpets when danger was sensed.[47]

When the Amish read the New Testament, they extended the analogy of Christ as the Great Shepherd to the church. The ministers were said to be shepherds, to whom the brothers and sisters were to respond, just as natural sheep respond to their shepherds.[48] On this their favorite verse was Hebrews 13:17. In Luther's version it called upon Christians to "obey your preachers [*Lehrern*] and follow them, for they watch for your souls, for which they must give an account" on the Judgment Day.[49] This verse had a two-pronged thrust. It called on the laity to obey the preachers and on the latter to obey God on the pain of suffering God's ultimate condemnation if they wavered.

God's punishment of an unfaithful minister might not wait until the judgment. Did not Bishop Jacob D. Yoder fall on evil days in the 1860s, financially and otherwise, after he had introduced stream baptism and some false doctrines into the Oak Grove congregation in Wayne County, Ohio?[50] Then Deacon Moses Kaufman of Middlebury, Indiana, died within a year after he left the conservatives to affiliate with the more change-minded Amish. And Preacher John Kenagy of the Clinton congregation, who was deprived of his ministry for some reason and later joined the Mennonites, died of cancer.[51]

Conscientious Amish ministers took all these injunctions and warnings seriously. Once chosen by God through the lot, were they not thereafter responsible to God alone? In a way the ministers, especially the full deacon and the elder, were in a no-win situation. If they tried to be strict enforcers of the *Ordnung* (the order of Amish discipline and lifestyle), they became something of tyrants in the eyes of many members of the congregation. But if they grew lax in enforcement, the more faithful of their members would say that they "kept house poorly" and were therefore unfaithful to God—an accusation every minister wanted to avoid like the plague.[52]

Choice by Lot and Ordination

The use of the lot requires further consideration. When a congregation wanted to ordain a deacon or another minister, a man was to be chosen from among the members of that congregation. Each member passed through the council chamber and named his or her nominee for the position to be filled. Then the names of all those nominees receiving two votes or more (in some congregations three votes were required) were put in the lot for minister or deacon, as the case might be. They were now on the list of candidates from which God would choose the person to fill the office in question.

Then as many books were lined up on a shelf or table as there were nominees, with one book containing a paper on which was written an appropriate passage of Scripture, such as that found in Proverbs 16:33: "The lot is cast into the lap; but the whole disposing thereof is of the Lord."[53] The lot "fell" on the nominee who selected the book containing this slip of paper. If only one person was eligible for an office (full deacon or full minister), the lot was not used.

Once selected by the lot or by vote, the candidate had to accept his ministerial assignment. He had given his word at his baptism that he would accept a call to the ministry if it came to him. If he married after his baptism this promise may have been exacted from him a second time.[54] The pledge allowed no exceptions. God did not make mistakes. If he called a man to the ministry he would also empower him to serve satisfactorily. As was asserted in the annual churchwide ministers' meeting of 1866, "the Almighty demands from no one [more] than He has entrusted to him and therefore such refusal is disobedience."[55]

Usually the response of the man who was chosen for an office was solemn, often accompanied with considerable anguish. His family shared those feelings.[56] In some instances this kind of demonstration may have been a result of the Amish emphasis on humility. It would indicate that the chosen person had the virtue so essential for a faithful follower of the Lord. Ministers were to be good examples as they walked before their flock. More likely in most cases the one called had been observing enough to realize that he was now faced with the prospect of a life not unlike that of Bishop Jacob Swartzendruber. As a boy, C. Henry Smith, Amish Mennonite of central Illinois, observed that "strong men" cried only at funerals and at their own respective ordinations. He consequently·"came to regard these events as the two great tragedies of life."[57]

The most extreme response of an Amishman faced with the call to preach was to reject it or to attempt to escape it. Numerous stories recount such efforts. One of the most poignant of these is told of another John Stoltzfus, this one of the Buffalo Valley congregation and grandson of Deacon Christian Stoltzfus of that same community. In 1883, the congregation was already well advanced in the process of disintegration after more than four decades of infighting. Preacher Christian King was moving back to Lancaster County, leaving a vacancy in the office of minister of the Word. When the congregation proceeded to fill this position, the lot fell on Stoltzfus who, when informed, promptly fainted.

"They carried him out," the account continues, and

> he frothed at the mouth. They called a doctor and he worked with him for half a day. He never fully recovered. Some thought he should be ordained. Had he not been chosen of the Lord? Should he not yield himself to be His messenger? He was not ordained but the matter weighed heavily upon him. He became a carpenter and worked with Samuel Kennel [who] said that sometimes he would stop in his work, hammer in hand, and gaze off into space for five or ten minutes. [Then] he would resume his work.[58]

"Little" David Stoltzfus, so-called because of his small stature, son-in-law of Christian, was then ordained in John's place. Knowing fully the conditions in the congregation, Grandfather Christian looked down at David and said commiseratively, "*der glanie David* (the [poor] little David)." Christian thought that David's first sermon on August 5, 1883, was "a good beginning."[59] But David became depressed at times, actually asking to be excommunicated on one occasion so he could escape from his ministerial duties. His move to Lyon County, Kansas,[60] less than two years after his ordination, may have been an attempt to escape from a particularly difficult situation. Moving away from a troubled congregation was a rather common and acceptable maneuver. Even so, the newly moved minister would be expected to accept ministerial duties in his new location.

Only a few years earlier, possibly in the late 1870s, and far to the west, in Johnson County, Iowa, Noah Troyer (1831-86) had refused to permit his name to be entered in the lot for minister. He was dissatisfied with some of the regulations of the congregation. Surprisingly, according to Sanford C. Yoder's account, "it may not have affected his membership," although it "greatly affected his standing" in the congregation. Soon thereafter he identified with the change-oriented group of Amish who were to form the nucleus of the new Union Amish Mennonite church. By some he is credited—or charged—with being the original and primary instigator of that separation.

In the midst of these events Noah began to have trances, during which he would preach for several hours. Conceivably, but far from certainly, the trauma associated with his refusal to submit to the lot may have helped to bring on these trances. In his record of the activities of Noah Troyer, Amishman S. D. Guengerich may have been hinting that the untimely death of Troyer, caused by a faulty breech pin in his gun, was God's judgment on him for his disobedience.[61]

In another instance at the end of the century, at an ordination service in one of the Somerset County Amish Mennonite congregations,

> the lot fell on a young man with little ability. When the truth of the situation seemed to dawn on him he jumped up in a frenzy and started to run for the door with several men in pursuit. One man grabbed him while he clung to the door kicking at his pursuers. He would not submit to ordination.[62]

Amish belief and practice with respect to the call to the ministry are both illustrated by the life and writings of David A. Troyer (Treyer; 1827-1906), of Holmes County, Ohio. On April 30, 1848, just before his twenty-first birthday and less than three years after his marriage, he was ordained to the ministry. Ten men had received votes, but three of them only one vote each and were not taken into the lot. Of the seven men remaining in the lot, one man received thirty-one votes while David received only three. Nevertheless, the lot having fallen on David, he was duly ordained. Within a year or two, if his biographer is correct, he was ordained as bishop.[63]

In this case, as in many other instances, the use of the lot obviously resulted in the choice of an able man. Troyer became a highly respected leader in the Amish church, remaining with the Old Order in the early 1860s when the Great Schism reached Holmes County. He also did considerable writing, including at least one article for J. F. Funk's *Herold der Wahrheit*.[64] A volume of his articles and meditations, the *Hinterlassene Schriften*, was published fourteen years after his death.

Troyer defended the Amish view of the ministry, including the use of the lot. By using the lot the choice of ministers is left to God alone. He wrote:

we are bound to the ministry by our baptismal vow . . . [and] we mortals do not have the power and the right [either] to take away the ministry from anyone, or to call anyone to the ministry, but only to vote and to cast lots and then charge him who is chosen by God in the name of the Lord and the congregation. . . . And what we may not give to him, neither may we take away from him.[65]

Troyer was thus explaining and defending the use of the lot. In addition, he was arguing with his fellow ministers about what really happens when an ordained man, for reasons thought to be biblical, is forbidden to function in his office. Troyer felt that as soon as such a minister demonstrated that he had corrected his life so that he again had the biblical qualifications for his office, the congregation had no choice but to reconfirm him in his ministry. If sin had been involved, as soon as he had been restored to full fellowship in the congregation, he should be reconfirmed.

Given the Amish theology of the calling of the minister, Troyer's position was entirely logical. But it seems that opinions, both among the conservatives and among the change-oriented Amish, varied on this question. A nineteenth-century minister's manual contains the formulary for silencing a bishop:

Just as you were ordained to the ministry and to the bishop's office in the name of the Lord and of the church, so are you now in the name of the Lord and the church again removed from the ministry and the bishop's office.[66]

This statement of congregational action implies that a silenced minister could be restored to his office once again only by selection through the lot, as had been the procedure at his original ordination.

The minutes of the annual churchwide ministers' meetings of 1862-78 indicate a reluctance to restore fallen ministers to their office. But they were willing to allow individual congregations considerable discretion in the matter.

Already in the 1864 meeting John Kanegy had inquired as to the proper procedures for restoring such ministers,[67] but an answer was not forthcoming until 1868. The meeting of that year rejected the idea that restoration of a silenced or a fallen minister was automatic or even routine after he had repented and been restored to full fellowship in the congregation. It was agreed without dissent that he could only be restored "by a unanimous counsel [united consent of the congregation] or if called to it by the lot."[68] In the instance of a minister who had been silenced but not put under the ban, the annual meeting of 1874 urged that he be restored "to his ministry as soon as possible if he has made his mistakes entirely right."[69]

The origin of the use of the lot in the selection of ministers in the Amish church in America lies in mystery. Its use among the Amish in Europe was not common. None of the minister's manuals which had their origins in Europe calls for any use of that instrument. Bishop Hans Nafziger's minister's manual of 1781 directed that "the one who has received the most votes" shall be selected for the office to be filled. The presiding minister then says to this candidate that "since the most votes have fallen on you [suggesting only a plurality, and not necessarily a majority], you are appointed to the office of minister." A deacon was to be chosen in the same fashion. Another eighteenth-century document, known as the Unzicker Manual, provides for similar procedures in the choice of brethren to be ordained.[70]

The record book of the Montbéliard congregation for almost the entire period of 1750-1896 consistently records the choice of men to be ordained by "vote of the congregation," "voice of the congregation," "vote of the brotherhood," a "plurality vote (die meisten Stimmen)," or a "majority (die Mehrheit)." There is no record indicating that the lot was used at Montbéliard until 1879. At that time, and only then, were two ministers ordained by lot (*durch das Los*).[71]

The lot was in general use whenever feasible in the Amish congregations of America throughout the nineteenth century. The Amish settlement in Lewis County, New York, was an exception. It retained the European procedures until 1874.[72] John Stoltzfus' "Short Account," written in 1862, indicates that in America at that time the use of the lot was standard procedure and a practice of long standing. In the time of his forefathers, he wrote,

> ministers were first nominated by vote of the brethren and sisters of the congregation. Then those who had the most votes were taken into the lot. Scattered votes were not taken into the lot.[73]

Two theories may be advanced to explain the difference between the earlier practice of the Amish in Europe and the almost universal use of the lot by the Amish in America. It is possible that the early Amish migrants to this country came from areas of Europe where at least some use was made of the lot and brought this practice with them. A second possibility seems unlikely but conceivable—that the Amish borrowed the lot from the Mennonites, who were using it.

The structure of the ministry among the early Anabaptists, it has been asserted, was unfettered and fluid,[74] a not unusual circumstance in the early years of a religious movement. However, long before the beginning of the nineteenth century, many Anabaptist groups, including the Amish, had moved to the opposite extreme. Among the Amish, ordination had become almost a sacrament.

In Amish church polity, one kind of minister must take great care not to encroach upon the assigned duties of another. Conditions for advancement to a senior or higher position were quite rigid. Moving sideways in the ministerial hierarchy, from deacon to minister, was in some areas of the church all but impossible. The individual had no choice in the matter, and even the call of the congregation was muted through the interposition of the lot. The Amish of that day and this, however, would say that the arrangement was and is strictly scriptural.

4

Nineteenth-Century Amish Beliefs and Lifestyle

The Dordrecht Confession of Faith

Early in 1861 Deacon Christian Stoltzfus of Union County, Pennsylvania, became involved in a discussion with Bishop John K. Stoltzfus (1805-84) of the Millcreek congregation of Lancaster County. The subject was the duties of deacons, particularly the extent of their participation in the Sunday morning congregational worship service. Christian thought deacons should preach occasionally in such meetings, but he did not assert that this should happen on a regular basis. In supporting his position he referred to article 9 of the Dordrecht Confession of Faith. This document, said Christian, "we acknowledge as being God's Word, and already so many thousands [of baptismal candidates] have been instructed according to it."

Christian received an unusual response from the bishop, who countered by saying that the Dordrecht "articles are made by man . . . [for] the names of the men are right there with it [appended to the document]." To this the deacon replied with good logic that with such reasoning "you might just as well say that the [New] Testament was made by man."[1]

Bishop Stoltzfus may have been taken off guard or even misquoted by the deacon. In any event, Christian, along with almost all Amish people, was not willing to put the Dordrecht Confession much below the Scriptures in authority. In 1632, after decades of struggle and effort, this confession had been drawn up at Dordrecht in the Netherlands and was eventually confirmed by most of the functioning Mennonite groups of the seventeenth century.

Devised about sixty years before the Amish division of the 1690s, it was now, in the nineteenth century, the accepted statement of faith for both the Amish and the Mennonites. The latter, however, were inclined to apply article 16 (on excommunication) and especially article 17 (on shunning) with less rigor than were the Amish.

Had one pressed an Amish church leader to rank the Dordrecht document with the Scriptures, he would have given the higher authority to Scripture. He might not have done it with the boldness exhibited by Bishop Stoltzfus, but he might well have added that the question was immaterial. Had not the participants in the conference at Dordrecht searched the Scriptures diligently and prayed earnestly for divine guidance? How could they have erred?[2] This confidence in the spiritual purity and doctrinal integrity of their forefathers accounts to a considerable extent for the respect given to this day to religious custom and tradition by the Amish.

This confidence in the Dordrecht Confession of Faith is a recurring theme in nineteenth-century Amish writings. In the third quarter of the century, when some Amish leaders in the annual conference of 1864 were ready to propose a few carefully selected changes in Amish custom and practice, they nevertheless asserted that they meant to hold fast to "our eighteen Articles [of the Dordrecht Confession] of Faith, which were always recognized by our forebears, and which are still recognized by us."[3] Again at the 1872 conference a committee exhorted some dissident ministers in Illinois

> to hold on to the articles of faith as they were put together at Dordrecht . . . which, according to our understanding, is the true Christian faith which the apostles believed and taught in their time, and have sealed with their blood and death.[4]

In 1897 the Amish Mennonites and the several district conferences of the Mennonite Church were contemplating closer cooperation through a biennual general conference. Even then it was proposed that membership should be open to those district conferences which, along with other qualifications, "are in harmony with the eighteen articles of faith adopted . . . at Dordrecht in 1632."[5] Used as the basis for the instruction of applicants for baptism, it might well have been called the Amish (and Mennonite) catechism.[6]

The Amish have the same Anabaptist roots as the Mennonites. They draw their doctrinal position from the same confession of faith. Thus it is not surprising that the respective positions of the Amish and the Mennonites in the nineteenth century were, in the words of J. C. Wenger, "quite similar."[7] For the most part, therefore, this description of Amish beliefs will be concerned with distinctive Amish nuances of

Anabaptist doctrines. It will give nineteenth-century Amish leaders considerable liberty to describe their doctrines in their own words.

The Holy Scriptures

The holy Scriptures, *Die heilige Schrift* were just that, the sacred writings. The word *Bibel* (Bible) was not used by the Amish until the end of the century. Along with many other denominations the Amish spoke of the Scriptures as "God's Word." What Norman Kraus has said about the nineteenth-century Mennonites applies equally to the Amish:

> The Bible is accepted as completely trustworthy and inspired by God for man's guidance, but emphasis falls upon the content and unique value of its message . . . , not upon verbal inerrancy. . . . They simply assumed its divine origin and validity,

a stance which Kraus appropriately labels "pre-theological biblicism."[8] This assumption was nevertheless conscious and considered, at least for the more studious of the Amish church leaders.

A few Amish leaders were *asserting*, rather than merely *assuming*, the authority of the Bible. In 1865 the well-known Amish layman, Shem Zook (1798-1880), observed that the Amish Mennonites "consider the Scriptures as the only rule of faith."[9] This statement is in line with the nineteenth-century Amish and Mennonite view of the Scriptures and in contrast to the twentieth-century fundamentalist position on the verbal inspiration of the Bible.

The conservative Bishop David Beiler of Lancaster County came much closer than Zook to claiming verbal inerrancy for the Scriptures. Already in 1857 he had reminded his readers of Deuteronomy 4:2, where the Israelites were warned not to "add unto the word which I command you," neither to "diminish ought from it." He then added to this reference another from Revelation 22:18-19 (also cited in article 5 in the Dordrecht Confession of Faith), which warned against adding to or taking from "the words of the prophecy of this book."[10]

The Amish used both Luther's translation and the Froschauer printings of the Zürich translations of the Scriptures, both of early Reformation origin. They made comparisons between the two without asserting the superiority of one over the other. This supports Kraus's statement that they were more concerned with the message of the Bible than with the question of its verbal inspiration. Even in the midst of the divisive controversy of the 1850s and the 1860s over stream baptism, both parties to the dispute quoted Scripture from both versions. The change-minded faction sought to prove that true New Testament baptism took place *in* water, the traditionalists that the Scriptures merely called for baptism *with* water.

In contrast, the preoccupation of the fundamentalists of the first half of the twentieth century was with the unique authority of the King James Version of the Bible. Probably most of the Amish leaders in America would have settled for the affirmation of Christian Peterschmitt, Amish minister in Europe. In 1871 he wrote that he was sure "the Word of God has been handed down to us flawless (*lauter*) and pure (*rein*) and unadulterated (*unverfälscht*)."[11]

Concerning the ultimate authority of and respect for the Scriptures, however, Amish spokesmen were adamant; these must be shored up. "The Lord wants His Word to be proclaimed," said David Beiler, "and not man's learning or philosophizing."[12] When the annual ministers' meetings were initiated in 1862, it was resolved that the proceedings be "based entirely on the Word of God."[13] That statement was reiterated and amplified by the conferences of later years.

Any deviation from the traditional use and interpretation of specific passages of Scripture was regarded as tampering with God's Word. When Bishop Jacob D. Yoder, of Wayne County, Ohio, introduced a new interpretation of the temptation and fall of Adam and Eve, he was immediately faulted by one of his fellow ministers in the congregation.[14] And when the news spread to the neighboring congregations in Holmes and Stark counties, he incurred much additional criticism. Amish tradition called for the careful scrutiny of every sermon by the preacher's fellow ministers, and especially by the full deacon, for possible heresy.

The Bible was clearly not a "flat book" to the Amish. If there was any question about the final word or will of God on a certain matter, the *Evangelium*, the New Testament, was the final authority. The Old Testament was to be interpreted in light of the New. They attempted to find in the Scriptures, either through precept or example, the answer for every question relating to their faith or their lifestyle. When they found no answers in the *Evangelium*, they were quite ready to turn to the Old Testament.

The Old Testament also served as a preface to the New. Recorded Amish sermons literally teem with references to Old Testament "types and shadows" of persons and events described in the New. Samson as a deliverer was a figure of Christ, as were Moses and Joshua. The temple was a type of the spiritual temple or church of the New Testament, with Jesus Christ as the cornerstone. Noah's ark typified the New Testament ark of salvation. The dead lion in which honey was found (Judges 14:5-9), was a figure of the "dead believer." The earthly land of Canaan was a figure of heaven, the promised land for every true follower of Christ. Just as the Israelites strove against enemies, so must Christians fight against their spiritual enemies, albeit with spiritual weapons only. The serpent in the wilderness (Numbers 21:9) was a type of Christ, as confirmed by the New Testament (John 3:14).[15]

Then there was the Apocrypha. This body of writings was included in both Luther's and Froschauer's translations as well as in the early printings of the King James Version. It was not generally thought to have equal authority with the remainder of the Old Testament, yet it was used and quoted freely. Deacon John Stoltzfus observed in the annual ministers' meeting of 1868 that merchandising in itself is not dishonest, but "sin sticks between the buyer and the seller like a nail between two hard rocks." Everyone no doubt recognized this well-known quotation from Sirach 27:2.[16]

In condemning the taking of photographs, a ministers' meeting of 1876 called attention to the Wisdom of Solomon concerning the origin of this sinful practice. The entire passage (14:15-21) was included in the minutes of the session.[17] In 1885 Bishop David A. Troyer (Treyer) of Holmes County, Ohio, chose to quote from Sirach (16:12) on the nature of God: "Although God is merciful, he is also wrathful. He is reconciling, but he also punishes fearfully."[18] In spite of the respect shown for them, there was some recognition that the Apocryphal books were not "to be counted among the books of Holy Writ," as stated in one of the minister's manuals.[19]

The most extensive use of the Apocrypha was made in connection with the instruction of couples about to be married and in the marriage ceremony as well. Since marriage is referred to elsewhere in the Bible only in generalities, the Amish resorted to the book of Tobit, chapters 5-9. There Tobias's marriage to Sarah, daughter of Raguel, is described in considerable detail.[20]

Other Sources of Amish Doctrine

Along with the Dordrecht Confession of Faith, the Amish used and respected greatly another document which predated Jacob Ammann, the *Martyrs Mirror*. It told of the sufferings of those who were faithful to Christ from the age of the New Testament through and beyond the Protestant Reformation. First published in 1660, it was considered an authentic record, a history of the true church. Large portions of it told of the sufferings of nonresistant Anabaptists during and since the Reformation. In the controversies and divisions which plagued the Amish church in the third quarter of the nineteenth century, the *Martyrs Mirror* was quoted frequently by opposing parties. References to the *Martyrs Mirror* appear alongside those to the Dordrecht Confession of Faith and the Scriptures.[21]

The Amish regarded highly several other books from which they derived considerable instruction in doctrine and style of living. Two of them, the *Foundation Book* of Menno Simons and the *Enchiridion* of Dirk or Dietrich Philips, were broad in content. They provided instruction on a wide variety of subjects relating to Anabaptist life and doctrine.[22] The support which these two Anabaptist leaders gave to applying the ban and shunning may account in part for the widespread acceptance and use of their writings by the followers of Jacob Ammann.

A third book, the *Ausbund*, also predated Ammann. This hymnbook without musical scores was used for centuries by the Mennonites as well as the Amish. It provided support for a wide variety of Amish beliefs and practices. A considerable number of songs were primarily doctrinal in nature. The several editions of the *Ausbund* in the eighteenth century were greatly enlarged over those published previously. One of the later supplements was a confession of faith, although not that drawn up at Dordrecht.[23]

The prayer book used by the Amish, *Die ernsthafte Christenpflicht*, was the fourth volume on which the Amish depended for their religious instruction and edification. Its origin lies with the Mennonites of the Palatinate soon after the Jacob Ammann schism. Yet it came to be used—perhaps *adopted* is the more appropriate word—by the Amish for both public and family prayers. Like the *Ausbund*, it grew larger from edition to edition. An early American edition, printed in 1770 at the Ephrata Cloisters, was the first to include the Dordrecht Confession of Faith.[24] The pietistic flavor of this prayer book has been noted by many writers.

Similar in pietistic flavor was a small book of Lutheran origin, the *Geistliches Lustgärtlein*,[25] which described, in the words of Robert Friedmann, "what the continuing attitude of a truly pious Christian should be."[26] In the nineteenth century this volume ranked a close second to *Christenpflicht* among American and European Amish and Mennonites.[27] In addition to its widespread use, Amish respect for it is indicated by the fact that, in the course of the nineteenth century, two Amishmen published parts of it. In 1854 Michael Lapp, Amish deacon in Lancaster County, Pennsylvania, embodied the first section in his

Handbook or Wholesome Instructions for a Godly Life.[28] In 1878 Amish schoolteacher Samuel D. Guengerich of Johnson County, Iowa, reprinted the same section again in his periodical, *Der Christliche Jugenfreund.*[29]

The Church, a Body of Obedient Believers

In formulating a doctrinal statement for the annual Amish ministers' meeting, the delegates assembled in May 1866, at Danvers, Illinois, paraphrased certain parts of 1 Corinthians 12. They declared that Christ was the head of the entire body of believers, "in whom the whole body is put together, and one member to the other member, so that one assists the other, each in his own way, so that the body may grow in self-improvement."[30] This description of the church as a close-knit body of believers, and of its relationship to Christ—whom they referred to constantly as the "chief cornerstone"—will be recognized immediately as typical Anabaptist doctrine.

This church of Christ was to be a "holy, unspotted and blameless church." If any known sin or impurity were to be tolerated, "the whole body would be ruined." Christ "demands of His disciples a godly life, a walk in accordance with the Gospel, a frank acknowledgement of the truth before men, a denial of oneself, a faithful following in His footsteps, a willing bearing of the cross, a renunciation of all things, [and] an earnest striving after the kingdom of God and His righteousness."[31]

Using an Old Testament analogy, as the Amish often did, George Jutzi, a minister of the Amish congregation at Richville, Ohio, southwest of Canton, asked:

> May anyone rightly call himself a Christian or a follower of Jesus and believe that his sins are washed away through the grace of God with the blood of Jesus, if he actually thereafter chooses to remain in the slavery of Satan, in the lust of the eyes, the lust of the flesh, and the pride of life? Truly this is as little possible as if an Israelite had remained in Egypt but nevertheless had said: "I follow after Moses, or I am a follower of Moses."[32]

In similar vein an unknown Amish minister challenged his listeners to a life of obedience to God's Word.

> Before you is placed life and death; whichever you choose, that will be given to you. If you have your desire for the evil, for death and for the world from which all unrighteousness comes, such as lying, cheating, swearing, cursing, backbiting, hatred, envy, drunkenness, pride, idolatry, covetousness, unchastity and dirty talk, dancing, copulation . . . if you

have your delight in such works you have already sold your birthright for a bowl of boiled vegetables.[33]

Becoming a disciple of Jesus was a deliberate choice, a matter of the will, to be followed by a life of obedience. In their baptismal vow Amish applicants for baptism declared that they believed they were uniting with the true church of the Lord. They promised to obey God and "the *Ordnung* of the church . . . to abide by the accepted truth, to live by it and die by it with the help of the Lord."[34]

The Amish considered the principal functions of the church to be maintaining the purity of the body of Christ and helping its members live a life of sustained obedience. Writing in 1885, Bishop David A. Troyer of Holmes County, Ohio, concluded that most of the denominations had reneged on this responsibility and had allowed all kinds of impurity to come into the churches. They had come to be "built only on sand, [only the] Old Amish and the Old Mennonites" excepted.

In saying that these alone "are yet a remnant of the old apostolic church," Troyer explicitly claimed a greater distinction for his church than did most other nineteenth-century Amish leaders.[35] However, Melvin Gingerich, speaking primarily for the Amish of Iowa, asserted that many Amish "were convinced that they alone had the true light and a few even questioned whether any but Amish could get to heaven."[36] Maintaining such a pristine level of purity required the imposition of a strict discipline, even to the excommunication and social avoidance of unruly members living in known sin.

In keeping with the belief of the Amish that the Old Testament was a preface to the New, some Amish ministers found prototypes of the church in the Old Testament. One minister proposed that "the church of God had its origin with the angels in heaven." When there was revolt among the angels the church was reestablished with Adam and Eve in Paradise. But this first pair disobeyed also. With Noah another beginning was made, although one of Noah's sons, Ham, is made responsible for a "new beginning of the church of Satan on earth." Then the church made still another beginning with Abraham. Much later came the law under Moses, "but grace and truth" awaited the coming of Jesus Christ. By him "the lost sheep of the house of Israel have been sought out and led into the true sheepfold."[37]

This sermon was likely a variation of the first sermon in the Sunday morning worship service which traditionally dealt with Old Testament themes. Yet it attempts to provide a historical-theological definition of the church not quite in keeping with the Amish tradition of letting the Scriptures speak for themselves.

As suggested earlier, obedience to Christ and his church was thought to be the essence of discipleship. *Gehorsamkeit* and *gehorsam* (*obedience* and *obedient*), with their opposites, *disobedience* and *disobedient*, were probably the most frequently used nouns and adjectives in the typical Amish sermon. They were probably used even more frequently in the shorter *Zeugnisse* (testimonies) which followed the principal Sunday morning sermon. Even when the change-minded Amish parted company with the traditionalists in the third quarter of the century, they softened their emphasis on obedience not one whit.

Was not the Amish position on obedience based on clear New Testament teaching? Entrance to "the eternal blessed life . . . is not dependent on saying Lord, Lord, but on doing the Lord's will." This truth the preacher frequently illustrated by calling attention to the two men, one of whom built his house on sand while the other built on a rock.[38] Christ had demanded the utmost when he said that one who is not willing to leave his house, his lands, his wife, and his children, and even to give up his own life, could not be his disciple. Faithful Amish ministers did not flinch at reminding their hearers of such severe, almost devastating, demands of discipleship. David Beiler called them *kräftige* or *wichtige Lehre* (strong or weighty teachings), but nonetheless mandatory on every disciple of Christ.[39]

Amish preachers and writers found much in the Old Testament concerning the rewards for obedience and the punishment of the disobedient. The sin of Adam and Eve was disobedience, a sin which brought travail upon the entire human race. Cain was rebellious and killed his brother. Lot's wife defied God by looking back toward Sodom. And Moses smote the rock when he was told to speak to it.

The Israelites repeatedly disobeyed and dishonored their God. When Saul deviated from God's command to utterly destroy the Amalekites and their cattle, Samuel reminded him that "to obey is better than sacrifice" and that "rebellion is as the sin of witchcraft" (1 Samuel 15:22-23).[40] Achan, who appropriated some war booty in disobedience to the command of Joshua, was stoned to death together with his family.

If such punishment was meted out under Old Testament law, said preacher Peter Lehman,

how much more severe discipline and punishment do you think someone would deserve who [in this dispensation of grace] treads the Son of God under foot, and dishonors the Spirit of grace and considers impure the blood of the Testament by which he is sanctified [paraphrase of Hebrews 10:29]?

Lehman concluded his comments concerning Achan by noting that, in contrast to the treatment of this man, "our Savior did not come to kill men, but to call them to repentance." Yet there remains the implication that the sinner is to be punished as well as redeemed, a duty which the congregation and the ministers were expected to perform.[41]

To show the contrast to disobedience, Amish preachers constantly noted the obedience of Abel, Noah, Abraham, Joseph, Joshua, and Caleb in order to encourage faithfulness in the church. An oft-quoted Old Testament admonition which was thought to sum up the entire duty of a Christian was lifted from Ecclesiastes 12:13: "Let us hear the conclusion of the whole matter: Fear God, and keep his commandments: for this is the whole duty of man."[42]

The obedience expected of members of the church included obeying the Ordnung and observing the established patterns of congregational life. Since the Amish had confidence in the integrity and spiritual discernment of their forefathers, who had handed down the Ordnung to them, their acceptance of it as having scriptural and spiritual significance is not difficult to understand.

The Nature of Man

In a manuscript of the 1840s consisting largely of four-line stanzas addressed to his posterity and published posthumously, George Jutzi wrote at length about the Fall of Adam and Eve. God had told this pair that if they ate of the forbidden fruit they "must die the death." So when Adam disobeyed God, all

> . . . the million multitudes
> All mankind without number
> Who were born of him
> Were caught in the Fall.
>
> All followed Adam's footsteps,
> Fell into need through sin,
> To this our footsteps witness
> That we lie in death.
>
> Always death nibbles. . . .
> Oh how has man fallen
> Who had been a child of God.
> No tongue can stammer out
> This pride, fall, and sin.[43]

Robert Friedmann has said that Jutzi's work portrays "the sturdy and concrete biblical faith [of the Amish] without much emotion."[44] But this writer finds, quite to the contrary, that this segment, along with many other extended passages of Jutzi's volume, is loaded with feeling. In any case the Amish believed that the sin of Adam resulted in the bent to sinning experienced by all mankind, even to some extent by Christ's followers. Friedmann notes that Anabaptists spoke of an inherited inclination or tendency toward evil, but denied the concept of inherited sin (Ezekiel 18:4, 20). They tried to avoid the Calvinist-oriented term, "original sin," which suggests total depravity and the damnation of children.[45]

For the Amish, one did not become guilty of the sin of Adam until one had reached the age of accountability and had become conscious of committing sins of one's own. In his book of verse Jutzi devoted page after page to a description of human sinfulness. "I want to find one soul," he moaned, "among all numbered peoples who is not flecked with sins and has had no part in the fall."[46]

Bishop Jonas D. Troyer (1811-97), a rolling stone who spent most of the years of his active ministry in various parts of Indiana, agreed with Jutzi. He wrote of man's inner *Bosheit* or tendency toward wickedness as the source of many kinds of evil conduct.[47] David A. Troyer observed that "we are such poor stubble and dust of the earth so that we can scarcely *think* rightly in ourselves and much less *do* good," in our own strength.[48] This is fittingly Amish in its description of the nature of man.

The pull toward corruption was and is recognized and resisted in the Amish baptismal formula. The applicant for baptism renounces the devil, the world, and his "own flesh and blood."[49] These prescribed words may also reflect the Anabaptist view that especially the body is tempted by evil.[50] Alluding to the baptismal vow which he had made approximately forty-five years earlier, Deacon Christian Stoltzfus said that of the above three enemies of a follower of Christ, "my own flesh and blood are for me not the smallest one."[51]

The New Birth

Given then the requirements of discipleship, how might any specimen of sinful humanity possibly become a follower of Christ? In spite of their emphasis on striving and doing, the Amish had a ready answer to this question. This wretched mortal could be recast as a victorious and obedient disciple through the transforming effect of the new birth, a miracle effected on the inner person by God. The new birth was a central doctrine 'of the Amish, as it had been for the early Anabaptists, according to Friedmann. He called the new birth "an existential event of tremendous power" for the early Anabaptists, an event by which "man is transformed," making one "less willing to yield to the temptations of the 'natural world.' "[52]

The importance of the doctrine of the new birth is everywhere apparent in Amish religious literature of the nineteenth century. David Beiler's *Wahre Christenthum* is described by John A. Hostetler as coming "the nearest to being a book on Amish church doctrines than any other known volume ever written by an Amish person."[53] Its longest chapter (59 pages) is given over to an exposition of the third chapter of the Gospel of John. This passage contains the account of Nicodemus's encounter with Christ, in the course of which he was told that he must be born again in order to enter the kingdom of heaven.[54]

Bishop David Beiler was a conservative who stayed with the Old Order Amish through the turmoil of the second half of the nineteenth century. He frequently disagreed with his slightly more change-minded brother, Bishop Solomon Beiler of Mifflin County, Pennsylvania. But in large measure David would have approved of the following statement of Solomon on the nature and necessity of the new birth.

> We must have the true drawing from the heavenly Father, the true inward illumination, a repentance of the heart, a genuine new birth, a Holy Spirit joy, and the crucifixion and burial of the old man, from which transformation arise the true friends of the Spirit.[55]

An even more pietistically oriented description of the new birth than that of Solomon Beiler, above, may be found in John Umble's translation of an anonymous preliminary sermon. It was to be delivered in a Sunday morning service "after the first prayer" (according to translator John Umble, although Amish custom would place this admonition *before* the first prayer). Those who repent, confess, and turn from their sins, believe the gospel and accept Jesus Christ as Savior, so reads this sermon,

> are the newborn of God through His eternal Word in the power of the Holy Spirit that they may be renewed and sealed unto the day of redemption and have free entrance to God and to the throne of grace through faith in Jesus Christ. Here the Law, previously astounding, is silent. Stilled are the thunder peals, the earthquake, the storm, the frightful face of Mt. Sinai. The bright light of the Gospel shines forth, the sun of righteousness in the hearts of the believers. Here is an entirely new person, a new mind,

heart, and disposition, a child of God and fellow-heir of the Kingdom of Heaven united with God and newly born of God, strengthened with His power and prepared for everlasting life.[56]

The new birth Scriptures were to be read twice a year in the Sunday morning services, once in the spring and again in the fall, as the principal Scripture for those particular Sundays. This signifies something of the importance placed on that doctrine.[57]

Many Amish ministers were aware that certain members had conformed outwardly and might "yet have a wicked heart."[58] They had been baptized and become a member of the congregation. They had participated in congregational council meetings and partaken of the Lord's Supper. However, witness Lot's wife, who obeyed God to the extent that she fled Sodom, but left her heart there.[59] Indeed, some such outward conformers even insisted on "keeping house according to the letter," that is, on maintaining a strict church discipline.[60]

It may have been this emphasis on obedience which confused less thoughtful Amish persons, leading them to assume that obedience—conforming to the Ordnung—was the essence of faith. Ministers may have contributed to this confusion by sometimes emphasizing the effects of the new birth on the conduct of the believer with only scant reference to an inner commitment to God. Disciplining those who violated some provision of the Ordnung automatically emphasized the importance of proper conduct.

In a church which regulated the lifestyle of its members with firmness, even in the smaller details, discipline (*Strafe*, which can be translated *punishment*) was frequent. The *Ordnungs Gemeinde* (the semiyearly congregational council meeting which preceded the observance of the Lord's Supper) provided the greatest emphasis of all on keeping the Ordnung. In this meeting those who had deviated from the accepted Amish lifestyle as required by the Ordnung were disciplined, the severity of the punishment depending on the gravity of the offense.[61] To be chastised in the presence of and by the congregation was extremely humiliating. Since passing the ordeal of the *Ordnungs Gemeinde* was the requirement for admission to the table of the Lord's Supper which followed, the importance of the *outward* sometimes came to overshadow the *inward.*[62]

In the practical outworking of the Amish emphasis on lifestyle, perhaps Lilian Kennel's observation that the Amish saw the new birth "as a command rather than an experience". deserves some serious consideration.[63] It was in this vein that Christian Peterschmitt, European

Amish preacher, wrote in 1871 that "the haughty, honor seeking, selfish, and fleshly hearts must be circumcised; the evil hearing ear plugged; the unnecessary backbiting tongue tamed; the impure bloody hand purified; and the unclean, unchaste flesh chastised."[64]

Gelassenheit and Related Virtues

Current literature on Amish thought and lifestyle has been pointing out that *obedience* may not be the best comprehensive term for the Amish attitude toward life. The Amish considered certain virtues to be essential for entry into the kingdom of God, and thereafter for the maintenance of a proper relationship with God. The all-encompassing term for those virtues, it is asserted, is *Gelassenheit*. While found only rarely in nineteenth-century Amish writings, it was used by the early Anabaptists who, in turn, borrowed it from the medieval mystics.

Incorporated in this term, according to Sandra Cronk, are the personal attributes of *yieldedness* and *powerlessness*. One is to be yielding both in one's relationship to God and in one's association with others. Observing the principle of powerlessness deprived the Christian of the right to use coercion in any form. Only the restraining and enabling power of love remained to the Amish for influencing or controlling the activities of others.[65] Cronk's attempt to explain the lifestyle of the Old Order Amish (and Old Order Mennonites) wholly on the basis of this fundamental Anabaptist virtue may be attempting too much. Then too, if Gelassenheit actually has "many meanings," as claimed by John A. Hostetler,[66] Cronk's choice of that term may be less than ideal. In spite of these limitations, however, the concept of Gelassenheit has sufficient coherence and substance to be useful in the study of Amish religious thought.

Cronk admits that the Amish of the nineteenth century rarely used the word Gelassenheit. The term is used in the *Wahre Christenthum* of Bishop David Beiler, and in an 1862 letter from Christian Stoltzfus of Union County, Pennsylvania, to John Stoltzfus.[67] Further research is required to ascertain its use by Amish writers in general.

The verb *lassen*, however, which forms the root of the noun, was used frequently. Sometimes it was used in describing God's gift and sacrifice of his Son, and in connection with Christ's insistence that one be ready to give up one's spouse and children for the sake of the gospel.[68] Deacon John Stoltzfus, in the halting, almost garbled, style of his old age, may still have described the spirit of Gelassenheit as well as anyone. Good Christians, he said, do not want to cheat anyone out of a cent, and with Abraham do not wish to take honor by as much as a shoelace, and give out no show of self-esteem . . . ; they would rather let themselves be overcome (*sich über-vortheilen lassen*) and pushed back by others than to take their part by strife. . . .[69]

Rather than using the all-encompassing term Gelassenheit, the Amish of the nineteenth century preferred to use two simpler terms to identify those virtues so basic to Amish faith and practice. One of these was *Gehorsamkeit* (obedience). The other was *Demut* (humility). These two terms were often conveniently paired together by Amish ministers.[70] The emphasis given by the Amish to the Christian virtue of humility can scarcely be exaggerated. When John P. King addressed the ministers' conference of 1870 at Archbold, Ohio, he first spoke concerning the "fundamental principles of pride and humility." Only after that presentation did he move on to a consideration of "the renewing of the spirit through re-birth. . . ."[71] This progression from humility to the new birth is typically Amish, perhaps Mennonite as well.[72] Humility is a prerequisite to the experience of the new birth.

The Amish generally preferred the word *Demut* when they spoke of humility. But they had a considerable store of synonyms upon which they occasionally drew, such as *Niedrichkeit* (lowliness), *Sanftmütigkeit* (meekness), and *Nichtigkeit* (nothingness). Of somewhat similar meaning was the term *geistliche Armut* (spiritual poverty). Only the "poor in spirit" could hope to approach God, although, continued David Beiler, "there are many who think they are Christians . . . who have never rightly come to spiritual poverty."[73]

It follows that to have a sense of spiritual poverty—to be humble in one's evaluation of one's own spiritual condition—was an indication of spiritual strength and maturity! Indeed, the more one deplored his poverty of spirit the greater were his true spiritual resources! One should think of oneself as the most insignificant (*Geringsten*), the smallest (*Kleinsten*), and the most lowly (*Demüthigsten*).[74] Given this mindset, Amish persons and communities felt constrained to express humility and its companion virtue, yieldedness, in every aspect of life.

Amish ministers found in the ground wheat used to make the bread and the crushed grapes used to make the wine of the communion table a perfect illustration of Gelassenheit. Just as each grain of wheat must be ground and lose all identity and each grape must likewise be crushed, so must it be with the members of the body of Christ. It is impossible for unground kernels to be a true part of the bread and for uncrushed grapes to mingle their juices in the wine.[75]

Foot washing always followed the communion service and was considered an exercise in humility. Brothers paired off to wash each other's feet and sisters likewise. The observance of the Lord's Supper also provided an opportunity to remind the congregation that Christ's voluntary acceptance of the cross was the ultimate expression of yieldedness and humility.[76]

In addition to recurring admonitions to practice humility, verbal expressions of it abound in Amish literature written in the first person. These include private correspondence, letters between church leaders, and especially instances in which an elderly grandfather recorded his thoughts and admonitions for his posterity. A few of the latter were written by church leaders who, it seems, sometimes wrote for publication or considered that possibility. Any such formal composition was unusual in Amish circles and even suspect as an effort to exalt oneself above others. Consequently, such writers introduced their reminiscences and admonitions with extended remarks. They wanted to convince those who would read their admonitions or memoirs that their motives were honorable, not ambitious.

Said Bishop David A. Troyer in the introduction of what his descendents were to call his *Hinterlassene Schriften*:

> I have written these admonitions to you, dearly beloved children, because of my fatherly duty for your eternal welfare and in my great poverty and weakness with a very insignificant gift which I have unworthily received from the Lord, [and] since I am a very poor, incompetent writer [my writing] will not be found entirely without fault.[77]

Even letters between laymen dealing with mundane family affairs or matters of business occasionally began with expressions of self-abnegation. Shem Zook, the devout but extremely able and worldly-wise Amish layman of Mifflin County, Pennsylvania, wrote to John Stoltzfus in 1863. He spoke of his good health, but confessed that "spiritually" he was "very unworthy and insignificant." He signed this letter, as he closed all of his letters, as "your insignificant (*geringer*) friend, Shem Zook."[78]

Letters from one minister to another invariably began with a lengthy spiritual greeting, suggestive of the salutations found at the beginning of many New Testament epistles. But they always included self-deprecating remarks about the writer's deficiencies, weaknesses, or insignificance.[79] The highly respected David Beiler was asked to express his opinion about a controversial church issue. He replied haltingly that "you have asked a hard thing of me, because I find myself in great poverty and weakness at home, and often I have had to deal with myself, so that I can say: Miserable man that I am, who will save me from this suffering of death?"[80] In spite of such expressions of humility, one finds that Beiler and Jacob Swartzendruber (see chapter 3) and many other bishops found it difficult to walk humbly before their God and yet enforce the Ordnung.

Interestingly, when these Amish laymen and ministers wrote business letters, even sometimes to their fellow church members, much of their humility disappeared. The same Deacon John Stoltzfus, who so well described and enjoined what others call Gelassenheit, wrote a business letter to a Daniel Miller in an entirely different mood. He scolded Miller roundly for making a business deal with his (John's) son-in-law based on a "durty [sic] foundation." The letter actually had some legal overtones in it, for it bore the names of two witnesses. John informed Miller that he was keeping a copy of the letter. However, to prevent the matter from going to court, John indicated grudgingly near the close of his letter that he would make good Miller's claims against his son-in-law two months hence.[81]

According to Joseph C. Liechty, members of the Mennonite Church manifested this same kind of dichotomy in the 1860s. They expressed a self-effacing humility when corresponding on subjects relating to church affairs, but dropped that stance completely when writing business letters.[82] One must conclude that such verbal expressions of humility were sometimes more rhetorical than real.

5

The Amish View of Christ
and His Church

Amish View of the Person of Christ

One of the relatively few recorded sermons by Amish preachers
of the latter part of the nineteenth century includes a beautiful imaginary monologue. Christ is speaking to lost humanity on the eve of his
crucifixion. This discourse is actually one of those numerous Amish
paraphrases of the writings of others, in this instance of Menno Simons.
Yet the minister's selection of this remarkable passage indicates his appreciation of its beauty and power and implies his own appropriation of
its message. "See, dear children," Christ began in this imaginary scene,

> how far the love which I have had and will forever have for you and the
> human race has driven me, that I left my Father's glory and came into this
> sorrowful world as a wretched human being to serve you. For I saw that
> you were marked for death, and there was no one who was redeeming
> you; that you were mortally wounded, and that no one could heal you.
> Therefore I came down from heaven and became a poor, weak, mortal
> human being like you in every respect except sin. I have so earnestly
> sought you in my great love, you miserable, wretched and disagreeable
> [mortals]. Yes, half dead I found you. . . . I bound up your wounds, washed
> off the blood, poured oil and wine into your festering wounds, led you out
> of the mouth of hellish bears and wolves. I have taken you on my
> shoulders and carried you into the tents of peace, covered your naked-
> ness, pitied your wretchedness. I fulfilled the Law for you, I took away
> your sin, I proclaimed to you the peace, grace and favor of my Father. I
> have opened for you His good will, showed the way of truth—that I am the
> true Messiah, Prince and promised Savior. . . . See, little children, so long
> I have walked with you, taught, admonished, and punished [disciplined]
> and comforted [you] with my Father's Word. But now my hour is here, for
> this night I shall be mocked. . . . So I . . . will now perform my last service
> for you with my bitter suffering, flesh, blood, cross and death. Amen.[1]

Although packed with emotion, this beautiful and moving monologue is also explicitly doctrinal. It expresses succinctly the Amish view
of the person and work of Christ. In addition to Menno Simons, the
Amish derived their Christology chiefly from the writings of Dirk
Philips and the Dordrecht Confession of Faith.[2] They believed that
Christ was with the Father and worked (*gewirket hat*) with him before
the foundation of the world.[3] In the words of the Dordrecht Confession
of Faith, article 4, they believed that this Christ was

> the same one "whose goings forth have been from of old, from everlast-
> ing": who has "neither beginning of days, nor end of life." Of whom it is
> testified that he is "Alpha and Omega, the beginning and the end, the first
> and last." That this is also he—and none other—who was chosen,
> promised and sent; who came into the world; and who is God's only, first,
> and proper Son; who was before John the baptist, before Abraham, before
> the world; yea, who was David's Lord, and who was God of the "whole
> earth," "the firstborn of every creature. . . ."[4]

That Christ was with the Father from the beginning and was born
of a virgin, the virgin Mary,[5] was universally accepted by the Amish.
Reflecting the influence of Menno Simons and Dirk Philips, some
Amish writers did not believe "that he received his flesh and blood
from Mary." Or, in the words of another, did not think that he was the
"natural seed of the woman,"[6] Mary merely providing the womb for the
Son of God until his birth.

This Christology has been described by a non-Mennonite as "essentially Docetic"[7] and by a Mennonite as "coming perilously close to it
[Docetism] at times."[8] In the thought of some, had Christ been from
Mary's natural "seed," he would have inherited her Adamic nature. He
would therefore not have qualified as the perfect Lamb of God, the
spotless sacrifice for the sins of mankind. But the Amish were not
united on this question. One anonymous writer called attention to the
fact that Mary is called a wife in the Scriptures, which also state that
"Jesus is her seed and fruit of her womb."[9] This position was also taken
by Deacon John Stoltzfus.[10]

Probably most Amish ministers would have settled for the ambiguous statement in article 4 of the Dordrecht Confession of Faith. It
reflects the deliberate intent of the framers of that historic document
to remain aloof from the theological differences in the area of Christology within the several Anabaptist groups: .

But how, or in what manner . . . the Word became flesh, and He Himself man, we content ourselves with the declaration which the worthy evangelists have given . . . that He is the Son of the living God, in whom exists all our hope, comfort, redemption, and salvation. . . .

For the Amish, Christ was equally God's perfect disciple, the "way-shower" (*Wegweiser*)[11] and God's perfect or unblemished Passover Lamb whose blood was shed to atone for the sins of the world. Christ is "the way, the truth, and the life," said Christian Peterschmitt, quoting John 14:6.

He is the way with His holy life and is an example for us to follow . . . He is the truth which He brought from His Father in heaven; He is the life with His grace and with His merit, yes with His innocent death, which is our life, and with His precious blood, through which we receive forgiveness of sins.[12]

Petershmitt gave equal emphasis to Jesus as Savior and Jesus as the Christian's example of a perfect disciple. That is what especially distinguishes this Christology, as well as that of other bodies of Anabaptists, from the Christology of the mainstream Protestant churches. To the Amish writers of the nineteenth century, two postures of Jesus were inextricably intertwined and were not to be irreverently severed: that of the spotless Passover Lamb and that of the obedient disciple. Jesus' voluntary acceptance of death on the cross was the ultimate expression of obedience and self-denial. At the same time, by that death he made atonement for the sins of mankind.

Of the biweekly Sunday services, two Sundays were given to the observance of the Lord's Supper. In these services the dominant theme was always that of Christ the *Erlöser*, the Redeemer. He was the perfect sacrifice, the Pascal Lamb whose blood atoned for the sins of the world.[13] By the gift of his Son, God ransomed the believer from hell and the grave. He was the "trampler-under-foot" of Satan.[14]

At these services the elder (bishop), if he was emotionally inclined and a forceful speaker, would frequently bring his congregation to tears.[15] In his *Ermahnungen* George Jutzi builds up an enormous case against sinful mankind and then points to the Savior as God's answer to the cry for a deliverer. The buildup, consisting of scores of stanzas, is overwhelming. Mankind's sins, beginning with those of Adam, have accumulated until they "heap up from here to God's throne." All have "followed Adam's footsteps" and there is no one "who is not flecked with sins . . . who might have the power to blot out our guilt."

The crescendo continues. Even "angels' tears" will not propitiate a righteous and just God. There are none so "bold and wise in speaking" that they can persuade God to turn away his wrath. Jutzi eventually gets to the point. God finally shows "the light of grace" to his fallen creation. The king comes, who "will redeem the people from sin and death's power, and tread on the serpent's head, overtake his might, break Satan's lock and bolt, and free young and old on that victory hill [Golgotha]."[16]

Jutzi may have been more pietistically inclined than the majority of Amish ministers, but this is certainly not true of David Beiler. Yet Beiler wrote in a similar vein concerning God's

> precious ransom for us and all mankind. For no one was found worthy, whether in heaven or in earth, to loose the bonds which were between God and mankind, other than the unspotted Lamb, who was before the foundation of the world and made His appearance in the fullness of time, according to the outward appearance of a weak mortal.[17]

The easy and probably unconscious shift of thought at the close of this quotation from Christ as the Lamb without blemish to Christ the humble man of Galilee is typical of Amish statements concerning the person and work of Christ. In the same breath by which Christ is called Savior, his humility and lowliness is pointed out. Deacon John Stoltzfus said,

> God sent His Son into this wretched world out of love and offered Him up to a painful death on the cross, providing an example of [self] denial to the whole world, which natural man cannot or will not comprehend, who usually retaliates against evil with fist, sword, reviling, or insults, or in some other way.[18]

From birth to death Jesus' life was an expression of humility, of *Gelassenheit*. Did he not plead: "Take my yoke upon you and learn of me for I am meek (*sanftmüthig*) and humble (*demüthig*) of heart"?[19] Strangely, the Amish made little use of Philippians 2:3-8, in support of their characterization of Christ as the ultimate example of humility. That text portrays Christ's progressive degradation ending in his ignominious death on the cross.

To the Amish, Christ was the "way-shower"—not only by example but also by precept. He was the Great Teacher and the Great Prophet.[20] He urged his disciples to be like little children in guilessness and meekness.[21] He told them not to resist the evildoer and the oppressor, and to swear not at all. In the Sermon on the Mount he gave extended instructions to his disciples, instructions not merely for some future never-never dispensation, but maxims for everyday living.

The Sins of Christians

Christ's sacrifice provided atonement potentially for all mankind, removing the curse resulting from Adam's fall. Yet with respect to sins which Christians commit, Amish theology provided a less clear, more complicated avenue of forgiveness.

However, before dealing with the matter of the forgiveness of the Christian's sins, it is necessary to consider Amish theology which treats such sinning. A disciple of Christ was to be obedient and the church of Christ was to be pure. Nevertheless, it was admitted freely—actually taken for granted—that the life of a Christian involves constant spiritual warfare in which the soldier may occasionally experience temporary defeat. In the words of David Beiler,

> Perfection will come to no one as long as we are in this hut [mortal body]. If we could or would become perfect why should we daily pray and say: Forgive us our trespasses, if we no longer have any? And why does James teach: "Confess your sins to one another and pray for one another, that ye may be healed"? It would after all be vain for a healthy man to ask God for health. But since we fail manifold times, we therefore have great reason to ask God daily to forgive us our sins and weaknesses which we daily commit.[22]

The new birth reduced but did not remove one's bent to sinning. It made available God's power to resist temptation. Using this power was an option which the Christian might sometimes neglect, although to his peril.

Entering into the "ark of the New Testament,"[23] a phrase sometimes used for the rite of baptism and admission into membership in the congregation, did not insulate one from the temptations of the world. With baptism the conflict only began, a recurring warning given in instructional meetings to those applying for baptism. The fight is against one's own flesh and blood, against one's spiritual enemies, against the "prince of this world" and the "evil spirits under the heaven," and against "the many false doctrines" and "temptations of all kinds." This spiritual warfare convinces the follower of Christ that "the true Christian life is a daily struggle until [one is] in the chill of the grave," warned Bishop David Beiler.[24]

In the words of another Amish preacher, "living a long time is sinning a long time. Even if the believer decides that he will keep from sinning, he is sometimes led astray by the evil world and overcome by his own flesh so that he sins grievously."[25] It was this kind of human fallibility which led Amish ministers to emphasize "enduring to the end." This phrase found in Matthew 10:22 and 24:13 became an overriding theme for perhaps a majority of the admonitions and many of the sermons one heard in an Amish service, whether at a regular Sunday morning meeting, a baptismal occasion, or a funeral.[26] Amish ministers did not hesitate to list and carefully define sins to which Christians are especially prone.

The warfare of the Christian was described in various ways, but usually in some form of biblical language or illustration. As the Israelites were wholly to "root out" the Canaanites and destroy their idols, so must the "spiritual warriors of Jesus" destroy and root out the "indwellers of his heart," and that "without ceremony."[27] Ephesians, chapter 6, was sometimes used to describe the proper stance of the Christian toward sin. Here Paul warns Christians of their supernatural enemies and exhorts them to "put on the whole armour of God."[28]

The Amish believed that the sacrifice of the Lamb of God on the cross atoned—more correctly, potentially atoned—for the sin of Adam and Eve and for the sins of the whole world. An anonymous writing offered a model for the communion sermon: Christ "broke His body and shed His blood on the cross to redeem and save us from the sin of Adam and Eve."[29] In other words, the default of the first Adam was reversed by the sacrificial death of Christ, the second Adam. This doctrinal position allowed that "salvation is for all men as long as they are in innocence or childhood." But "when they come to their understanding" (that is, arrive at what Arminian theologians call the age of accountability) and continue in sin, then they become participants in the Fall of man and incur the guilt of their own sins as well.[30]

To escape from this load of guilt the conscious sinner must throw himself or herself on the mercy of God and ask for forgiveness on the basis of Christ's substitutionary sacrifice on the cross. There was an important condition, however, for the remission of sins. God's pardon would be forthcoming, *provided* the penitent would then walk consistently in obedience to God and his Word.[31] In the words of an anonymous preacher, Christ shed his blood "in order that all those who live and walk according to His rules and regulations" might "possess and enjoy His heavenly possessions in eternal peace and joy."[32]

Conversely, if a disciple of Christ became disobedient and reverted to his former life of sin, then all the guilt which had formerly been his would be heaped upon him once more. The Amish insisted on making God's grace contingent on walking in obedience to God. This explains why Amish ministers were inclined to view deathbed conversions with skepticism and reluctant to perform deathbed baptisms.[33]

Personal Assurance of God's Grace?

Given the Amish position on the proneness of Christians to commit sins, how may they know whether they have been obedient enough to continue to merit God's grace? Salvation depended on the complete yieldedness and obedience of the believer until death. Bishop David Beiler would probably have admitted, as he did about several Amish beliefs, that such conditional salvation was a "hard" or harsh doctrine, but nevertheless biblical. Since salvation was for those who endured to the end, how could one assert that one was saved before this life had ended?

In one of the most lucid statements of the Amish position on assurance, David A. Troyer (Treyer) wrote that "all promises of God are given to us conditionally," including the promise of eternal life. True, said Troyer, according to John 5:24 anyone that "heareth my word, and believeth on him that sent me, hath everlasting life." But such a believer "does not yet possess it; it is only set aside for him," to be claimed only if he has endured to the end.[34]

Anyone audacious enough to assert that he was saved was by that very token extremely likely to fall, or may already have fallen. Such boasting was a manifestation of the terrible sin of pride. The belief that one could be assured of a present state of grace, and that one should witness to this fact, gained an entrance into some of the change-minded factions of the Amish church, including the Amish Mennonites, in the last decades of the nineteenth century. Yet even in 1900 its acceptance by these groups was considerably less than unanimous.

The Amish steadfastly insisted that God's continuing grace depended on continuing obedience. But with a little searching one can find expressions of the blessedness of resting on God's promises which closely border on the doctrine of assurance. This statement runs counter to popular understanding of Amish beliefs and requires some substantial evidence. Said George Jutzi: "The children of the New Testament, if they follow Jesus' example and command, together with those of the apostles, and honor their parents . . . they . . . may await eternal life over there on the other side of the grave with certainty (*mit Gewissheit*)."[35] While the assurance described by Jutzi is highly conditional, yet the suggestion of the possibility of awaiting eternity already in this life "with certainty" is surprising.

Likewise, the conservative David Beiler was bold enough to quote from John 10:27: "For my sheep hear my voice and they follow me. And I give unto them eternal life, and they shall never perish, and no man shall pluck them out of my hand. The Father which gave them me is greater than all, and no one shall pluck them out of my Father's hand." Beiler followed this quotation with a reference to Peter, who faltered in his faith while walking on the water and was rescued by Christ. Then follows a portion of Psalm 121: "The keeper of Israel neither slumbers nor sleeps. . . . The sun may not strike you by day nor the moon by night. The Lord looks upon your out-going and your in-coming from now on and forevermore."[36]

In the same vein Jutzi compared those who had decided to follow Christ to the Israelites who chose to follow Moses out of Egypt. He declared that "if then such a [spiritual] Israelite wants to go out [of Egypt], truly then no power of hell can hold him back. . . . If the spiritual Israelite only looks continually to Jesus Christ, the author and finisher of his faith, looks at the spiritual Moses, does not leave him but rather truly follows after [him], then Satan can do nothing. . . ."[37] In "An Evening Poem," a gentle devotional piece, Bishop David A. Troyer seemed to bask in the protection of the Almighty. As we go to bed we want to ask God to send his guardian angel, said Troyer, "to stand by our side. Then we will shut our eyes and sleep under your care. The wicked enemy in his defiance can attach no harm to us." May we commit ourselves to "God's care and say amen."[38]

Deacon Christian Stoltzfus' nighttime meditations may illustrate the thought-process by which the Amish reconciled God's requirement of obedience with the Christian's recurring and inevitable bent to sinning. Christian poured out his heart in a plaintive and introspective letter to his brother, Deacon John Stoltzfus:

> I often have to think of it, especially at night when I often lie sleepless on my bed. After all, how are we poor mortals to do everything which the Great Prophet teaches us in His Gospel? Oh, I believe that I have fallen far short of doing everything that I am responsible for. And if I should say that I have done all that I am responsible to do, I am fearful that my daily commissions and omissions, and my imperfections would not wholly show it. [But] then I find comfort in the Word of God, for I believe that good intent is acceptable as genuine, that our Creator knows what poor, weak creatures we are, and that we even yet must strive against an evil enemy. . . . I need to confess that if I regard my poverty and imperfection, I dare not and cannot truthfully say that I have done what I am responsible to do, so I do not dare to, nor can truthfully say that I have received

such witness [that he has pleased God]. But yet I hope and believe that the loving heavenly Father is moved to pity me, poor sinner, and that He wants to forgive my past sins if I am to appear before Him on that great Judgment Day. But through unending grace and mercy, and the price of the shed blood of Jesus Christ, I hope to meet a merciful judge.[39]

In the last year of his life Christian continued to claim "the promises of the Lord what he promis[es] to his Saints or to them that Strive with all there hart and hands to doe his words. . . ."[40]

Christian Stoltzfus, himself a kind and gentle disciplinarian as deacon, was able carefully to sort out the doctrines of his church and find comfort and solace in them. Others, perhaps less tough-minded individuals, were never quite sure they were obedient enough to merit God's forgiveness. It should also be noted that our knowledge of nineteenth-century Amish theology comes to us largely through the writings of a few of the more able bishops and other leaders. In their efforts to enforce the *Ordnung* of the church, many less-discerning Amish preachers and elders stressed obedience so much that they themselves and their congregations appeared to slight God's mercy. Those who left the Amish church have frequently charged that the Amish had lost sight of God's grace.[41] The increased emphasis on personal salvation and personal assurance which the second- and third-generation Amish Mennonites came to adopt will be considered in chapter 12.

Amish Eschatology

The Amish view of the end time was amillennial, as described in article 18 of the Dordrecht Confession of Faith. The last trumpet will sound at a time to be determined by God alone—on the judgment day or the great day of revelation. Christ will return to the earth from which he ascended after his resurrection, and time will be no more. Christ will come as a thief in the night or like the bridegroom who came at midnight and surprised the five foolish virgins.[42] This time his coming will not be to save the world, but rather to judge it. All the peoples of the earth will be gathered before him and "all who are in the grave will hear his voice and come forth." Just as God's long-suffering came to an end in the days of Noah, so will God's wrath be poured out on the judgment day, resulting in a "terrible, indescribable eternity for all unbelievers."[43]

Amish preachers invariably indicated, when speaking about the judgment day, that each would be judged according to the life he or she had lived. Those "who had done good" in their respective lifetimes would receive life eternal and those "who had done evil" would receive the Lord's judgment.[44] One of the anonymous sermons translated by John Umble makes this point clear:

> Yes, if God asks you then at the Judgment Day: Why have you desecrated my Sabbath? Why have you drunk yourself full of wine? Why did you transgress all of my commandments? And if you will then say: Because the majority of the people did so, that will be a wretched answer! God will say to you at that time: Because you sinned with the multitude, you may now also ride to hell with the multitude.[45]

Sharing the Gospel

The Amish have consistently rejected any responsibility for preaching the gospel to the unchurched. In particular, they have not participated in the foreign missionary movement of modern times. They had a generally accepted interpretation of the great commission to go into all the world and preach the gospel (Matthew 28:19-20 and Mark 16:15-16). The Amish said that Jesus gave this command to "the eleven" apostles (Judas had taken his own life) and it does not apply to anyone else, not even to pastors (*Hirten*), preachers (*Lehrer*), or bishops (*Bischöfen*).[46] These church officers who led the church in later New Testament times did not have the same duties nor manifest the same miraculous signs as did the chosen eleven.

In a five-page discourse, "A Word Concerning Mission Work," Bishop David A. Troyer defended this Amish position at length. The Mennonites, he said, have accepted the command to preach the gospel to every creature as applying to "all preachers and ministers" of every age. However, he continued, "After much reading and thoughtful consideration, I do not find, up to now, any applicable basis in the Word of God to support this belief."

There was also a pragmatic consideration. At the time of the apostles, communication was extremely difficult, but in recent times the availability of the Scriptures in print and increased literacy throughout the world has made mission work unnecessary. Actually, said Troyer, the heathen are probably as well off without the gospel, "perhaps better." If they should be enlightened by having the gospel preached to them but nevertheless continue in disobedience as do the multitudes in Christendom, it will have been better for them "at the judgment of God" to have remained in ignorance. In the parable recorded in Luke 12:47-48, was not the servant who knew his lord's will but disregarded it beaten with "many stripes," while the servant who disobeyed out of ignorance was to be beaten with "few stripes"?

Troyer did, however, give left-handed deference to the missionary. He conceded that "whoever has the gift and the means and goes out and teaches the heathen according to the right way—unless he neglects something or is derelict—without doubt will not remain unrewarded on the judgment day."[47]

The Amish may not have felt constrained to preach the gospel to those who had never heard it, but they believed in witnessing of another kind. We must not only confess Christ with our mouth, said David Beiler (possibly referring to one's baptismal confession), "but also with [our] life and conduct" so that the "meekness and humility of Christ . . . manifests itself in effective power in us." Amish preachers frequently urged their listeners to "let your light so shine before men, that they may see your good works, and glorify your Father which is in heaven [Matt. 5:16]."[48] Such "preaching" through one's conduct and lifestyle has been found wanting by the evangelists and the missionary societies—Mennonite and other—of the nineteenth and twentieth centuries. Yet fairness requires that it be recognized as one church's version of witnessing to the truth of the gospel.

Witnessing to one's children, however, and to the children of one's fellow believers in the congregation was to be by precept as well as by example. The Amish constantly reiterated biblical admonitions to teach the commandments of God to one's children (Deuteronomy 6:6-9 and 11:18-20) and to "bring them up in the nurture and admonition of the Lord" (Ephesians 6:4). This concern for the spiritual welfare only or primarily of one's children is reflected in those few admonitions from Amish "house-fathers" to their "left-behind ones" which have been printed or otherwise preserved. The prayer of D. Stutzman reflects this single-minded preoccupation with the spiritual health of one's posterity:

> Be gracious to my children.
> Make them tired of every sin.
> Give them pure silk
> To clothe themselves with righteousness.
> Anoint them with your Spirit.
> Give your help to them
> So that the blessing of your hands
> Will accompany them to the end.[49]

The minutes of the annual Amish ministers' meetings, 1862-78, are replete with pleas "to bring the tender young heart to the beloved Jesus at an early age."[50] In 1871 the fluent Bishop Samuel Yoder of

Mifflin County, Pennsylvania, admonished the parents attending the yearly conference in similar vein "so that the [spiritual] seed of Abraham might be multiplied through us and our children."[51] Appended to the minutes of the 1871, 1873, and 1875 conferences are adaptations of a tract on motherhood published by the American Tract Society.[52] This was a further indication that the Christian nurture of one's children was considered a sacred duty. Nevertheless, even the change-minded Amish who dominated the annual ministers' meetings of the 1870s never wrestled with questions relating to missionary outreach or the establishment of Sunday schools.

The Amish View of Government

In America the Amish came to experience the freedom of the land of liberty. In that extended period between the War of 1812 and the Civil War (1861-65), they increasingly took this incomparable independence for granted. Government touched these little Amish communities only minimally. They were left to concentrate their efforts on the acquisition of land and other forms of wealth, and on maintaining and strengthening the faith and identity of the Amish church. They lived in virtual autonomy, with little governmental interference, delivered from the conscription practices of tyrannical European governments. In most localities regulations for serving in the local militia had lapsed. This life situation may account for the virtual absence of any consideration of the principle of nonresistance in the ecclesiastical literature of the Amish church in that period. Prohibitions may be found against serving on juries (disciplines of 1809 and 1837), holding public office, or participating in elections in any way (discipline of 1837). But no pronouncements may be found forbidding military service.

For the Amish, forced service in the army had been left behind, or so they thought. Nonparticipation in the military was probably taken for granted. It was not an issue which threatened the unity of the church. But then the Civil War destroyed this utopian assumption and brought the issue of army service to the doorstep of the Amish church. In this conflict which rocked the nation to its foundations, intense pressures were put on Amish and Mennonite young men to volunteer for service in the army. All this, followed by several federal draft laws, induced many of them to join the army. The number and percentage of Amish (and Mennonite) young men who yielded to these pressures is not known, in spite of intensive research, especially by James O. Lehman.[53]

The most well-defined and consistent response of the Amish church to the draft laws of the war period was to help young draftees raise money to hire substitutes or, later, to pay a fine in lieu of serving in the army.[54] The conscientious Amish bishop, Jacob Swartzendruber, of Johnson County, Iowa, thought this policy to be inconsistent and dishonorable. Those who hired substitutes, he said, were surely as guilty of killing as was King David in causing the death of Uriah (2 Samuel 11), even though he personally did not commit the deed.

In a letter which he wrote to the annual Amish ministers' conference of 1865, Swartzendruber incorporated a comprehensive concluding paragraph on this subject. He broadened his observations to include all relationships between nonresistant Christians and temporal authority, and alluded also to the recent assassination of President Lincoln. "If it is true," he said,

> as I have heard tell about the Dunkards [one draft has "Quakers"] in regard to nonresistance, we are behind them and could well take them for a pattern. Who will be responsible for the much blood which has been shed in the war and finally the President's blood? Here sin is piled upon sin. Our people should all keep themselves apart from all party [political] matters . . . where brother votes against brother and father against son. What a poverty this is throughout our congregations that we want to help to rule the world, we who are chosen out of the world by God. . . . Nowhere is it required that we should help to rule the world, but as Christian subjects we should be subject in all things that are not contrary to the Word of God for conscience sake, Romans 13.[55]

Some sensitive Amish youths bought substitutes who were then killed in the war. They may have carried the scars of such experience in their hearts for many years. Tradition says that John S. Stoltzfus, a free-spirited but gentle Amishman of Lancaster County, kept a blue coat in his attic. It was from the man he had hired as a substitute, later killed in battle. Occasionally John retrieved the coat and reverently polished the brass buttons in remorseful meditation.[56]

The first several of those annual churchwide Amish conferences of 1862–76 and 1878 came in the midst of the war. The fighting reached, or threatened to reach, into some of the very areas in which Amish settlements were located. One might expect that the Amish leaders would be preoccupied with the problem of remaining nonresistant. But those conferences had been conceived and called together to settle controversies unrelated to the war then in progress, issues which threatened to divide the entire denomination. The detailed minutes of the first annual conference, June 9-12, 1862, make no reference to the war or its impact on the church.

Even in the 1863 conference, May 25-27, the issue of serving in political office received more attention than did serving in the armed forces. Bishop Jonathan Yoder (1795-1869), of McLean County, Illinois, thought it "very unseemly for someone who professes non-resistance in faith to go to political meetings with a big mouth."[57] The question of military recruitment did surface. However, it required little discussion to conclude unanimously that service in the militia, including working as a teamster, was to be forbidden. This likely referred to service in the federal army as well as in the traditional local militia.[58] Neither was the war given any attention as such in the 1864 and 1865 conferences, although the question of voting and serving in political office was discussed again at the 1864 meeting.[59]

In only one instance did those annual conferences, either during or after the war, attempt to draw up a relatively broad statement as to how members of the Amish church should relate to government. This took place in the conference of 1868. Following usual procedure, a specific question was formally put before the assembly of ministers: "If something is stolen from us, is it right, according to the gospel, to pursue the thief and let the government throw him into prison and punish him?"

The meeting referred this question to a committee of five ministers and bishops. They drew up a resolution (as conferences of the early twentieth century would have called it) for consideration by the entire body of ministers. The committee declared, in response to the question, that it was "contrary to the gospel to turn a thief over to the authorities to have him punished, since we call ourselves nonresistant and, according to the apostles' teaching, should not take vengeance."

Although a majority of the ministers attending the 1868 conference accepted the committee report, some dissented. Deacon John Stoltzfus of Lancaster County, Pennsylvania, was the most vocal of the dissenters. He read 1 Peter 2:13-14, which indicates that governments are for the punishment of evildoers. Then he asked whether a Christian should not cooperate with the government in this task at least to the extent of turning the thief over to the officers of the law.

Bending to the expressions of dissent, the moderator added Deacon Stoltzfus to the committee and enlarged the question to read: "May it be permitted, according to the gospel, to use the power of the civil authority in any way?" But the enlarged committee could not come up with a well-considered answer to this wider question, although a report of sorts was attempted.[60] These annual conferences lacked the resources and structure essential for solving such broad issues.

Mostly submerged, but sometimes coming to the surface in this debate about what to do with a thief, was the concern of Amishmen for the protection of their property. Many were experiencing a prosperity denied them or their forebears in Europe. In the midst of that lively discussion, Bishop Elias Riehl (1818-1901) of Union County, Pennsylvania, remarked that one's actions should not be determined by concern for "how we will live," but by the dictates of his faith. Riehl meant that when one proposes to report a thief to the civil authorities, it is to be suspected that he is concerned for his property and his material welfare, that is, for how he "shall live."[61]

Bishop David Beiler was even more concerned than Riehl about the new affluence which Amish families were experiencing, as shown in his writings of some years (1857-62) before the 1868 conference. He had already perceived that with prosperity and accumulation of property came also a readiness on the part of some to use the law courts to protect their possessions or to recover them if stolen or seized illegally.[62] In property disputes involving members of the congregation, Beiler described approvingly the traditional means used by the Amish to settle financial disputes: a type of bankruptcy procedure supervised by the congregation.[63]

Later, at the end of the century, another bishop, David A. Troyer, gave support to Beiler's position. Said he: "I think there is nothing more clearly forbidden in the entire New Testament than using the force of the courts to protect our material possessions."[64] Beiler's and Troyer's concern reflected a keen observation of their own times. It may also have been prophetic concerning the effect of the even greater affluence of the twentieth century on the use of the law by Anabaptist property owners and business persons.

Only near the end of the century did an Amishman attempt an extended treatise on the subject of the Christian and the government. In 1898, Bishop David A. Troyer published a nine-page essay entitled "An Exposition Concerning the Worldly [or Secular] Government." In this carefully formulated commentary Troyer said that there are two kingdoms, the kingdom of this world and the kingdom of God. One must choose between these two kingdoms in terms of citizenship and allegiance. For Christians only one choice is possible. Their primary allegiance is to the heavenly kingdom, of which they are citizens.

Their relationship to the kingdom of this world is that of visitors (*Gäste*) and strangers (*Fremdlinge*). "It is impossible for us to be at once citizens (*Bürger*) of both the worldly kingdom and the heavenly kingdom." If "we are citizens with the saints and God's fellow lodgers we may take no part in the worldly kingdom, hold no worldly office, nor resort to the sword, swear no oath, nor avenge ourselves against our enemies." Neither may one go to court to claim or recover possessions. One may not serve on juries nor participate in political elections. Earthly rulers and princes are, in a limited sense, God's ministers—even that vain king Nebuchadnezzar—but this fact does not make them citizens of the heavenly kingdom, who should therefore have the support of nonresistant Christians.[65]

Many of the more change-minded Amish differed somewhat with Troyer. They showed some inclination to distinguish between those political officers who, potentially or actually, used or had access to the use of force in the course of their duties, and those who did not. Local road commissioners and rural school district directors were examples of the latter.[66] Recent and current research suggests that the participation of Amish people in the election of such local officers, Amish or other, was considerably more common than the writings of Amish spokesmen would lead us to suspect.[67]

Summation and Interpretation

Lacking any formal instruction from their founder, Jacob Ammann, the Amish relied largely on the writings of earlier Anabaptists for their interpretation of the Scriptures. Their claim that they followed Menno Simons more closely than did those who called themselves Mennonites was not entirely without foundation.[68] However, the Amish of the nineteenth century, along with the Mennonites to a lesser degree, had moved appreciably in the direction of Pietism. The reader may judge this from the devotional nature of large sections of David Beiler's *Wahre Christenthum*, David Troyer's *Hinterlassene Schriften*, and especially George Jutzi's *Ermahnungen*. Perhaps their appropriation of that pietistically oriented prayer book, *Die ernsthafte Christenpflicht*, accounts for some of this trend.

Richard MacMaster, however, has a more penetrating analysis of why Anabaptist spirituality shifted from the "bitter Christ" to the "sweet Jesus." Anabaptist theology was born and nurtured in a setting of persecution and frequent martyrdom, circumstances which did not obtain in America. As a consequence, the earlier emphasis on yielding to and accepting persecution gave way to an emphasis on humility and a yieldedness to Christ "in the course of repentance" and, in particular, a yieldedness to the Ordnung of the church.[69]

6

"Keeping House":
Banning and Shunning

The Amish Concept of Discipline

Deacon Christian Stoltzfus of Buffalo Valley experienced considerable difficulty in maintaining discipline in his congregation, and also in his family. He had eleven children by his first wife, followed by six more after his second marriage. Lydia Beiler, his second wife, was seventeen years younger than Christian. Their youngest child was born when Christian was fifty-nine years old.[1] Thus in his seventies he was faced with the responsibility of parenting the last of these teenagers.

Though well-intentioned, Christian's children were fun-loving and inclined to take lightly the regulations of the church concerning dress and other aspects of their personal appearance. Contrary to church regulations, his daughters had their pictures taken.[2] Sons Ben and Eli gave their long-suffering father much trouble as he attempted to keep them in the order of the congregation. They were conforming to "new fashions in dress and hair cuting and Beard shaving." In a letter to the two sons written while they were temporarily away from home, he complained that some members of the congregation had

> threatened to leave our meating all cause of your in the Spring promising to come under our church rules, and not kept your promise as you know and I had neglect to bring you & others right before the church and have you courtmarshalt [sic] for that reason I could not give you a certificate [of membership] & cannot doe it before you give Satisfaction to the Church. It caust me much troble to get so far as to have communion held here And when done many dit not goe along.

But kindhearted Christian was not willing to condemn these sustained infractions of church regulations by his own sons as partaking of that terrible sin of disobedience, as the theology of his church would have him to do. Rather, he ended his exhortation with a gracious plea, saying:

> I do not want to Say a member that does not live up to his promise is not newborn of the Spirit and holy goest [Ghost] but he is not a true member in Jesus. think of this hereafter And do not show pride or [here Christian lapses into German] disobedience to the ministers in the congregation where you are now living.[3]

Christian had not been able to give his sons a certificate of membership in good standing, a *Zeugnis*, from their home congregation in Buffalo Valley. He hoped that by careful observance of the regulations of the congregation where they were attending, they could obtain one from there. Such maneuvering to get a Zeugnis from a second congregation without having brought such a certificate from one's home congregation was contrary to established church polity. This procedure would permit an unruly church member to escape from the disciplinary power of his home congregation.[4] Perhaps Christian, aged seventy-nine when the above letter was written, was tempted to try to bend the rules of the church a little for the sake of the sons of his old age.

The Ordnung

As indicated earlier, the Amish believed that the church should maintain its purity at all costs. This purity was defined and safeguarded by the *Ordnung*, the ordered or prescribed lifestyle of the Amish community and its members. In adhering to this principle they were following established Anabaptist tradition. From the first these radical dissenters from the state church had, in the words of Robert Friedmann and Harold S. Bender, given the "final authority over their behavior" to the "corporate body" of believers.[5]

Basically, the Ordnung was unwritten and determined by the traditions of many generations. Nevertheless, the disciplines of 1809, 1837, and 1865 attempted to codify some of these generations-old practices. While rooted in tradition, the Ordnung was "built and founded on the Word of God," said Bishop David A. Troyer (Treyer). He added that it was a "spiritual fence" without which "a church cannot survive for long, [for] where there is no Christian ordering there also can be no real divine service."[6]

Ideally, the Ordnung was timeless, something like God's ordering of the universe, according to a contemporary Amish minister. Its formation "over generations and centuries [was] directed by Almighty

Powers and led by the Holy Spirit." However, in the last half of the nineteenth century the personal accoutrements formerly accessible only to the aristocracy, the new machinery, "and many other things" became available to the common person. Then the role of the Ordnung came to be principally that of "holding the line" against the incorporation of such in the lifestyle of the Amish, although that line may bend a little from time to time.[7]

Binding and Loosing

Although the Dordrecht Confession of Faith made no reference to Matthew 18:18, the Amish did not hesitate to claim Christ's statement that "whatsoever ye shall bind on earth shall be bound in heaven; and whatsoever you shall loose on earth shall be loosed in heaven" as his grant of authority and disciplinary power to the church.[8] In addition to this forthright statement, the several passages in the Scriptures calling for faithfulness and abstinence from sin were accepted as regulations to be enforced by the church, the body of Christ.[9]

Discipline in the formal sense was only the means of last resort in keeping the church pure. Its use was not spared, however, if it was thought that circumstances required it. Thoughtful Amish leaders constantly admonished the parents in their congregations to rear their children "in the nurture and admonition of the Lord," which meant to teach them to accept and live according to the Ordnung. For the adults, likewise, instruction and exhortation, including discourses on the subject of God's wrath on the disobedient, were useful in preserving the Ordnung.

Those, however, who stepped outside the boundaries of the Ordnung were to be disciplined. In his letter to his sons, Christian Stoltzfus used an unorthodox term to describe this disciplinary procedure. Some members of the congregation, he said, thought that they, Ben and Eli, should be "courtmarshalt" (court-martialed), a term used for the trial of an uncooperative or disobedient soldier in a military court. It was an inappropriate and opprobrious term to describe the disciplinary proceedings in an Amish council meeting. By using that word, Christian must have meant to express some personal and family disapproval about the way in which disciplinary actions were taken in the Buffalo Valley congregation. Surely Christian would have been faulted severely had his use of the term in this way become known to the church.

In spite of Christian Stoltzfus' inappropriate use of the term *court-martial,* Amish disciplinary procedures did contain elements suggestive of a courtroom trial. In 1866 when Christian Conrad of the

Clinton congregation east of Goshen, Indiana, built an unusually large and presumably modern house, leading bishops and ministers from Iowa, Ohio, and Pennsylvania came to the community and held what one young spectator called a "process." This word was clearly a transliteration of the German word *Prozess*, meaning a civil trial. Conrad's trial lasted for two days, and when the observer, twenty-one-year-old Malinda Stoltzfus, took the train for West Liberty, Ohio, it was even then "not altogether finished." Eventually Conrad was excommunicated.[10]

Also suggestive of a trial in a court of law was the way in which the Amish spoke of *witnesses* in connection with such hearings or trials.[11] Even the word which the Amish used for discipline—*Strafe*, the verb form being *strafen*—has legal overtones, often being translated "punish." John Umble and others have adopted this translation, although "discipline" or "rebuke" are acceptable alternatives. As used by the Amish, *strafen* probably incorporated all three meanings.

A principal purpose of all Amish discipline was to bring the transgressor to repentance which, in turn, would result in God's forgiveness. If there were indications of a contrite heart, the offender would be restored to full fellowship in the church. In some of the documents, however, appear undertones implying that the punishment of the erring one was intended or appropriate. The idea of chastisement is implied in a statement made by Bishop John K. Yoder at the annual ministers' meeting of 1868. For transgressors who conform belatedly and only under duress, said Yoder, there must "first be a reconciliation [evidently involving a confession before the congregation] before the disobedience is overlooked."[12]

Some offenders, principally those who were guilty of serious offenses, were required to wait for some time after they had made their confession to the congregation before they could be restored to full fellowship in the body of believers. In 1860, Henry Yoder of Holmes County, Ohio, who had labored for fifty years under the awful guilt of murder, finally confessed his crime. He was immediately excommunicated. Although his bishop, Levi Miller, and others provided wise counsel to Henry which might have led to the dismissal of charges against him, yet in spite of his pleading, they would not restore him to full fellowship in the congregation. His case was later reviewed by the public courts, and he was released from any criminal charges. Only then did his congregation restore him to membership.[13]

The reason usually given for such lengthy suspension of membership was that time was required to allow the transgressor to express his penitence in his lifestyle, although punishment was sometimes implied.[14] Had not Dietrich Philips, the Amish favorite among the early Anabaptists writers, justified both purposes? Said Philips:

> One who truly repents will be satisfied to have imposed on him by God and the church the punishment that belongs to him and which he richly deserves. [Should] one who has sinned before God and desires to repent not be content that the church of the Lord punish and mortify him a little in the flesh?[15]

Nineteenth-century Amish ministers and bishops did not hesitate to classify sins and specify degrees of discipline. Some sins were against one's brothers and sisters and some were against God. Some sins were "gross" or "mortal," and some were mere mistakes committed in weakness.[16] Peter Lehman attempted to apply the parable of the unjust servant (Matthew 18:23-34) to this problem of classifying sins. He likened the debt of one hundred pence, which the one servant owed to the other, to the sins which one person commits against another. These are the sins, said Lehman, which "we are to forgive." But the sins which "come under the [category of the] ten thousand talents . . . might be [the] grossly wicked sins against which the kingdom of heaven is closed." Such sins, he said, are "not ours to forgive one another."[17]

By far the largest number of violations of the Ordnung coming before the congregation related to clothing, hairstyling, and other forms of personal adornment; embellishment of buildings, carriages, and furniture; and every other evidence of pride. Such adornment constituted clear evidence that the offender had a proud heart. Having one's picture taken or playing a musical instrument fell in the same category. As humility and yieldedness were essential to the Christian life, so all evidence of pride and arrogance was to be eradicated. First Peter 3:3, which forbids the braiding of the hair (*Haarflechten*), the wearing of gold (*Goldumhängen*), and the putting on of apparel (*Kleideranlegen*), was an oft-quoted verse.[18]

This concern about pride as expressed in all kinds of embellishment increased as the decades of the nineteenth century moved ahead. Those landmarks of Amish discipline—the disciplines of 1809, 1837, and 1865—progressively gave increasing attention to the matter of adornment. Regulations were multiplied and spelled out in greater detail with each new discipline.[19] As twentieth-century Amish writers have pointed out, the increased specificity so evident in the later disciplines came about for historical reasons. It was only in the nineteenth century that the "common class" acquired sufficient affluence to enable them to change styles frequently and to adorn themselves and their houses with all kinds of decorations.

According to Amish minister J. F. B., the Ordnung, as it is structured today, is the response of the Amish church to the affluence and glitter which had come to the common person in America.[20] The superfluity in dress among all classes may account for a moderate but discernible late-nineteenth century shift in emphasis from simplicity, humility, and modesty in dress, to imposed uniformity. This happened in both the Old Order Amish church and among the Amish Mennonites.[21]

If one's violation of the Ordnung in some aspect of adornment was a one-time or short-lived offense, it was considered minor and required only a public confession before the congregation. This was followed by a request for forgiveness and a promise to walk more circumspectly in the future. Upon such contrition, according to a pronouncement of the annual ministers' meeting of 1865, "the angels of God in heaven will rejoice."[22] After making a confession the offender was restored immediately to good standing in the congregation.

However, if offenders in these minor sins persisted in their prideful ways, they could expect much more severe discipline. They were providing unmistakable proof of a proud heart. In addition, they were also guilty of that terrible sin of disobedience. Even the smallest violation of the Ordnung became a gross sin—disobedience—if one persisted in it.[23]

The first response of the ministers and the congregation to such defiant conduct was to bar the disobedient from participation in the Lord's Supper. But this expedient was only temporary, an expression of patience (*Geduld*). It permitted the offender to reconsider his or her attitude and conduct and perchance to repent. The person who returned to obedience might be required to make a more formal and abject confession, called a full (*hoechst*) confession,[24] before restoration to full communicant status.

Disbarment from the communion service also constituted a warning to the sinner. Like the barren fig tree (Luke 13:6-9), disobedient members might be given one more chance before being cut off. If they persisted further in disobedient conduct, they would be subjected to the ultimate disciplinary instrument. They would be banned from the congregation—that is, "cut off" (*absondert*) from membership and shunned (socially ostracized) by all faithful members of the Amish church.

The Ban and the Shunning

Likely the most controversial issue in the Amish division of the 1690s was the use of shunning (*Meidung*) as a disciplinary measure. The difference was not on the ban (*Bann*) or excommunication of unruly or disobedient members. On this Jacob Ammann and his opposers were agreed. Ammann thought that, in addition to excommunication, such members should be "avoided" or shunned in social and business affairs (*im Handel und Wandel*) as well.

Shunning was to be complete. Members of the congregation were not to eat with nor pay social visits to persons under the ban.[25] According to accepted practice in the nineteenth century, faithful members were not to engage in any business agreements with such backsliders, not even to purchase or sell farm produce or food, or any other item of convenience. All these restrictions applied to other members of the backslider's family, including a spouse—who was not to sleep with the marriage partner. Shunning was to be observed regardless of such personal relationships (*ohne Ansehen der Person*).[26] This was a standard phrase used to indicate that an excommunicated person was to be shunned by everyone, even his closest friends and the members of his or her own family.

Thus when Deacon John Stoltzfus and several of his children with their families decided to move to Tennessee, a son-in-law (John S. Stoltzfus) who was under the ban scarcely knew what was afoot. When Tennessee John and several of his sons and sons-in-law decided to make an exploratory trip to Tennessee, John S. was evidently excluded from the traveling group. Not knowing the name of the town to which they were going, he tagged along behind the group on the way to the railroad station and asked the station agent for a ticket "to the same place." Later, when the Stoltzfus group actually made the move to Tennessee by train, John S. kept himself aloof from his relatives, "like if he dit not belong to us," as his father-in-law described it.[27] In this instance one suspects that Betsy, the kind and gracious wife of John S., had found ways to slip bits and pieces of information to her otherwise shunned husband.

Although banning and shunning were carefully differentiated in Amish theology, these two disciplinary procedures were inseparable. Without exception, shunning must follow banning. By the ban the sinner was isolated spiritually. The person might not fellowship in any way with the congregation and of course not partake of the Lord's Supper. Shunning extended this isolation to eating at the family table and to virtually every other kind of social contact. Thus, while banning and shunning were two distinct steps, they were nevertheless considered to be of one cloth. When the congregation banned a person, the members were to shun him or her immediately. When the congregation cut one off from membership, the members were to cut that person off from their society.[28]

This unalterable sequence from banning to shunning is well-illustrated by a discussion which took place in the Ohio ministers' conference of 1826. In this meeting some ministers urged that banned-shunned former members of an Amish congregation should no longer be shunned once they were received into a Mennonite or Dunkard church. The more conservative ministers, however, argued against this proposal on the ground that this would be separating the inseparables, banning and shunning. Former members, they observed, although still banned from the table of the Lord's Supper in the Amish congregation from which they had departed, would no longer be excluded from the tables in the homes of the members of that congregation, nor from other social relationships. Such dichotomy could not be tolerated. Banning without shunning was not a biblical option.[29]

The ostracism imposed by shunning was not airtight, however. It was appropriate, according to the Dordrecht Confession of Faith, to admonish the offenders "as brethren." And if one of them should come to be "in need, hungry, thirsty, naked, sick or visited by some other affliction," the faithful members of the congregation were obligated to come to that person's aid. But there could be no reciprocation. Members of the congregation could not accept favors from the backslider, not even payment for goods or services rendered.

Jacob Ammann did not introduce the practice of shunning or avoiding persons who were excommunicated or banned from the church. Avoidance had its advocates already among the early Dutch Anabaptists, particularly Menno Simons and Dirk Philips. The Dutch Mennonites predominated in the framing of the Dordrecht Confession of Faith of 1632. In it article 16 affirmed the ban and article 17 asserted that a person who had been banned should also "be shunned and avoided by all the members of the church . . . whether it be in eating or drinking, or other such like social matters. In short . . . we are to have nothing to do with him."

As Amish preachers so often did in affirming church doctrine, they found a "shadow" or "type" of shunning in the Old Testament. Persons who had touched a dead body were to be ostracized until cleansed.[30] But they had no difficulty in finding New Testament texts as well which, if taken literally, called for the social ostracism of backsliders. In 1 Corinthians 5:11 Paul admonished the members of the congregation at Corinth "not to keep company . . . no not to eat" with those backsliders guilty of certain gross sins. Other Scriptures on social avoidance which were quoted by the Amish were 2 Thessalonians 3:14, Romans 16:17, 1 Timothy 6:3-5, and Titus 3:10-11.

Still other passages of Scripture were interpreted by the Amish as supportive of their position on banning and shunning. Frequently quoted or alluded to was Christ's statement that "every branch in me that beareth not fruit he taketh away" (John 15:2). Just so should unfruitful members be cut off from the church, according to Amish teaching, for they "are the unfruitful branches of the vine."[31]

Somewhat more strained may be the Amish interpretation of Christ's statements about cutting off one's hand or foot, or plucking out one's eye if one of these should offend the body (Matthew 5:29-30 and Mark 9:43-47). They applied these sayings not to the individual but to the congregation, the body of Christ. Peter Lehman wrote that these passages of Scripture "probably" do not refer to

> the literal eye, hand or foot, but may indicate the members of the congregation. The eye might refer to those who are to have oversight in the congregation, declare the Word of God and administer the rules and regulations. If such people were to lead a wicked life, they should not be spared because they are needed, but torn out; for he says: Tear it out and cast it from you. . . . The hand might possibly indicate the minister who cares for the widows and orphans [the deacon]. . . . If a disorderly life were to be led by such persons, they are not to be spared because they are needed, but cut off. . . . The foot might well refer to the members of the congregation who have the power to lead opinion and to choose ministers and elders. If a disorderly life should be led by such persons, they should not be spared but cut off and cast away. For he says: Cut it off and cast it from you. It is better for you that one of your members should perish than that you should have two feet and be cast into everlasting fire.[32]

A virtually identical explanation of the above Scriptures concerning the eye, hand, or foot as an offending member of the body of Christ was made by David Beiler.[33] It appears that this interpretation was widely, perhaps generally, accepted by Amish ministers and bishops.

These metaphors which compared the pruning of vines and the amputation of limbs of the body to the disciplinary acts of banning and shunning troubled Bishop Joseph Stuckey of Danvers, Illinois. In 1867 he inquired at the annual ministers' meeting how such severed branches and "irreparable, rotten, and cast-off" limbs could ever be restored.

If they were actually severed from the vine and "withered" and cast "into the fire," did they not fall in the category of those persons described in Hebrews 6 who could not be "renew[ed] . . . again unto repentance"?

Stuckey may have been troubled by this question but not sufficiently to prevent him from attempting an answer to his own inquiry. After lengthy discussion by the assembled ministers, Stuckey noted that "all things are possible with God," including the restoration to the body or the stem, of severed limbs and branches.[34] Nevertheless, whether a good analogy or not, ministers continued to talk about cutting off unprofitable vines and limbs.

John Umble's description of the excommunication process as it was carried out in the Buffalo Valley congregation is poignant:

> The excommunication of members was an awful and a solemn procedure. The members to be expelled had been notified in advance and were absent. An air of tenseness filled the house. Sad-faced women wept quietly; stern men sat with faces drawn. The bishop arose with trembling voice and with tears on his cheek he announced that the guilty parties had confessed their sin, that they were cast off from the fellowship of the church and committed to the devil and all his angels. . . . He cautioned all the members to exercise "shunning" rigorously.[35]

To those who respected the authority of the church to bind and loose, this virtual imprecation—committing offenders to the devil—was terrifying, for quite possibly "the Lord might take them away [in death] in such circumstance unprepared."[36]

In spite of the severity of the discipline of banning and shunning, the Amish exercised great tenacity in retaining the practice throughout the nineteenth century and since. It was one of the principal concerns of Jacob Ammann and, as he and his followers understood the Scriptures, was foreshadowed in the Old Testament and commanded in the New Testament. No matter that it seemed a harsh practice and difficult to administer. It was felt that without this heavy instrument "the church of God cannot stand."[37] As the Scriptures provided for water baptism as the rite for admission into the church, so did banning and shunning provide for expulsion from the church. John P. King of West Liberty, Ohio, said "he considered avoidance [shunning] as important as water baptism. . . ."[38] In short, banning and shunning were necessary to maintain the purity of the church, to bring the offender to repentance, and to preserve the integrity of the church as observed by people from without.[39]

Most of the sins for which the ban and avoidance were accepted forms of discipline may be classified into four categories. One of these, (1) the sin of persistent disobedience to the church even in the smallest detail, has already been noted. This became a gross sin if the person, after being treated with patience and after repeated warnings (Matthew 18:15-18), persisted in it defiantly. The three other kinds of sins to be penalized by shunning were to be treated more brusquely. These were (2) leaving the denomination and joining with another church; (3) marrying an unbeliever or anyone outside of the denomination; and (4) committing one of the gross or deadly sins, primarily those of violence and those related to sex.

By their nature most of these three categories of sins were public so that guilt could scarcely be denied. Even the sexual sins which came to the attention of the congregation were mostly those which resulted in the pregnancy of the woman, making the establishment of guilt almost automatic. Expulsion from the congregation and avoidance were automatic for those guilty of such acts.

The Discipline of 1809 asserted that "all those of our members who leave us to join other churches shall be treated as apostate persons" and were to be banned and shunned.[40] But this disciplinary practice was to be challenged by dissenters from within the church throughout the century. Already in 1826 in an ad hoc ministers' meeting in Ohio some leaders proposed that if someone left the church and was later taken in by the Dunkards or Mennonites, shunning should be lifted. Bishop Christian Yoder, Sr., of Somerset County, Pennsylvania, the recorder of this discussion, called the proposal a manifestation of a "liberal spirit," and of a "planting not planted by the Heavenly Father."

The liberal spirit was thereby suppressed and the ruling of 1809 retained. Such unfaithfulness to one's baptismal vow was considered to be the spiritual equivalent to unfaithfulness to one's marriage vow. The Scripture quoted—or paraphrased—by the conservatives was 1 Corinthians 5:11: "If any man that is called a brother be a fornicator, with such an one you shall have no dealings and shall not eat."[41] In this spirit Jacob Swartzendruber later (1864) posed a question at the annual ministers' meeting. Should not leaving the Amish church for any other denomination be considered an immoral act (*Unsittlichkeit*), as well as those deeds more commonly put in that category?[42]

Whether those who left the Amish church to join another nonresistant denomination—Mennonites or Dunkards—should be shunned was a question which would not go away. It was to become one of the issues over which the conservatives and those who were somewhat more change-minded were to differ in the course of the Great Schism. Still later, among the Old Order Amish at the end of the century, the debate reappeared in the Moses Hartz controversy; and again early in the twentieth century in the events which led to the formation of the Beachy Amish Mennonite Fellowship.

Marrying someone who was not a member of the Amish church also made a member subject to the ban. As applied to an outsider who was not a professing Christian or one who was in the ban, the rule remained unchallenged to the end of the century.[43] By that time, however, the change-minded Amish Mennonites were no longer shunning those who had been placed in the ban.

In the early 1800s it had been possible for such an offender to be restored, "after the lapse of some time," to full fellowship in the church without bringing his or her spouse along with him.[44] But as the church tightened its controls over the community and the family, it was decided by the 1837 conference at the Glades that "those who marry outside are no longer to be received again so lightly into fellowship, unless they bring their marriage partners with them into the Christian discipline. . . ."[45] If the wife of the banned member refused to come back to the church with him, there remained only one other way for him to be restored to membership in the congregation. He must separate from his wife and refrain from conjugal relations with her.[46]

Sins which the Amish classified under the "lust of the flesh," primarily fornication, adultery, and sins of physical violence, were dealt with summarily. The bishop merely announced to the congregation that the party or parties involved had confessed to sin and had thereby cut themselves off from the fellowship of the church.[47] Young people, however, usually did not ask for baptism until about the time of their marriage or shortly thereafter. As a result, the sins associated with courtship, such as bundling and fornication, usually occurred before they had come under the discipline of the church. Consequently, the only way to bring the authority of the church to bear upon courtship practices was through the parents.

This approach was attempted in the Discipline of 1837, which decreed that, "with regard to the excesses practiced among the youth, namely that the youth take the liberty to sleep or lie together without any fear or shame, such things shall not be tolerated at all. And when it takes place with the knowledge of the parents and something bad happens on account of it, the parents shall not go unpunished."[48] This ruling was largely ineffective, for the practice of bundling (*unehelich Beischlaf*) continued throughout the century and beyond.[49]

Clearly banning and shunning were relatively effective in keeping the church "pure," that is, uncorrupted by those who would and did violate the Ordnung. How effective they were in bringing offenders to repentance is difficult to determine. At some point and in some manner the aforementioned John S. Stoltzfus was restored to the church. The procedure of restoration has not been determined. There was a different outcome for Ezra Yoder, who was banned and shunned in 1867 by the Oak Grove congregation of Wayne County, Ohio, under the leadership of his uncle, Bishop John K. Yoder. Ezra never accepted his guilt and the judgment of the congregation. To his bishop uncle, Ezra wrote belligerently that "it must afford you satanic pleasure to look down upon such fallen creatures as me."[50] However, Ezra's spirit later mellowed, even though the ban against him was never lifted.

The ban and shunning were not to be removed on the first indication of penitence. In fact, this disciplinary action was often imposed *after* the offender had already clearly indicated sorrow for the sin by a voluntary confession. The congregation must wait for evidence of repentance in the life of the transgressor. Henry Yoder, the murderer, had to wait not merely until he had begun his efforts to give satisfaction to the state for his crime, but until he had completed that process. The length of time for which the ban was imposed indicated the seriousness of the sin and served as a warning both to the sinner and to the congregation. However, one must conclude that the ban was sometimes used to hold the penitent one in spiritual limbo for a time. Acquiescence to one's punishment and humiliation were viewed as an act of penance.

But eventually there would be reconciliation for the penitent. Even Henry Yoder was restored. "There is no sin so great [but that] God's grace is still much greater"[51] or words to that effect, were to be expressed as the penitent waited on bended knee to be restored to the church.

The formulary for the *Aufnahme*, the reinstatement, varied in detail with time and place, but not in principal features. With the applicant kneeling before the congregation the bishop would first ask three questions:

> Do you acknowledge and confess that the punishment of the Lord and the church was put on you rightly?
>
> Do you hope also that your sins have been forgiven of God and ask for forgiveness?
>
> Do you promise that you will seek to live and abide by your faith foundation and your baptismal vow as you promised in your baptism?

If the applicant answered these questions in the affirmative the bishop would then say,

> In the name of the Lord and the church it seems appropriate to extend the hand and kiss [of fellowship] to you again.[52]

Some formularies provided opportunities for the penitent or for members of the congregation to make informal statements.

In the course of the nineteenth century, differences within the Amish church concerning the use of the ban and shunning widened. At the end of the century only the conservative wing of the splintered church, the Old Order Amish, continued to practice shunning.

The Great Schism

7

The Coming of the
Great Schism, 1848-62

Portents of Division

Events of the late 1840s in the Amish church in America portended trouble for the future of that body. Only four years after their founding, the twin settlements in northern Indiana experienced a temporary division (1845–47). One Amish community was in Clinton Township, Elkhart County, and the other straddled the Little Elkhart River in Eden Township, Lagrange County, and spilled over into Middlebury Township in Elkhart County.

For two years those who had come from Wayne and Holmes counties, Ohio, worshiped separately from those who had moved to Indiana from Somerset County, Pennsylvania. During the separation the Ohio party, led by Bishop Isaac Schmucker, ordained a preacher and a deacon, evidently in order to have a more complete complement of ordained brethren in the congregation. However, with the help of Moses Miller (probably Bishop Moses P. Miller), Peter Gerber, and Jacob Coblenz from Ohio, the two congregations were reunited for a time. As to the causes of this temporary break in fellowship, we know only that they related to the "rules and regulations (*die Regeln und Gemeinde-ordnungen*) of the church."[1]

Another division took place in the later 1840s—this one permanent—in the Amish congregation in Mifflin County, Pennsylvania. The first resident Amish elder in this county had been Hans Beiler, who had held this office from about 1807 to his death in 1842. Evidently his successor, Samuel King, was not able to provide the type of leadership which Beiler had given to the congregation. In 1846 King was temporarily silenced. In 1849 his ministry was taken away from him, upon which he and his followers withdrew from the main body and formed a new congregation. Other than that he at one time used seventy-two unnecessary words in one sermon, the charges against Bishop King are not known.[2]

Also in the late 1840s trouble arose in what was then known as the Wooster congregation (later Oak Grove) in Wayne County, Ohio. In 1848 Bishop Christian Schantz took eight young people to a stream at their own request and baptized them as they knelt "shoe-deep" in the water. At the same time he baptized eight other persons in the traditional way, in the house where the service was being held.[3] The difference in the procedure of baptism was not that of mode; in both instances baptism was by pouring. In house baptism the water was poured by the deacon into the cupped hands of the bishop, the bishop then releasing the water on the head of the kneeling applicant. In stream baptism the applicant knelt in a stream or creek while the bishop stooped down, scooped water from the stream with his cupped hands, rose, and released it on the head of the applicant.

Likely the man responsible for promoting this change in the baptismal procedure in the Wooster congregation was the newly ordained minister, Jacob D. Yoder. Tradition says that when Jacob was ordained (around 1847), he accepted ordination only after making it clear that, if he were ever involved in baptismal services as a bishop, he would be allowed to baptize in a stream. In spite of this condition, Bishop Schantz ordained him. In the next decade Jacob Yoder was to become a controversial figure in the Amish church in the Wayne County–Holmes County area.[4]

By baptizing converts in a stream Bishop Schantz had opened Pandora's Box. From the time of the Amish division of the 1690s, baptism in a home had been the time-honored pattern in the Amish church. Some leaders, including the conservative-minded bishop, Levi Miller, theorized about the origin of this Amish (and Mennonite) practice. They thought that from the beginning of the Anabaptist movement, those who believed in adult baptism observed it in homes because they had been subjected to severe persecution.[5] Bishop David Beiler, however, rejected this explanation, saying that it belittled the true martyrs to say that they altered a practice based on God's Word because of "fear of pain or of death."[6]

In any case Bishop Schantz's departure from tradition in his baptismal procedure was viewed with alarm. In the 1850s the issue of stream baptism was to preoccupy the attention of Amish church leaders much as, in the same period, the issue of slavery dominated national politics. Interestingly, stream baptism seemed to become the identifying characteristic and rallying point for most of those persons wanting to introduce a few other carefully chosen innovations into Amish life and practice.

Frederick Hege, bishop of the Martin's Creek congregation in neighboring Holmes County, took immediate umbrage at Schantz's departure from tradition. In a letter to Bishop John K. Stoltzfus of Lancaster County, Hege poured out the story of the baptismal service in the Wooster church, charging Schantz with breaking his ordination vows to maintain the standards and practices of the church.[7]

Although some links in the story are missing, it seems fairly certain that the ministers' meeting in August 1849 at Berlin, Ohio, dealt primarily with this innovation in the rite of baptism. The half sheet (the other half was lost) with writing on both sides, which constitutes our sole source of information on this meeting, suggests that it was attended by ministers "in all America," that it dealt with some problems "in the Wooster congregation," and that the ministers of said congregation "acknowledged their mistakes." The extant part of this document indicates that it was signed by ministers from Ohio, Indiana, Illinois, and Iowa.[8] Possibly the lost half of the sheet listed the ministers in attendance from Pennsylvania, although there is no reference to this meeting in the extensive correspondence and other documents on this subject coming out of that state in the 1850s.

By 1850 forces for change were evident. Already in evidence were harbingers of what the editor of the *Herald of Truth* would later (1882) call the "great schism" in the Amish church.[9]

Schism in Northern Indiana

As the decade of the 1850s unfolded, church troubles in three large Amish communities—northern Indiana, Wayne and Holmes counties in Ohio, and Mifflin County, Pennsylvania—would not go away. Rather, they multiplied. In northern Indiana the progress of the division between the conservatives and the change-minded leaders was somewhat faster than in Ohio and in Mifflin County, Pennsylvania. Here Isaac Schmucker, first resident bishop in northern Indiana (ordained in 1843), presided over both settlements until 1848, although he lived in the Clinton district. That year a second bishop was ordained with jurisdiction over the other settlement, sometimes called the Lagrange district.[10]

The ordination in 1848 of Joseph Miller as bishop for the Elkhart congregation (as the Lagrange congregation was sometimes called) may have been a part of the agreement of 1847. Miller was more conservative than Schmucker. In that year the two parties came together after they had been meeting separately for about two years. Likely Miller's ordination was also an adjustment to the demography of the twin colonies, separated by a five-mile stretch of land.

In 1851 Bishop Schmucker moved to central Illinois and affili-· ated with the Rock Creek congregation. Here he served as a junior bishop under the older Jonathan Yoder, recently arrived from Juniata County, Pennsylvania. After only a year in Illinois, Schmucker and his family decided to move back to Indiana, influenced by illnesses which they evidently associated with the poorly drained prairie land.

However, Bishop Schmucker may have experienced a reinforcement of his liberal tendencies during that short sojourn. In the 1850s the Amish in Illinois were gradually moving away from the old order of church affairs with only a minimum of resistance from conservatives. While at Rock Creek (as noted in chapter 2) Schmucker helped the congregation plan for a meetinghouse, an innovation which the traditionalists in other parts of the church sometimes resisted as strongly as stream baptism. Contrary to statements by his biographers, however, he left the area before the meetinghouse was built.[11]

Bishop Isaac Schmucker may have moved to Illinois in part to escape the impending storm in northern Indiana. This way of escaping a nasty congregational squabble was a common practice. In any case, by the time Schmucker returned to Indiana in 1852, trouble was in the offing. Although he located at the Haw Patch (an area near Topeka and straddling the border between Lagrange and Noble counties) on his return to Indiana, rather than returning to or near his former property in Clinton Township, he did not escape the impending storm. Within two years he had organized a congregation at the Haw Patch over which he had bishop oversight. Only two years later (1856) this young congregation built a meetinghouse.[12]

Already in 1854, as bishop in a neighboring congregation, Schmucker had evidently provided counsel and exercised leadership in the choice of a new bishop in the Clinton congregation. Preacher Jonas D. Troyer (1811-97) was selected for this office only months after he had moved from Ohio to Indiana. Since Schmucker and Troyer were of one mind in church affairs, it may be that the former exercised his influence—not necessarily unethically—in favor of Troyer as bishop.

For the story of the critical years of 1852-57 from the conservative point of view, the reminiscences of John "Hansi" E. Borntreger, who was a youthful eyewitness, merit quoting at some length:

Jonas D. Troyer (1811-97), ordained a bishop in 1854. Leader of the change-minded group in Elkhart and Lagrange counties, Indiana, in the Amish division of 1854-57. Photograph probably taken about 1890. (Courtesy of Linda Wojciechowski, Mishawaka, Indiana.)

Up to this time both congregations had grown large in numbers and got on very well, and most of the preachers were very zealous to feed the church with the Word of God, to maintain the rules and regulations of the church, to continue steadfast in the truth as they had promised at baptism, [and] not to dress according to the world. . . .

Most of the church members were in agreement with their ministers, but some preachers, namely, Jonas Troyer, Christian Plank, Christian Miller, and John Schmeily, and a part of the congregation, no longer desired to be subject to the old rules and regulations, and had much to say in opposition, causing the faithful ones much concern and grief. The rebels got together, counseled among themselves, declared their freedom, and started a new congregation, based on their own notions. This began perhaps already in the spring of 1854 and occurred in the Clinton District. But J[onas D.] Troyer [of the Clinton congregation], who was a gifted speaker and exercised a strong influence, brought it about that a considerable number from the Lagrange congregation [also] joined with him. . . .

The result thereof [of this rebellion] was a critical, regrettable, and complete division in these congregations. Children were separated from their parents and siblings [from one another]. This [split] was completed [became irreversible] in 1857.[13]

More specifically Troyer, the new bishop, was charged with tolerating expensive clothing and worldly adornments in his congregation, the holding of worldly (civil) offices, engagement in all kinds of commercial activities, and "the wisdom of this world." The latter phrase possibly implied that he was ready to accept more education than the conservatives would allow.[14] It is not clear whether baptizing in a stream was originally an issue, or whether the practice was introduced by Troyer after his party had begun to meet as a separate congregation. Meetinghouses were not built by the liberals in Clinton and Eden townships until the early 1860s. They were likely not an immediate issue in 1854–57.

While Borntreger's account must be accepted in the main, it should be observed that, with two bishops—Isaac Schmucker and Jonas D. Troyer—leading those who were ready to accept some changes in Amish church practices, followed by several other ministers and a large part of the Clinton congregation, it is not entirely correct to treat this party as a rebellious splinter group.

Borntreger's observation that the results of the division were devastating and that it was complete and irreversible by 1857, is likewise subject to some modest revision. Before he died, Jeremiah Yoder, also a youthful witness to this schism, told Daniel Bontrager that feelings weren't really as bitter as Hansi Borntreger described them. He added that, nevertheless, the memory of that division led him to determine never to be involved in a church split.[15]

Borntreger himself has provided a small shred of evidence that the bitterness engendered by the division was not all-consuming. Two entries in his diary (August 14 and September 25, 1864) indicate that he and his bride, conservatives, attended meetings at the Forks and the Clinton Township meetinghouses. Both buildings had been erected the preceding year by the change-minded Amish who had followed Schmucker and Troyer in the split of 1854–57.[16]

More substantive evidence that the schism of the midfifties in northern Indiana was not totally irreversible in 1857 is provided in a letter written by Bishop Jonas D. Troyer himself. On July 11, 1860, Troyer wrote to Bishop John K. Yoder in Wayne County, Ohio, that he hoped "with God's help and great diligence that the schism may perhaps yet be healed." Evidently at that late date Troyer was still envisioning some possibility for a reconciliation of the two parties. He realized, however, that it was a forlorn hope, for several sentences later he commented that "it seems unlikely to me that we can settle the matter here without a split. This I admit between me and you."[17] Troyer's letter suggests that the door of reconciliation had not been slammed shut in 1857, but remained open a crack as late as July 1860. Other ministers from both parties did not consider the 1854–57 division irreversible. This is made clear by the consultations between the two groups in the annual Amish ministers' meetings of 1862–65.

In addition to the Elkhart County–Lagrange County division of 1854–57, similar divisions took place in the Amish settlements at

Nappanee, Indiana, and in ·the Miami County–Howard County area, eighty miles to the south. For the schism in these two locations, little information is available. The division at Nappanee probably occurred in 1854. Preacher John Ringenberg led the group that was ready for some modest changes, and Tobias Hochstetler led the conservatives. Some persons assert or surmise that those of the Nappanee settlement who had recently migrated from the Palatinate (via Wayne County, Ohio) identified largely with the change-minded faction. Also, that those who had come from Holmes and Tuscarawas counties in Ohio—with longer and stronger American roots—identified largely with the traditional faction.[18]

For the division in Howard and Miami counties, oral tradition has handed down dates ranging from 1854 to 1863. In the course of this division "the members called each other nicknames of all sorts." This routine led the only minister in the liberal group, Benjamin Schrock, to move north to Elkhart County, or at least contributed to his decision to leave the area.[19] The Amish settlement in Allen County, just north of Fort Wayne, divided in 1861.[20]

Comparable and parallel to the schisms occurring in the northern Indiana congregations was the division which took place in the infant Amish settlement in Lawrence County, in northwestern Pennsylvania, under the leadership of Bishop John C. Gnagey. Like the Indiana Amish, this settlement was young—possibly even younger than the Elkhart–Lagrange counties settlement —when the split occurred (early 1850s). The issues involved were comparable to those in northern Indiana.[21] In contrast, the major issue in the Amish settlements in Mifflin County, Pennsylvania, and in Wayne County, Ohio, was stream baptism.

Baptism in Water and the Preaching Deacon Controversy in Mifflin County, Pennsylvania

In 1849 that remarkable Amish layman Shem Zook published a new edition of the *Martyrs Mirror*.[22] On the title page of part 2 of this volume appears a picture of a baptismal scene. It probably depicts the baptism of Christ, with the baptizer and the baptized standing slightly less than waist deep in what appears to be a river. This picture is not found in any other edition of that tome.[23]

Zook's choice of a baptismal scene to embellish the title page is appropriate, for this treasured book gives extensive coverage to the baptism of converts in the face of persecution and martyrdom. Zook may also have been influenced in his choice of this scene by a short

Baptismal scene appearing on the title page of part 2 of Shem Zook's edition (1849) of the Martyrs Mirror. *Zook was deeply involved in the controversy among the Amish concerning stream baptism, and may have chosen this scene to indicate his position on this issue.*

paragraph in the *Martyrs Mirror*. It stated that a certain Walfridus Strabo, who evidently lived in the second century A.D., had proved that "in these early times it was not customary to baptize otherwise than in running water (*fliessendem Wasser*)." Mention is also made of two young women who were baptized similarly in the same era.[24]

It should be noted too that the question of the proper mode of baptism was filling the religious atmosphere in nineteenth-century America. The subject was extremely controversial and, in the mind of John F. Funk, was bandied about in such a way as to create confusion in the minds of his Amish and Mennonite readers. Funk published article after article on the subject, probably primarily to combat the claims of the immersionists.[25] Funk's articles in the *Herald of Truth* postdate the early phases of the controversy in the Amish church concerning baptism. Nevertheless, they reflect the preoccupation and concern of religious thought of the nineteenth century over the proper mode of baptism.

The attention of Shem Zook and other Amish leaders may have been drawn to the rite of baptism by the controversy of the 1820s concerning the rebaptizing of Mennonites who wished to join the Amish church. In searching the New Testament to determine the answer to this question, Amish leaders may have been reminded of how Christ and the Ethiopian eunuch were baptized in a stream or in a body of water. In searching the *Martyrs Mirror*, they may have been attracted to the passages concerning baptism in running water. Yet, amazingly, no instance has been found in which the proponents of stream baptism referred to or quoted them to support their position.

The most immediate source of this new doctrine of stream baptism among the Amish was probably the Mennonites. Sometime previous to 1841 this question had arisen among the Mennonites of Ontario and upstate New York and was given some attention in their annual conferences. After "much discussion" in one of these conferences, it was decided that "the form of baptism hitherto in use should be held to in the main." It was to be administered to candidates who did not object to the traditional procedure of pouring in a home or meetinghouse. But if someone "should insist . . . upon his preference for the new form, this should be allowed." The "new form," as described by Preacher Jacob Krehbiel, was "in water, with water,"[26] the same pair of phrases used by the Amish to indicate stream baptism.[27]

In any case Amish historian David Luthy has good reason for his notion that the baptismal scene in Zook's edition of the *Martyrs Mirror* was placed there by the latter because of his vigorous espousal of stream baptism.[28] For the next three decades Zook continued his advocacy of stream baptism, as did Solomon K. Beiler, the bishop of Zook's home congregation in the Middle district of the Kishacoquillas Valley in Mifflin County, Pennsylvania. Although a businessman and surprisingly worldly-wise, Zook was also very much an Amish churchman. As a result of his interest in church affairs, he got caught up in those controversies which eventuated in the Great Schism as it widened in Mifflin County. Whether or not Zook chose that baptismal scene in his edition of the *Martyrs Mirror* deliberately to promote the idea and practice of stream baptism, it is clear that he supported his bishop wholeheartedly in this matter. To Zook the entire division took place because of differences concerning stream baptism.

Zook's preoccupation with the importance of this question surfaced again in 1865 when wrote for the *Herold der Wahrheit*. In his article Zook resurrected the story of some primitive Christians from Thessalonica, Greece, who had visited the early Anabaptists. After comparing beliefs these Thessalonians and Anabaptists had found themselves in general agreement and had composed a confession of their common faith.[29] The story in some of its parts is likely authentic.[30] This confession stated that "a baptismal candidate must be standing with his feet in water like Christ was standing in the river Jordan." Zook could not have found a better manuscript to support his position on stream baptism. As late as 1880, when he was 82 years old, Zook wrote up his version of the Great Schism in Mifflin County. Even though the controversy concerning stream baptism had completely dissipated, he viewed it as the one and only issue in that division.[31]

The question of stream baptism emerged simultaneously in two locations in the Amish church—in Mifflin County, Pennsylvania, and in the Wayne County–Holmes County area of Ohio. The first stream baptism in an Amish congregation probably took place in the Wooster church in the spring of 1848. If it is correct that Jacob D. Yoder, the aggressive advocate of stream baptism throughout his ten-year ministry in the Wooster congregation, had already moved from Mifflin County to Wayne in the previous year, it becomes plausible—even probable—that he brought the idea with him.

For the first few years of the controversy in Mifflin County concerning baptism, we are completely dependent on a short paragraph in the account by Shem Zook. His partisan espousal of stream baptism has already been noted. Some time during the 1840s, the Amish settlement in the Kishacoquillas Valley of Mifflin County was divided into three districts. By 1849, possibly earlier, new bishops had been ordained for the Upper and Middle districts—Abraham Peachey for the former and Solomon Beiler for the latter. These two bishops quarreled continuously thereafter and became the principals around whom the two respective parties in the Great Schism in Mifflin County rallied.

Zook's account says that Solomon Beiler began to advocate this new baptismal procedure "not long after he had come to the bishop's office." Already in May 1851 three ministers (all bishops) had been called in from other areas of the church to adjudicate the dispute.[32] Shem Zook and his bishop, Solomon Beiler, had been preoccupied for several years with the issue of stream baptism. It is therefore a plausible conjecture that these men played a central role in influencing other Amish leaders, such as Jacob D. Yoder, and possibly Jonas D. Troyer. The latter lived in several locations in Ohio in the years immediately preceding 1854.

The three bishops who had been called to Mifflin County in 1851 to settle the quarrel were David Beiler from Lancaster County, Abner Yoder from Somerset County, and Levi Miller from Holmes County, Ohio. The report of these men is a study in the way Amish churchmen wrestled with the problem of reconciling the traditions of the church with the Scriptures. "Concerning the dissensions which exist about the administration of baptism in water" in the Kishacoquillas Valley, so ran the report, we are minded to stay with the Word of the Lord, and bind and loose with the same. So we agreed to make no rule (*Gebot*) against it since we have no word [Scripture] against it. But since disunity and discord have come from it, so it would be our wish that it would be discontinued and the applicant for baptism not advised to it, since we have no commandment to that effect, but rather only the example [of baptisms performed in water].[33]

Concern for the unity of the church permeated this report. It urged that, "since the church has suffered much harm [as a result of this dispute], and since it serves more to discord than peace and unity and love," the practice of stream baptism be discontinued. The statement encouraged the ministers involved not to burden themselves "with that to which we cannot easily give an answer." The visiting bishops were apparently saying that, whether biblical or not, the disagreeing parties should desist from talking about baptism in water. Finally, although these arbitrators were not willing "to make a ruling that it [baptism] must always be done" in the traditional way, they reminded the parties to the dispute that they had agreed to accept the decision of this bishop committee and would be expected to comply with it.

The part played by David Beiler of Lancaster County in this Mifflin County quarrel throughout its duration requires special consideration. Apparently baptism in water never became a critical issue among the Amish in Lancaster County. Nevertheless, this highly respected senior bishop felt compelled to exert his influence far beyond the boundaries of his local area. In the same year in which he served on the above-described panel of bishops in Mifflin County, Beiler responded to an inquiry concerning baptism in water from Moses Miller (probably Moses P. Miller) of Holmes County, Ohio. Beiler wrote:

When I consider all those places in the Scripture [where baptism occurred] . . . I come to the conclusion in my simple way that in the time of the apostles baptism was performed in both ways. . . . In my youth I was baptized in a house, and I was never disturbed by that, for God sees the obedience of the heart by His grace. . . . I count the Holy Spirit second baptism much more important than water baptism.

David Beiler ended this letter with a statement which the proponents of stream baptism would never let him forget:

If any person is burdened in his heart and feeling, and feels firmly in his heart that it [stream baptism] is nearest to the divine order and wants to follow it in lowliness and meekness as he feels is the example given by Jesus Christ, I do not want to make that person weak, for where there is no law there can be no transgression. I for my part am content if it can bring peace, but for me the old order is preferable.[34]

In his *Wahre Christenthum*, the manuscript of which was completed in 1857, Beiler included a lengthy chapter on baptism. Repeatedly he maintained therein that baptism "with water" (in a house) is as scriptural as baptism "in water" (kneeling in a stream). So why not simply abide by the time-honored procedure, he argued, and avoid strife and ill-will?[35]

Those on the other side of the stream baptism issue, however, felt that beneath these gracious and patient pleas for voluntary compliance with the old order of church affairs was an adamant determination to see that it happened.[36] Thus, although David and Solomon Beiler were brothers, they came to be leaders of opposing sides in the Great Schism. Mostly David took on the role of senior bishop and adviser to the younger Abraham Peachey. The latter was Solomon Beiler's opponent, neighbor, and counterpart in the Upper district of the Kishacoquillas Valley. Perhaps some unresolved sibling rivalry exacerbated the differences between David and Solomon.

According to Shem Zook's account, the aforementioned visiting brethren held parting conversations with Solomon Beiler and his supporters. They indicated that if the latter persisted in their divergence from custom, thus "provoking discord and disagreement," "the matter must be turned over to the congregation for counsel." What was not anticipated, evidently, was that the congregation would, after some hesitation, ultimately support their beleaguered bishop.[37] Solomon Beiler's recourse to the authority of his own congregation in order to thwart a decision made by a delegation of visiting bishops illustrates again the basic congregational polity of the Amish denomination. It also constitutes a harbinger of future events in this dispute which was increasingly to become a struggle between Bishop Solomon Beiler and Bishop Abraham Peachey.

Finally, in 1855, when Beiler found that he could not quiet the minority in his own congregation, he proposed that his accusers choose another delegation of visiting ministers to settle the matter. Upon the advice of Bishop Peachey and members of his congregation, four ministers, all from Lancaster County, were selected. They were Full Deacon Michael Schwartz, Bishop John K. Stoltzfus of the Millcreek district, Preacher John Stoltzfus of Groffdale ("Groffdale Johnnie"), and Preacher Christian King. These men, all of whom were to remain with the conservative party in the 'Great Schism, ruled that "the accusers of Beiler must be satisfied with him whether he baptizes in the house or in water." This decision, says Zook, was accepted unanimously by both Peachey's and Beiler's congregation, the four accusers excepted. This time it was Peachey who found it convenient to disregard the decision of a delegation of visiting ministers.[38]

Faced with Peachey's persistent opposition, in January 1857 Beiler appealed to the Lancaster ministers who had made the ruling in his favor in 1855. These ministers wrote an impassioned letter to the Mifflin County congregations urging unity based on their agreement of 1855. The dissenters were first admonished and then warned that they were really guilty of that sin of all sins, disobedience.[39]

When Peachey disregarded the letter and continued to demand that Beiler return to the traditional way of administering baptism, Beiler and his congregation again asked for help. This time they appealed to Moses Miller (probably the senior bishop Moses P. Miller rather than the younger Moses J. Miller) from Holmes County, Ohio; Jonas Troyer of Elkhart County, Indiana, but formerly also of Holmes County;[40] and Abner Yoder from Somerset County, Pennsylvania. These men came to Mifflin County in November 1857, but Troyer and Miller (Yoder having been called back home) failed even to get the dissident parties together for a consultation.

According to Shem Zook, Bishop David Beiler had advised Peachey not to meet with the visiting bishops.[41] Miller and Troyer evidently were forced to be content with compiling excerpts from eight pastoral letters of previous years relating to and favoring stream baptism.[42] These excerpts lend some support to the views of conservative-minded Amish leaders of the 1860s and by later Amish writers. They assert that the issue of stream baptism would not have been sufficiently divisive in itself to have caused a churchwide schism.[43] As for Solomon Beiler's congregation, the Middle district in Mifflin County, it was decided that "it should continue with the help of God on its course."[44] In 1861 Solomon was still performing "baptism in water whenever it is requested."[45]

Until the late 1850s the only visible issue on that iceberg called the Great Schism, as far as the Kishacoquillas Valley was concerned, was baptism in water. No doubt other questions lurked in submerged parts of the iceberg.

In 1859 an issue surfaced which would be superimposed on that of stream baptism. The question concerned the role of deacons, particularly of full deacons, and centered around Solomon Beiler's full deacon, Samuel Yoder.[46] Yoder had been ordained a deacon in Solomon's congregation in 1850. Only a year earlier he had married the bishop's daughter, Elizabeth—a cozy arrangement, but not particularly unusual.[47] Yoder was well liked by the congregation, and about as early as custom would allow, probably in 1858, he was advanced to full deacon.

However, this full deacon was evidently not staying within the bounds prescribed for that office by Amish tradition. His bishop (and father-in-law) was accused of allowing him to take a regular turn with the ministers in preaching and of using him too frequently in opening and closing the services.[48] Given the Amish penchant for a strict delineation of ministerial duties among the ordained brethren of a congregation, perhaps this criticism was to be expected.

Nor is it surprising that those who had supported Solomon Beiler on stream baptism now also backed him in allowing his deacon to preach. Conversely, those who were opposed to baptism in water were also opposed to letting deacons preach on anything like a regular basis. David Beiler's position already in 1860 reflects this alignment. The conservative faction of the Amish church in Pennsylvania and perhaps beyond was beginning to define its position. Beiler reportedly said that "those who administer baptism in water, who perform marriages closer than second cousins, and who permit deacons to preach, these he does not consider to be his brethren."[49]

On both sides of this debate concerning preaching deacons, the participants quoted the Dordrecht Confession of Faith, the Bible, and the *Martyrs Mirror*. Article 9 of the Dordrecht statement said that deacons might assist the bishop by exhorting the church "in word and doctrine." This statement could be interpreted as allowing deacons to preach or not to preach, depending on the predisposition of the expositor.

The critics of Solomon Beiler found in the Old Testament a strict division of duties between the several religious orders—Levites, priests, and high priest. So it should be, they said, with the offices in the church. It follows that a deacon should not infringe upon the duties of the minister or the bishop. Solomon Beiler's supporters noted from the New Testament that Philip, whom they assumed to be the deacon of Acts 8:5-8, went into Samaria preaching and baptizing. His opponents claimed that the Philip who preached in Samaria was not the deacon but the apostle by that name. Finally, Solomon's supporters called attention to stories in the *Martyrs Mirror* which indicated that deacons preached in post–New Testament times.[50]

Within a few years Samuel Yoder may actually have assumed the role of bishop. A letter of 1864 written by one of Samuel's fellow ministers speaks of "Sem [Samuel] Yoder's congregation" and "Sem Yoder's ministers."[51] This activity may not have been as controversial as that of preaching, for Amish practice allowed a full deacon to perform all the functions of a bishop (with the exception of taking his regular turn in preaching) if circumstances required it. Bishop Solomon Beiler had turned sixty years of age at about the time that Yoder had been raised to full deacon (1858) and may have desired or needed an assistant already at that time. Facilitating such a shift of responsibilities was the fact that Yoder was Solomon Beiler's son-in-law.

John A. Hostetler has described the formal break (perhaps in 1862) in fellowship between Solomon Beiler and his congregation, and Peachey and his congregation:

> It seems that the occasion for the outbreak of the division occurred one Sunday during preaching service. While admonishing the brethren, Solomon Byler [or Beiler] again brought up the subject of creek baptism. Abraham Peachey, who had already heard too much about this creek baptism, turned to Solomon Beiler and said, "In Gottes Nahme, wann du net zufrühte bist mit wass mir dühne, geh un duh wie du witt (In God's name, if you don't like what we do, go and do as you please)."[52]

Although this break in fellowship between Peachey's and Beiler's congregations proved to be final, it was not so regarded at that time. Attempts to achieve a reconciliation through the annual ministers' meetings and by other procedures continued throughout the critical years of 1862-65.

The Great Schism in Mifflin County produced ripples—more accurately, heavy waves—which reached to the neighboring counties. Little is known of what happened during this period southward in Juniata County, except that Bishop John Esh maintained fellowship with Solomon Beiler and his congregation and participated freely in the liberally dominated ministers' meetings of 1862-78. Esh was one of the few ministers who attended as many as ten of the sixteen annual meetings.

To the northeast, the Amish congregation of Union County was almost swamped when the waves from Mifflin County converged in Buffalo Valley with other waves from Lancaster County. Like the satellite nations in world politics, this small congregation was torn between alignment with David Beiler's Upper Pequea congregation in Lancaster County and Solomon Beiler's more liberal congregation to the southwest.

In Union County, Bishop Elias Riehl and Deacon Christian Stoltzfus were prepared to introduce some changes into the church, but other leaders were more conservative: Christian's son-in-law, Preacher Christian King, Jr., and Michael Schwartz (after his reinstatement as full deacon in 1869).[53] Evidently King and Schwartz sought to strengthen their position by keeping close ties with the Lancaster County Amish. Stoltzfus and Riehl, on the other hand, insisted on keeping close fellowship with Solomon Beiler who, asserted their opposers, "allows S[amuel] Y[oder] to preach and baptizes in water."

Already in the spring of 1860 Stoltzfus thought that a division in his congregation was imminent. A year later the group that opposed Stoltzfus and Riehl was holding separate Sunday services.[54] Finally, in the fall of 1862 Stoltzfus was able to write to his deacon brother, John Stoltzfus, that the differences had been patched up, with only a couple of families remaining unsatisfied.[55] Although the Buffalo Valley congregation would soon adopt stream baptism and support a Sunday school, it appears that the issue in the 1860–62 crisis was whether the congregation should continue to fellowship with Solomon Beiler and his church. The disintegration of this congregation in the 1880s has been told in chapter 3.

Stream Baptism in Wayne and Holmes Counties, Ohio

Jacob D. Yoder may have come from Mifflin County to Wayne County as early as 1847. Likely his coming was not later than 1850, his ordination to the ministry occurring soon after his arrival. Whether Yoder was the "carrier" for the idea of baptizing in water or not, this innovation apparently came to the Wooster congregation at about the same time as did Yoder. Jacob's ordination to the office of full minister or bishop had shortly followed his ordination to the ministry—in the early 1850s.

The congregation may have moved too rapidly in ordaining Jacob Yoder and then promoting him to the office of bishop. This new arrival brought trouble to this Wayne County congregation. His ordination to the ministry itself may have been the signal for the defection of a few conservatives under the leadership of preachers Hannes Yoder and Emanuel Hochstetler. They were concerned about deviations from the *Ordnung* in the congregation.[56]

Most of the records available concerning Jacob Yoder's ministry reveal more of the procedures taken to dispose of his troubles than the substance of the controversies which surrounded him. In the course of these difficulties, Yoder at first maintained the upper hand. For several years he received strong congregational support when he placed several of his adversaries under the ban, presumably followed by shunning. A series of letters bearing dates from 1853 to 1857, each signed by a considerable number of lay members of his congregation, bear witness to the backing of Yoder from his flock.[57]

In 1853 Frederick Wenger of the Wooster congregation and his son Joseph raised their voices against stream baptism. They were informed by a letter that they were "no longer considered brethren in the church." The letter inferred that disrespect for the ministers of the congregation was the principal offense of the Wengers. A majority of the seven signers were laypersons.[58] But the matter did not rest here. Consultation with the Beech congregation in neighboring Stark County followed. At some point in these conversations, Frederick and Joseph were constrained to make the usual confessions and were restored to membership in the congregation.

Preacher Christian Graber, recent immigrant from France, gave Jacob Yoder more trouble than did the Wengers. As a minister, Graber's opposition to stream baptism was more formidable than that of the Wengers. The well-known letter of 1855 from Christian Brandt (one of Bishop Yoder's ministers) indicates that Graber had been making his views known for some time. Evidently the latter was finding support among the conservatives of Stark and Holmes counties.

Bishop Frederick Hege of the Martin's Creek congregation in Holmes County had raised his voice against stream baptism already in 1848. He found support among the members and possibly the ministry of the Canton congregation (actually located in the Richville area southwest of Canton).[59] In Holmes County, Hege may have been instrumental in disposing the bishops of neighboring congregations, including Levi Miller, against stream baptism. Originally quite tolerant on the matter of stream baptism, the latter soon came to position himself with the conservatives.[60]

In promoting stream baptism, Jacob Yoder could find considerable support from New Testament accounts of baptisms which took place "in water." Yet one of his critics, Bishop David A. Troyer (Treyer) of Holmes County, rather astutely observed that the baptisms described in the Scriptures took place at the location where the instruction of the converts took place. There was no deliberate removal to a stream for the purpose of baptizing.[61]

Christian Graber soon found an even more questionable interpretation of Scripture in Yoder's version of the fall of Adam and Eve in the Garden of Eden. According to Bishop Troyer, Graber charged Yoder with saying that the sin of Adam and Eve was lying. This ran counter to the traditional Amish interpretation of Adam and Eve's fall, which emphasized their defiance of the Creator. Therefore, this deviation from Amish theology may have been of greater substance than meets the eye at first glance. Graber took Bishop Yoder to task. "If you teach such a thing," he said to him, "then you are an angel of the pit [the abyss]."[62]

Yoder's congregation continued to support him and ratified Graber's excommunication. Graber appealed to the Canton (Richville) and the Holmes County congregations. When attempts were made to confer with Yoder in the traditional manner—through ad hoc ministers' meetings—he would never appear.

Even under these circumstances Yoder's congregation remained loyal to him. On March 15, 1857, nineteen laypersons sent a congregational letter to Moses Miller of Holmes County (either Bishop Gross Mose or Bishop Klein Mose). They told those who wanted to examine Yoder that the congregation had placed Graber under the ban with due process and after careful deliberation, and considered the case to be closed. The congregation was not answerable to the Stark and Holmes County ministers. If the latter wanted to examine Yoder, it would be necessary for them to bring neutral ministers along with them and come to Wayne County. He would not be coming to the appointed place in Holmes County on April 2, to which he had been summoned.[63]

Soon after the Christian Graber affair, within the space of two or three years at most, Jacob Yoder's world crumbled about him. His wife died early in 1858 and at about the same time he became bankrupt. His secular activities came under censure—racing against a train up the steep grade from Wooster to Weilersville in a sled pulled by mules (and winning), dealing in horses, and engaging in unidentified "rather grave social misconduct." He was relieved of his ministry and soon thereafter he moved to Indiana without a reconciliation with his congregation.[64]

Yoder next tried to relate to or affiliate with Jonas D. Troyer's congregation in Clinton Township, Elkhart County. This caused much dissension within the latter congregation, and some misunderstandings between that congregation and the Wooster church from which he had come. Only then did the Wooster congregation feel compelled to adjudge Yoder (in absentia) guilty of misconduct.[65] Apparently this action by the Wooster congregation disqualified Yoder for membership in Troyer's congregation,[66] and he joined the Church of the Brethren.

According to David A. Troyer, Jacob Yoder's novel interpretation of the story of Adam and Eve and the serpent "was really the main reason for this regrettable division" in the Holmes County–Wayne County area. This is difficult to accept. Yet Troyer was a central participant on the conservative side in the dispute.[67] This quarrel no doubt stirred up animosities which would not go away. But there clearly were other ingredients which contributed to the falling out of Yoder and his Holmes County critics. At a later point in his narration, Troyer himself lists other deviations from the old order of things, of which Yoder and his congregation were guilty. "Now the good reader may judge who caused this separation," wrote Troyer in 1898;

> was not J[acob] Yoder the chief instigator of this separation? By him great confusion was introduced into the congregations, and by him and his followers the division was completed, and also many other innovations were introduced into the congregations here and there. It was no longer considered good or necessary for the ministers to go into the preservice ministerial counsel meeting (*Abrath*). At times [the congregational] counsel [meeting] was held with open doors in the presence of nonmembers. The old thick hymn books [the *Ausbund*] were discarded, and the new fast tunes introduced. The prayer books, too, they used no more. The ban and avoidance were seldom practiced. Pride, splendor, and haughtiness took the upper hand. Almost anything was permitted. People said: The outside does not matter if the heart is good, and so on. The houses were splendidly furnished. All this and yet much more of such a nature arose through the above-mentioned J. Yoder and his following.[68]

In examining these charges against Bishop Jacob Yoder, one is drawn toward the conclusion that Troyer was actually enumerating all the differences in religious practices which gave rise to the Great Schism. However, some of them were not even considered in the Amish congregations of Wayne and Holmes counties until after Yoder's departure. Not until 1860 or 1861 did the formal break in fellowship occur between the Wooster congregation and the conservatives of Holmes County under the leadership of bishops Frederick Hege, Levi Miller, David A. Troyer, and (Klein) Moses J. Miller. According to Troyer, these conservatives met and decided to "withdraw from J[acob] Yoder and not to serve (*dienen*) with him any more so long as he continued with his unscriptural teaching . . . in regard to the serpent and Eve."[69] Yoder had certainly left or was leaving the Wooster congregation by the time of this consultation.

However, the Holmes County bishops failed to achieve a united front at that meeting. For reasons which have not been ascertained, (Gross) Mose P. Miller of Walnut Creek stood with Bishop Jacob Yoder. Perhaps he thought the issue too trivial to justify a division. More likely, judging by his words and conduct in the years immediately following, he identified with Yoder and the Wooster congregation primarily with respect to other issues. These other points which he considered more important would receive increasing attention in the Amish church in the crisis years of 1862–65.

This decision of the several Holmes County bishops to break fellowship with Jacob Yoder and, as it resulted, with his supporter Moses P. Miller, was not thought to be permanent. An attitude prevailed similar to the earlier views on the division in northern Indiana. Breaking fellowship was an improvised response to a critical situation which, judging by past experiences, might well be rectified. In June 1862 the first annual churchwide ministers' meeting assembled near Smithville, in Wayne County, Ohio. The recent Wayne County–Holmes County division was to receive much attention from the delegates.[70]

The Great Schism Elsewhere

The Amish settlement in the Logan County–Champaign County area of Ohio largely followed the pattern of the Wooster congregation. The several families who chose to remain conservative withdrew and moved either to Holmes County or to Indiana.[71]

In those Amish congregations and clusters of congregations formed by nineteenth-century migration from Europe, the issues of the 1850s produced only a minimum of dissension. Although the influence of the recent immigrants for change has been overemphasized, yet it can scarcely be denied that the majority of them were more change-minded than their native American brethren. The Ropp brothers—Christian and Andrew—in Illinois were exceptions to this generalization. The only division of that decade in Illinois occurred when Bishop Jonathan Yoder felt compelled to impose some restrictions on the Hessians, the "button Amish," who had been worshiping in his Rock Creek congregation.[72]

Although not all was calm in the recently settled Fulton County Amish community in northwestern Ohio, no schism related to the relaxing of the Ordnung would occur there.[73] In the 1850s the Beech church of Stark County, Ohio, had challenged some of the actions of Jacob D. Yoder in neighboring Wayne County, but nevertheless pursued a path similar to Yoder's congregation.

A small group of about six families in this Beech church, however, were not prepared to approve the changes which the congregation was making. The new things included the use of "English-style" overcoats and shawls, "so that one cannot be distinguished from the gentlemen in the town," and the "decoration of the hair." These families, led by Preacher Joseph Ramseyer, were meeting separately already in the spring of 1862. Deacon David Maurer was the leader of the majority party in the Beech congregation.

The other Stark County congregation, the Canton church at nearby Richville, remained conservative. Nevertheless, a messy situation muddied the waters considerably and added a new element to the friction already existing between the Beech and the Canton congregations. The scene involved a vain and evidently unprincipled young woman named Mary Eicher and the son of Minister Henry Sommer.[74]

In Iowa the congregations at least partially made up of European immigrants, those at Wayland and Pulaski, were making considerable adaptations to the broader American culture.[75] In addition to the divisions noted above, there were mass defections to the Apostolic Christian Church in a few congregations in this period, as described in the forepart of chapter 10. The century-long drain to the Dunkards and Mennonites continued also.

The Amish Church, 1850–62; An Analysis

Although a comprehensive analysis of the Great Schism must follow a description of the crisis period of 1862–65, some comment about the initial stage of this division is required at this point. From the viewpoint of the broader society, the schism appears to have been a consequence of the inevitable trend toward the acculturation of a minority group in the milieu of the American melting pot.

One notes the efforts of Amish church leaders and faithful lay persons to maintain the faith and the identity of the group. On the other hand can be seen the forces conducive to acculturation, or at least to accommodation with the larger society. The Amish church in each succeeding generation had suffered mightily from attrition. Nevertheless, by strengthening the authority of the Ordnung and expanding its scope, the faithful had preserved the integrity of the denomination. Finally, in the 1850s, the retaining walls of the Ordnung had burst and one-half or more of the members of the Amish church eventually chose to move out of the old channel.

The cause of the Great Schism emphasized by the conservatives among the Amish, deserves more attention than has been given to it thus far in this volume. The Amish had come to America to flee religious persecution and military conscription, and to escape economic discrimination especially with respect to landholding. In large measure those who survived the voyage to America and the trauma of adjusting to their new environment had found what they came for, and more. Second-, third-, and fourth-generation Amish Americans had found prosperity and had accumulated wealth, primarily in the form of land. At the same time, as the benefits of technological change became available, their lifestyle was affected. New things included factory-made clothing, household furnishings, and improved farming implements.

What David Beiler described so vividly and decried so vociferously, were the expressions of this modest affluence in the activities and personal appearance of members of the church. Not only were members of the Amish church living more and more according to the "world mode" in following the fashions of the world. They were even resorting to the courts to protect their property. Had Beiler been acquainted with the term, "conspicuous consumption," as introduced half a century later by the economist Thorstein Veblen, he might well have applied it to the lifestyle of the more progressive Amish of his day.

Beiler and his fellow conservatives felt that these adaptations to the ways of the world were in violation of the Amish principles of humility and simplicity. "I verily believe," David Beiler observed in his lament,

> that sixty years and more ago, if anyone . . . would have dressed and conducted himself in the high fashion as is too much the case today and would not have heeded the warning of the church, he would have had to be put out of the church as a disobedient person. . . .
> Nearly all of our ancestors came to this country poor and had to manage with scanty food and clothes and had to live almost in huts. And we, their descendants, live in superfluity, in pride and luxuriousness in dress, in expensive comfortably furnished houses, and many lead a sensual life.[76]

What of that visible tip of the iceberg, the preoccupation of the Amish church in the 1850s with the issue of stream baptism? In the first place, the baptism-in-water issue, at first a matter of sincere difference of conviction, soon came to symbolize the entire package of moderate adjustments which the change-minded church leaders were proposing. Second, when push came to shove in the critical years of 1862–65, stream baptism would be eclipsed by other issues. In terms of the unity of the Amish church, those years would be critical.

8

The Diener Versammlungen, 1862-65

The Amish Church in 1862

In 1862 the Amish church was in considerable confusion. The conservatives and the change-minded factions in the several Amish settlements in Indiana had not fellowshiped with each other since 1857, perhaps since 1854. It is probable that the breakdown of relations between the two factions in the Holmes-Wayne-Stark counties area of Ohio had been formalized in 1861. In Mifflin County (Pennsylvania) fellowship was terminated between two congregations sometime in 1862, or possibly would be in 1863. Abraham Peachey's conservative group (supported by David Beiler and some of his fellow ministers in Lancaster County) was at odds with that of his change-oriented neighbor Solomon Beiler. In Iowa the change-minded congregations at Wayland and Pulaski were openly rejecting the conservatism expressed by the growing Amish settlement in Johnson County.

Of the larger Amish settlements, only Lancaster County (Pennsylvania) and central Illinois had escaped division or the threat of division. Lancaster had avoided schism thus far by maintaining a conservative position. The Illinois congregations had maintained their unity by moving together in the direction of some selective changes. Thus the differences between the Lancaster congregations and the Illinois congregations were likely greater than those which separated the factions within one given settlement. In the long run those East-West differences may have constituted the gravest obstacle to denominational unity. Only distance prevented the differences between the Amish churches in Illinois and those in Lancaster County from adding to the discord prevailing in the Amish church. David Beiler, who completed his *Vermahnung* in 1862, wrote that "divisions and vexations have arisen and the split appears to be all but irreparable."[1]

Although Amish church polity was congregational, there was no lack of communication between congregations and between geographical areas. Amish leaders were frank with each other and as honest as participants in any dispute could be expected to be. In the 1850s, when some leaders were advocating stream baptism, many candid and sincere letters were exchanged between the leaders of the several Amish communities in Ohio and Pennsylvania.[2]

Such communication reached across the entire church. Bishop Jacob Swartzendruber of Johnson County, Iowa, heard of the dissatisfaction with Bishop Solomon Beiler because he permitted his full deacon, Samuel Yoder, to preach too frequently. He wrote to Shem Zook or possibly to Solomon Beiler in Pennsylvania, proposing a solution: Why not ordain this full deacon to the office of bishop?[3] When Solomon Beiler felt his voice was not being heard he wrote a position paper of ten large, closely written pages, which probably was copied and sent to several church leaders.[4] The major obstacle to unity in the church appears not to have been lack of communication. By 1862 this same network of communication made evident to many leaders throughout the church that the situation required emergency treatment.

Assessing the Blame

As has been indicated repeatedly, the conservatives laid the blame for the schism on the spirit of disobedience and pride which they detected in the words and actions of the liberals. To these conservatives, tampering with the *Ordnung* of the church was tantamount to haughtiness and smacked of disobedience. They equated unity with uniformity, so that inconsequential differences became indications of disunity in the body of Christ. For most questions of lifestyle and personal conduct, there was a correct answer. Any deviation from it was nothing less than a departure from the narrow way (*schmale Weg*). With this thought pattern, *compromise* signified *concession* to evil, a most unholy arrangement. Thus attitudes on both sides hindered a restoration of unity. In addition, the conservatives were inclined to equate traditional practices with scriptural authority. The possibility of a healing of the schism appeared remote.

One must hasten to add that the mind-set of those who wanted a few carefully selected changes in Amish faith and practice differed only slightly from that of the conservatives. In his position paper Solomon Beiler, change-minded bishop, repeatedly decried the use of "unnecessary and shameful clothing ornaments," a practice which was creeping into the church. In 1861 the change-minded ministers of Mifflin and the adjoining Pennsylvania counties decided "to punish this terrible pride with sharpness . . . for there is finery among the young brothers and sisters with the head hair parted on the side."[5] What the liberals considered evidence of pride in 1862 differed only a little from the conservative view.

While the liberals were less insistent on uniformity than their conservative brethren, they were willing to tolerate only slightly greater diversity in faith and practice than the latter. Solomon Beiler was demanding that others follow his interpretation of the Scriptures concerning the administration of baptism and the duties of deacons. As late as 1871 mutual commiseration and concern was shared between liberals Shem Zook and Deacon John Stoltzfus as the former observed that brethren in both of their congregations could be found with "their hair styled according to the way of the world." Zook may have exhibited almost as much concern for uniformity and for preserving the Ordnung as did his more conservative brethren. He observed to Stoltzfus that "we should all work at preventing such things, and when they do come up, *to get rid of them* [emphasis added]."[6]

Back of the rejection of the process of compromise by both factions was the firm conviction that, with biblical procedures, opposing views could evaporate. But first a body of believers, such as the ministers of a congregation or of a cluster of congregations, needed to give themselves up wholly to the Lord's leading and seek to determine what the Scriptures said on a particular subject. Then they would all come to the same conclusions, even in the minor details of the Ordnung. Repeatedly they called on each other to use the Word of God as "the plumb line" in determining or maintaining church standards.[7] Were not the five thousand converts who were added to the church soon after Pentecost "of one heart and one soul"?[8]

It was only in the process of division that the change-minded faction began to think in terms of toleration (within a narrow range of differences to be sure) as a means of keeping the denomination together. Even then this obnoxious concept (formerly considered to indicate evidence of lack of zeal for the truth) would be advocated on the basis of expediency, rather than of a biblical principle.

With respect to this critical problem of conflict resolution in the Amish church in the 1860s, a close parallel obtained in the Mennonite Church. Joseph Liechty's analysis of conditions in the latter church in the 1860s applies equally to the Amish. The parallel is uncanny. According to Liechty, conflict was inevitable in the Mennonite Church of the 1860s. Since Mennonites did not divide faith into essentials and nonessentials, issues such as what kind of clothing to wear, or what type of buggy to drive, or whether or not to sing in parts did not seem petty. . . . Where every facet of life was significant, Mennonites inevitably differed with each other. . . . Frank Epp has suggested that Mennonites divided frequently because they "had not yet learned, perhaps had no intention of learning, the process of resolving differences and conflict through discussion, negotiation, and compromise." [Furthermore, whereas] compromise offers no more than coexistence, Mennonites sought nothing less than a common mind.[9]

In many ways the Amish and the Mennonites were clearly at the same place in the 1860s. Perhaps external forces contributed to this, but it seems likely that some continuous communication between the two churches was taking place.

Even though the motives of those who took sides in this Great Schism in the Amish church cannot be accurately measured, they must be examined. Our Amish forebears on both sides were manifestly unaware of the self-delusion which even the most careful person who feels constrained to take sides in a controversy may bring upon oneself. Solomon Beiler's letters and his position paper, as well as the letters of Shem Zook, his loyal lay supporter, show that Beiler originally advocated stream baptism out of personal conviction. But after twelve years of opposition, personal vindication had become more important to him than stream baptism.

Although Beiler's opposer, Abraham Peachey, has not left any of his writings for historians to analyze, the letters of others lead one to believe that his motives paralleled that of Solomon.[10] Other leaders of both factions may have suffered the same deterioration of motives as did Peachey and Beiler. However, for most of the leaders the evidence is not sufficient to draw definite conclusions. The running account of the crisis of 1862–65, below, will provide information and further insight into the motivation of those who participated in the Great Schism. It will also expose other forces which helped to produce that division.

A Radical Remedy: The Annual Ministers' Meetings of 1862–78

What was to be done? The old informal structures for maintaining the identity and unity of the Amish church with its congregational form of church polity were proving inadequate. Throughout the 1850s both liberals and conservatives had thrashed about in their search for a solution. A onetime churchwide meeting to consider issues and draw up conclusions or rulings had ancient precedent in the 1779 meeting in Europe and in more recent meetings of the nineteenth century in America.

None of the earlier meetings were clearly and deliberately set up to be churchwide. However, some of them, notably the 1849 meeting at Berlin, Ohio, had approached that dimension. By 1849 the steam locomotive on rails had made it possible for ministers from Iowa to cross over the Mississippi River into Illinois and "take the cars" to the meeting at Berlin. By 1862 the railroad network in the Union (but not in the Southern Confederacy) was well advanced. It was almost ideally routed to accommodate travel from the several Amish communities located in southeastern Iowa to Lancaster County (Pennsylvania) and to points lying between these extremities. Thus it made sense to hold the first of the annual ministers' meetings near Smithville, Ohio, only two miles from the depot at the Summit (later Weilersville), the highest point on the Pittsburgh to Chicago railway.

The ministers' meetings begun in 1862 did depart from tradition in that they were continued on a yearly basis. More importantly, they attempted to constitute an umbrella over the entire church. Of all the innovations which were proposed between 1848 and 1862, the idea of having annual churchwide ministers' meetings was the most far-reaching. In the end, it was the conservatives who would reject this departure from the ancient pattern of church polity.

In the 1850s, however, the conservatives had on at least two occasions proposed an ad hoc churchwide ministers' meeting to determine the Amish position on stream baptism. They no doubt remembered that several ad hoc regional ministers' meetings of the first half of the century had returned conclusions or rulings upholding the traditional practices of the church. Judging by the fragmentary information available, the Berlin, Ohio, meeting of 1849, which brought ministers from states east and west, had resulted in at least a temporary victory for the conservatives; the Wayne County ministers had agreed to desist in their practice of stream baptism. Therefore, the conservatives may have hoped that another meeting would result in a more definitive settlement of that question.

The first suggestion proposing a churchwide ministers' meeting was made by none other than Bishop David Beiler. In that Lancaster ministers' epistle of 1851 concerning stream baptism, written by Beiler and signed by most of the Lancaster County ministers, the writer added a postscript. He had "often thought," said Beiler, "that a churchwide ministers' meeting would be very useful so that we could make oral inquiry and *give a directive* [emphasis added]."[11] Then in 1855, in the midst of continued acrimonious dispute concerning stream baptism in the Holmes-Wayne-Stark counties area, Bishop Frederick Hege again proposed that the matter be settled by a general ministers' meeting. In view of Hege's rigid conservative position, one may assume that he expected such a meeting to rule against innovations such as stream baptism. In commenting on Hege's suggestion, the change-minded Preacher Christian Brandt of the Wooster congregation groaned at the thought of convening such a ponderous body.[12]

However, when a churchwide ministers' meeting finally convened, it was not at the initiative of the conservatives but rather under the auspices of the change-minded ministers of the church. The process of planning for and calling the meeting of 1862 can now be reconstructed in considerable part. This is possible because of the discovery in 1982 of documents now in the Lydia Mast Collection, photocopies of which may be found in the Lancaster Mennonite Historical Society Library.

It appears that on March 8, 1861, Deacon John Stoltzfus sent an open letter "to all peace-loving Amish congregations in 'nort america.'" In this letter Deacon Stoltzfus proposed the introduction of yearly churchwide ministers' meetings and set forth the rationale for the introduction of this new church agency as a means of restoring unity to the Amish church. Stoltzfus' proposal was stated quite formally. His first *whereas* recounted the persecution of the forefathers in Europe; his second *whereas* reminded his readers of the freedom of religion which they had enjoyed in America. Included in his third *whereas* was his proposal for the aforementioned meeting. "Whereas," he began

> our forefathers and ancestors were few in number when they first viewed this land of freedom, and endeavored to live by the rule of the Word and the gospel and to teach that way, and so in the course of time from their seed and that of those who followed them, has evolved a rather large people, consisting of some fifty congregations in the United States and Canada, who now live in widely scattered and remote areas. In the course of time the result of this was that the Word of God, which came to be taught by many ministers . . . is no longer understood and taught alike [uniformly throughout North America], yea, even in living and teaching, in keeping and doing, which can easily happen due to human weakness on the one hand, and through the power of the Spirit on the other, without any evil intentions; and for the same reason [and] sometimes for other [reasons], interpretations result which are held to be even more true than the Word from which they are derived.

Given such circumstances, Deacon Stoltzfus proceeded to inquire whether it would not be wise to follow through on the proposal of the elders, evidently referring to David Beiler's suggestion of 1851 for a churchwide meeting. "Would it be contrary to the rule of the Word and the example of the apostles [Acts 15]," he asked rhetorically,

> to select men or a man in each congregation . . . and send them to a ministers' and peace [restoration] meeting . . . to discuss the differences and to bring peace with the help of God on all points and questions? To this end we wish the grace of God and the blessing from above from Him who makes us complete and mature through the power of the Spirit and the Word of truth to His peaceable kingdom through Jesus Christ. Amen. Written by me John Stoltzfus, in the year 1861, the 8th of March.

In the original manuscript the above letter is followed by a postscript. Embodied in this addendum is a concrete proposal for a churchwide ministers' meeting, indicating time and location. The use of "we" in this section suggests that some ministerial group, perhaps self-appointed, was issuing this call. Below are the principal portions of that summons:

> To all peace-loving congregations in *nort america* a greeting of love and peace. We think that at this time something is necessary to bring about a greater churchwide love. A churchwide *Conferenz* or ministers' meeting could do no harm if it takes place according to a godly ordering, for He is a God of order. And if such [a meeting] can take place in a peaceful atmosphere and for the sake of peace, it can and indeed will bring forth much fruit . . . because it is now the case that patience in many places has grown cold, so much that defections and divisions have crept in which could perhaps be corrected with God's help. . . . If there is disunity, it should be brought to this meeting to be discussed. Such a meeting should provide ways and means to deal with and treat such a situation, [and not] to originate a [new] kind of church rule (*Kirchenregel*), but rather to stay by the old foundation, that which has been our confession of faith for 238 years.[13]

Finally came the stipulation of time and place. This first conference was to be held in Holmes County, Ohio, on the first Tuesday in September 1861, "if they will provide a place for it there." Having made such arrangements for this meeting, the framers of this call indicated that the delegates to the first conference "should determine when and where the second shall be held." In calling a ministers' meeting a *Conferenz*, he may have startled his readers. This word was used by the Mennonites; the Amish term was *Diener Versammlung.*

This open letter of John Stoltzfus is a remarkable document. It is so well written and composed that one suspects that the best writers in the Amish church, and Shem Zook in particular, were involved in its composition. The composers of this document sought to allay the fears of the conservatives that the conference would be used as an instrument for introducing changes into the denomination. They committed the conference in advance to operating as an instrument of conciliation rather than as a legislative body to reconstruct the Ordnung of the church.

Nevertheless, the suggestions of Stoltzfus and his collaborators involve two daring departures from Amish church procedures. Most daring was the explicit assumption that the first conference would be followed by another and perhaps by still more meetings. Thus far the Amish had not followed their Mennonite neighbors in setting up annual or semiannual conferences by regions. Equally divergent from Amish practice, but possibly with less serious implications, was the proposal that each congregation choose one or two of its ministers as official delegates to the meeting. In the Amish tradition, a minister was a minister was a minister. All ordained brethren should be eligible to participate in a ministers' meeting. As will be noted later, the old tradition prevailed when the ministers' meetings of 1862–78 got under way, for all Amish ministers in good standing were permitted to participate in the deliberations of the conference.

While Deacon Stoltzfus' letter sheds considerable light on the background of the *Diener Versammlungen* of 1862–78, it leaves many questions unanswered. The identities of those who collaborated in drawing up this document are not revealed. Neither do we know why the plan to meet in Holmes County in September 1861 miscarried. Why this call for a series of ministers' meetings came from a deacon rather than a bishop, and from an area of the church in which no division was imminent, also remains a mystery.

The date for the proposed ministers' meeting may have been moved from September 1861 to June 1862 because the lead time was too short for the completion of the necessary arrangements. The open letter was sent in March 1861. The location of the meeting may have been changed to Wayne County because not all of the Holmes County leaders were sympathetic to the idea of a churchwide conference. They may have been reluctant to cooperate in making the necessary arrangements. It is even possible that this invitation was never sent out to each of the approximately fifty existing Amish congregations. That may explain why no other copies have come to light over the years as historians have searched for the origins of these meetings.

However, the idea of a churchwide ministers' meeting to deal with this crisis in the Amish church persisted. On November 7, 1861—two months after the proposed date for such meeting—Shem Zook inquired of Deacon John Stoltzfus about the status of renewed planning for such a gathering. In a short paragraph constituting the principal part of the letter Zook reports that he had

> received a letter from house-father and minister Jacob Swartzendruber [of Johnson County, Iowa]. He is wondering . . . whether there has been no effort to call a ministers' meeting. And so I wondered too if you had discussed it this fall in your [Lancaster County] ministers' meeting, and how far you got with it. Because you, as I understand it, worked at the matter in the spring in the hopes that perhaps peace might be made.[14]

This letter indicates that the idea of a churchwide conference had become widespread, reaching from Iowa to Lancaster County. Even more significant and more intriguing is Zook's understanding that the Lancaster ministers had "worked at the matter [of a general ministers' meeting] in the spring in the hopes that perhaps peace might be made." Had John Stoltzfus' open letter and invitation of the preceding spring (March 8, 1861) been the product of this effort by the Lancaster County ministers? Perhaps Stoltzfus had been the principal promoter of the idea of such conference and had come to the Lancaster ministers' meeting with his proposal in hand. Was it rejected by his fellow ministers under the leadership of the conservative senior bishop, David Beiler? Such a scenario would account for the fact that no other copies of Stoltzfus' proposal and invitation have been found.

Eight days after Zook wrote this letter, he followed up with a second letter to Deacon Stoltzfus to report startling developments on an entirely different front. Zook reported that his bishop, Solomon Beiler, had just come home from a visit to Butler and Wayne counties in Ohio. He and Bishop John Esh of nearby Juniata County had gone there "to smooth out some church matters." In Wayne County these two traveling bishops "and others" had got together and finalized plans for the much-discussed ministers' meeting. The Wayne County congregation had offered its facilities and services and the offer had been accepted.

"So the churchwide ministers' meeting is to be held on Monday after Whitsuntide [Pentecost], June 9, with the congregation in Wayne County, Ohio," Zook concluded. "Ministers from all congregations of the brotherhood in the entire country are to be invited. I believe you also will receive an invitation." John Stoltzfus might have been offended that the initiative for setting up the meeting had been taken over by others, but his moral support of the yearly conferences as they occurred indicates that he may have been pleased that his ideas had produced results.[15]

The plans developed by Solomon Beiler, John Esh, and the Wayne County congregation were evidently carried out. The date and place of the first annual conference coincide with those indicated in Zook's letter. Accordingly, a number of the men who brought the ministers' meeting of 1862 into being may now be identified. Obviously Solomon Beiler and John Esh are high on this list. Apparently the chief collaborator in the Wayne County congregation, which had offered to host the conference, was John K. Yoder, ordained as bishop there in 1859. Of the 72 or more ministers who attended the 1862 meeting in Wayne County, ten were from the host church, an indication of strong support from John K. Yoder's congregation.

Jonathan Yoder, bishop of the Rock Creek congregation in central Illinois, must be credited at least with wholehearted support of the conference. Possibly he had also participated in the planning, for he served as temporary chairman of that first Monday morning session on June 9, 1862, in which capacity he expounded on the purpose of the conference. That he was then retained as permanent chairman of the 1862 conference may have been unplanned, but may well constitute additional evidence that his role in arranging for this meeting was known and appreciated.

Shem Zook, best known layperson in the Amish church, probably had a hand in planning this conference. Clearly he was in close touch with two of the planners of the meeting, Bishop Solomon Beiler and Deacon John Stoltzfus, and served as a channel of communication between these two ordained brethren. Deacon John Stoltzfus must be included in this list because of his efforts as evidenced by his open letter and his frequent correspondence with Shem Zook on this subject.

The shrewd observer may have noted that this coterie of men credited with bringing the conference to fulfillment had more in common than at first meets the eye. Clearly all but one of them identified with the change-minded faction of the church. All but the same one likewise came from the two areas of the church which were in the midst of division. Only Deacon John Stoltzfus does not fit into this pattern. His area of the church, Lancaster County, was relatively calm—although it proved to be the calm before the storm. And he could scarcely be classified as change-minded in 1862. Yet he was opposed to breaking fellowship with those who did want to make some changes in the Ordnung of the church.

A more subtle relationship, however, ties these five men together. Three of them, Beiler, Esh, and Zook, lived in the contiguous counties of Mifflin and Juniata in central Pennsylvania and were in close contact with each other. Two others, bishops John K. Yoder and Jonathan Yoder, had formerly lived and been active in the ministry in this same area before moving farther west. They were certainly personally acquainted with their fellow ministers in central Pennsylvania. Deacon John Stoltzfus, again, does not fit quite so neatly into this scheme. But even he had close contact with Shem Zook and his brother-in-the-flesh Deacon Christian Stoltzfus of Union County (just northeast of Mifflin County) through his frequent correspondence with these brethren in central Pennsylvania.[16]

These six men then—the four bishops, Solomon Beiler, 64 years old; John Esh, 55; John K. Yoder, 38; and Jonathan Yoder, 67; along with Deacon John Stoltzfus, 57; and layperson Shem Zook, 64—must be credited with having launched the yearly conferences of 1862–78. This narrow base of operations made the proposal for a ministers' meeting somewhat suspect to the conservatives. The circumstances are not improved when one considers that not one of these promoters represented the conservative viewpoint, nor is there evidence that any effort was made to draw conservatives into the planning.

Levi Miller of Holmes County, principal spokesman for the conservatives, complained that not all of the Amish congregations had been properly consulted as the conference was being planned.[17] These circumstances led many of the conservatives to feel that the structure of the conference was rigged against them. While some of them attended the first four annual sessions in good faith, many others, notably most of the ministers from Lancaster County, boycotted the meetings from the beginning.[18] On the other hand, these promoters of a denominational conference were probably as honest and as conscientious as any party to a serious dispute could be. They sincerely hoped that the ministers' meetings would be instrumental in restoring unity to the Amish church. In retrospect, however, men as opinionated as Solomon Beiler were clearly prepared to make peace only on their own terms.[19]

The Ministers' Meeting of 1862

Deacon John Stoltzfus attended and was an active participant in the first annual churchwide Diener Versammlung which convened on

June 9, 1862, in Samuel Schrock's barn near Smithville, Ohio. He likely lodged in the home of Samuel Yoder, who was a first cousin to John's wife. The members of the Wayne County or Wooster congregation, soon to be renamed the Oak Grove congregation, must have been extremely busy that summer. Not only did they host this large conference,[20] they also built their first meetinghouse. This structure was not completed in time for the June meeting, but even if it had been it probably would not have been large enough to accommodate the crowds. Furthermore, the use of a meetinghouse would certainly have offended the conservatives.

This first annual meeting was also the longest, starting with Pentecost Sunday services and continuing through four days of business. Of the fifteen annual meetings which followed, all were in business session for three days except that of 1869, which adjourned after two days.

Stoltzfus was thrilled with the prospect before him. He participated in the special Pentecost Sunday services. On Monday evening, following the first day of business, he wrote home to his wife that

> we have beautiful weather for the great work in which we are engaged. Yesterday I saw the largest church group (*Gemeinde*) assembled that I have ever seen. Between 4[00] and 500 persons were together, 40 [of them] ministers. The assembly was addressed by Andreas Rupp from Illinois and Solomon Yoder from Maryland, who live 900 miles from each other. Today more ministers were present. The ones from the congregations in Holmes County came only today. . . . Today two congregations which had been divided in Indiana were brought together again by the help of 5 [the writer and 4 ministers] who were appointed to make inquiry into the matter. This afternoon it [the discussion or dialogue] was between the Wayne "Countiers" and the Holmes "Countiers." I believe now that through the help of God and his blessing much good will be accomplished. . . . I do not know at this time when we will be finished or when I will be coming home.[21]

Deacon Stoltzfus was obviously elated. He perceived that he was witnessing a new day in Amish church affairs. It was his understanding that the division of some years ago (1854–57) in Indiana had been healed on that first day. He also thought that progress had been made in bringing the Holmes County and Wayne County congregations back together.

But John Stoltzfus was too optimistic. This first *Diener Versammlung* was not able to stem the tide of division, nor were those

Left: First page of the
Church Record Book
kept by Jacob S. Gerig
(1866-1964), telling of
the building of the first
meetinghouse of the
Oak Grove Amish Men-
nonite congregation,
Wayne County, Ohio, in
1862. Gerig was bishop
of the congregation
from 1912 to 1955.
(Courtesy of Harold
Thut and James O.
Lehman.)

Below: First
meetinghouse of the
Oak Grove Amish Men-
nonite congregation,
Wayne County, Ohio,
constructed in 1862.
(Courtesy of Harold
Thut and James O.
Lehman.)

which followed any more successful. His letter does confirm, however, that the principal—almost the sole—purpose of these annual meetings was to restore unity to the Amish church. If further evidence is needed to establish this fact, one may examine the minutes of these meetings for the first years, especially the addenda calling attention to the meeting of the following year.[22]

Seventy-two ministers registered for this first annual conference (Stoltzfus' count was incomplete), the second-largest participation of all of the sixteen meetings of the series. If the total attendance, including laypersons, was as high as Stoltzfus indicated, preparing for this assemblage was a considerable undertaking. Considering these circumstances, the apparent ease with which this new organization moved into operation is amazing. Ministers' meetings were not new in the Amish church, but they had not been of this size. Here more structure was required. Officers had to be chosen. Participating ministers needed to know or to learn how to conduct themselves within this structure.

The men who arranged this meeting had planned carefully. One evidence of their thorough preparation may be found in the minutes which were kept of the meeting. As far as can be determined, no such official minutes, providing a running account of the proceedings, had been kept for any of those earlier ad hoc ministers' meetings. Only the findings or conclusions or rulings of each meeting were usually preserved. The secretary was none other than Shem Zook, probably the most literate man in the Amish church at that time.[23] Although the keeping of minutes was officially the result of a request from John Stoltzfus' Lower Pequea (Lancaster, Pennsylvania) congregation[24] to the assembled ministers, one suspects that this proposal had been planned in advance by the initiators of the conference. If so, the introduction of a resolution to that effect by one of their group was to secure acceptance and approval of this departure from previous practice.

That Monday morning session on June 9 was opened by the elderly Bishop Jonathan Yoder from Illinois, followed by a prayer by a bishop from central Pennsylvania, Elias Riehl. When Jonathan Yoder, temporary chairman, proposed the selection of a moderator, Bishop Solomon Yoder, formerly of Union County, Pennsylvania, but presently of Long Green, Maryland, was nominated. Solomon had preached one of the sermons of the previous day, Pentecost Sunday. When Solomon begged to be excused, the assembly unanimously fell back on the temporary chairman Jonathan Yoder. Jonathan then asked that John Esh be approved as his assistant, which was done.[25]

In terms of parliamentary procedures, only a few elementary ground rules were adopted at that first annual ministers' meeting. It was agreed without debate that "the proceedings of this assembly shall be based entirely on God's Word." "Weighty questions" were to be submitted to a committee or council ("Committee" *oder Rath*) of five to seven ministers (ordained men). That committee was to consider the question at hand and bring a proposal or recommendation back to the assembled ministers for discussion and action. Presumably the moderator exercised the significant power of appointing these committees, although this is nowhere indicated. However, no minister was to sit on a committee if objection were made to his appointment.[26] It was not until 1875 that "Comite" replaced *Rath* (council) as the word generally used in the minutes to designate these ad hoc study groups.

Over the course of the first five conferences, the rules of procedure under which the meetings operated were expanded. At the beginning of the 1863 conference in Mifflin County, the newly elected chairman, Abner Yoder of Somerset County (Pennsylvania) asked whether attendance at the meetings should not be restricted to the brotherhood (members of the Amish church). He may have thought that unbaptized young people of Amish families should not be allowed to sit in the meetings (a restriction of long standing in congregational council meetings). But more likely he was concerned about the attendance of observers from other local groups, such as the Mennonites, the unaffiliated Samuel King (Amish) congregation, and conceivably the local press. At first Abner seemed to have the support of the majority, but when Jonathan Yoder argued that the meetings should be open to the public "since we do not intend to do anything for which we are ashamed," the conference decided to conduct the meetings openly.[27]

At the 1864 conference near Goshen, Indiana, under the chairmanship of Bishop John K. Yoder, two changes in procedure were introduced which presumably were followed thereafter. All committees were to have a majority of bishops. The second innovation is indicated only by a secretarial interpolation in the minutes. Perhaps Moderator John K. Yoder introduced it on the basis of prerogative as moderator, to expedite the business of the conference. It provided that, in case of indications of disagreement with a committee report, a vote should be taken. If a majority of those voting favored a proposal or a committee report, the report was to be considered as accepted, even if some of those opposed to the report had abstained from voting.[28] Previously an informal system of approval by consensus had been in effect. Thus in three years, in the words of one appraiser, "the decision-making process had degenerated to a simple majority vote."[29]

In checking the names of the men participating in the organization of the 1862 conference that first morning, only two appear outside the coterie of six mentioned above. These are Solomon Yoder and Elias Riehl. The former had served earlier in central Pennsylvania, and Riehl was still located there. Thus the Mifflin County–central Pennsylvania connection applied to these as well as to the six. Missing from these first-morning-participant names are the change-minded bishops from Indiana, Isaac Schmucker and Jonas D. Troyer, although they were active in the discussions which followed. And that first-morning record does not identify any ordained brethren with conservative inclinations.

Most of the ministers who attended the 1862 conference may be identified either as conservatives or liberals (if one may be permitted to classify them by whether or not they had chosen or would eventually choose to remain with the Old Order Amish wing in the course of the Great Schism). On the basis of this criterion, about twenty of the ministers in attendance in 1862, possibly one or two more, were conservatives (slightly less than one-third of the total). From the time of that first conference these conservatives were conscious that control was in the hands of the liberals and that they constituted a minority. On the first day Levi Miller of Holmes County, spokesman for the minority, had complained that his congregation had not been properly involved in the planning for the conference.[30] Had representation from the conservatives been as full as from the liberals, the balance between the two parties may well have been quite even. Not until the conference of 1865 did the conservatives plan and make a concerted and organized effort to present their position and to support it with their attendance.

9

Point of No Return, 1865

Conference Procedures

Possibly three somewhat-overlapping avenues of approach were open to these annual Amish conferences and could have been followed in the effort to restore unity in the church. A new churchwide discipline could have been devised, such as those of 1809 and 1837. Second, the conference might have attempted to establish itself as a legislative body with authority, as the occasion demanded, to make specific regulations binding upon the entire denomination. The third option for the conference was to serve as a fire-fighting brigade whose role would be to extinguish local and regional brushfires of dissension and schism.

The first of the above options was never considered. Indeed, it was openly and repeatedly repudiated. Why the conference turned its back on this traditional device is obscure. Perhaps the change-minded ministers who controlled these meetings were opposed in principle to taking this route, as James N. Gingerich has implied.[1] More likely the liberals rejected this device for more practical reasons. The option of a disciplinary code did not lend itself to their purposes. If they had introduced their proposed changes forthrightly in the form of a revised code, it would certainly have added to the distrust already brooding in the minds of the conservatives. The failure to draw up a new discipline may have come back to haunt some of the original change-minded leaders. Later, near the end of the century, a number of them expressed alarm and resistance to change as they viewed with dismay the sustained escalation of change. When the tables were turned, they apparently would have welcomed a new disciplinary code to stem this alarming drift in their branch, the Amish Mennonites.

Neither was the second approach—that of establishing the conference as a continuing and controlling legislative body—ever envisaged in its entirety by its leaders. It would have been impossible to centralize authority in a denomination heretofore strictly congregational in organization. Repeatedly the leaders and the corporate conference body declared that it was not in the province of the conference to make laws. Probably Deacon John Stoltzfus's "Short Account of the Life, Doctrine, and Example of Our Old Ministers" was read at the first conference. If so, its purpose must have been to assure the conservatives that the old order of things would not be unduly disturbed.[2]

Two years later, when John K. Yoder was chosen moderator of the third annual conference, his first statement was to assure his listeners that "the purpose of the assembly was not to introduce innovations or to make laws (*Gesetze*), but to proceed according to the Word of God and to seek after a noble peace."[3] Still, two years later (1866), when the conference devised and adopted ten rules of order, rule two asserted in similar language that the conference shall not "make laws (Gesetze) or unbiblical rulings (*unevangelische Beschlüsse*)."[4]

In spite of such assurances, what was actually attempted was certainly a considerable modification of the congregational structure of the Amish church. The conference leaders obviously hoped these ministers' meetings would constitute an umbrella over the entire denomination and that compliance with its decisions by member congregations would be forthcoming. Already in 1862 the conference attempted to set up guidelines with respect to the duties of deacons—particularly of full deacons, and to the practice of shunning as exercised between husband and wife. Even more sharp and clear was the agreement that if a congregation should impose the ban and avoidance on one of its members, other congregations should respect and observe the same discipline. Most significant of all was the imposition of sanctions against the Hessian Amish congregation in Butler County, Ohio. The conference would send bishops to supervise the ordination of a bishop for this congregation only if the "musical instruments and other worldly entertainments" were put away.

Already in 1863 some proponents of the authority of conference, such as Solomon K. Beiler and John K. Yoder, were complaining emphatically about those ministers who "help to decide something, but afterward do the opposite."[5] And in the same year the participants in the conference were speaking of conference decisions as conclusions or rulings (Beschlüsse). At the same time statements had been and were being made to the effect that the function of the conference was not that of making new rules. It is difficult to reconcile those disclaimers with what was actually happening.

The problem of enforcement was never solved. Repeatedly

thereafter the yearly conferences sought ways and means to secure compliance with what were called the rulings (Beschlüsse) and laws (Gesetze) which that body had previously made. The minutes of these conferences repeatedly give evidence of the frustrations of energetic conference leaders, such as Solomon Beiler, John K. Yoder, John P. King, and Samuel Yoder, especially the first three. As indicated by Gingerich, efforts to secure compliance with the rulings of conference increased in intensity as the years passed.[6] But somewhat contrary to Gingerich, it appears that the intent to give a measure of authority to this body existed in the minds of the original coterie and its supporters from the beginning.

Wrestling with Local Schisms; the Conference of 1862

Whether by design or by force of circumstances, the annual ministers' meetings of 1862–78, particularly those of 1862, 1863, and 1864, were preoccupied with regional divisions. Of the three options mentioned above, this approach to the problems which the Amish church faced was the least radical and probably the one most available to the conference. By 1864–65 these local splits, these brushfires, were joined together, and the conference was faced with one all-consuming conflagration. Leaders of both the change-minded and the conservative factions had become quite aware that the divisions within the several regions—in northern Indiana, central Ohio, and central Pennsylvania—had merged and become churchwide. Many of these leaders sincerely wanted and tried earnestly to effect a reconciliation.

Jonathan Yoder chaired the conference of 1862. Early in the meeting he tried to direct the attention of the assembled ministers to the older (1854–57) division in the Lagrange-Elkhart counties area of northern Indiana. He proposed that they "begin with the oldest matters first." These "matters" related to "the difficulties between the Elkhart and Lagrange congregations." The "Elkhart congregation" referred to the settlement in Lagrange County on the "Forks" of the Little Elkhart River; that community stretched over into Middlebury Township in Elkhart County.[7]

Before the end of the first day of the conference, the committee which was appointed to expedite a reconciliation was able to report that "the ministers in these congregations had forgiven each other." However, forgiveness apparently did not mean reconciliation of differences, for the ministers of the more conservative group, the "Elkhart people" at the forks of the Little Elkhart River, were not sure whether the "new things" could be accepted by the congregation.[8] Two years later, when the conference met in northern Indiana, a much more concerted effort would be made to heal the schism there.

Because the 1862 conference met in Wayne County, a greater concentration of effort was given to the recent division between the "Holmes Countiers" and the "Wayne Countiers." The site of the meeting also accounts for the fact that one-third (27) of the ministers attending the meeting were local, from Wayne, Holmes, and Stark counties. The discussions were frank, sometimes blunt, but evidently conducted in good order. Of the Holmes County congregations, only Bishop (Gross) Moses Miller and his congregation at Walnut Creek sided with Oak Grove in Wayne County.

The issue of stream baptism was discussed at length even though, according to several of the conservatives, it was no longer a matter of major concern for them. Probably the greatest achievement of the conference was the reluctant consensus which Moderator Jonathan Yoder extracted from the assembled ministers. "Patience" would be exercised toward one another in the matter of stream baptism. Bishop Levi Miller, spokesperson for the Holmes County ministers, affirmed that "baptism in water was not the reason for their holding back," then indicated what he considered to be the real stumbling blocks to unity. People were conducting themselves "like the world." In particular, he was opposed to lightning rods, photographs, lotteries, large meeting-houses, and insurance. He could not continue in fellowship with those ministers who approve of such things.[9]

Curiously, there was no specific mention in this conference of personal adornment or the embellishment of household furnishings or houses. Those concerns were strongly emphasized by David Beiler already in his *Vermahnung* of 1861–62, but did not come to the attention of the conference until its 1865 meeting.[10]

A few questions arose in the 1862 conference which were not directly related to the schisms in the Indiana and Ohio congregations. One of them concerned the practice of shunning. The change-minded ministers (Solomon Beiler excepted) generally expressed concern about the possible unhappy results of imposing avoidance on someone. The conservatives insisted that it be applied "without respect of person." Yet they discussed these differences concerning the discipline of shunning with dispassion in the context of the Amish church as a whole and not as a part of the Holmes County–Wayne County controversy.

Concerning the Trenton congregation of Hessian Amish in Butler County, Ohio, which allowed the use of musical instruments, the conference was united. These instruments associated with worldly amusements must be put away. As noted above, the conference decided to defer the ordination of a new bishop in that congregation until this was done.[11] Considerable attention was also given to a delineation of the duties of deacons,[12] a subject of great controversy at that time in Logan and Champaign counties in Ohio and in Mifflin County, Pennsylvania. The matter was to receive more attention in the conference of 1863.

The conference ended on Thursday afternoon, and the secretary, Shem Zook, added to the minutes his observation that

> although no complete uniformity of attitude or viewpoint was arrived at, it seemed after all that all were concerned to move hindrances out of the way and to promote the well-being of the church, which showed itself in good order, Christian moderation, and brotherly behavior.[13]

But good intentions were not enough. Peace was not restored in any area of the church.

Bishop David Beiler, his fellow bishops, and most of the other ordained brethren of Lancaster County had boycotted the meeting. Beiler judged that according to the minutes and other reports which had come to him, "not much was decided about how it is to be." He was of the opinion that, in trying to maintain a conciliatory spirit, the ministers had not come to grips with the points of difference. "If we wish to destroy a weed," he concluded, "we must pull it up by the roots. . . . Just so it is with evil in the church. If the causes of offense are not put away, then . . . no real unity can be restored."[14]

The Conference of 1863 and the Pequea Ministers' Meeting

By invitation from Solomon Beiler and his fellow ministers, the conference of 1863 was held near Belleville, Mifflin County, Pennsylvania. Attendance was poor (42) compared to that of the 1862 conference (72), of 1864 (71), and of 1865 (89). The number of conservatives attending was not more than ten and, lacking a spokesperson such as Levi Miller, their voice was scarcely heard.

Bishop Abner Yoder of Somerset County, Pennsylvania, was chosen moderator. Of all the moderators of the sixteen annual conferences, Abner was the only one who would eventually cast his lot with the conservatives and remain with the Old Order Amish. At the time of this conference he was probably one of the few participants whose position and future direction was not discernible. That he was undecided about which side he should take in the Great Schism is suggested by his continued cooperation with the conference as late as

1872. He attended four of the first five conferences, including that of 1866, by which time most of the conservatives were no longer attending. Even later, in 1871, evidently in absentia, he was assigned by the conference to serve with two other bishops in examining the circumstances existing in several congregations in Illinois. Abner served as requested and signed his name to the report submitted to the conference of 1872, although, according to the roster of attendance, he was not present.[15]

Solomon Beiler and his fellow ministers had probably invited the conference to come to Mifflin County for the 1863 meeting to deal with the long-standing differences between himself and Abraham Peachey. The issues involved stream baptism and preaching deacons, but by 1863 the dispute had degenerated into a personality clash between the two bishops. Solomon had the support of the congregations in the adjoining Juniata and Union counties, and Peachey had the support of David Beiler and some of the other ministers in Lancaster County. However, the Lancaster County supporters of Peachey were not present at the meeting.

The minutes of the 1863 conference suggest complete success in bringing the Solomon Beiler and Abraham Peachey congregations together. The committee which worked on this problem in private consultation with the principals and their respective backers reported to the full assembly that

> Solomon Beiler and his fellow ministers acknowledge that mistakes have been made on their side and ask for patience. Solomon Beiler is willing to come into Peachey's congregation and confess to such, and to ask the congregation for patience, if such is required, and to put behind what is in the past. Abraham Peachey asks for time in order to come together, and desires to inform his congregation concerning this. He then asks that Solomon Beiler shall come to them and explain himself before the congregation.
>
> They confess on both sides, as far as their immediate persons are concerned, to be somewhat upset. A. Peachey and his fellow ministers are also willing to come to S. Beiler's congregation and give an account of themselves if it is requested. S. Beiler is willing, with the Lord's help, to serve baptism in the house if it is requested.[16]

The above minute identifies only one point of dissension between Beiler and Peachey, that of stream baptism, and implies that otherwise the quarrel was largely personal. Other sources, however, indicate that as early as 1859 or 1860 Peachey had added to his complaints. He charged that Beiler had allowed his full deacon, Samuel Yoder, to preach more than was appropriate for one who held that office.[17] The 1863 conference gave considerable attention to the debate about whether or how much Yoder and other deacons should preach. Nevertheless, the minutes do not connect this question directly with the Peachey-Beiler quarrel.[18] That such was the case is supported by other documents indicating that by 1863 this new complaint was about to eclipse the earlier dispute in the Mifflin County congregations concerning stream baptism.[19]

Chairman Abner Yoder and the members of the committee which had attempted this reconciliation between Peachey and Solomon Beiler were optimistic. They hoped that the agreement would signal the end of the Peachey-Beiler controversy of more than a decade. The conference closed with the bright prospect that it would be so. The secretary recorded that "various difficulties have been cleared away and a good part of the divisions brought into such a state that there is hope for healing."[20]

Perhaps a reconciliation was too much to be expected. In any case the procedure arranged for at the conference of 1863 was never implemented. Peachey did report to his congregation concerning the compact which had been drawn up at the conference. But he announced that he had reconsidered the whole matter and felt constrained to recommend "another way to get united" with Solomon Beiler's congregation. He said that he had never supported the churchwide ministers' meeting anyway and would have preferred all along to "depend entirely upon the congregation." Nevertheless, he assumed that outside help would be needed and favored a meeting "of the ministers of Pennsylvania [only]."

This congregational meeting over which Bishop Abraham Peachey presided did not proceed smoothly, but he evidently had his way in the matter. Two of his own ministers opposed him and later joined Solomon's congregation.[21] Just such a meeting of Pennsylvania ministers as he suggested took place on April 20, 1864, at Pequea (less than two miles north of Gap) in Lancaster County. Although the evidence is not quite conclusive that this well-known Pequea meeting resulted directly from Abraham Peachey's proposal, it certainly fits the circumstances. The date of the meeting, its composition, and the subjects considered, all support this conclusion.[22]

The attempt of the churchwide ministers' meeting to effect a reconciliation between Peachey and Solomon Beiler had failed. Would a meeting of Pennsylvania ministers be more successful? According to

John Yoder, a minister in Solomon Beiler's congregation, this Pequea meeting was David Beiler's idea.[23] If so, it follows that Peachey, who was David's understudy, probably was prompted by the latter in the first place to propose such a meeting to his congregation. Representation of Pennsylvania congregations at this ministers' meeting was broad, including those of Mifflin County (Peachey's and Solomon Beiler's), Buffalo Valley in Union County, Tuscarora in Juniata County, Long Green in Maryland, and three Lancaster County congregations.

The attempt at Pequea involved greater attention to specific issues than did that of the 1863 general conference. Several agreements were reached. First, it was not proper for deacons to preach on a regular basis. However, in the case of Deacon Samuel Yoder, the problem could be solved if he were ordained as a bishop, providing his home congregation approved of this procedure. Second, both forms of baptism—in the house and in water—were to be permitted, but with the understanding that "David Beiler and his fellow ministers [and] Abraham Peachey and his fellow ministers do not wish [to administer] baptism in water." Third, "[higher] education, Sunday schools, showy clothes, fancy vehicles, and so on are harmful." And fourth, the ban should be applied "as Christ and the apostles instituted it." These agreements were to be submitted to the congregations represented at the meeting. If approved by them, they were to be considered "a conclusion of peace."[24]

Shem Zook probably got his account of the Pequea meeting from Deacon John Stoltzfus. In 1880 Zook put together a history of the Amish division in Mifflin County and wrote that "the proposal to advance Samuel Yoder to the office of bishop was accepted." He then added that "the meeting did not come to full agreement; neither was it [afterwards] accepted by all congregations. . . . The secretary said he had written what Bishop David Beiler had told him to write, which was . . . not the unanimous opinion of the assembly."[25] The conclusions reached at Pequea were shaky. Both Solomon Beiler and David Beiler, the principal protagonists at the Pequea meeting, opposed the ordination of Samuel Yoder as bishop, although for different reasons. After the meeting both of them found ways to continue their opposition to Yoder's ordination.

David Beiler said he opposed the ordination of Samuel Yoder as bishop because he found "no basis in the gospel for doing such a thing," and did not "know that our forefathers ever did it."[26] He felt that once a man had promised to take on the duties of a deacon he could not be released from these to assume new duties as bishop.[27] Solomon Beiler opposed Yoder's ordination as a bishop simply because he thought such was not required to qualify him to preach occasionally.[28] To support his position, Solomon turned again to the annual churchwide conference. He had appealed to the conference in 1863 and he would turn to it again. However, by the time of the 1864 conference (June 16–18) he was facing growing pressure from his minister-friends as well as from a considerable portion of the conservative-minded ordained brethren.[29] Even Solomon's own congregation, including the influential Shem Zook, was pressing him to ordain Samuel Yoder as bishop.

Being in "great distress and heartache because of the circumstances in [his] congregation,"[30] Solomon found it impossible to attend the 1864 conference in person. He was compelled to present his case in writing. Was it ever proper, he asked, to ordain a full deacon as a bishop? If Solomon was looking for support in his determination not to ordain Samuel Yoder as bishop, he was not to find it in the response which the conference gave. The assembled ministers found no "basis in the Holy Scripture to prevent this if one has those virtues and those gifts for it which the apostles prescribe."[31]

The final chapter in the story of Solomon Beiler's opposition to Yoder's advancement to bishop is parenthetical to the history of the Great Schism. Yet it requires telling as a part of nineteenth-century Amish church affairs. His capitulation to those who insisted on Yoder's ordination may be traced in considerable detail through a series of letters from Shem Zook to Deacon John Stoltzfus.[32] Although Beiler eventually gave reluctant consent to this step, he was in such distress at the time of the ordination on March 15, 1865, that he left the meeting. Following the service he called his ministers together and asked to be relieved of his ministerial duties, which they properly refused to do.[33]

For several months thereafter Solomon sulked, absenting himself from Sunday morning services, including a communion service. Even later, when the ministers of his congregation met with him, primarily to quiet their frustrated senior bishop, he produced a forty-eight page document opposing the ordination of a deacon as a bishop, which he began to read. According to Zook, some people were beginning to think that Solomon was "a little mixed up in his mind."[34]

The conference of 1862 had not resulted in much real progress in healing the division in northern Indiana nor that in the Holmes-Wayne-Stark counties area of Ohio. Similarly, the 1863 conference failed to restore peace in Mifflin County. The quest for peace among the Pennsylvania congregations was continued in the Pequea meeting of April 1864. But this schism seems to have moved beyond hope of healing sometime in the course of those 1863–64 events. In any case, the scars acquired in the controversy about stream baptism would not heal, and Samuel Yoder's ordination to the office of bishop was evidently too little and too late. Even with all that, Shem Zook reported that some hope for healing loomed for a time in 1866.[35] In 1868, in still another letter, he hinted that a reconciliation was in prospect.[36] Unfortunately, it never happened.

Ultimate Failure: The Annual Conferences of 1864 and 1865

The most significant development coming out of the 1864 conference was an informal understanding that the conservatives would attempt to prepare for a comprehensive approach to the Great Schism. They would bring a fuller representation of their people to the 1865 meeting, people who would be prepared to discuss the issues on a churchwide scale. Before dealing with this subject, however, an analysis of some of the specific concerns raised in both the 1863 and 1864 conferences is required if one is to catch the spirit and intent of these meetings.

The application of the ban (the shunning which followed was assumed) was a major topic of consideration in the 1862 conference as well as in those of 1863 and 1864. That the use of that ultimate instrument of discipline was biblical was not in dispute. Only Joseph Goldsmith of Henry County, Iowa, indicated some misgiving about the practice of shunning. He inquired whether those who had been excommunicated should be avoided "only at the Lord's Supper or also in everyday affairs (*im Handel und Wandel*)."[37] The discussions reveal not only differences of opinion as to the circumstances under which the ban should be applied, but also concern for occasional perceived unfavorable or even disastrous results of its application.

The application of the ban against persons who married outside the Amish church or who left the church for another nonresistant denomination received much attention. In the case of a person who had joined another church while in the ban, there was little question. The ban should be continued.

The question of how to treat persons who merely chose to leave the Amish church but who were otherwise not guilty of any "immoral conduct," was a more difficult issue. A committee which studied this question at the 1863 conference was released from duty without making a report because they could not agree on a conclusion or ruling.[38] The following year a new committee appointed to consider the same subject reported back to the conference body as follows:

We do not find any reason in God's Word to judge a person without investigating what his motive might have been. We therefore leave such matters to the congregation where such things have happened, to act in accordance with the circumstances.[39]

A minority objected to this conclusion and Bishop Jacob Swartzendruber, as spokesperson for this conservative group, wondered whether leaving the Amish church was not in itself an immoral act.

A parallel consideration to that given those who left the church was given to persons who married a member of another nonresistant faith. The conference of 1863 gave an ambiguous answer to this question,[40] but in 1864 it was answered with greater clarity. The committee which reported said that "it must be determined whether or not such person [the spouse from without the Amish church] is a member of the spiritual tribe of Jesus Christ and of the true church of God." In defending this committee report against potential criticism from the conservatives, one of its members, Joseph Stuckey, said: "We have all worked hard on this problem, and if someone can give us a better solution, we will gladly accept such, but do not press us to judge."[41]

Whether one should shun one's spouse if the latter had been put in the ban, was probably the most controversial of all the questions relating to shunning. It must be remembered that shunning required the cessation of conjugal relations with the shunned spouse. The secretary of the 1862 conference, after listening to the discussion of this question, recorded that "the whole assembly seemed to be pretty much agreed that avoidance should be observed without considering the person, except in cases involving married couples, where it does more harm than good."[42]

The question of whether a wife or husband should be expected to shun his or her spouse was lifted up again in the 1864 conference. In a letter to the conference, Solomon Beiler, who had found it impossible to attend in person, took a relatively rigid position. He insisted that shunning by spouses in cases where the marriage partner was banned, was scriptural. The wife's (or the husband's) earthly marriage relationship must "yield to the spiritual" union or marriage with Christ. Beiler made one small concession to those who opposed shunning between spouses. If a spouse "is unable to practice shunning" against her partner, the congregation is not obligated to punish the former by banning and shunning, but should impose other kinds of punishment on her. She should be excluded from the Lord's Supper and from the congregational council, and the kiss of peace should be withheld from her. Only six ministers voted against Beiler's pronouncement.[43]

John K. Yoder, who pleaded for tolerance of differences on this aspect of shunning, was likely one of the six dissenters in this case. In counseling restraint in the application of the ban, Yoder did not quote from the Scriptures, as he might have. He merely said that marital shunning was impractical. It wouldn't work! It did more harm than good. It could result in the loss of the custody of the children by the innocent party. Rather than referring to the Bible, Yoder cited actual cases to prove his point. His approach was strictly pragmatic. In 1870, in a lengthy essay pleading for toleration of minor differences in dress and related practices, John K. Yoder would again resort to the same line of reasoning.[44] To Yoder's practical reasoning Jacob Swartzendruber responded simply that he was "in favor of shunning without respect of person." The minute of the conference which recorded Swartzendruber's comments ended with an indirect quotation: "He means to hold to Holy Writ."[45]

With regard to voting in political elections and holding local public offices, an appreciable difference was again discernible between the conservatives and the liberals. The conservatives advised against both, especially during the current Civil War. Change-minded bishops John K. Yoder and (Gross) Mose Miller urged that voting be left up to the individual and his conscience. If a ruling were made concerning voting, they said, it would be divisive. As to local office holding, the only restriction imposed was that no one should hold an office involving criminal or military jurisdictions or any other in which the use of force was required.[46]

In 1863 many change-minded congregations were building, or had recently built, meetinghouses. Consequently, the topic received considerable attention in the conference of that year, appearing as a subheading in the minutes. Not surprisingly, the conservatives questioned this innovation, although their position on the issue was not rigid.[47]

The conferences of 1863 and 1864 were dominated by the change-minded wing of the Amish church and some toleration of differences in minor matters was urged. However, the limits of this toleration were quite narrow. Photographs were "likenesses" and therefore forbidden by the second of the Ten Commandments. Serving in the militia or as a teamster in the army was not to be tolerated. The use of musical instruments was forbidden. Membership in secret societies was unacceptable.

1865, the Watershed Year·

For some reason Bishop Jonas D. Troyer of Clinton Township, Elkhart County, Indiana, was not able to attend the 1863 conference in Mifflin County. His absence did not indicate disinterest in the conference, for he sent a letter proposing that in the following year it meet with his congregation. In extending this invitation Troyer set in motion a train of events which eventuated in the watershed conference of 1865. Troyer's letter of invitation referred to some "complaints which have been brought against him and other ministers." He implied that he wanted the help of the conference in dealing with these "complaints." The conference body accepted Troyer's invitation[48] and convened on June 16, 1864, at the home of Daniel Schrock, about five miles east of Goshen, Indiana.[49]

The complaints to which Troyer had referred in his invitation were identified by Moderator John K. Yoder. He announced to the 1864 conference that "as is well known, we want to deal with the misunderstanding between the Clinton and Elkhart congregations, in which other congregations are also involved."[50] The Clinton congregation was Troyer's church and change-oriented. The Elkhart congregation was Joseph Miller's tradition-oriented congregation, centered around the forks of the Little Elkhart River in Newbury Township on the western edge of Lagrange County.[51]

Troyer had invited the conference to come to Indiana to attempt to heal the schism which the Amish chronicler and eyewitness, John (Hansi) Borntreger, reported to be final as early as 1857. He added that it had resulted in bitter alienation between the two parties.[52] In the intervening years, both parties had formalized the division by completing the organization of separate congregations and ordaining additional ministers. Meetinghouses had been erected in Clinton Township and at the "Forks" in Lagrange County.[53] To have attempted a reconciliation after a decade of separation seems, in hindsight, unrealistic.

Evidently Troyer and his conservative counterpart in the Elkhart-Lagrange counties area, Bishop Joseph Miller, had done their homework well. Northern Indiana (including the Nappanee area) was represented by twenty ministers in the 1864 conference.[54] Of these, Miller and his fellow conservatives numbered eleven or twelve, and Troyer and his fellow liberals numbered eight or nine. The forenoon session on that Monday morning of June 16 adjourned after choosing two secretaries because "some of the ministers whose presence was desired for the beginning were still absent and not expected until noon."[55] The Clinton-Elkhart division was to be the first order of busi-

ness, and it required full representation from the congregations concerned.

The hopes of many years seemed to surface that afternoon when
Moderator John K. Yoder "asked the ministers of the Elkhart congregation whether they desired to examine the matter." Assistant Moderator
(Gross) Mose Miller then "exhorted the ministers of these congregations very earnestly." Although both parties appeared willing to
proceed with peacemaking, there was a problem of logistics. "Not all of
the congregations which were involved had ministerial representation" in the conference. Some thought that arriving at "a comprehensive peace" required "representation from all the affected congregations." Moderator Yoder then became somewhat impatient and
said he felt "that the matter should not be postponed."[56]

On the following day, Tuesday, the conservatives made it clear
that they did not want to proceed with comprehensive peacemaking
without representation from the conservative congregations of Holmes
County, Ohio.[57] Their facts were correct. Holmes County was
represented by only two ministers—(Gross) Mose Miller and Eli Miller—both of whom were known to be liberals. It is puzzling that, with
all the concern which the conservatives of Elkhart and Lagrange
counties expressed about needing the help of fellow conservatives
elsewhere, no mention was made of Mifflin County conservatives.

Already in that Monday afternoon session (Gross) Mose Miller
had recognized this problem of ministerial representation. He had
asked: "Do you want to try to unite yourselves now, or do you want to
wait until the next annual meeting attended by [hopefully] all the congregations?"[58] Evidently the conservatives chose the latter alternative.
They came to the next conference (1865) in larger numbers than ever
before and fully prepared. Northern Indiana and Holmes County
(Ohio) were especially well represented.

However, only days before the ministers assembled in Wayne
County for this fourth annual conference, thirty-four of those conservative ministers met in preliminary session in adjoining Holmes County.
They drew up what may well be called a position paper. By every indication it was the paper referred to as a "letter signed by thirty-four
ministers" when it was presented to the 1865 annual conference only
days later.[59] Included in this group which met in Holmes County were
Levi Miller of Holmes County and Joseph Miller, bishop of the Elkhart
congregation. These two had served as spokespersons for the conservatives on several occasions in the previous annual conferences.

The tradition-oriented ministers had been challenged by the

leaders of the 1864 conference to prepare themselves and come to the 1865 conference ready to deal with the schism on a comprehensive scale. They were doing just that. Their method was to draw up a statement indicating their position on the issues that were dividing the Amish church. This would be their method of dealing with a ministers' meeting dominated by liberals. This document read as follows:

Holmes County, Ohio, June 1, 1865

Now my beloved brethren and sisters in the Lord, may the loving God purify us through his Holy and Good Spirit that we may continue in the faith which we have embraced until a blessed end, that we may leave behind what is destructive to our salvation and contrary to God's Word and help to root out all plants which our heavenly Father has not planted. But at the present time a spirit has come to light which allows that this and that signifies nothing and may be considered either as good or as bad. Now we should consider whether this is a spirit from God or a spirit of enticement. Therefore we the below named ministers of the Word have assembled in the name of the Lord and agreed on the following: First, some things are appearing which we think serve to express pomp and pride and lead away from God. These are a disgrace to the church and should justly be rooted out and not be tolerated in the church, namely to attend worldly "Conventionen" and "Fairs," or annual fairs, and to take part in them or to take out insurance on our earthly property with insurance companies or to put lightning rods on our buildings.

Likewise [the use of] speckled, striped, flowered clothing made according to the style of the world on women and men. Also not to trim the beard according to the style of the world. Likewise to carry hidden photographs made in the likeness of men or to hang them on walls in the house to be seen.

Likewise the overcoat of oilcloth or rubber or other overcoat made according to the style of the world.

Likewise false shirt bosoms and such like.

Likewise merchandising according to the ways of the world, for the Savior cast such out of the temple; also the pompous carriages according to worldly pomp and pride. Also it is considered entirely unseemly to hold [the congregational] council with open doors and permit outsiders to sit in the council, but rather [to counsel] only with [the members of] the congregation.

Also it is considered proper that the ministers go into the preservice ministerial council (*Abrath*), as our forefathers did, and we are not agreed to forsake this custom. The apostle says: Consider your preachers (*Lehrer*) who have proclaimed to you the Word of God, etc.

Also we declare that spiritual songs and also spiritual tunes should be used in worship services and not notes or fast tunes, which belong to the world.

Also we declare it to be unseemly for one who professes to be a Christian to mingle God's creatures, such as the horse and the donkey, which produces the mule, since God did not create such in the beginning.

Also we think it should not be allowed for members of the congregation to serve in worldly offices, especially those which use force and also the military or penal offices.

Also we consider it to be unseemly [to decorate] the houses with all kinds of unnecessary, gorgeous, household furnishings such as speckled wall and window paper, large mirrors on the walls, along with all kinds of pictures and such like. The above listed [recommendations] we declare as right and good and similar to and in agreement with the Word of God and our Articles of Faith, and thus we have been taught and instructed by our forefathers and [we] intend to stay with the same, as we agreed to do and promised in our baptismal vow. And all those who affirm such with us and demonstrate with works and deeds we are willing to recognize as brothers and sisters and resume fellowship with them with hand[shake] and kiss and to minister with them in the Word and in doctrine, and to maintain spiritual unity with them, for the Savior says: "Whoever does the will of my father in heaven, the same is my brother, sister, and mother." And the gate is portrayed for us as strait and the way as narrow, but is not therefore ever closed, but stands open for all repentant souls, and as the Savior says in Luke 14:33, "Whoever does not forsake all that he has cannot be my disciple."

Thus concluded [or agreed upon] and undersigned by us as follows.[60]

The signatures which follow include those of eighteen ministers from Holmes County, seven from the Elkhart-Lagrange counties area (including Nappanee), three from Somerset County (Pennsylvania), three from Ontario, two from the Howard-Miami counties area of Indiana, and one from Wayne County (Ohio). None of the conservative ministers from Mifflin or Lancaster counties attended.

This position paper was just that. As has been noted by James N. Gingerich, it did not list points of difference for possible negotiation. Instead, it stated the position of the conservative wing and indicated that the position was right and biblical. The paper invited those who had deviated to repent and return to the fellowship of the church, noting that the gate "always stands open for repentant souls."[61]

This document was in the tradition of the disciplines of 1809 and 1837, except that the 1865 discipline was much more detailed than the earlier ones in attempting to codify the *Ordnung* of the church. In the context of the progressive stages of the Great Schism, the paper has great significance. No concern is indicated about the use of meetinghouses for worship or about stream baptism. The latter was a deliberate omission.[62] Much more distress is expressed with respect to the adornment of persons and the embellishment of buildings and furnishings than heretofore.

The year 1865 marks the high point in total attendance at the conference, the total registration list numbering eighty-nine. This record attendance is explained largely by the presence of an unusually large number of conservatives, approximately thirty-seven, constituting two-fifths of the assembly of ministers. Attendance by conservatives at the 1862 conference had numbered in the lower twenties, in 1863 the number was down to nine or ten, and in 1864 their number had risen to only about sixteen. Of the approximately thirty-seven conservatives who came to the 1865 conference, twenty-nine had attended the conservative ministers' meeting held in Holmes County only four days previously. They came as a self-appointed delegation and presented their position paper. The minutes of the 1865 conference speak of it as "a letter signed by thirty-four ministers . . . in which many things were mentioned which were harmful for the church."[63] Both the description of the contents of this "letter" and the fact that it was signed by thirty-four ministers (the exact number of those who had signed the Holmes County position paper) make it evident that the "letter" read at the conference was the position paper of the conservatives.

The 1865 conference was not managed well. The minutes which were taken were poorly kept, certainly the most poorly recorded by far of all the sixteen conferences. They were also the shortest. Neither the moderator or his assistant are named, nor the secretary or secretaries. Most of these minutes are in the nature of a summary which might have been written after the conference, with no reference to the sequence of time and topic as these unfolded in forenoon and afternoon sessions and from day to day. Finally, the minutes included no copy of that extremely important "letter" from the conservatives who had met in Holmes County just before the conference.

In particular, procedures followed in the 1865 conference left something to be desired, if the minutes indicate to any degree of accuracy what actually transpired. This document was read to the assembly quite late, perhaps in the third and final day, judging by the location in the minutes of the reference to the Holmes County letter. Such a procedure, if intentional, was deplorable. The paper may not have been presented to the moderator until that time, in which case the timing was not his fault.

Even conceding the possibility of a late presenting of the paper, one must conclude that only indifferent attention was given to it and to the thirty-four ministers who had spent a day or possibly several days in drawing it up. It was concluded, evidently with little or no discussion, that the paper need not be acted upon, since the concerns presented therein had already been covered by a ruling made earlier in the conference. This assertion was only partly true. The earlier ruling of the conference had dealt entirely with the matter of personal adornment, whereas the Holmes County position paper covered a multitude of concerns. Furthermore, such an offer of peace, even on conditions quite unacceptable to the liberals, should have been given the courtesy of more discussion and a dignified response.

Obviously more information is needed to make a definitive judgment concerning the relations between the two factions at the 1865 conference. There definitely was a basic difference in the thinking of the two parties. The liberals were slightly more prepared to consider the points at issue as negotiable. They were probably restrained from making concessions to the conservatives, however, because their lay members would have rebelled against any rollback of changes already effected. For the conservatives a principle was at stake. Negotiation was compromise and compromise was sin. Given the unbending stance taken in the Holmes County paper, and possibly displayed by the conservative delegation personally, the liberals may well have been discouraged and nonplussed.

Speculation as to what might have been the ultimate outcome of a reconciliation between conservatives and liberals is interesting but not helpful. One may note, however, that a reconciliation between liberals and conservatives without some representation from conservatives in Mifflin and Lancaster counties might have separated the western Amish from the eastern congregations.

What is clear is that the last opportunity for the liberally dominated conference to make peace with the traditionalists on anything like a churchwide basis had passed into history. From the beginning the bishops and most of the conservatives of Lancaster County had boycotted the conference.[64] From now on, with a few exceptions, the conservatives throughout the Amish church would do likewise. Even then, this "rump" conference would not be able to maintain unity among its own constituent congregations.[65]

10

The Annual Conferences of 1866-78

The Amish Mennonites, 1865-1900

The annual conferences of 1862-65 had failed to effect reconciliation. In the 1870s, when the leaven of the Great Schism reached Lancaster County (Pennsylvania), the ministers' meetings would be as powerless as ever in providing any balm of healing. They were wholly estranged from the ecclesiastical structure of the Amish congregations of that area. In the 1880s the same issues of the Great Schism reached into the congregations of Johnson County (Iowa) and Ontario (Canada). By then the conferences had been discontinued.

Judging by the procedures followed in the 1865 conference and the results, these first four ministers' meetings may actually have hastened the process of division. They served to polarize the differences between the two parties and crystallized the schism. As of 1865, therefore, it becomes appropriate to speak of the conservatives as Old Order Amish and of those who continued to affiliate with the annual conferences as Amish Mennonites. These names, however, did not come to be used in this way until later. Of the Old Order Amish, only Frederick Swartzendruber and Abner Yoder, both from Johnson County (Iowa), attended the conference of 1866.[1] The two conservatives who attended the 1868 conference ("Groffdale" John Stoltzfus and Moses Hartz) were, surprisingly, from the Lancaster-Berks counties area, but thereafter Lancaster County was completely unrepresented.

Curiously, the most frequent conservative attendants of the annual conferences after 1865 were the Graber brothers of Allen County, Indiana: Peter, John, and Jacob. All three of these brothers attended the 1872 conference. Attendance by Old Order Amish ceased completely after that year. Significantly, after their 1865 experience, not a single conservative minister ever again attended from the major centers of strife: the Elkhart-Lagrange counties area of Indiana, the Holmes-Wayne-Stark counties area of Ohio, or Mifflin County (Pennsylvania).

Probably the Amish Mennonites were aware following the 1865 conference that the schism was irreparable. The situation was recognized three years later in an "Addendum" to the minutes of the 1868 conference. This Addendum consisted largely of a welcome to the conference of 1869. All were invited "who have been baptized by one Spirit into one body and who *a few years ago were one church* [emphasis added]," but who were no longer thus united.[2] Although this invitation attempted to keep open the door of reconciliation, it also acknowledged the fact of schism.

No longer restrained by the traditionalist Old Order Amish, the change-minded leaders may have expected that unity within the conference and its constituency was assured. But, although change-minded, they were not agreed on what to change.

Indicative of the troubles ahead for the conference and for the Amish Mennonites was the division which took place in the Martin's Creek, Holmes County (Ohio), congregation. This occurred during the same years in which the conference was attempting to restore unity to the Amish church.[3] Two of the first four conferences had been held in nearby Wayne County, and although they might well have given some attention to the Martin's Creek division, there is no indication that they did.

Another harbinger of future trouble was the quarrel between Full Deacon John P. King and Bishop John Werey of the Logan-Champaign counties area of Ohio. That dispute had started in 1860 and continued until about 1880. Elsewhere, Bishop Henry Egli (Egly) of Adams County, Indiana, began to disturb the quiet of his congregation by calling for a personal conversion experience for all applicants for baptism. Soon Benjamin Eicher and Philip Roulet of Iowa, followed by Joseph Stuckey of Illinois, proposed relaxing the personal dress code and the restrictions on other kinds of embellishment. They introduced protracted evening meetings, Sunday schools, and congregational outreach in evangelism and missions.

Other distracting forces were at work. Since 1850 the Apostolic Christian Church had been proselyting Amish in a number of communities. The first congregation thus disrupted was that at Croghan, New York. Over a period of twenty-five years, three-fourths of the Amish congregation united with this group.[4] In the 1850s (and also later) defections to the Apostolic Christian Church in several Amish congregations in central Illinois followed.[5] In 1862 and following, the Amish of Allen County, Indiana, lost members to this church.[6] And in the mid-1860s about half of the congregation near Pulaski, Davis County, Iowa, was won over by two Apostolic Christian ministers from Illinois.[7] There was also a continuing drain to the Mennonites and the Dunkards.[8]

In 1865 and following years, this emerging body faced two other situations, perhaps only peripherally related to the problem of unity. But they were factors affecting the well-being and even the survival of the Amish Mennonites. The first of these was the diaspora of the Amish Mennonites from their relative concentration in Amish communities in Pennsylvania, Ontario, Ohio, Indiana, Illinois, and Iowa, to points south, north, and west. The pages of the *Herald of Truth* from 1864 to the end of the century teem with reports from newly established Old Order Amish, Amish Mennonite, and Mennonite settlements. Mostly the direction of migration was westward, following that amazing expansion of the general American population after the Civil War.

This dispersion was not forced like the Diaspora of the Jews. Neither were the older established settlements depopulated—with a few notable exceptions. Like other settlers, the Amish and the Mennonites moved westward because the government was giving away western lands to settlers. This land was now accessible to the settler for the first time by means of the railroad, which provided fast, cheap, and relatively safe and comfortable transportation to almost all regions of the country. Amish from Ontario trekked westward to points such as Bayport, Michigan, and the area around "Troyer's schoolhouse," eight miles west of Mancelona in the same state. Others went to Worthington and Fulda in the southwest corner of Minnesota.[9] Before 1900 at least three settlements had been made in Tennessee—in Knox County in 1871-72, in Coffee County in the mid-1880s, and in Dickson County in the 1890s.[10] A few other settlements were attempted in the South before the end of the century.

Enumeration and description of all the permanent or short-lived Amish Mennonite settlements made in 1864-1900 await much additional research. Communities were established in Missouri, Kansas, Nebraska, the Dakotas, Arkansas, Oklahoma, Idaho, Oregon, and Washington Territory. Pending further research, the Amish Mennonite colonies in the prairie country of Wright County, Iowa, and in Lyon County, Kansas, provide keyhole perspectives on the several settlements which failed.

The Wright County location was settled largely by dissident Amish Mennonites from Johnson County. Included among the settlers was the youthful Sanford C. Yoder and Solomon J. Swartzendruber, already a minister. The settlement mushroomed, built a meetinghouse, and disintegrated in the course of about eighteen years (1892-1910).[11] In this instance the major cause for decline was disagreement among these change-minded emigrants from Johnson County as to how far the congregation should deviate from the traditional *Ordnung*. On the other hand, drought and the invasion of insects caused the disintegration in the 1890s of the one-decade-old Amish Mennonite settlement at Hartford, Kansas. It suffered a lingering death in the following decade.[12]

The correspondence which came to the *Herald of Truth* and the *Herold der Wahrheit* from these remote communities in that last third of the nineteenth century is repetitious. The land is cheap. Frequently the climate is salubrious and the soil productive. The settlement needs only some additional families and a resident minister to prosper spiritually and economically. The most frequently expressed immediate need was for more visits by ministers from the large, established congregations in Amish Mennonite communities.[13]

The second situation which challenged the Amish Mennonites was the converse of the first. While new congregations were forming outside the older Amish Mennonite communities, a few previously well-established congregations were dying out. Conferences and leaders, both of the Mennonites and the Amish Mennonites, addressed themselves rather vigorously to the problem of providing spiritual instruction and pastoral care for their remote congregations. Yet they curiously manifested much less concern for these older communities which were disappearing.

By 1900 the Amish Mennonite settlements in the northern part of Somerset County and southern Cambria County, Pennsylvania, were nearing extinction.[14] Yet immediately to the south, the Old Order Amish in the Grantsville area had increased in numbers.[15] Well to the north of Somerset County, the Buffalo Valley congregation had practically disintegrated already in the 1880s. Contributing factors were the silencing of Bishop Elias Riehl, the removal of Preacher Christian King to Lancaster County, the death of Deacon Christian Stoltzfus, and the relocation of a considerable number of the latter's extended family to Lyon County, Kansas.[16]

The Tuscarora settlement in Juniata County, Pennsylvania, followed much the same course as that of Buffalo Valley and in the same time period. With the death of Bishop John Esh in 1879 and the removal in the late 1880s of the conservatively inclined remaining ministers, Benjamin and Jacob Hertzler, to Mifflin County, this congregation likewise fell apart.[17]

Similar tragedies could be recounted for the congregations in Fairfield County, Ohio; at Richville in Stark County, Ohio; and at Pretty Prairie in Lagrange County, Indiana. The chroniclers of these events list several causes for the demise of the congregations: strife and division, the lure of cheaper land to the west, poor leadership, and attrition to the Mennonites and Dunkards.

The Annual Conferences, Continued, 1866-78

The conference of 1866 met from May 20-23 in the vicinity of Danvers, Illinois. The decision of the 1865 meeting to convene next in this liberal Amish territory in central Illinois may reflect again some insensitivity on the part of the conference leaders of 1865 to the feelings of the conservatives. Bishop Joseph Stuckey was soon to have a predominating influence over this area of Amish concentration. In February of 1866 Bishop Jonathan Yoder's wife had passed away, and he had moved to Woodford County just north of Danvers to live with his daughter and son-in-law, Leah and John Sharp. He resided there until his death in 1869.[18]

Of the original leadership of the conference, Solomon Beiler would attend no more. Although he lived until 1888, his name virtually disappears from the annals of Amish Mennonite church affairs. Jonathan Yoder would attend only the conferences of 1866 and 1868. Deacon John Stoltzfus, who wrote that original invitation to a general conference in 1861, was to attend the conferences of 1867 and 1868, but none thereafter.

The leadership of the conference from 1866 to the final meeting in 1878 was in the hands of three men, John K. Yoder, Samuel Yoder, and John P. King. Samuel Yoder served as moderator for five of these conferences, and John K. Yoder and John P. King each served three times. Only once—in 1867 when Elias Riehl chaired the conference—was a moderator chosen outside the three. John K. Yoder also served twice as assistant moderator. Otherwise the latter office was passed around judiciously from year to year, no one else holding it more than once. Shem Zook was a fourth leader. Like John K. Yoder, he was a carryover from the earlier conferences. As a layperson his role as unofficial business manager and expediter had to be unobtrusive, but it was nonetheless real until at least 1868.[19]

Attendance of ministers at these annual conferences is shown in the chart below, although some may not have registered and been counted. Never again would the tally of eighty-nine (for the 1865 conference) be reached, and when the conference was held in Washington County in relatively remote Iowa, it dropped to twenty-eight. Attendance even from states with the larger concentrations of Amish Mennonites sometimes dropped as low as one. In ten of the sixteen conferences the state in which the conference was held accounted for half or more of the participants. In four of those same years attendance from the home state approximated or exceeded two-thirds of the total. One may deduce that attendance of specific individuals was sporadic, making continuity of planning and administration difficult. Attendance records of the three leaders were the best in the conference. Of the entire sixteen conferences, John P. King attended twelve, John K. Yoder fourteen, and Samuel Yoder all sixteen.

Attendance of the laity, but not participation in the discussion, was taken for granted from the time of the first conference. The observer role of the laity was officially recognized in 1866. According to the title page of the minutes for that year, the name of the conference was changed from Ministers' Meeting (*Diener Versammlung*) to the Gathering of the Amish Mennonite Ministry and Brotherhood (*der . . . Zusammenkunft der Amischen Mennoniten-Diener und Brüderschaft*). In 1868 the name on the title page was changed back to Ministers' Meeting, but the following page retained the 1866 revision. Total attendance at the 1866 conference was estimated by the Amish Mennonite schoolteacher Christian Erismann to be 1200.[20] Bishop Joseph Stuckey's guess was 1500.[21] Estimates for the remaining conferences are available only for 1874 at Washington, Iowa ("more than 1000");[22] 1875 at Hopedale, Illinois ("at least one thousand");[23] and 1878 ("some 400 or 500 People").[24] The following chart counts ministers only.

Attendance at the
Amish Mennonite Diener Versammlungen, 1862-1878

Date	County & State of Meeting	PA	NY MD ONT	OH	IN	IL	IA & West	Total
9-12 June 1862	Wayne, OH	11	1	40	14	5	1	72
25-27 May 1863	Mifflin, PA	24	4	10	1	2	1	42
16-18 June 1864	Elkhart, IN	7	0	20	31	10	3	71
5-7 June 1865	Wayne, OH	10	4	47	24	2	2	89
21-23 May 1866	McLean, IL	4	0	14	7	45	5	75
10-12 June 1867	Logan, OH	7	2	19	7	7	0	42
1-3 June 1868	Mifflin, PA	19	1	11	2	1	0	34
17-18 May 1869	Holmes, OH	4	0	19	3	1	0	27
6-8 June 1870	Fulton, OH	5	0	14	10	10	1	40
29-31 May 1871	Livingston, IL	2	2	3	5	41	3	56
20-22 May 1872	Lagrange, IN	5	0	11	22	17	1	56
2-4 June 1873	Wayne, OH	7	0	18	4	11	1	41
25-27 May 1874	Washington, IA	2	0	6	2	11	7	28
17-19 May 1875	Tazewell, IL	1	1	4	4	25	3	38
5-7 June 1876	Fulton, OH	3	0	14	8	4	1	30
10-12 June 1878	Woodford, IL	1	0	4	2	32	4	43
Cumulative Attendance Totals		112	15	254	146	224	33	784

The only extant description in detail of the physical arrangements under which these conferences were held is in the form of a newspaper reporter's account of the meeting of 1878. The setting for the several conferences of 1862-78 must have varied considerably. Yet this rare description of one of these Diener Versammlungen provides a close-up view not available elsewhere. "The Amish," so runs the account,

> who number only about ten thousand in the United States and Canada, meet annually in Conference, which is their most important ecclesiastical event. . . . The Amish Conference this year was held in or near Eureka, Ill. in June. On the first day some 400 or 500 People met together in A Chapel which is four miles from any town, or, rather in a large shed, for the church proper was occupied by women and babies. As there are many Amish families in the surrounding country, the delegates from A distance were taken to and from the place of meeting morning and night by the farmers who became their hosts. This was their Sixteenth Annual Conference and it continued in session four days [Pentecost celebration plus three days of business]. Notwithstanding the unfavorable weather and the

almost impassable roads, the attendance was good. The meeting-house being too small to accommodate the people, a huge shed, covered with fencing boards, was erected at one side; and in the center of this a platform, occupied by the preachers and a few of the elder and elect ladies. The listeners were carefully separated. The women and girls, with heads covered by tidy black silk caps or stiffly starched sunbonnets (none wear hats) meekly and modestly looked up to the preacher from the rough board seats on one side of the platform. While the men and boys with coats and vests fastened with hooks and eyes, occupied the seats on the other side and with honest and attentive faces gave heed to the spoken word. . . . The preachers, as has been mentioned, occupied the platform, and were called out by him [the moderator J. K. Yoder] to address the people. The addresses [called *admonitions* by the Amish Mennonites] were in German, and usually were from fifteen to twenty minutes in length. They were largely hortatory in their character, calling the people to practical godliness and simplicity in dress. . . . The expenses of delegates are always paid, and in all cases where a Preacher is forced for the sake of his people to neglect his farm he is paid for his time. . . . When the meeting broke up, the brethren saluted one an other with the holy kiss. They regard the "kiss" as an ordinance of equal importance to the Lord's Supper, baptism, and feetwashing. The leading missionary or evangelist of the church is elder J. K. Yoder. He regards the Amish as aggressive and says they hope not only to hold the ground they now have, but also to extend their conquests among the German and even among the English speaking population. . . .[25]

Further corroboration is required for the comments concerning the payment of ministers for their time and expenses in attending the annual conferences. Some compensation may have been given to some of the ministers. However, judging by the lack of such supplemental support for Amish Mennonite ministers early in the twentieth century, the statement seems to describe the exception rather than the rule. Likely the minister-delegates were dependent on their respective home congregations for any such remuneration.

Probably most of the half-day sessions of these three-day conferences were "somewhat lengthy," a description given to the sessions of the 1870 conference.[26] Increasingly, through the years much time was used in the delivery of those impromptu "hortatory" addresses. These probably consumed well over half the time in several of the conferences of the 1870s. One gains the impression that sometimes they were utilized to take up time. In the later conferences they may also have been used to permit the audience to hear especially gifted speakers not ordinarily available to them. It may be unkind to suspect that some of these Amish exhorters sought, or at least welcomed, the opportunity to demonstrate their speaking skills. Singing at the beginning and the close of a session was standard procedure. For the conferences of 1875 and 1876 the book used was *Eine unparteiische Liedersammlung zum Gebrauch beim öffentlichen Gottesdienst und der häuslichen Erbauung,* a book reputedly compiled by Shem Zook of Mifflin County.[27]

On only two occasions in the history of the sixteen yearly conferences did the ministers withdraw from the laity to meet in what today would be called executive session. In 1868 the ministers decided to stay over another day (Thursday) and meet in a postsession to deal with "an event in Ohio which [had] caused disunity in the brotherhood in the Logan and Champaign Cos."[28] The second such closed meeting took place on the last day of the 1871 conference. The ministers met in the *Rathskammer* (council room) in the morning before the public session to discuss the problems relating to Joseph Stuckey's congregation.[29]

The closing of a yearly conference sometimes became a lengthy ritual. Such rites occupied a major part of the afternoon session on June 4, 1873, at Orrville, Ohio. Moderator Samuel Yoder delivered his closing admonition, after which Assistant Moderator Christian Werey exhorted for a time and reviewed "all that we have heard in these days." Then the moderator called on Minister Joseph Yoder for some remarks. "After this as a closing there followed an instructive admonition and prayer by Sem King." Then "after the prayer the blessing was pronounced by J. K. Yoder." Almost comical to a twentieth century "observer"—but proper and appropriate to the participants—was the choice of the closing hymn, "Now, Praise God, It Is Finished," which followed Yoder's blessing.[30] Even more prolonged was the closing of the 1875 conference.[31]

Surely the ministers who attended the 1866 conference noticed that the conservatives were almost completely unrepresented. Yet the minutes do not record their awareness or whether they were disappointed in the withdrawal of the tradition-oriented Amish. Instead, the conference in effect covered its tracks and looked to the future. The first order of business was a proposal to adopt ten carefully formulated additional rules of procedure, which were accepted with little or no debate. These rules represent an increased institutionalization of the conference and continued in force for most, probably all, of the conferences which followed.[32]

The indicated procedures in these ten regulations reflect a considerable concern for orderliness. Participating ministers ("co-workers") might express themselves freely but not speak for more than twenty minutes at one time. (This time limitation was dropped in 1870.) When engaging in discussion, a minister was to stand up to speak and to lead out in a loud and clear voice. Only one person was to speak at a time and no one was to interrupt or "cut down" another speaker. Any participating minister was to be ready, at the request of the chairman, "to use his gift [of exhortation] which he has received from God." This regulation was carried over from a minute in the 1864 proceedings. Items for discussion or questions for solution were to be presented in writing. The moderator and his assistant had "the right to keep back all matters or inquiries which [were] not considered useful or upbuilding by them."[33]

This set of rules bears the imprint of Bishop John K. Yoder, although his authorship cannot be documented. Already in 1864, when acting as moderator of conference, Yoder had exercised a chairman's prerogative in choosing not to read an epistle to the conference from Jacob Rupp, dissident and follower of Henry Egli. His reason was that "it would take almost a whole week to discuss all the questions contained therein." However, he would be willing, he said, to submit his decision to a committee of seven ministers for review if Rupp so desired.[34] This control over the agenda of the conference, formally stated in the ten rules adopted in 1866, seems rather firm, but there is little indication that this power was abused or even used much.

John K. Yoder was also the most likely author of two resolutions which were introduced into the next conference (1867), again as the first order of business and passed without discussion. These resolutions asserted the binding force of conference decisions. They read as follows:

> First it is decided that all proceedings of former meetings [conferences] which were brought to a conclusion [i.e., in which rulings were made] are in force at present, unless a scriptural proof is presented to the general assembly that those which are not being observed are unscriptural.
> Second, no minister who is a participant in the meeting shall have the right to make any changes afterward unless he hands in a scriptural proof that the ruling is unscriptural or deviates from the Word of God and in that way is harmful.[35]

It will be noted that this assertion of the binding force of conference rulings applied only to those ministers, perhaps with their congregations, who had taken part in the original decision making. It was never claimed that nonparticipating congregations and ministers were bound by the rulings of conference. The supporters of conference were merely asking that those who had participated in making a ruling in a ministers' meeting, as was the custom of centuries, have the integrity to abide by it. However, the regulations were now being made by a conference which met yearly, rather than by an ad hoc ministers' meeting, a distinction of major importance. Meeting yearly provided the conference with the opportunity to follow up on its decisions which, in turn, opened up the possibility of imposing sanctions on uncooperative or wayward ministers and congregations.

The ten rules of conference procedure were drawn up in 1866. In 1867 the meeting adopted those additional statements concerning the responsibility of ministers to abide by the rules which they themselves had approved. All these were reaffirmed by most of the succeeding conferences thereafter, with the exception of the conferences of 1871, 1872, and 1878. But reiteration did not produce performance. The problem of noncompliance with the rulings of conference had arisen already in 1863, when someone asked what to do about "ministers who help to decide a matter, but afterward do the opposite." To this concern Solomon Beiler had responded: "Such a thing cannot be tolerated; to approve of such would ruin the effect and the results of our conference rulings. What is the use of our coming together, if afterward we overthrow what we have decided. . . ? [Such persons should] make their peace with conference." Then the entire ministerial body "expressed by rising that they were not satisfied with such ministers until they provide further explanation."[36]

These extended quotations from the minutes of 1863 indicate that virtually from its beginning the conference sought vigorously to secure compliance with its decisions. A threat to apply the sanction of breaking fellowship with the offenders is clearly implied in the above resolution.[37] Those two rules concerning obedience to conference regulations drawn up in 1867 were nothing more nor less than a codification of this impromptu resolution of 1863.

James N. Gingerich has pointed out that the annual conference never resorted to the kind of legalism represented by the disciplines or codes of 1809 and 1837, and by the position paper drawn up by the conservatives in 1865 in Holmes County, Ohio.[38] Rather, the conference chose to deal with individual problems as they arose, thus providing a dynamic approach to Ordnung, as compared to the static approach of the conservatives. However, the distinction can easily be overdrawn. As Gingerich himself has noted, the all-inclusive broadside against worldly attire and hairstyling, adopted at the conference of

1865, represents something of an exception to the dynamic approach. This more static approach on the same subject was reaffirmed in 1872. The conference, recalling the ruling of 1865, provided for the inclusion in the minutes of 1872 an extensive quotation from the 1865 record. The notes observed guardedly that the 1865 regulation had been recalled "not in order to correct it, but in order to admonish us to live up to it better in the future than what we have in the past."[39]

Similarly, in 1875, when membership in that farmer's organization called the Grange was questioned, the answer was found, not through any dynamic process, but by referring to a decision made in 1864.[40] Exactly the same procedure was used in 1876, when the question of the propriety of having one's photograph taken was answered by referring to an action taken in 1863. "Since it was not approved then," it was observed, "[it] can therefore not be approved now."[41]

Observance of the rulings made by conference continued to be a problem, for there were few sanctions which could be imposed on non-cooperating ministers or congregations. Again in 1870 someone asked how to relate to "ministers who help to make rulings and then are not willing to enforce them, declaring them to be unscriptural, but refusing to come to the meeting to explain their position." The committee which was assigned to this question rightfully urged first the exercise of patience and the use of exhortation. But if this procedure proved ineffective, they said, one must cease fellowshiping with and "withdraw from" those who are recalcitrant.[42] The application of the ban and of shunning was not implied in this answer. They advised only the withholding of cooperation in the sharing of ministerial duties and ministerial consultations, and the withholding of the spiritual kiss and handshake.

What the committee failed to indicate was who should do the withholding. Should individual congregations take this action? Or should conference break fellowship with the offending minister or ministers, and perhaps refuse to seat them as delegates in the annual meeting? Only in the matter of the Joseph Stuckey schism, 1872-73 (to be described later), did the conference itself accept such responsibility—that of breaking fellowship with one considered to be an uncooperative minister.[43]

A great hindrance to the exercise of effective leadership and some measure of control by the conference lay in its structure and composition. As suggested earlier, the arrangement under which the conference operated provided no continuity from one conference to the next. A glance at the attendance chart (shown above) will make it clear that regular attendance by any one minister was the exception. Then too, in accordance with traditional Amish procedures, no permanent structure provided continuous supervision from year to year. The ministers assembled without officers and without any established rules of order, making reorganization a yearly procedure. There was never an official agenda, although in some years it was known before the meeting convened that certain concerns were to be taken up.

The conference of 1871 provides a striking example of the absence of an agenda. On Monday forenoon the election of officers took place, but even the yearly readoption of the rules of order was neglected. That afternoon, when the time for business had arrived, there was no business to be taken care of, for "no questions had been handed in."[44] Consequently, the afternoon was spent in listening to impromptu admonitions from a variety of ministers. In that 1871 session only two items of business were taken up, the record of which occupies only two pages of the twenty-page *Verhandlungen* of that year. Only the distribution of these minutes to the participating congregations following each conference, the informal initiative of the three leaders, and the relatively faithful attendance of a few others provided any semblance of continuity. Given such circumstances, effective leadership by the conference was virtually impossible.

The conference and its supporters, however, tried diligently to make the ministers' meetings function properly and were frustrated when they failed. Probably a majority of the minister-delegates sincerely attempted to conform to its rulings. In 1868 twenty-three ministers of central Illinois met together and studied the minutes of the conference for the preceding years. They "came to the agreement that the actions [recorded therein] were scriptural and that they were minded to follow them more carefully than heretofore."[45]

Bishop John K. Yoder, in particular, was quite preoccupied with the problem of enforcing the decisions of conference. As moderator in 1874 and again when he served in the same position in 1878 he called on the assembled ministers to join hands in implementing the directives of the conference.[46] Yet he also realized that other less-heavy-handed means could be employed to maintain unity within the group which was soon to take the name Amish Mennonite. At the 1870 conference he read a prepared paper pleading for toleration of what today would be considered minor differences from East to West in standards of dress. The differences, he thought, could be kept to a minimum if ministers from the West would visit eastern congregations and ministers from the East would visit western congregations.[47]

Clearer communication, both within and without the confines of the annual conference, was gaining increasing recognition as an instrument for maintaining the unity of the church. This was to be flavored with a pinch of toleration (but no more than a pinch).[48] In the conference of 1878, the last one of the series, John K. Yoder was to propose some significant changes in the church polity of the Amish Mennonites.

More Brushfires

The record of the conferences after 1865 in dealing with schism is as dismal as before that date. The first of these, the Egli schism, followed hard on the heels of the decisive 1865 conference. Other than Henry Egli's onetime attendance in 1865, the Adams County (Indiana) Amish congregation over which he became bishop in the early 1860s had not participated in the annual conferences and would not in the future. In 1864 and later years attempts were made to have the conference discuss Egli's teachings. Evidently because the conference dealt only with problems brought to its attention by delegates, Egli's activities in Adams County never came under the direct scrutiny of that body.

Henry Egli's autobiography indicates that he came to experience God's forgiveness after several years of ill health and much introspection. Ordained a deacon (1850) soon after his experience and a minister in 1854, he began to call for an experiential conversion as a prerequisite for baptism. In the early 1860s, probably after he was already under considerable criticism, he was ordained a bishop. It was only then, when he was in a position to implement his convictions, that schism became imminent. "Even the older ministers were against me," he wrote, "and threatened me to quit preaching." Those, he said, who "were baptized without repentance . . . had no more promise than the one that was baptized in infancy."[49]

In 1866 he resigned his pastorate under pressure and formed a new church with the half of the congregation which followed him. Already by that time—or in some cases soon thereafter—he had won other Amish Mennonite ministers to his position, including Jacob Rupp and the latter's son Joseph of Fulton County, Ohio; Joseph Rediger of Gridley, Illinois; Joseph Gerig of Leo (Allen County), Indiana; and others.[50]

Except for insisting on an experiential conversion, Egli was a typical Amish bishop. In a letter of 1864 to a fellow bishop in Ontario, Peter Litwiller, he had deplored "the sinful pride in splendor of clothing as well as in building houses, and in insurance companies, lightning rods, helping to elect government officials, seeking honor and a good name from the government, seeking help from it in recovery of money or property, or also permitting all kinds of impurity and unchastity [bundling?]."[51] Even shunning as the ultimate instrument of church discipline was practiced against the recalcitrant ministers Joseph Rupp of Fulton County, Ohio, and John A. Rupp of Illinois.[52] As late as 1887 Egli's congregation decided against "having organs in our homes."[53]

It was only as Egli's teachings led to schism in participating congregations elsewhere that the annual ministers' conference got involved. Egli was convinced and taught that baptism should be administered only to those who had an "experiential knowledge of conversion and regeneration."[54] This may have, already in the 1863 conference, provided the impetus for the discussion on baptism, although the tenor of that interchange does not give much support to this hypothesis. However, a letter to that same conference from Jacob Nafziger of Fulton County, Ohio, probably was concerned with the growing difficulty which the congregation in that county was having with Jacob Rupp, an adherent of Egli.[55] The contents of the letter are not recorded.

Jacob Rupp then attended the conferences of 1864 and 1865 in person and registered as a minister, although it is not certain that he was ever ordained by the Fulton County Amish Mennonite congregation.[56] An entry in the 1864 minutes implies that the assistant moderator, Moses P. Miller, was questioning Rupp's right to participate as a minister-delegate.[57] Under Moderator John K. Yoder's leadership, the conference of 1864 had refused to hear Rupp's appeal.

Jacob Rupp, probably accompanied by Egli, got his petition heard in the 1865 conference. The conference minutes said the petition consisted of "complaints and accusations against other ministers and congregations." Bishops Abner Yoder, Samuel Yoder, and Jacob Kanagy were appointed to investigate the situation in the Fulton County congregation.[58] This committee reported back to the 1866 conference that Rupp could not substantiate his charges, refused to withdraw them, and "could not provide us with sufficient reason to justify a division."

The 1866 conference also responded to a report from "the congregation in Livingston Co., Ill." This evidently referred to the Gridley congregation, where Joseph Rediger, adherent of Egli, was a minister.[59] Although Joseph Yoder, John Werey, and John Esh were appointed to visit this congregation and report back to the 1867 conference, no such visit is recorded in the minutes of that meeting. The involvement of the conference in the Egli schism thus ended on an uncertain note, for this body pursued reconciliation with the Egli faction no further.

The influence of the Egli movement remained with the Amish Mennonites indefinitely. In 1870 the conference wrestled with two questions which were undoubtedly inspired by the teachings of Egli and his adherents. The first inquiry asked whether one "is worthy of receiving baptism without knowing by feeling and sensing that he is reconciled to God through Christ." The second question asked "how one should consider people who say that their entry into the church is not right, and are again baptized and have much to say about the [Amish Mennonite] church."

The gracious answer of the conference to the latter question requires quoting in full:

> We are not ready to say much about this question, since the circumstances are reported only from one side. Still we counsel those who have gone out of the church and have had themselves rebaptized, that they do not revile or scold in return, for such is not pleasing to the Lord. We also counsel the other side to take care that they do not judge too severely those who have left the [Amish Mennonite] church.[60]

Egli, on the other hand, did not distance himself too far from the Amish Mennonites. He submitted an occasional article to the *Herold der Wahrheit*, including one of 1890,[61] and was corresponding with John K. Yoder as late as 1880.[62] According to the authors of the *History of the Salem Evangelical Mennonite Church of Gridley, Illinois*, Joseph Rediger and Henry Egli often said afterward that "had all of them [on both sides?] been riper in experience and exercised more forbearance with one another, the outcome might have been different."[63] In similar manner, Nicholas King, a minister in the Fulton County Amish Mennonite congregation, spoke for the Amish Mennonites. He "lamented later that maybe if they had shown more charity, the breach [between Jacob and Joseph Rupp on the one hand and King's own congregation on the other] might have been healed."[64]

The Egli Amish, founded in 1865, held their first annual conference in 1883 as the Defenseless Mennonite Church of North America. In 1947 the name became Evangelical Mennonite Church. Since 1890, according to the chronicler of the history of the church, it has moved into the mainstream of evangelical Protestantism and there is little of an Anabaptist orientation.[65]

In the decade following 1865, the Hessian Amish of Butler County, Ohio, and of Danvers, Illinois, along with two non-Hessian congregations in Iowa, gradually drew away from the annual conference. The congregation in Marion Township, Washington County, Iowa, underwent a considerable transformation under the leadership of Benjamin Eicher, first resident minister of that church. Eicher had registered as a delegate at the conferences of 1865 and 1866. He appeared again at the conference of 1874 near Wayland, Iowa, adjacent to his own congregation. This time he probably did not attempt to register as a delegate, for he was wearing buttons on his coat, a serious deviation from the Ordnung of the church. Appearing in this costume may have constituted his public declaration of freedom from "the old custom,"[66] although his views were certainly well-known before the time of the meeting at Wayland.[67]

In similar fashion Philip Roulet, ordained to the ministry in 1869 in the Pulaski congregation in Davis County, Iowa, led his congregation away from Amish Mennonite traditions in style of clothing and works-oriented theology. Both also espoused the Sunday school movement and missionary outreach.[68] In Butler County, Ohio, the Hessian Amish eventually absorbed the other two Amish Mennonite congregations.[69]

Apparently Eicher's personal appearance at the 1874 conference was more than that advocate of tolerance, John K. Yoder, could tolerate. It was probably as moderator of the conference that Yoder "insisted that a minister should wear clothing that would make it possible for anyone to distinguish between a preacher and a lawyer or banker."[70] In 1865 at the conference in Wayne County, the Old Order Amish had insisted on acceptance of their position as a basis for peace. Now in 1874 at the conference at Wayland, Iowa, the spokesperson for the Amish Mennonites took the same position, evidently again with little openness for dialogue. In the case of the Butler County congregations, no effort was made to retain their affiliation with the annual conferences.

While the cases of the Eicher, the Roulet, and the Butler County congregations disturbed the composure of the annual conferences little, the case of Joseph Stuckey was different. Under the leadership of Bishop Jonathan Yoder, the Rock Creek (Illinois) congregation had called Stuckey to the ministry in 1860. In 1864 he was ordained a bishop to aid the aging senior bishop. In 1866, when Bishop Yoder moved to Montgomery Township, Woodford County (Illinois), to live with his daughter, additional responsibility for the congregation gravitated to Stuckey.

Stuckey was ready to relax the Ordnung of his congregation and his church in matters of personal adornment and other forms of embellishment, attendance at fairs, higher education, and participation in politics. It soon became evident that even when discipline was admittedly required, he would proceed more slowly than Amish tradition allowed.[71] Already in the conference of 1866 Stuckey had revealed a surprisingly latitudinarian attitude—surprising, that is, for an Amish bishop. On that occasion he called the attention of the conference delegates to an article by John M. Brenneman in the *Herold der Wahrheit*, proposing that the Amish and the Mennonites unite.[72]

For unknown reasons Joseph Stuckey did not attend the conferences of 1868-70. By the time of the 1871 conference, differences had developed between Stuckey and his congregation on the one hand and some of the surrounding congregations on the other hand. The specifics of the quarrel did not surface in conference records until 1872. The minutes of the 1872 conference reveal that Stuckey's principal opponent was Bishop Christian Rupp [Ropp] of the Mackinaw congregation (the mother church of Stuckey's Rock Creek congregation).

A committee had been appointed by conference in 1871 to investigate the "circumstances in Joseph Stuckey's congregation."[73] Its findings imply that Stuckey had been admitting people into his church from neighboring congregations without a church letter and was allowing "unnecessary [personal] adornment." The committee urged that ministers "work toward some kind of a label or mark of recognition." The implication was that Stuckey's clothing or that of his fellow ministers was not plain enough or did not use the distinctive Amish hooks-and-eyes.[74]

Previous historical accounts of the attempted disciplining of Joseph Stuckey suggest that the process was abrupt and abrasive; and so it was, but perhaps not as much as heretofore thought. It might well be that the breach was already in process from the time Bishop Jonathan Yoder moved out of the immediate community in 1866. Stuckey may have absented himself from the ministers' meetings of 1868-70 because he did not care to experience the sting of criticism which he could expect there.

The 1870 conference posed a question concerning measures to be taken against ministers who help to make rulings "but are not willing to enforce them, declare them to be unscriptural, and refuse to come to the meetings to explain themselves."[75] Perhaps that was directed at Stuckey. Certainly the circumstances support this hypothesis. Stuckey had been a participant in the 1865 conference, which had adopted that strong statement against personal adornment.[76] Then later—perhaps when Christian Ropp and others had begun to criticize his lax discipline—for three years he had not attended the annual conferences. If the entry in the minutes of the 1870 conference had reference to Joseph Stuckey's lax discipline, then the confrontation with Stuckey in the 1872 conference seems not to have been quite as sudden as historians have considered it to be.

The alienation of Joseph Stuckey and his associates from the conference occurred in 1872. That year the committee previously appointed to investigate the controversy surrounding Joseph Stuckey's congregation and the neighboring congregations reported that the parties concerned had made peace on their own initiative. They had agreed that change of membership from one congregation to another required a church letter, that personal adornment should be curtailed, that ministers should work toward some distinctive mode of clothing, and that they should cling steadfastly to the Dordrecht Confession of Faith.

Evidently some delegates were dubious and asked whether the above agreement was actually being observed. This led to the appointment of another committee of five—Joseph Burkey, John K. Yoder, Elias Riehl, John Yoder, and Abraham Mast—the first three named being bishops. Evidently sensing that much of the problem was personal, this committee soon came back with the single recommendation that "Joseph Stuckey should be more patient, and should promise that, with the help of God, in the future he would be more careful."[77]

In suggesting that Stuckey was impetuous and hasty, without making any unfavorable observations about his counterpart, Christian Ropp, the above committee may well have insulted Stuckey. On the next day Stuckey closed the forenoon session with the usual admonition, but then requested that the message not be recorded "and that he does not want his name to appear in the *Proceedings* [*Verhandlungen*] booklet, since he did not hear everything that had been discussed, for he had not attended on the previous day on account of not feeling well."[78]

Stuckey probably did not stay for the third day of the conference, but this did not deter the assembled ministers from bringing charges against one of the members of his congregation. Joseph Yoder, brother of Bishop Jonathan Yoder (by then deceased), had been writing poetry for some time,[79] some of it in English and evidently a bit heretical. Not until he had written one such piece, *Die frohe Botschaft*, "The Good News," in the language of the church, did he incur the denunciation of many Amish Mennonites.[80] The conference minutes stated that "the main thought and assumption in this poem was that all people will be saved and there will be no agony of hell or pain."[81]

This "universalism," as Joseph Yoder's heresy was called, was not entirely of his own deduction. The doctrine had received considerable public attention and was making its effects felt in many denominations.[82] Already in the 1850s Minister Daniel Holly of the Bureau Creek congregation had left his church and espoused universalism.[83] In the mid-1870s it was rumored that Isaac Schmucker was a universalist. Although entirely groundless, the rumor frightened Schmucker. In letters to John K. Yoder, Elias Riehl, and Jacob D. Yoder (formerly bishop of the Wayne County congregation), Isaac tried to squelch the rumor and determine the perpetrator.[84]

Already at the conference of 1870 someone had asked, without naming a suspect, how to "deal with those who claim there is no eternal punishment or pain."[85] When the question was restated in 1872, reference was made to the 1870 discussion. The conference of 1870 had decided that such should first be excluded from the congregational council meeting, and if they persisted they should be "put in the ban until there is repentance and reform." Although no one had been accused by name in 1870, it is probable that the participants knew the offender was Joseph Yoder, for his poem had been written and publicized already in 1869.[86] In any event, the answer to the question posed in 1872 was thus found in the minutes of the 1870 conference. What had been declared in principle should now be applied to Joseph Yoder. He should be excommunicated if he did not repudiate his false doctrine.

Stuckey was now at odds with the conference with respect to two matters. He was not enforcing the common Amish Mennonite standards of dress, and he was tolerating universalism in his congregation. According to customary procedure the conference would have appointed another committee to continue the investigation of Stuckey's lax discipline, but the minutes do not record such action. Perhaps the confrontation with Stuckey had been so traumatic that the assembled ministers were not prepared to follow through in accordance with normal procedure. Only four months after that confrontation in the conference of 1872, Stuckey's congregation dedicated their new church building. They sang the *Kirchweih Hymne* as the dedication hymn, composed by none other than the heretical Joseph Yoder. Stuckey's respect for the pronouncements of conference was not thereby confirmed.[87]

What the conference did not initiate was nevertheless carried out. Evidently on the basis of "an urgent request of the brethren in Illinois to visit them,"[88] John K. Yoder, John P. King, and John Yoder responded. One immediately recognizes two of these men as influential leaders and the third, John Yoder, as a brother of the third leader (Bishop Samuel Yoder), and a minister in the latter's congregation. In October 1872 these men visited the churches of Illinois and also some congregations in Iowa, holding more than thirty public meetings, including a preaching service in Stuckey's congregation on October 10.[89] While with Stuckey the touring group confronted him concerning his universalist church member. The following is a report of this meeting, which was taken back to the conference the next year:

> Mention was made by Christian Rupp [Ropp] from Ill., about the withdrawal [breaking of fellowship] which took place last fall, October, 1872, between the three eastern ministers, J. K. Yoder, J. P. King, and J. Yoder [on the one hand] and Joseph Stuckey [on the other]. Since there is a misunderstanding in the matter and some believe and say that the three eastern ministers did not withdraw from Stuckey, but only the western ministers, it was considered appropriate to make the matter clear to all, so that each might know just how the matter stands.

At this point John K. Yoder himself took the floor and reported that

> the three above named ministers visited the congregations in the west and when they came to Joseph Stuckey they asked him before they left whether he considered the writer of that poem, entitled "The Good News," to be a brother. J. Stuckey declared that he did and had also gone to communion (*die Einigkeit*)[90] with him. And so the three ministers withdrew from Stuckey in the matter of the kiss and in spiritual fellowship.[91]

Although the three conference leaders had not been formally commissioned to continue the Stuckey investigation, it appears that the 1873 conference was ready to accept and approve what they had done.

Of significance is the fact that the bishop of a congregation neighbor to that of Stuckey took the initiative in asking for help from those eastern brethren. The same then led in making this report on the outcome of their examination of Stuckey to the conference. It is also noteworthy that the withdrawal of Bishop Christian Ropp and his adherents from Stuckey was more clearly established in the minds of the assembled brethren than was the withdrawal of the three eastern ministers. Finally, the action of Ropp's group appears to have been independent of that of the three eastern ministers and may well have preceded that taken by the latter. Perhaps the eastern ministers and the conference should be given less blame for the Stuckey schism than some historians have tended to give.[92] A final irony is that Stuckey, in his own good time, finally did exclude Joseph Yoder from the communion table, although he did not expel him from the congregation.[93]

Stuckey's fellow ministers and his congregation stood with him in this crisis. Two other congregations gave support to Stuckey's North Danvers church at the time, the Washington Prairie and the Weston congregations.[94] By the end of the century the number of congregations under Stuckey's leadership had risen to a dozen.[95]

The conference-related events of 1871-73 generated obvious hard feelings. Nevertheless, the break between Stuckey with his associates, and Christian Ropp and the conference, was not as sharp as one might assume. According to Willard Smith, relations between the ministers of the North Danvers congregation "and the old group continued in various ways." However, the instances he cites are primarily of personal relationships, common participation in funeral services, and occasional attendance at each other's church services.[96] Even the severance of all relations with the conference was delayed by the attendance of John Stahly, one of Stuckey's associates, at the 1873 conference. Perhaps John K. Yoder was pointing his finger at Stahly at that 1873 conference when he remarked that if "the head of the congregation is in agreement with the above mentioned [doctrine of universalism], then one must also withdraw from his co-workers."[97]

The decision of conference to break fellowship with Stuckey was given less than united and sustained support by all Amish Mennonites. Some of those who had attended the conference of 1872, including Bishop Isaac Schmucker of the congregation at the Haw Patch in northern Indiana, had reservations. Schmucker ceased attending the annual conferences after 1872 and, along with his son, Bishop Jonathan P. Smucker, continued to share pulpits and other ministerial functions with Stuckey to the end of the century.[98] In 1878, Joseph Stuckey, along with Isaac Schmucker, "officiated" in the ordination of Isaac's son Jonathan to the office of bishop for the Nappanee, Indiana, congregation.[99]

In the 1880s something of a rapprochement took place between Stuckey and other Amish Mennonite leaders of Indiana and Ohio. Evidence for a restoration of fellowship with the Illinois Amish Mennonites, however, is largely lacking. In 1882 Stuckey visited a number of Amish Mennonite churches in northern Indiana. George Z. Boller of the Haw Patch church near Topeka reported that Stuckey had attended and presumably participated in baptismal services at the Nappanee Amish Mennonite church and in communion services at the Forks church and at Clinton Frame.[100] At the service at Clinton Frame Daniel Johns was ordained to the ministry, again with the participation of Stuckey. From northern Indiana, Stuckey was scheduled to go to Stark County, Ohio, to "do some church services," after which he would return to Indiana "to visit for several weeks and hold meetings in the above named churches." On his return to northern Indiana, he participated in the ordination to the ministry of Jonathan Kurtz of the Haw Patch congregation and preached again at Forks and Clinton Frame.[101]

Two years later Bishop Jonathan P. Smucker of the Amish Mennonite church in Nappanee, Indiana, returned Stuckey's visit by attending baptismal services at the North Danvers church.[102] In 1885 Stuckey again visited "the Amish brethren in Elkhart County, . . . holding meetings in their various places of worship. He was present at a number of communion meetings and conducted the services." From Elkhart County he planned to go on to visit the churches in Champaign and Logan counties in Ohio. A year later he was visiting these same Ohio congregations again.[103]

Then on November 17, 1889, the incredible happened. Bishop John K. Yoder visited Stuckey's North Danvers church and "preached to a large congregation." (Sharing or refusing to share pulpits with other ministers and cooperating in other ministerial duties was exactly what the ecclesiastical term, *dienen*, was all about.) Stuckey himself reported to the *Herald of Truth* that "it afforded us much pleasure to see and hear the brother." Adding to the significance of the occasion was the presence of old Bishop Christian Ropp of the nearby Mackinaw congregation, Yoder's collaborator in the attempted disciplining of Stuckey in 1872. In his report to the *Herald* Stuckey hoped that Yoder's visit might "long be remembered and that much good [might] result therefrom."[104]

The last time previous to 1889 that John K. Yoder had preached in Stuckey's church had been on that momentous occasion on October 10, 1872. Yoder and those traveling with him had told Stuckey—after the evening meeting—that they would no longer maintain fellowship or serve (*dien*, they said) with him. Certainly John K. Yoder understood Amish tradition clearly enough to realize that in preaching in Stuckey's church he was publicly reversing the position which he had taken in 1872. Bishop Yoder's visit to Danvers took place at the very time when the Western District Conference of Amish Mennonites was in the process of organizing without the inclusion of the Stuckey congregations.[105]

Although the years which had followed that rupture in fellowship between Yoder and Stuckey had probably mellowed both of them, nevertheless this gesture of reconciliation seems remarkable. Stuckey's evident pleasure concerning the event suggests that he too considered Yoder's participation in a service at the North Danvers church as a reversal of the "sentence" imposed upon him in October 1872.

For John K. Yoder the date for his return to North Danvers is significant. At that time his home congregation was in the midst of a serious crisis. He was experiencing tremendous pressure to relax the dress standards and to make other concessions to the younger generation in his flock. In less than two months he would concede to most of those demands.[106] That he should leave his community at this time for a trip to Illinois is quite inexplicable. Perhaps he wanted to observe a congregation in which the old standards had already been relaxed for most of two decades.[107]

But the glue of restored relations did not hold very well. In 1890 the Western District Conference of Amish Mennonites was organized without the inclusion of Stuckey's congregations.[108] In 1907-08, after almost a decade of informal meetings, the latter organized independently as the Central Conference of Mennonites.[109]

Probably, given the mind-set of the respective parties, the Stuckey churches and the Western District of Amish Mennonites were incompatible, making "marriage" quite impractical. The Amish Mennonites were moving toward the church polity of the Mennonites. A bishop's oversight of several congregations was becoming more common, and the idea of annual or semiannual district conferences was probably borrowed from the Mennonites. The differences in the dress codes of the two parties—the Stuckey Amish and the Amish Mennonites—were becoming more pronounced. In the decade of the 1880s neither party was prepared to enter into any kind of organic union with the other. Actually, at the same time that Stuckey was participating in ministerial activities in Amish Mennonite congregations, he was also cultivating relationships with the more like-minded congregations of Ben Eicher and Philip Roulet in Iowa, and with the General Conference of Mennonites.[110]

In dealing with the foregoing divisions the conference had become, to some degree in each case, a party to the dispute. In other disagreements, however, that body served primarily as a referee. A quarrel in one of Bishop Jacob Swartzendruber's two congregations in

Johnson County, Iowa, was of·this nature. Although it would eventually take the Old Order Amish track, this Johnson County community had not yet finally withdrawn from the conference. It was asking for the help of conference in a local dispute involving layman Moses Kauffman's behavior in the settlement of an estate.[111] Two consecutive conferences—1866 and 1867—wrestled with the problem and failed. Finally, the assembled ministers recommended "that the Iowa ministers and brethren get together in the name of God and try once more to solve the quarrels." They left the door open for future help from the conference as a last resort.[112] No further word of that quarrel can be found in the conference minutes.

A much larger and longer-standing quarrel with which the conference dealt perennially was that between John Werey of Logan County (Ohio) and Jacob C. Kanagy of neighboring Champaign County. In 1866, when Kanagy moved to Cass County, Missouri, in part to escape from the dispute, Werey continued the quarrel with Kanagy's successor, Full Deacon John P. King. The original issue was evidently that King had been advanced from deacon to full deacon entirely too quickly and that, as a deacon—albeit a full deacon—he was doing entirely too much preaching. King was ordained a bishop later, but that did not end the quarrel. Other differences surfaced. In particular, King tended to be stricter in discipline than Werey, resulting in some attrition from King's congregation to that of Werey.[113]

This Werey-King controversy began in 1860, about two years before the first annual conference, and outlasted the entire series of sixteen annual meetings. The debate in the conferences of 1862-64 concerning the advancement of a deacon to the office of full deacon and the duties attached to the latter office, related in considerable part to John P. King.[114] In 1867-68 the dispute came to the attention of the conference again. A committee was appointed in 1867 to go to Logan County and seek a reconciliation of the two parties. It was apparently unsuccessful.

In 1868, after initial consideration in the open meeting, the ministers stayed over another day to deal with the quarreling in Logan County in closed session. At this deliberation the committee appointed the previous year reported that repentance was necessary before unity could be restored,[115] suggesting considerable stubbornness on one or both sides. Although the minutes do not record the action, an investigating committee was appointed in this closed session. Joseph Stuckey reported to the *Herald of Truth* in September 1868 that he, Samuel Yoder, Shem King, Joseph Augsburger, and John K. Yoder had gone to the Logan-Champaign counties area. There a three-day "examination and consultation was held concerning certain difficulties."[116]

The Werey-King quarrel was a perennial one. At the conference of 1875 it surfaced again. King himself was serving as moderator that year when he proposed again that a committee of conference should "go to Logan County, Ohio, to examine the matters which are to be put right between the two congregations." In 1876 it was reported that no work had been done on the matter. David J. Zook and John Smiley were appointed to "go over there and see whether they are still willing to have the matter adjusted and want to have peace restored."[117]

The conference did not meet in 1877, and finally in 1878, King in his absence was indicated by name to be the center of the problem. A committee was chosen "to examine the letters and also the witnesses concerning J. P. King's situation." This committee reported back shortly that they could not "pronounce him [King] guilty or innocent on the basis of the evidence which we have received." To make a proper judgment a committee should be sent to Logan County to make an on-the-spot investigation.[118] However, no such committee was ever appointed, and there were no more annual conferences. Consequently, as far as conference involvement is concerned, the story of the King-Werey quarrel ends on an unsuccessful and uncertain note.

Finale: The Conference of 1878

Trouble which developed in the mid-1870s within the circle of the three leaders may account for the discontinuance of the annual conferences. From 1866 to 1876 the three bishops, John K. Yoder, Samuel Yoder, and John P. King, had worked together and exercised strong leadership in conference affairs. In 1872 Bishop Isaac Schmucker of the Haw Patch near Topeka, Indiana, had invited the conference to meet with his congregation in 1873.[119] Within months, however, Schmucker and his fellow ministers announced in the *Herold der Wahrheit* that a "majority of the members in this and the surrounding congregations are not in agreement with this, that it should be held here."[120] They wanted another meeting place to be chosen and announced.

But who should pick up the pieces and make new arrangements for the next annual conference? No executive secretary or other official had ever been designated to carry on the business of the conference between sessions. The meeting of 1873 might not have taken place had not two of the three faithful leaders stepped in. A month later John K. Yoder and two of his fellow ministers put a notice in the *Herald of Truth*. They stated that, after consultation with John P. King and with the counsel of other ministers, it was "unanimously decided to have the general conference for 1873 . . . in Wayne County, Ohio."[121] The informal leadership of Yoder and King had supplied what the conference lacked in organization.

Pieces of evidence, some circumstantial and some more direct, indicate that differences which arose among the three leaders in the years 1876-78 account for the discontinuance of the conference following 1878. An exchange of letters in September 1876 between John P. King and John K. Yoder indicates some estrangement between the two bishops. King wrote to Yoder that "I exonerate the brethren so far as the evidence exonerates them, and hold you . . . and all offending persons in patience." The meaning of some parts of these letters, written in German, is obscure. It appears that, as a representative of the conference, Yoder had become involved in the chronic Logan County-Champaign County quarrel. In so doing he had incurred the displeasure of his erstwhile associate in the leadership of the conference.[122]

A news reporter who covered the 1878 conference wrote that "the three men who are pillars in the church (J. K. Yoder and J. P. King of Ohio, and Samuel Yoder of Penn.) disagreed last year, and this prevented the meeting of the Conference." This information apparently came from an interview with John K. Yoder or some other responsible delegate.[123] Certainly this document provides the best clue yet discovered as to why no conference was held in 1877.

The sixteenth, and last, annual Amish general conference assembled on Pentecost Sunday, June 9, 1878, at Eureka, Illinois. John K. Yoder gave "a powerful introductory address," followed by the traditional exposition of the second chapter of Acts by Joseph Slegel from Henry County, Iowa. The day was rainy, so in the afternoon the "sisters and the older people stayed in the meetinghouse." There Christian K. Yoder, of Logan County, Ohio, and brother to John K. Yoder, gave the introductory message, followed by Paul Hershberger. The younger people gathered in the large shed, described earlier, where Joseph Burkey from Bureau County, Illinois, spoke first, followed by an exposition of Acts 3 by John K. Yoder.

When the business meeting convened on Monday morning, Christian Ropp of McLean County, Illinois (with whom John K. Yoder had worked closely in disciplining Stuckey in 1872), opened the meeting. Then, following established procedure, Samuel Yoder explained

Above: Christian Sutter's barn, built in 1868, in which the Diener Versammlung of 1875 met. The host congregation later became known as the Hopedale Mennonite church. This barn has been moved (1989) to the grounds of the Illinois Mennonite Historical and Genealogical Society near Metamora, Illinois, and will be used to house a Mennonite agricultural museum. Picture taken about 1907. (Courtesy of the Illinois Mennonite Historical and Genealogical Society.)

Right: Title page of the Proceedings of the churchwide Diener Versammlung of 1875, held at Hopedale, Illinois. (Courtesy of the Mennonite Historical Society.)

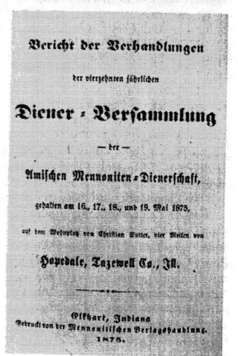

Bericht der Verhandlungen

der vierzehnten jährlichen

Diener = Versammlung

— der —

Amischen Mennoniten = Dienerschaft,

gehalten am 16., 17., 18., und 19. Mai 1875,

auf dem Wohnsitz von Christian Sutter, vier Meilen von

Hopedale, Tazewell Co., Ill.

Elkhart, Indiana
Gedruckt von der Mennonitischen Verlagshandlung.
1875.

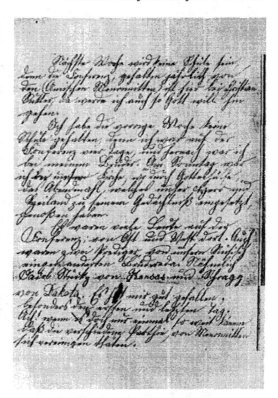

Left: Description of the Amish Mennonite Ministers' Conference of 1875 appearing in the Delavan Times, *May 22, 1875. (Courtesy of the* Delavan Times, *Delavan, Illinois.)*

Right: Schoolteacher and Amish Mennonite layman Christian Erisman's account of the 1875 ministers' meeting at Hopedale, Illinois, as recorded in his Tagebuch *(Diary). He wrote that the yearly Amish Mennonite conference would be held at Christian Sutter's place. After attending the conference, he added that many people had come from the East and the West. He enjoyed all four days of the conference, especially the first and last days, and hoped for the day when all Mennonite groups would be one. (Courtesy of the Archives of the Mennonite Church.)*

"the reason for the meeting." Following Yoder's comments, Ropp nominated John K. Yoder as moderator and then, again following customary procedure, the latter was approved "by a unanimous counsel." John K. Yoder chose the aforementioned Joseph Slegel as his assistant.[124] The hands of John K. Yoder and Samuel Yoder are apparent in these early sessions of the 1878 conference.

The third conference leader of years past, John P. King, did not attend the conference of 1878, suggesting again that he was at odds with John K. Yoder and possibly with other conference leaders. He had missed only three conferences previous to that and had attended all of the immediately preceding five conferences. As indicated earlier, he was the subject of some considerable investigation in 1878.

The most significant order of business taken up in the 1878 conference was a proposal to alter appreciably the structure of the Amish Mennonite church. After Moderator John K. Yoder had spoken a second time about the need for better cooperation in carrying out the rulings of conference, a committee was appointed "to try to find a means and a way" to achieve this goal. The committee reported back already in that same forenoon session that

> all matters should be examined first in the congregation in which they originated, and that all efforts should be made to straighten out the matter there. If it cannot be resolved there, then it should be brought before the *distrikt* meeting in the same *Distrikt* where it occurred, where such is held or will be held, and be brought before the [district] church council. If it cannot be settled there, then it should, with the counsel of the church, be brought before the general *Conferenz.*[125]

The news reporter who wrote "The Amish in Conference" thought that the above proposal arose out of unhappy experiences in the annual meetings. "It had been customary," he wrote,

> for petty differences to find their way into the Annual Conference and to be cast upon it in such an informal and unbusinesslike manner as to create not a little trouble. . . . The first business this year was to erect barriers against this nuisance.[126]

The plan was bold. Handling matters in the local setting first could be regarded as an extended application of Matthew 18:15-20. In any case, the regional or district meetings or conferences of Amish Mennonites spoken of in the recommendation did not exist. Perhaps there were prototypes of such district meetings, such as the Mackinaw ministers' meeting in Illinois or a similar arrangement which may have obtained in Lancaster County. However, the term *district meetings* and the idea of their being adjuncts to the general conference were both new. In the 1880s ad hoc regional meetings would be held, but not until 1888-93 were the three district conferences of Amish Mennonites organized.

The minutes of the 1878 conference provide no hint that the conference was about to expire. Rather, the assembled ministers were engaged in making plans for a new day in the Amish Mennonite church. In the last session on Wednesday afternoon John K. Yoder "explained . . . very clearly to everyone's satisfaction" how the conference would function in the future under the proposed plan of reorganization.[127] A report of the conference which appeared two months later in the *Herald of Truth* was also upbeat, with no hint that the conference was dead.[128]

Probably the dissolution of the informal leadership team of Yoder, Yoder, and King was the immediate cause of the demise of the conference. Friction within this trio had already led to the failure of the conference to meet in 1877. By several indications, that trouble had intensified by the time of the 1878 conference.[129] Perhaps J. S. Hartzler and Daniel Kauffman, writing in 1905, knew more than they were telling. They wrote that "the principal reason for abandoning this conference was a lack of unity among the brotherhood."[130] One gets the impression that, because of the collapse of the leadership trio, John K. Yoder was carrying, or attempting to carry, the entire load of the conference on his own shoulders. When the writer of "The Amish in Conference" said that "the leading missionary or evangelist of the [Amish Mennonite] church is elder J. K. Yoder," he may have unwittingly affirmed this impression.

The annual Amish general conference was not highly institutionalized. Its operation was based on no constitution and even its bylaws had to be reenacted each year. No permanent secretariat carried on its business between sessions. The conference was a step removed, however, from the earlier ad hoc, unstructured, and unscheduled local and regional conferences. It was as great an addition to the polity of the Amish Mennonites as could be tolerated by an emerging church whose people brought with them a strong tradition of congregationalism. In spite of its weaknesses, the conference was a major force in the formation of the church which M. S. Steiner listed as Amish Mennonite in his 1905 directory of Mennonite groups.[131] The conference had forged this church, however, not so much by drawing a circle which included all Amish groups—an admittedly impossible task—but by lopping off groups which would not or could not conform to the standards of the majority, and then building a fence around the nucleus which remained.

Hartzler and Kauffman wrote that "much good was accomplished through these annual meetings,"[132] the Amish conferences of 1862-78. They probably had in mind this process of forming a church and enclosing it within well-defined boundaries. Not all appraisers of these conferences came to the same conclusion. In 1899 an anonymous writer, a "Constant Reader" of the *Herald of Truth*, reflected on these meetings of an earlier era. He wrote that

> when in 1862 our Amish Mennonite brethren held their first General Conference, your humble servant, who was then a young man of twenty-four years, was an enthusiastic friend of the General Conference. . . . I was a friend of the conference because I longed for more light to be let into our church from God, and for a more general union, more love and life in our hearts, and more active work in the white harvest fields around us. But alas! my bright hopes of development and progress in our churches were blasted. The good for which I hoped did not appear, but instead of the good which might have been there was failure. There was a tendency to assume authority that did not belong to the conference; to do things which did not come within its jurisdiction. The result was dissatisfaction with some, alienation with others, and finally a collapse of the General Conference after it had been held about eighteen years.
>
> Many dear brethren took part in the conference and far be it from me to say anything harsh or unkind of them. If there was any lack of charity and of humble whole-souled dependence on God, and also an undue love of authority on the part of others, let it only be sadly and reluctantly named as a lesson for us that we do not fall into the same snares. . . .
>
> In 1866 [after the conservatives had withdrawn from the conference] some rules of order were adopted, the second of which stated that the conference should aim to establish ourselves upon the foundation laid in God's Word, and *not make laws* (*Gesetze*) or unevangelical decisions (*unevangelische Beschlüsse*). It seems fair to me to take these words as *disclaiming all legislative function* on the part of the conference. Yet probably, without noticing the inconsistency, the conference the very next year (1867) adopted two additional rules of order *which in effect claimed legislative authority for the conference over the churches.*
>
> This bold and radical assumption of mandatory authority over the churches without their consent, by which the decisions and enactments of former conferences were to be enforced (*in Kraft gesetzt*) in the churches without first submitting them to the churches for their acceptance or rejection, produced a deep and widespread feeling of indignation throughout the brotherhood, and henceforth as attempts were made to exercise mandatory authority over the churches, the indignation increased and the collapse of the conference was only a question of time.[133]

Obviously the evaluation of the conference by "Constant Reader" is quite opposite to that of Hartzler and Kauffman. One's position on this question will quite certainly be determined by one's understanding of the nature of the church. Perhaps it is sufficient to observe once more that the conferences of 1862-78 mothered the Amish Mennonite church in its infancy.

Amish, Amish Mennonites, and Mennonites

11

Amish Mennonites

A New Church

The printed minutes of those first four annual Amish ministers'
conferences, 1862-65, bore the title, *Verhandlungen der Diener-
Versammlung der Deutschen Täufer oder Amischen Mennoniten* (Proceedings of the Ministers' Meeting of the German [Ana]baptists or
Amish Mennonites). For the years thereafter the term *German
[Ana]baptist* was dropped, but *Amish Mennonite* was retained for the
entire series. As is implied by Harold S. Bender, *Amish Mennonite* was
and is the most appropriate name for the Mennonites who had followed Jacob Ammann in the division of the 1690s back in Europe.[1]

It follows that those responsible for the printing of the minutes of
these conferences used the proper term to identify the church under
the auspices of which the meetings were held. However, with the withdrawal of the conservatives following the 1865 conference, the continued use of this name is problematic. After 1865, for about two
decades, the terms *Amish, Amish Mennonite, Old Amish Mennonite*, and
Old Amish were used with little precision. Commonly those who
remained under the umbrella of the annual conference and those who
later affiliated with that group were called Amish (sometimes spelled
O-m-i-s-h) Mennonites, but on occasion they were called Old Amish
Mennonites, or simply Amish.[2] For many years the followers of Joseph
Stuckey were called Stuckey Amish, and the followers of Henry Egli
were called Egli Amish.

The church which came to be called Amish Mennonite got its
name primarily from those annual conferences out of which the new
body of believers was born, the Amish Mennonite ministers' meetings.
The name became as official as possible, given such a loose structure,
when three district conferences were organized in the five-year period
from 1888 to 1893—the Western, the Indiana-Michigan, and the Eastern districts—all bearing the name Amish Mennonite. In the first *Men-*

nonite Yearbook and Directory, compiler M. S. Steiner accepted this nomenclature. He found it convenient to classify the congregations and conferences which had their roots in those annual conferences of 1866-78 as Amish Mennonites. A few congregations which had not joined an Amish Mennonite conference were listed as "Amish Mennonite Churches (Conservative)."[3]

Church Accretions and Church Structure

In the 1870s and 1880s new divisions in three additional Amish communities provided significant accretions to the emerging Amish Mennonite church. These separations occurred on the fringes of that belt of established Amish communities stretching from eastern Pennsylvania to Iowa. They were on the same issues which had divided the traditionalists and the change-minded in the first four annual conferences. It therefore is not unrealistic to think of them as ripples or waves emanating from the Great Schism of the 1860s.

The Amish congregations of Lancaster County had not been untouched by the divisions of the 1860s to the West. These congregations, and particularly the Lancaster bishops, exercised considerable influence over some of the western congregations and regions in which separations were occurring. In Mifflin County some of the Amish of the Kishacoquillas Valley could be said to have had a primary allegiance to the "mother church" in Lancaster County. Others preferred a westward orientation, particularly with the Wayne County or Wooster congregation in Ohio. In nearby Union County the two factions of that fragile Amish community in Buffalo Valley were torn in the same two directions. In Lancaster County, however, actual schism had been avoided or, more accurately, postponed.

From the first, representation from Lancaster County and environs in the annual conferences had been extremely weak. No bishops from the area ever attended. Of the ten ordained men who attended, eight went only once, a ninth twice, and even Deacon John Stoltzfus was present at only four meetings. Most significant of all, not a single minister from Lancaster County attended any conference after 1868. Probably in that year, what the bishops had been opposing—attendance of their ministers as delegates to the annual conference—was forbidden.

Evidence that 1868 was a crucial year in Lancaster County Amish church affairs may be found in the correspondence of Amish leaders of Pennsylvania. Late in 1868 Deacon Christian Stoltzfus of Union County wrote to his brother, Deacon John Stoltzfus. He asked how the

Lancaster County ministry could have had the temerity to break off fellowship with all churches west of the Susquehanna River. How could he, John, vote for such a ruling against his own blood brother?[4] In a letter to Abraham Peachey, which reads like a reply to the Christian Stoltzfus inquiry, John flinched. He would like to forget the whole thing if he could. He had voted for breaking fellowship with all western churches in order to avoid division in Lancaster County.[5] The laity of the five Lancaster County congregations rejected this decision. Nevertheless, no ministers, not even Deacon John Stoltzfus, attended any of the annual conferences thereafter. It appears that the ministers of Lancaster County were able to implement their decision without the support of their congregations, merely by mutual agreement among themselves.

Until 1868 Bishop Christian Ummel and the other ministers of the Lower Pequea and Conestoga congregations on the eastern edge of Lancaster County were about equally divided between liberals and conservatives. However, they were able to maintain a semblance of unity among themselves. They tried to maintain normal relations with their more conservative ministering brothers in the three other Lancaster County Amish congregations immediately to the west of them—and also with the liberal Amish congregations west of the Susquehanna River.

In 1864 the Conestoga and Lower Pequea ministers stood together in supporting the ordination of Full Deacon Samuel Yoder as bishop—likely in the face of some opposition from the other Lancaster congregations.[6] In 1868 the conservative ministers of these two congregations, or at least Bishop Ummel, disregarded their unease and consented to the ordination of Deacon John Stoltzfus' son Gideon as a minister in the Lower Pequea congregation. They did this in spite of knowing that he had parted his hair on the side and that his avowed intention was to maintain fellowship with the western liberals.

The issue over which the Lancaster County Amish divided was just that: Should they maintain fellowship with the change-minded ministers and congregations to the west? In addition to this dispute, agitation for the construction and use of a meetinghouse for worship services may have contributed to the division in the Conestoga congregation. In neither congregation, Lower Pequea or Conestoga, was there any appreciable agitation in favor of stream baptism or the introduction of Sunday schools, or any related innovations. Already in 1869 Shem Zook had responded to the discouraging reports about conditions in the Lancaster County congregations which Deacon John

Stoltzfus of the Lower Pequea congregation had relayed to him. Zook asked Stoltzfus whether he thought the congregations in Lancaster County would "be able to continue together."[7]

By 1870 the strife had become so sharp that communion could not be observed in either the Conestoga or the Lower Pequea congregation. This condition continued from year to year until the final separation in 1876-77. Although Deacon Stoltzfus moved to Knox County, Tennessee, in 1872, he did not remove himself from the tangle of events back in Lancaster County. He returned to his former home community for several months each summer and became deeply involved in the negotiations—more accurately, the failure of negotiations—which preceded the final division in both congregations.[8]

Probably the final break in the Lower Pequea congregation in the late fall of 1876 was precipitated by the silencing of Gideon Stoltzfus. The charge against him was that he associated too closely with some of the more change-minded western ministers. About two-thirds of the congregation, seventy-five members, followed Gideon and thereafter met separately as a congregation. In the Conestoga congregation one of those traditional ad hoc ministers' meetings met on March 8, 1877, in a final effort at reconciliation, only to fail after a two-day consultation.

John M. Mast, one of several lay persons allowed to attend a part of that meeting, later recounted the steps leading to that futile consultation as well as the events which followed it. One Sunday morning, Mast wrote, Minister "Groffdale" John Stoltzfus announced to the congregation

> that if ower Preachers would not withdraw from all the Preachers that had churches to worship in and sunday schools and Baptise in watter, they could not go along with us. That did not take with us as god had not forBid Eney of that and we had not Enney of the three [forbidden practices] at that time. . . . The Konferance [the two-day consultation mentioned above] did not amount to enething. [On] June 24, 1877 . . . Samuel Yoder from Mifflin County, Pa., and John Stoltzfus from Tennessee held communion for us and ordained John P. Mast for Bishop by A vote. He had all the votes except the Eight famles wich did not go with the Conestoga meatting. . . . So October 28th, 1877, Moses Hartz withdrew from us and got John [K.] Stoltzfus of Milcreeke to hold communion and startedt A Millcreeke meatting hear in Conestoga with a number of Eight famles.[9]

The ordination of Mast without the presence or consent of Bishop Ummel was, of course, a forthright rejection of the latter's authority. The visiting bishop, Samuel Yoder, will be recognized as one of the leaders in the annual conferences of 1866-78.[10] In later years, although both of these Lancaster County congregations identified themselves as Amish Mennonite, the relationship of the Millwood congregation (the name adopted by the Lower Pequea liberals) with the Eastern Amish Mennonite Conference was much more tenuous than that of the Conestoga church.[11] The conservative minority in this division, the Conestoga Old Order congregation, grew and was divided into two districts in 1931.[12]

A few years later, in the first half of the decade of the 1880s, the ranks of the Amish Mennonites were augmented again by a division in the Amish congregations in Johnson County, Iowa. This settlement, composed largely of migrants from Somerset County, Pennsylvania, had been served from 1851 to 1868 by Bishop Jacob Swartzendruber. He was succeeded by Abner Yoder, already ordained a bishop in Somerset County before he moved to Iowa in 1866. By 1877 the Johnson County settlement had grown to four congregations.[13]

This Amish settlement in Johnson County should probably be categorized as conservative, although the classification is not neat or exact. In contrast to the conservatives elsewhere, the Amish in this area had maintained relations with the annual conference until at least 1872. Bishop Swartzendruber's son Frederick, along with newly arrived Abner Yoder, had attended the conference of 1866. And the bishop himself had asked for help from the conferences of 1866 and 1867 in solving a congregational squabble.[14] In 1871 Abner Yoder, the remaining bishop after Jacob Swartzendruber's death, had accepted appointment to a committee of conference to examine the circumstances relative to Joseph Stuckey's congregation.[15] In the early 1870s Sunday schools were organized in both of the two Johnson County congregations then in existence.

Johnson County, however, was not an island. An early cause of dissatisfaction was not unlike that which had caused dissension in Lancaster County. Visiting ministers from more liberal Amish Mennonite churches were not allowed "to preach when they visited friends and relatives in that settlement."[16] As a consequence some families began to meet separately. For a time, 1878-79, some of these families actually transferred their membership to the Sugar Creek congregation, two counties southward. Following that impossible arrangement, Preacher Sebastian Gerig of Sugar Creek went to Johnson County occasionally to preach for the group. This action caused much resentment against him on the part of the conservative ministers of that community.

One member of this dissident group in Johnson County was Noah

Troyer. At some point, probably in the late 1870s, this unusual Amish-man had refused to allow his name to be entered in the lot for minister because he could not support some of the regulations of the church. Later two of his sons withdrew from the baptismal instruction class only shortly before they were to be baptized.[17] Both events caused resentment on the part of the ministers and the congregation. To these circumstances was added a third. In 1878 Troyer, who had declined to allow his name to be entered in the lot for minister, began to preach in his sleep. Soon large crowds were attending these nightly exhortations by an unordained Amishman. Apparently without malicious intent, Troyer was challenging the authority of his church. Perhaps for this reason the Amish historian, Samuel D. Guengerich, placed the major blame for the division in the Johnson County congregations on this man.[18]

Noah Troyer is tied to the Johnson County division by another thread. In 1884 his brother-in-law, Preacher Christian Werey of the Pretty Prairie Amish Mennonite congregation in Lagrange County, Indiana, moved to Johnson County, Iowa.[19] In Indiana, Werey had been affiliated with the change-minded Amish Mennonites. In spite of this, he first attended services in Iowa with the Old Order Amish, with the intention of joining that group. He may have made this attempt to join with the conservatives because of his friendship with, and possibly his admiration for, the latter's senior bishop Abner Yoder.[20]

Werey did not take it kindly when the Amish ministers did not ask him to preach because he had a buggy with a folding top and wore a raincoat. He was not inclined to give up these conveniences because they protected his health. When the seceding members (including Noah Troyer), still without a minister, heard of Werey's experience, they proposed that he preach for them. Werey accepted and the following year was ordained bishop of the congregation by Joseph Birky, Amish Mennonite bishop from Tiskilwa, Illinois, and Jonathan Smucker of Nappanee, Indiana. A meetinghouse was built in 1889.[21]

Also in the 1880s the five Amish congregations in Ontario, Canada, initiated a slow-paced transition to Amish Mennonite with the building of meetinghouses. Conservative dissidents in the Wellesley and the Mornington congregations rejected this step and formed a "house Amish" congregation, soon divided into two districts. In the case of the change-minded faction of the Wellesley congregation, the shift to the use of a meetinghouse for church services was facilitated by gathering in the congregation's "funeral chapel." By 1900 other changes had been or were occurring, such as the departure from the use of the *Ausbund*, followed by the introduction of four-part singing, evening services, and Sunday schools. The *Mutze*, or frock-tailed coat, and hooks and eyes fell into disuse.[22]

With the demise of the annual conferences in 1878, the earlier pattern of congregational polity again obtained for those congregations which had accepted in some measure the authority of conference. This kind of autonomy was traditional and normal for an Amish congregation. What was new was the infinite variety of Amish Mennonite congregations. No longer was there agreement on the use of hooks and eyes, the importance of unparted hair, the use of slow hymn tunes, what constituted the new birth, when the ban and shunning should be applied, and still other issues. In the face of these discordant tendencies, the Amish Mennonite leaders of the 1880s, with their congregations, fumbled, regrouped, and then began to devise an organizational structure. They set up denominational fences that would include the middle-of-the-road Amish Mennonites, but would deliberately exclude those who had departed too far in the direction of "worldly popular religion."

Speakers at that last annual conference in 1878 had spoken of *distrikt* conferences as though they already existed and were functioning. The term was new and such conferences are not known to have existed. One must conclude that these leaders were recommending the establishment of regional assemblies, probably patterned after the existing conferences of the Mennonite Church. If the advocates of these district conferences expected that they could be organized quickly and would provide regional support for a continuing general conference, as the records suggest, they were mistaken. The formal structuring of district or regional conferences required a decade.

Much of the fumbling and regrouping of the 1880s consisted of regional ad hoc ministers' meetings, called in part to resolve common problems, but sometimes also with the intent of setting up a continuing organization.[23] Preliminary to the establishment of the Western District Amish Mennonite Conference (the entire area west of Indiana and Michigan), a number of meetings were called. These gatherings were held in Illinois (1882); in Cass County, Missouri (1883); and in Henry County, Iowa (1884 and 1887). At the 1884 meeting, plans for yearly meetings were finalized. Although such meetings were held thereafter, the Western District Conference was not formally organized until 1890 at Sycamore Grove, Cass County, Missouri.[24]

The Indiana-Michigan Amish Mennonite District Conference was the first of the three district conferences to be organized. The first meeting took place in the spring of 1888 at the Haw Patch church (Maple Grove), near Topeka. Congregations represented at that meeting were Nappanee, Clinton (Frame), Forks, Haw Patch, and Pretty Prairie (several miles north of Lagrange). Unrepresented were Barker Street, the Townline, and the Howard County–Miami County congregations. Barker Street was in Michigan, just across the state line north of Bristol, Indiana. Bishop Joseph Yoder of that congregation had moved away, leaving the congregation without a minister. Under the leadership of the recently ordained Jonathan J. Troyer, the Townline church may have already begun to resist the drift away from the traditional Amish lifestyle so evident in other Amish Mennonite congregations. Distance may help to explain why the Howard-Miami congregation was not represented.

The senior bishop of the host congregation at the Haw Patch, Isaac Schmucker, was not in attendance, possibly because of the infirmities of old age. Isaac's son, Bishop Jonathan P. Smucker of Nappanee, Indiana, was chosen "President" of the conference, which office he also held at the second meeting in 1889. The "Church News" section of the *Herald of Truth* commented on this first Indiana-Michigan Conference: "There was one noticeable feature ... that should characterize every conference: namely, the feelings and opinions of every member received the attention and consideration of all the other members, and especially by the president."[25]

The Eastern Amish Mennonite Conference became a reality in much the same way as did the Western Conference. Already in 1883 "the district conference of Amish Ministers [was] held in Wayne County, Ohio, [on] March 22, 23, 1883." Just as the use of the term *Distrikt* in the minutes of the 1878 annual conference seems ambiguous, so also does *district* as employed in this record of the 1883 conference in Wayne County. The district is not named. In attendance at this conference were representatives from Mifflin and Lawrence counties in Pennsylvania, from most of the Amish Mennonite congregations in Ohio, and from Barker Street in Michigan and Townline in Lagrange County, Indiana.

Of the twenty-four ordained brethren who participated, nineteen had attended one or more of the annual conferences, including Samuel Yoder, John K. Yoder, and John P. King. The roster of this eastern district conference and also the adopted regulations remind one of the earlier annual conferences. Members who conformed to worldly styles "and all else which contribute to outward adornment and ornamentation" and those who owned musical instruments were to be disciplined or punished (*bestrafen*).[26]

Another "District conférence" of Amish Mennonites was held in May 1888 at the South Union church in Logan County, Ohio.[27] In July 1890 M. S. Steiner reported to the *Herald of Truth* that the "eastern Amish conference" had been held in Lawrence County in the preceding April. The permanent organization of the Eastern Amish Mennonite Conference was finally accomplished at the 1893 meeting.[28]

Although these three Amish Mennonite district conferences were not joined together organically, they nevertheless were tied together by informal arrangements. Chief were the "visitation rights" which entitled—more correctly, encouraged—ordained men of one district to attend and participate fully in the deliberations of one of the other districts. Thus in 1893 Jonathan P. Smucker of Nappanee, Indiana, and Daniel J. (D. J.) Johns of Goshen, Indiana, served as moderator and assistant moderator, respectively, of the first Eastern District Conference. Two other ministers from Indiana, as well as two ministers from the Western District, also attended and evidently participated in the deliberations.

The following year Smucker again served as moderator and Sebastian Gerig of Iowa was his assistant. Six of the first seven moderators of the Eastern District Conferences came from Indiana: Jonathan P. Smucker served twice in that capacity, D. J. Johns three times, and Jonathan Kurtz once.[29] Similarly, John K. Yoder served as moderator for the Western District in 1891 and Jonathan P. Smucker served in the same office in 1893 and 1895. D. J. Johns was four times assistant moderator in the first ten years of the Western Conference.[30] In addition to those who held office, most of these district conferences of the 1890s were attended by a sprinkling of visiting ministers. Such reciprocity no doubt contributed to interdistrict cooperation and unity.

There was continuing Amish skepticism concerning a permanent conference structure. It therefore is not surprising that the first few district conferences "were marked for their extreme caution," as Hartzler and Kauffman characterized the early years, particularly of the Western District Conference.[31] This depiction of the beginnings of these conferences, however, may be slightly understated as it applied to the Indiana-Michigan Conference. In its second annual meeting (1889), it claimed "the right," after careful instruction and admonition to the offending minister, "to call into question any bishop, minister or deacon in any of the churches represented by this conference if he fails to lead his church according to the Gospel."[32]

In 1891 Moderator D. J. Johns took a softer position on the authority of conference, saying that the purpose of conference "was not to make commandments but to confer ideas and to get a better understanding of the Word of God and to work in greater harmony for the welfare of the several churches."[33] In 1892 the Silver Street group separated from the Clinton (Frame) congregation. In response, the Indiana-Michigan Conference "Resolved That those who become disobedient to the church of which any bishop, connected with this Conference has the oversight, cannot be owned as a part of this Conference."[34]

The Indiana-Michigan Amish Mennonite Conference and the Indiana-Michigan Mennonite Church Conference united in 1916. Hence, it is appropriate to examine the position taken by the latter body in the 1890s on the authority of conference. The first question presented to the Mennonite ministerial body assembled at the Holdeman Church near Wakarusa in 1896 was: "What is Conference? What is its object? Wherein lies the governing or ruling power, and who should obey the decisions?" "The Church," replied the ministers, "through God, is the ruling power. Decisions of conference are valid and can be enforced only when they are accepted by the Church as a body. They should be obeyed by all members, first, by the [minister-delegate] members of conference which made the decisions, and then by the body which accepts them."

Later in that same conference it was agreed that

> it is the duty of ministers to yield to the decisions of conference and also maintain these decisions among the laity. Christ is the head of the Church and has given the authority of Church Government to the Church. Conference is the representative of this authority and gives expression to the faith and practices taught in the Bible and maintained by the Church. Therefore, all members, including ministers, should be subject to the decisions of conference.[35]

The authority of conference was one of the issues in the schism of 1923-24 among the Mennonites and Amish Mennonites in Indiana and Ohio. In retrospect, this bold 1896 declaration on that subject carries ominous significance.

Maintaining the Amish Heritage—With Modifications

As indicated earlier, many of those leaders who began to deviate from the traditional Amish *Ordnung* in the third quarter of the nineteenth century wanted only a few changes. Although these change-minded leaders did not always agree among themselves as to what changes should be made, the majority were in sufficient accord to permit the formation of the Amish Mennonite church.

Judging by his letter "from One Full Minister to Another Full Minister," Solomon K. Beiler would have been satisfied with the adoption of stream baptism and an enlarged role for full deacons in the Sunday morning services. Beiler made a forceful attack on the "old customs." However, those paying attention may have heard more than he intended to say. The term "old customs" could well have been applied to other practices in addition to those of house baptism and a limited role for full deacons.[36] From the traditionalist point of view, Solomon Beiler and his kind had opened up Pandora's box.

In about 1890 Old Order Amishman and historian Samuel D. Guengerich was chronicling the history of the change-oriented congregation at Sugar Creek, Iowa. He wrote that the leaders were bowing to the wishes of the majority of the congregation, permitting some considerable deviation from the "ordinances and customs." All this seemed to avail nothing, for "the more concessions given, the more is wanted."[37] Old Order Amishman John (Hansi) Borntreger in 1907 recalled the split of 1854-57 in the congregations of northern Indiana. His opinion was that Bishop Jonas D. Troyer "allowed pride to enter, so that in a short time a great change became evident."[38] The reference to *pride* probably was a general description of the trend toward personal adornment and decorative house furnishings.

David A. Troyer (Treyer) in 1898 chronicled the division of 1861 in the Holmes County–Wayne County area. He dramatically described in detail the drift in the liberal congregations which followed the schism. Troyer said that one thing led to another. He was correct in many of his observations, including his comment that shunning soon came into disuse. From his point of view he felt justified in charging that "pride, splendor and haughtiness took the upper hand."[39]

In terms of the Ordnung, these evaluations by Old Order Amishmen were essentially correct. Buttons were accepted by the Illinois congregations already in the 1870s, albeit not without some struggle.[40] In Indiana and Ohio the use of buttons was resisted until the late 1880s.[41] Shingled hair for men and the trimming of beards followed a similar time schedule. Photographs and the use of musical instruments in the homes were resisted to the end of the century, although the church was unable to prevent their widespread appearance.[42] The many extant photographs of the 1880s and the 1890s of families and young people's groups testify explicitly to the transformation which was taking place in the personal appearance of Amish Mennonite men and women.

Young people of the Clinton Frame Amish Mennonite congregation, Goshen, Indiana, about 1893, showing no vestage of Amish garb. (Courtesy of the Archives of the Mennonite Church.)

A picture of twenty-seven young people of the Clinton Frame Amish Mennonite church located five miles east of Goshen, Indiana, taken in about 1893, included Bishop Daniel J. Johns's son Elmer. In evidence among the men are buttons, shingled and parted hair, watch chains, lapel coats, and turned-down shirt collars. Coverings and the traditional aprons for the women are conspicuous by their absence. The dress of the women is characterized by puffed sleeves, separate skirts and blouses, wide belts with prominent buckles, neckerchiefs tied prominently or small brooches at the neck, a couple of tight bodices, and a variety of modest hair styles. Says Editor Melvin Gingerich: "There is no evidence of the Mennonite [more correctly, Amish Mennonite] garb in this picture, although the excesses of stylish clothing are not in evidence."[43] Significant was the new emphasis on separation from the world and on some symbol of recognition (*Kennzeichen*) in one's clothing or personal appearance, in contrast to the earlier stress on simplicity and modesty.[44]

Marriage outside the denomination came to be accepted reluctantly, but even then only if the spouse was of a nonresistant denomination. According to a minute' of the Western District Conference of 1899, however, marriage to someone not a member of such a denomination was to be studied carefully before disciplinary action was to be taken.[45]

The Ordnung of the Amish church related primarily to the traditional standards of the simple lifestyle required of a member. The Discipline of 1865 drawn up in Holmes County, Ohio, was an attempt to codify the Ordnung.[46] A present-day Old Order Amish minister in Lancaster County states that the primary purpose of the Ordnung is to resist change, that is, concessions to worldliness.[47] Clearly, among the Amish Mennonites the very principle of Ordnung was breaking down. The "ordering" of the lifestyle of a congregation and its members had become a dynamic process rather than a holding pattern. The dynamic of change lay with the laity, and the ministry gave reluctant approval to one fait accompli after another.

The Old Order Amish view of this process, as expressed by John (Hansi) Borntreger and David A. Troyer, has already been indicated. David Luthy, Amish historian, has sharpened the distinction between the Amish and the Amish Mennonite pattern of church discipline by noting that

> "Admonish" [as contrasted with *discipline*] is the key word in understanding the Amish Mennonite and Mennonite pattern of drifting. Conference "resolutions" and "admonishment" lacked the teeth that the Old Order "discipline" had. Today it constitutes the vast gulf between the Old Order Amish and the Mennonites with whom the Amish Mennonites united.[48]

Judged by twentieth-century standards, however, the Amish Mennonites retained some rather rigid regulations and considerable severity in their disciplinary procedures. A resolution of 1889 of the Indiana-Michigan Amish Mennonite Conference was designed to keep members from false doctrines and especially from the influence of the worldly churches. It urged that the ministry should not only admonish and warn but also respond by "enforcing discipline and keeping the church clean of these innovations, not simply preaching against them."[49] As heretofore, if members persisted in minor offenses in the face of congregational disapproval, those deviances became gross sins of disobedience.[50] A contributor to the *Herold der Wahrheit* in 1867 compared those stubborn and stiffnecked (*Hartnäckiger und Halsstarriger*) persons who were "unwilling to confess their [lesser] transgressions before the church" to a "small wound, [which], if it is not healed it can kill the entire body [of believers]. And if a small wound has become large and deadly through the application of a mild [ineffective] and weak poultice, then one must turn to stronger and more biting (*fressende*) means; and this means is the ban and shunning."[51]

Ministers continued to use the biblical metaphor of the unfruitful vine which should be cut off from the vine stem as a biblical directive for the exercise of the ban and shunning, although with less frequency. It was usually accompanied by admonitions to exercise patience with offenders.[52] Certainly Amish Mennonites would have agreed with a decision made in 1898 by the Indiana-Michigan Mennonite Conference concerning a member who was guilty of adultery. Should such "be expelled or may he simply confess and be retained as a member?" The assembled ministers answered that "on account of the greatness of [the] sin, and the danger of such persons not seeing their real condition, we advise that such persons be [temporarily] expelled."[53]

Shunning as the ultimate recourse in church discipline was discontinued only by degrees and was never rejected per se by any Amish Mennonite conference.[54] The biblical basis for the discipline of shunning had never been questioned in any of those annual conferences of 1862-78. At the 1872 conference Moderator John P. King declared emphatically that "he considered avoidance as important as baptism, for without avoidance the ban is of no use."[55] Shunning continued to be thought of, in part, as punishment and also a procedure to bring sinners to repentance. This is indicated by a conclusion reached in the annual conference of 1874 to the effect that one could not be put in the ban "and again on the same day be taken out of it,"[56] suggesting that instantaneous expressions of repentance on the part of the one shunned should not immediately cancel the penalty.

However, the practice of shunning the disobedient and the gross sinners was on the way out. No doubt John F. Funk's *Herald of Truth* and *Herold der Wahrheit* contributed appreciably to this outcome. Already in the first year of those two papers "A Brother" requested the "true meaning of 1 Corinthians 5:9, 10, 11," one of the principal passages of Scripture used in support of shunning.[57] The responses to this question as printed in these papers were varied. On this subject, Funk exercised his editorial policy of allowing the expression of differing points of view in his papers. He printed both articles which took a rigid position in support of shunning and those which would ease the stringency traditionally practiced in the application of this discipline.

What can not certainly be determined in every case is whether the responses which Funk received were written by Mennonites or by Amish Mennonites. In any case one may be sure that the many Amish

Mennonites who were reading Funk's papers took notice of those responses which called for less-strict social avoidance than that dictated by Amish tradition. One such reply urged that only the grossest of sinners should be avoided.[58] Another suggested that shunning of banned persons need not be observed in unplanned or chance meetings at mealtime, nor against those who have joined some other church and have reformed, and certainly not between wife and husband.[59] In March 1865 Funk closed the dialogue in an editorial which gave support to this less-stringent application of avoidance.[60]

The Old Order Amish critics of the Amish Mennonites were correct in charging that the latter seldom resorted to shunning. However, a few instances of such shunning may be noted. The shunning of Bishop John K. Yoder's nephew, Ezra Yoder, is perhaps the best known of all such cases and illustrates how the administering of discipline in the form of shunning could be fraught with much pain and misunderstanding.[61] Ezra later wrote a gracious letter admitting some excessive arrogance on his part and seeking a lifting of the ban so that he could visit his relatives in the Oak Grove church without hindrance. The records do not indicate that the bishop ever relented. It is thought that the last instance of shunning in Bishop Yoder's Oak Grove congregation occurred in about 1890 with the excommunication of C. J. Miller and his wife because of their association with a "health cult that condoned rather crude social irregularities."[62]

In June 1888 Bishop Jonathan P. Smucker, was visiting another Oak Grove Amish Mennonite congregation—this one in Champaign County, Ohio. "The avoidance of Yoder and Fett was taken up."[63] Whether shunning had already been imposed on these persons or was merely under consideration at the time of Smucker's visit is not clear. The full identity of "Yoder and Fett" has not been determined. A rare instance of shunning, probably in the 1890s, occurred in the Conestoga Amish Mennonite congregation on the northeast border of Lancaster County. In this case a young man was brought to repentance and restored to the church.[64]

As the Amish Mennonites entered the last two decades of the century, contacts and areas of cooperation with the Mennonite Church multiplied. Not only did articles on the subject of shunning continue to appear in Funk's periodicals but, as the leaders of the two denominations attended each other's conferences and began to exchange ministerial services, this topic of necessity became a subject of discussion. Amish Mennonite ministers sat in the Mennonite conferences, and some no doubt were influenced by the freedom of opinion allowed to individuals on this subject.[65] Shunning, it will be recalled, was the largest issue between Jacob Ammann and his opponents in the Amish division of the 1690s. Now this centuries-old difference would need to be repaired if complete reconciliation between the Mennonites and the Amish Mennonites was to be realized.

The earliest outright repudiation of shunning by an Amish Mennonite that has been found is that made in 1885 by layman Jonathan K. Zook of Cass County, Missouri. He was a frequent contributor to the *Herald of Truth*. Zook argued that Christ associated equally with expelled brethren as well as Gentiles. Consequently, he reasoned, "we cannot otherwise but conclude, in order not to conflict with the precepts of Christ . . . that they [Scriptures used to support shunning in temporal affairs] allude to spiritual affairs only [exclusion from the communion table]."[66]

Several years later Funk allowed his young apprentice J. H. (presumably John Horsch) to insert an article in the *Herold der Wahrheit* entitled "Ist unsere Gemeine heute in gutem Zustande?" (Is Our Church Today in Good Condition?) In noting that the Mennonites and Amish were split into so many divisions, he referred particularly to differences in the practice of shunning. He addressed those who were clinging tightly to the teachings of Menno Simons and of some of the other early Anabaptist leaders concerning avoidance. "Neither [Hans] Denk nor Menno [Simons] should be our foundation, but rather Jesus Christ." So if "today we consider that on the basis of the teachings of Jesus Christ, Menno Simon's understanding of shunning was too sharp and not correct, then it is our responsibility not to apply shunning as stringently as Menno would have it." Horsch became even more adamant: "Only if we set Menno over Christ," he said, "may we practice the strenuous shunning."[67]

By the turn of the century shunning (but not excommunication) had been completely abandoned by the Amish Mennonites.[68] According to Hartzler and Kauffman, this removed the one difference of any substance between them and the Mennonite Church.[69] Photographs, fire insurance, and other innovations had come into the church through their widespread use, without ecclesiastical approval. Just so shunning had left the church through disuse, again without any formal reversal of church policy.[70]

Changes in Worship and Lifestyle

Some of the changes related to congregational structure and public worship in Amish Mennonite congregations have already been identified and described. Simply by discontinuing the ordination of full deacons, that office was gradually discontinued. Meetinghouses were erected wherever economically feasible. Baptism "in [flowing] water," with the applicant kneeling in shallow water, came to be widely practiced. Yet this innovation, so vigorously espoused by the change-minded ministers in the early years of the Great Schism, was not uniformly and permanently adopted by the Amish Mennonites as a distinctive denominational practice. Even in the congregation of Bishop Solomon Beiler—that archchampion of stream baptism—conformity to this new procedure was quickly made optional by Beiler's successor.[71]

Sanford C. Yoder offers a picturesque description of an impressive baptismal service administered according to the new Amish Mennonite formula. Yoder was reared in an Old Order Amish home but as a young man was gravitating toward the Amish Mennonites when he attended a baptismal service conducted by Bishop Christian Werey of what is now the East Union Mennonite (then Amish Mennonite) church near Kalona, Iowa. After a preaching service in the meetinghouse, the congregation drove south and west several miles to a river. The procession was "nearly a mile long." A steady rain did not prevent or change the order of service, which consisted of singing, Scripture reading, and prayer. Then twenty-five

> mature men and women knelt in the river as the old bishop dipped up the water with his hands and baptized them. Then with the trees dripping with rain and the whole congregation soaked, everyone moved out [from the trees] under the cloud-covered sky and the woods rang with the songs they sang.[72]

The Amish procedure of reading specifically prescribed Scriptures each Sunday was dropped by Amish Mennonites according to the pleasure of each congregation. Possibly at about the same time ministers began to preach from a "text," developing a theme based on one or more verses of Scripture.[73] In most Amish Mennonite congregations fast singing, followed by four-part singing, soon took the place of the slow tunes to which the hymns in the *Ausbund* were sung. Judging by comments made in some conference sessions, even the head covering, to be worn by women in public or family worship according to 1 Corinthians 11, may have been in some jeopardy.[74] Possibly the influence of the Mennonites contributed to the retention of this symbol.

Other changes related to the congregational services of the church were introduced. For the most part the ministers ceased meeting in counseling session (the *Abrath*) before the Sunday morning wor-

ship service. Unbaptized young people were no longer uniformly excluded from the counsel meetings of the congregation. The transition
to the use of the English language was in many instances not completed until after the close of the century. It was often resisted by a
rearguard action by the older members of the congregation. Even more
importantly, new types of services were introduced.

In many Amish Mennonite congregations Sunday schools were
initiated soon after the congregation had separated from the Old Order
Amish. At South Union, Logan County, Ohio (1863), and in Johnson
County, Iowa, Sunday schools had preceded the division. But in Lancaster County and in the Ontario churches, they were not introduced
until about the turn of the century, long after the division. Usually
Sunday schools were followed by protracted evening meetings (often
evangelistic in nature), Sunday evening Young People's Bible Meetings, and midweek prayer meetings, although the order in which these
innovations were introduced varied.

The old Ordnung may have been breached at many places, but it
was not completely demolished. As a whole the Amish Mennonites
were able to maintain relatively effective taboos against divorce, marriage outside the denomination or at least outside of nonresistant
denominations, membership in secret societies, suing at law, swearing
of oaths, active participation in politics, holding any public office which
involved the direct or indirect use of force,[75] patronizing astrologers,
and attending fairs and circuses. Concerning voting at political elections, ecclesiastical authorities who had earlier spoken out against the
practice in the post–Civil War years, lapsed into silence.[76]

Actually, while some taboos were being withdrawn, another was
added when the Amish Mennonites joined the temperance movement.
"Taking the pledge" against the consumption of alcoholic beverages
had been the theme of American temperance crusades already in the
1840s. For a time it was smothered by the preoccupation of the nation
with the slavery issue, followed by the Civil War. However, cultural
isolation, and perhaps the influence of the large numbers of more
recent Amish immigrants from Europe, had prevented this early
temperance movement from having any appreciable influence on the
Amish church. After the war between the states, as the Amish Mennonites emerged from their cultural and social shell, the situation had
changed.

The opinions expressed and the decisions made at the annual
Amish conferences related to temperance may probably be taken as a
gauge of Amish Mennonite practice. From them it is clear that the

manufacture of alcoholic beverages was becoming unacceptable to laity and ministers alike. The temperance movement was sweeping the nation. In 1874 Frances Willard organized the Women's Christian Temperance Union. Eight years earlier, prominent women had engaged in a "Women's War" by marching on saloons "singing hymns, praying, and pleading with saloon keepers to give up their traffic in liquor."[77] In that same year of 1866 the annual Amish conference had gone on record urging and begging church members to desist from the manufacture and sale of liquor on a commercial basis. Members were also urged to stay away from public saloons.[78] Much the same routine of discussion was engaged in at the conference of 1873.[79] In both the 1866 and the 1873 conferences, however, the finger was pointed primarily at the distiller and the dispenser of liquors. No mention was made of the production and consumption of alcoholic beverages in the home.

While the discussions in these conferences were forthright and unanimous in condemning the liquor business, no formal ruling was made against it. No one made the legalistic and punitive recommendation so often proposed in cases of violation of the Ordnung, that of cutting off the unfruitful vine from the vine stem. In the 1873 conference, however, excessive consumption of alcoholic beverages per se was condemned. In summing up the discussion the secretary wrote that

> no animal gets drunk except man, who was made in the image of God. Such a person thereby lowers himself beneath the animal. He destroys everything that is still there of the image of God. He diminishes his strength and confuses his mind. He weakens his memory. He blunts all his good feelings and sinks his poor soul into a sad depths where it will be eternally unhappy. Befogged senses cannot rightly find the way here on earth, much less the narrow way of life.[80]

By 1890 the commercial brewing of alcoholic beverages by church members had probably been successfully done away with in most Amish Mennonite congregations, but not without travail. In Bishop John K. Yoder's congregation the process covered most of a decade (1869-77). During that time one brewer eventually was able to dispense with his business and another was banned and shunned.[81] In 1888 the Walnut Creek congregation of Holmes County, Ohio, made a "unanimous decision." It was ruled that no member was to "keep a saloon and such person would no longer be considered a brother in the church." The proscription did not prevent two members from building a "still house" in 1890 or 1891. This brought on them the displeasure of the congregation and presumably some kind of disciplinary action. In the same congregation three cases of habitual drunkenness received repeated attention in the years 1888 and 1889.[82] The annual district Amish Mennonite conferences of the 1890s took essentially the same position as the earlier general conference.[83] In no instance was total abstinence called for. Moderate consumption in the home was left untouched.

Total abstinence as an unwritten addition to the Ordnung, if the latter term may be used at all in connection with Amish Mennonite church discipline at the end of the century, probably obtained in a large majority of congregations by 1900. The Stuckey Amish "were beginning to be strongly temperance minded" already by 1874.[84] In about 1890 Bishop John Smith of central Illinois espoused total abstinence, although some fellow ministers warned him "to preach the gospel, and leave such non-religious questions to the individual conscience."[85] As late as 1910, or thereabouts, at the ordination of Jeptha Troyer as a deacon in the Town Line congregation of Lagrange County, Indiana, Silvanus Yoder heard the minister condone moderate drinking in the privacy of the home.[86]

The use of tobacco, primarily chewing tobacco, completely escaped the censure of conference bodies. Yet many individuals, including Bishop John K. Yoder and at least one of his laymen, gave up the habit because they had developed scruples against it.[87] In 1873, in the *Herald of Truth*, Editor Funk apologized for "a little article" against the use of tobacco which had appeared in that periodical, saying that it "had altogether escaped our notice until after it was in print." Said Funk, "We do not want to censure anyone for using it," particularly older people who have used it for a long time. Yet he urged these too, to use tobacco moderately, "and then when you go to meeting," he continued, "do not spit too much on the floor, for sometimes I have seen persons in the meeting spit on the floor until a pool stood there, so that a person could hardly kneel in prayer, on account of it."[88]

The Great Schism prejudiced conservative Amish persons against almost any kind of change. But there is little evidence of resistance to technological innovation before 1865, particularly in the area of farm equipment and animal husbandry. Lightning rods, however, were rejected. On one hand, the Amish widely decried conspicuous consumption—the use of new consumer products made available by the new technology, such as factory produced clothing. On the other hand, what little ecclesiastical resistance had· been directed against new technology used in agricultural production had not prevented the Amish farmer from adopting such as it became available.

In Europe the survival· of Amish and Mennonite farmers had depended on the ingenuity of their tenant farming in the use of the land and the development of new strains of domestic animals.[89] Earlier in the century the Amish had adopted the grain separator powered by horses, horse-drawn drills and planters, and reapers. In the midst of the Great Schism, stationary steam engines arrived, sometimes portable but tractionless, and binders, which cut and bound grain in one operation.[90] All these the Amish adopted almost as rapidly as other farmers. However, when the Great Schism hardened and the differences between the Amish Mennonites and the Old Order Amish began to polarize, the latter began to resist on a broad front what they may have considered to be an enslavement to technology.

The change-minded Amish, on the other hand, whether Amish Mennonite or Stuckey Amish or any other liberal segment of Amish, embraced technological advance eagerly and indiscriminately. In 1881 Deacon John Stoltzfus, then living near Knoxville, Tennessee, was utterly fascinated with reports of demonstrations of machinery at the United States "Exabishion" (World's Fair) at Atlanta, Georgia. He thought that industrial equipment would be "a good thing for the South."[91] At about the same time he conveyed to his brother-in-law Levi King his amazement at a machine in Knoxville which made ice in the summertime.[92]

Bishop Sebastian Gerig, of Wayland, Iowa, was the first member of his congregation to have a telephone in his home and later one of the earliest to have his house wired for electricity.[93] In Illinois, Bishop Christian Ropp opposed Bishop Stuckey's rapid accommodation to "worldly" styles. Yet Ropp himself was a progressive farmer, quite ready to make use of "new methods and new machinery." His son, Christian, Jr., invented a "wind engine" in 1857 and a corn planter in 1859. That same son was eventually excommunicated for his heretical beliefs, but not for his inventions.[94]

As the Amish Mennonites emerged from their cultural seclusion a multitude of questions arose relating to occupational, business, and financial activities allowed a member of the church. There was slowly growing ecclesiastical acceptance of occupations other than farming and simple processing operations, such as running a grist mill or a saw mill. Merchandising, including storekeeping, "taking over the office of agent for the sale of all sorts of machinery," and especially dealing in horses, became respectable occupations for Amish Mennonites in spite of resistance by the ministry.

Merchandising was accepted as an occupation with difficulty.

Opponents liked to quote from Sirach, one of the apocryphal books, that in merchandising "sin sticks between the buyer and seller like a nail between two hard rocks."[95] When the Lord cleansed the temple of merchants and traders, he was not only objecting to the desecration of that sacred building, but also expressing disapproval of merchandising in general.[96] Dealing in horses requires separate consideration. It accommodated itself so well to deceit that, except for the most honorable operation, it was held in disrepute even by the public in general until autos and tractors diminished the business.

While the occupational options of Amish Mennonites were multiplying, other areas of economic activity were also opening up to them. Patenting a new invention was approved by the annual conference of 1875—but only for laypersons—if excessive profits were not the objective. Loaning money—presumably as a purely business deal—and receiving interest was allowed, but borrowing at a low rate of interest in order to loan again at a high rate was considered usury and therefore unscriptural.[97] Although the annual conference of 1875 had declared it to be "unscriptural to be a stockholder in a bank,"[98] John P. Mast, minister (1852) and then bishop (1877) of the Conestoga Amish Mennonite church was not only a stockholder but also a director of the Honey Brook Bank. He owned and operated the Morgantown Roller Mill and owned several farms. Evidently he separated his business affairs from his charities for "it was said that he would not consider an investment unless it realized 6 percent profit, yet he was always ready to extend a helping hand to anyone in financial stress."[99]

Likely some of Amishman John P. Mast's business activities predated the Great Schism, but it is nevertheless significant that he identified with the Amish Mennonites in the course of that division. Two other highly successful Amish businessmen followed this same course. Shem Zook of Mifflin County engaged in various business activities, including acting as agent for the purchasing of land in Mifflin County for the right-of-way for the main line of the Pennsylvania Railway. At his death he was a stockholder in the Kishacoquillas Turnpike project to the extent of nine shares.[100]

The other outstanding Amish businessman, Isaac Kaufman (1806-86), of Johnstown, Pennsylvania, may have been the wealthiest Amish person of the nineteenth century. Not only did he own seven farms conveniently located along the plank toll road between Johnstown and Hooversville, but he also was one of the owners, along with two other stockholders, of the toll road. He realized considerable income from this road and invested some of his wealth in Pennsylvania Railroad stock which came to be worth $23,000. His great-grandson later recorded that as a stockholder in the company he "cut an interesting figure among the Big Shots when he attended the [annual] stockholders [*sic*] banquets" in Philadelphia.[101] At the time of his death Kaufman was a stockholder in the First National Bank of Johnstown, with an investment of $2,700, and was serving as one of the bank's directors. A large glass-covered, heavy, framed picture (about 24 by 30 inches) of Kauffman in Amish garb, including a broad-rimmed hat and beard, hung in this bank.[102] He had already distributed property worth $96,000 to his children, with $150,000 remaining to be distributed after his death.

Kaufman's 2500-word obituary which appeared in the Johnstown *Tribune* makes it clear that he was a businessman of no small dimensions and highly respected. At the same time he was a practicing first-generation Amish Mennonite, although he must have helped to push the denominational fences outward at various points in the course of his lifetime. Even before the Great Schism came to Somerset County, he had served as county auditor (about 1846). And in 1853 or thereabouts he became the first president of the above-mentioned turnpike company. For a time he owned "some Government bonds, but these he sold, being able to use his money to better advantage in other ways."

Following in the footsteps of his father, Kaufman became an active Whig and in the late 1850s made the almost standard transition to the Republican party. "In the party's struggles Mr. Kaufman was always earnestly engaged," reads his obituary, "his wise counsel being sought to advantage on many occasions."[103] Again, probably in the late 1870s or early 1880s, when he consented to be photographed and permitted his picture to be hung in a public place, he was surely bending, if not breaking, the Ordnung of his day. In view of some of the ecclesiastical pronouncements described earlier, all of these men—Mast, Zook, and Kaufman—were clearly stretching the boundaries of economic activities permitted by the Amish Mennonite church.

Education beyond the rudiments of reading, writing, and arithmetic had little support among the first generation of Amish Mennonites. On Pentecost Sunday, May 28, 1871, the Amish Mennonite schoolteacher Christian Erismann from Illinois heard John K. Yoder from Ohio preach a sermon based on the first chapter of Acts. Yoder said "he believed it was not necessary to attend high school; that it was enough with the 'Common' school."[104]

Erismann, immigrant in 1857 from Hesse in Germany, probably became a schoolteacher because he had lost a hand in a farm accident soon after his arrival in this country. He became a lifelong advocate of more education for Amish Mennonites, especially for the training of schoolteachers and for ministers.[105] In spite of Bishop John K. Yoder's attitude toward education beyond the elementary grades, in the 1890s a considerable number of the young people in his congregation at Oak Grove disregarded his attitude and attended normal school (to prepare as teachers) at Smithville and went on to attend the more prestigious school at Ada, Ohio.[106]

This burst of interest in higher education manifested itself among the Amish Mennonites not only at Oak Grove, but elsewhere as well,

Portrait of Isaac Kaufman (1806-86), wealthy Amish Mennonite businessman of Johnstown, Pennsylvania. This picture, probably taken about 1882, hung in the lobby of the First National Bank of Johnstown, of which he was a director. On April 14, 1874, on the floor of the Senate, Senator Scott of Pennsylvania, spoke of Isaac Kaufman as "a man of great wealth who has given his time, his influence, and his money to the advancement of the building of railroads and other public improvements," and also of Shem Zook as "a man of very considerable literary culture" (Congressional Record, Forty-third Congress, First Session, volume II, page 3058). *(Courtesy of the Conemaugh Township Area Historical Society, Somerset County, Pennsylvania.)*

including the congregations in central Illinois.[107] The Amish Mennonites tended to follow rather than lead the Mennonites in supporting mission work and revival meetings. But this relationship did not obtain in the area of higher education, where the former were equal partners with the Mennonites. "Among the most influential" of those fifteen Amish Mennonites and Mennonites who "felt the need in the church for a school of higher learning were J. S. Coffman, D. J. Johns, J. S. Hartzler, Jonathan Kurtz, and others," wrote C. Henry Smith, the younger contemporary of these church leaders.[108] Of these men, Johns and Kurtz were Amish Mennonite bishops. Preacher Jonas S. Hartzler had transferred from Amish Mennonite to Mennonite in 1896, soon after he had left the Haw Patch community to teach at the Elkhart Institute.

The Elkhart Institute Association, organized in 1895, a year after the founding of the institution, had as its charter members the above-mentioned two Amish Mennonite bishops, preachers D. D. Miller (of the Forks) and J. S. Hartzler, along with nine Mennonites. This cooperative venture was not without its problems, for within two months of its organization J. S. Coffman noted in his diary that there was "just a little friction between some Amish and Mennonite members" and opined that care should be taken "by treating all parties with due deference."[109]

The rising interest in higher education among the Amish Mennonites lies, in part, outside the scope of this volume. Appropriate, however, is some consideration of the ecclesiastical response to this surge. In 1895 the Western Amish Mennonite conference said that it was not considered to be "scriptural and edifying that the Church build and support high school, where divine science and the Spiritless worldly sciences are taught together."[110] But in 1899 the Indiana-Michigan Amish Mennonite conference was recommending attendance at Elkhart Institute for those of "our young people who want to attend an institution of higher learning."[111] In 1898, at the first meeting of the General Conference of Mennonites and Amish Mennonites, a three-man committee was appointed to examine all church institutions. The members were D. J. Johns (Amish Mennonite), D. H. Bender (reared in an Old Order Amish home but baptized in an [Old] Mennonite church), and Daniel Kauffman (Mennonite). This committee reported back to conference favorably with respect to the Elkhart Institute.[112] The Amish Mennonites would be full partners with the Mennonites in the development of this new institution.

12

Toward Union with the Mennonite Church

The Great Awakening

In January 1891 Joseph Stuckey's congregation at Danvers, Illinois, experienced, in the words of Stuckey, "a great awakening." On January 17 a number of "ministering brethren" had come together in Stuckey's home for what today would be called a retreat. The next day some of these ministers went elsewhere to fill appointments, but some stayed at Danvers for the week of evangelistic meetings which was to follow. As a result "a number" had sought and received baptism and others had asked for the prayers of the church. Stuckey was thrilled. "Oh remember us in your prayers," he continued in his letter to the *Herald of Truth*, "that the victory may be on the side of the Lord of heaven and earth."[1] The revival movement, which had been gaining momentum in both the Mennonite and Amish Mennonite churches in the late 1880s, had come to a crescendo in the early 1890s. It resulted in many congregational experiences such as that recorded by Stuckey.

Mennonite historians have called this movement of revivalism and other changes, the Quickening,[2] or Great Awakening. It included many of the changes in the Mennonite and Amish Mennonite churches described in the preceding chapter. These modifications took place in the closing decades of the nineteenth century and the beginning of the twentieth. Here the focus is more directly on the Amish Mennonites rather than the Mennonites.

In 1876, at the annual ministers' conference, John Schrag from the Dakota Territory reminded his hearers of "what the Lord requires of us in order to be saved by grace."[3] This self-contradictory statement indicates that the theologically unsophisticated Amish Mennonites were experiencing some difficulty in incorporating into their faith, practice, and religious vocabulary some of the theology of Protestant evangelicalism.

A similar blend of the' old with the new is illustrated by the anatomy of a revival in Mifflin County, Pennsylvania, as described by Jacob Hooley, a layman who lived in Champaign County, Ohio. He had been informed that "some of the omish members Stuck up Posters telling the People if they did not quit using tobacco Elkahal & whisky they could never enter into the kingdom of heaven." The "unquickened" Jacob Hooley thought this kind of conduct and this addition to the *Ordnung* was "truly wonderful and lamentable."[4] Revival meetings continued to offend Hooley. More than a year later he was still complaining about that revival back in Mifflin County (or was it a subsequent series of meetings?) in which

> Some omish weaman Sprang to their feet & Said the[y] felt so happy that the[y] were Shure of going to Heaven if they were to die. did you ever hear of such talk in our omish churches. Such people you may set down as Religious Cranks as they have not Sense anough to Know that they are Blasfeaming the word of their maker.[5]

Dramatic changes were taking place in Mennonite and Amish Mennonite beliefs and activities. Harold S. Bender and Guy Hershberger have labeled them the Great Awakening, but Theron Schlabach and J. Denny Weaver called them the Quickening. The term chosen probably depends on one's own system of beliefs.

Weaver has described with great care the theological shift which provided the undergirding for this Quickening. The critical change, he says, was in the doctrine of the atonement, a change "from an unselfconscious assumption of the satisfaction theory of atonement to a deliberate requirement of the substitutionary aspect of atonement in a narrow, doctrinaire manner." This change, he continues, "correlate[s] directly to the removal of peace from the heart of [Mennonite] soteriology."[6] Much of this shift in emphasis was due to the influence of Fundamentalism.

Little of this new theology can be detected among the first generation of Amish Mennonites. Those founders of this church who attended the annual conferences from 1862 to 1878 spoke not one word about "the Great Commission," missionary outreach, and Sunday schools. They said almost nothing about protracted evening meetings, assurance of salvation, or other terms associated with the newer experiential emphasis. Articles by Bishops Jonas D. Troyer, John P. King, John K. Yoder, and others in the *Herold der Wahrheit* continued to emphasize obedience, humility, and perseverance.[7]

Deacon John Stoltzfus mixed a little of the new theology with the old. His infant congregation in Tennessee quickly opened a Sunday school (1871) and within a few years he personally financed the building of a meetinghouse. He reported to his preacher son, Gideon, that three young women had "responded to the call of our Redeemer to all the weary and heavy laden to come to Him, or to accept His yoke, that is to say, the sweet heavenly doctrine in which blessed rest for souls is promised in obeying the commandments of God." Although steeped with Pietism, Stoltzfus' description of the conversion of these women emphasized obedience and accepting God's "yoke." In that same letter he wrote almost testily that he was tiring of all the talk "about faith without works, and then faith with works . . . so I said yesterday that I now want to turn away from the argument about the truth of faith without works and faith with works and note that it is the fear of God which is the beginning of wisdom. . . . Oh beloved friend, how much can we read through the holy Scriptures where obedience was blessed and disobedience was punished?"[8]

In 1883 Bishop Joseph Yoder of the Barker Street congregation in Michigan mixed the old with the new when he charged that "vanity and pride and all manner of inconsistencies are almost overwhelming the churches. Watchmen of Zion," he continued, "sound loudly your trumpets over the land. . . . Preach not to please the people, but to please God, and to save souls."[9] In the 1890s the shift in soteriology is evidenced by the use of such terms as "lost souls," "neverdying souls," "the salvation of the unsaved," "the salvation of lost souls," and "winning people for the Lord." These expressions appeared frequently in the minutes of the Amish Mennonite district conferences and elsewhere.[10]

This terminology was borrowed by the Mennonites and Amish Mennonites from the Protestant missionary movement of the nineteenth century, as Theron Schlabach has described so well.[11] Especially significant at this point is the fact that among a score or more of names of men who were involved in this movement, Schlabach mentions only three Amish Mennonites—bishops Jonathan P. Smucker of Nappanee, Indiana; D. J. Johns of the Clinton Frame congregation east of Goshen, Indiana; and Preacher Jonas or J. S. Hartzler, who joined the Mennonites in 1896. Schlabach omits the names of two Amish leaders who, already in the 1860s, had manifested an interest in missionary outreach. This circumstance may have contributed to their deviation from what they considered to be the sluggish Amish Mennonite movement. These men, Philip Roulet and Benjamin Eicher of the Iowa counties of Davis and Washington, respectively, were no doubt influenced to missions by the general Protestant missionary movement. But they were more directly affected by the emphasis given to missions in the recently organized General Conference Mennonite Church. In the 1880s Joseph Stuckey also came to support the missionary movement.[12]

The Mennonite Evangelizing Committee was organized in 1882-83 and was the prototype of the later Mennonite Board of Missions and Charities. It was originally a "self-perpetuating committee of the Elkhart [Mennonite] congregation."[13] However, Amish Mennonites were said to have "contributed liberally to this [evangelizing] fund" almost from its beginning. In 1892 this committee reorganized. One of the three reasons given for the change was to include representation from the Amish Mennonites on what was now to be called the Mennonite Evangelizing Board of America. In harmony with this stated intention of the committee, the two principal addresses delivered in the 1892 meeting were given by Mennonite J. S. Coffman and Amish Mennonite Jonathan P. Smucker.[14] Even before this reorganizing meeting, the Western District Amish Mennonite conference had responded favorably to an invitation from the Evangelizing Committee to participate in its program. The motivation for its cooperation was concern for "scattered members" and for young people who had not yet joined the church, rather than a concern for the unchurched.[15]

Included in the fourteen-man membership of the Evangelizing Board were Amish Mennonites C. Z. Yoder, Christian Albrecht, Levi Yoder, Herman Yoder, and J. T. M. Miller. Only a month or two after this reorganization, Amish Mennonite Bishop Jonathan P. Smucker was authorized—and probably minimally funded—by the Evangelizing Board to visit the Mennonite congregations and especially the declining Amish Mennonite congregations in southern Cambria County and northern Somerset County, Pennsylvania.[16] Already in the 1880s, before reorganization, the Evangelizing Committee had served as the umbrella under which Smucker had made at least one trip to the West—probably more than one—as far as Colorado.[17] The Western Amish Mennonite Conference in 1892 adopted the most forthright nineteenth-century Amish Mennonite statement of acceptance of the great commission, to "preach the gospel to every creature" (Mark 16:15). It acknowledged that the great commission "is binding for us,"[18] thus rejecting the Old Order Amish position that this command applied only to the original apostles.

As suggested earlier, the doctrine of assurance, that one could know one was heaven-bound, came to the Amish Mennonites via the revivalists, including some who came with the Sunday school move-

Jonathan P. (1834-1903) and Salome Smucker (1837-93) and family. Jonathan Smucker was bishop of the West Market Street Amish Mennonite congregation, Nappanee, Indiana, from 1878 to the time of his death. After this 1887 picture was taken, Bishop Smucker asked his children not to display it, fearing the displeasure of those who continued to oppose having one's picture taken. (Courtesy of Silas J. Smucker, Goshen, Indiana.)

ment. This was in contrast to the "blessed hope" long treasured by the Amish, that God would have mercy at the judgment day on one who had "endured to the end." One of the prizes given to Sunday school pupils as early as the 1870s was a sixty-four page *A B C and Spelling Booklet*, 3 X 4 inches, written in German and published by the American Tract Society. It devoted five pages to "Jesus on the Cross." This section closed with the following appeal:

> Beloved children! May we mourn and be sad that we have caused the beloved Jesus so much pain because of our sins. But we may nevertheless rejoice that He loved us so much and so willingly endured death for us. Now whoever believes in Jesus and loves Him in return may die safely and

calmly. He may commit his spirit into the Father's hands, who loves all those who love Jesus.[19]

Conspicuous by its absence is the traditional Amish soteriology. As described by J. Denny Weaver, the Amish "understood salvation as an ongoing process which touches all of life and which focuses on a saved lifestyle, characterized by humility, with peace and nonresistance as a *sine qua non.*"[20]

In the 1880s John F. Funk gave this doctrine of assurance considerable support by publishing articles by others and by his own editorials.[21] Nevertheless, he observed in one editorial that he was not certain which was worse, to be careless about one's conduct because of indifference or because of one's (unwarranted) confidence that he was secure in the Lord. Still almost completely inexplicable is a series of articles which appeared in the *Herold der Wahrheit* (but not in the *Herald of Truth*) in the summer and fall of 1885. They went beyond assurance conditioned on one's continued personal loyalty to Christ, a doctrine which the Mennonites, and then the Amish Mennonites, were slowly coming to accept. These papers gave polemical support to the doctrine of the unconditional and eternal security of the believer. Evidently the support given to this heresy in those several issues of the *Herold* produced only a ripple of protest. Had such deviation from sound Mennonite doctrine appeared in the church paper—the *Gospel Herald*—in the first half of the twentieth century, it would undoubtedly have produced a storm of criticism. What damage was done to Funk's standing with his constituency was evidently soon repaired by a sequence of articles on the more acceptable doctrine of conditional assurance.[22]

As far as can be ascertained, the doctrine of conditional assurance was not openly espoused by any Amish Mennonite writers until the 1880s. In 1885 Joseph Gascho from Nebraska was preaching about a "saving faith and a firm confidence in God, of *which we should already here be possessed* [emphasis added]."[23] Among the Lancaster County Amish Mennonite congregations, John S. Mast, ordained a minister in 1896 and a bishop in 1908, is given credit for being the first minister to preach "assurance."[24]

J. Denny Weaver has noted that Mennonites have frequently borrowed from other traditions. "Historical analysis," says Weaver, "does not identify a pure and authoritative Anabaptist/Mennonite vision, but rather reveals that Mennonites have continually engaged in borrowing and repackaging."[25] The sources of these outside influences, as well as the resulting changes, have been identified at various points earlier.

An example of the process whereby these external influences infiltrated the Amish Mennonite church is provided by the Amish Mennonite schoolteacher in Illinois, Christian Erismann. While in school in Danville, Indiana, preparing to teach, he sometimes attended the local Methodist church. There he "came to a more fervent life in Christ through the preacher, Mr. Barnes . . .; to God be praise and thanks for that." Here also, he wrote in his diary, "I lost my prejudice against the Sunday School. . . . The first time they invited me, it was not with joyousness that I went; but later I did not want to stay away." In 1869, again while attending school away from home—this time in Bloomington, Illinois—Erismann heard some missionary sermons in the Congregational church. On one such occasion he went to his lodgings to pray in his diary: "Oh God, grant that we [Amish] Mennonites would also take part in proclaiming the gospel to the heathen."[26]

Another illustration of the way in which the Amish Mennonites were influenced by evangelical Protestantism may be found in the activities surrounding those protracted meetings of 1896 in Mifflin County, Pennsylvania. The visiting evangelist, Mennonite David Hostetler, and Joe Byler, one of the ministers from the home congregation, "got a Presbyterian minister to assist them. After they were through, that Preacher made an appointment for the Omish to meet in the Presbyterian church." Then Hostetler, Byler, and others "Preachet from the Same pulpit with the organ Playing in full blast."[27] In 1899, under similar circumstances, the Lutheran minister participated in the "night meetings" held in the Maple Grove Amish Mennonite church in Lawrence County, Pennsylvania.[28] One may be certain that peace and nonresistance were not presented as integral parts of the gospel in those cooperative ventures.

Which was it, Awakening or Quickening? One can agree with Schlabach that "whatever its content, the quickening certainly moved Mennonites [and Amish Mennonites] away from an earlier mood that had fed heavily on the martyr stories, that used 'pride' as its chief code word in an effort to warn against a wrong attitude towards life, [and] that systematically cultivated self-effacement and lowliness."[29]

If even today "the sin of human beings is arrogance," as some contemporary Mennonites are saying,[30] then the loss of the emphasis on humility is regrettable. With respect to the more strictly theological aspect of this movement, Weaver's conclusion that it resulted in "the removal of peace from the heart of [Mennonite and Amish Mennonite] soteriology,"[31] also seems true. Both of these historians would suggest that too much was lost in the movement to call it an awakening.

On the other hand, those who fostered the movement for Sunday schools and missions and were accepting the theology of Protestant revivalism, would certainly have called the movement an awakening. The revival of 1890 in the Oak Grove congregation illustrates the nature of this movement. In 1889-90 Bishop John K. Yoder, "the symbol of the authoritative old order"[32] of the Amish Mennonites, conceded to most of the demands of the young people of his Oak Grove Congregation. He followed up on his promises by providing for a series of evening revival services. The results were dramatic. A correspondent from Oak Grove reported to the *Herald of Truth* that "after several years of ups and downs during which 'husks of contention and criticism' formed a large proportion of spiritual food on which some of the poor starving souls at this place were trying to keep alive we have at last been favored by what seems to be a 'better breeze.' "[33] The visible result of those meetings was a baptismal class of forty-two applicants. In the three years from May 24, 1890, to May 20, 1893, revival meetings resulted in the addition of no less than 112 persons to the membership of the Oak Grove Amish Mennonite church.[34]

Equally impressive are the reports in the *Herald of Truth* of a revival in the churches of Logan and Champaign counties, Ohio. It occurred coincidentally with the initial revival at Oak Grove in Wayne County.[35] Reports of similar revival meetings in the early 1890s elsewhere virtually flood the pages of the *Herald*.[36]

Given the milieu in which the rapidly changing Amish Mennonite church found itself in the last decades of the nineteenth century and the propensity of the denomination to some degree of eclecticism, what sort of changes might one have anticipated? Perhaps a look at what actually did transpire is required first. Not all of the originally change-minded Amish took the same direction. The Egli Amish deviated from the Amish originally almost entirely in their emphasis on an inner experience of conversion, but soon came to be a mainstream evangelical Protestant denomination. The Stuckey Amish, together with the congregations of Benjamin Eicher and Philip Roulet, broke free from some of the personal lifestyle restrictions of the Amish and joined the Protestant missionary movement. As will be noted later, in the 1890s a few Amish Mennonite leaders and congregations took fright at the rapid pace of change in that denomination and eventually became a part of the Conservative Amish Mennonite Conference. Individuals and smaller groups went still other directions. Finally, there was the option of returning to the Old Order Amish. This was taken by Joseph J. Borntrager, one of the original ministers in the Townline congregation, Lagrange County, Indiana;[37] and John Yoder (brother of Bishop Samuel Yoder) of Mifflin County, Pennsylvania.[38]

The changes which took place in the Amish Mennonite church from the time of the Great Schism until its merger (1916-27) with the Mennonite Church differed to some extent from all those other options described above. One's opinion as to whether there was an alternative way than that taken by the Amish Mennonites will probably determine what label—the Quickening or the Awakening—one gives to the package of changes described in the preceding pages. And one's opinion as to whether there was an alternate way will probably be determined by one's theology, particularly by his definition of "salvation."

Amish Mennonites and (Old) Mennonites

After 1865 the Great Schism appeared to be beyond healing—at least in the Midwest. Quickly several of those who later came to be called Amish Mennonites began to make closer contact with the (Old) Mennonites. Two ministers of northern Indiana, John Ringenberg and Bishop Isaac Schmucker, led the way with what some must have considered unseemly haste. Even before the disastrous annual ministers' conference of June 1865, John Ringenberg of the change-minded Amish congregation of Nappanee, Indiana, had written to the editor of the *Herold der Wahrheit*. His purpose was "to address you as a brother, although we do not have the same name, for I am an 'Amonit' and you a 'Mennonit'; but Jesus says: Whoever shall do the will of God, the same is my brother and my sister." Ringenberg followed this greeting with a plea for the union of the two bodies.[39]

This advocate of union with the Mennonites was willing to make a large personal investment in his proposal. David Burkholder, long-time minister of the Mennonite church on the north side of Nappanee, evidently had returned for a time to his native Ohio to try his hand at farming there. When he moved back to his farm in the vicinity of Locke, near Nappanee, Ringenberg went to Warsaw and transported his household goods to his old home. When Burkholder arrived, he discovered that his benefactor had also cleared ten acres of woodland and sown it to wheat.[40] In 1869, at the death of Ringenberg's wife, Barbara, three Mennonite ministers had charge of the funeral.[41]

Ringenberg's 1864 note to the *Herold*, along with similar expressions by others, likely prompted the Indiana Mennonite Conference, meeting at the Yellow Creek meetinghouse in the fall of 1864, to resolve that,

> Inasmuch as some of our so called Omish brethren have a desire to unite
> and join in fellowship with us, a sincere and hearty welcome was ex-
> tended to such as desire to do so, and especially are their ministers invited
> to visit our Conference.[42]

The wording of this invitation to the Amish Mennonites suggests that
conversations with that group had been on a rather broad basis, and at
the latter's initiative.

In the 1860s northern Indiana was the center of the movement
for the merger of Amish and Mennonites. The 1864 gestures by
Ringenberg and by the Mennonite conference at Yellow Creek were
only the beginning of louder calls for the union of the two groups. John
M. Brenneman's large, four-column spread occupied neatly and
precisely the front page of both the *Herald of Truth* and the *Herold der
Wahrheit* for March 1866. In it he asked his readers to anticipate what
might happen "if all the so-called Mennonite and Omish brethren
should be united and joined together in love, working in harmony with
each other, to promote the honor of God and the salvation of men."[43]
He even suggested a trial run at a "general conference" which would
include "Old Mennonites," Swiss Mennonites, and "Omish brethren
. . . in order to . . . effect a more perfect union and enter into a more in-
timate relationship with each other." Of course Funk, again of Indiana,
supported this thrust for close cooperation and eventual merger, and
Brenneman lived just outside the borders of Indiana, at Lima, Ohio.

Brenneman's call for a union of Mennonites and Amish Mennonites brought at least a few favorable responses. Funk's periodicals
carried a response from the pen of Bishop Isaac Schmucker of the Haw
Patch, on the border between Lagrange and Noble counties, in Indiana.[44] In the year which followed, Schmucker would give further
evidence of his Mennonite proclivities. Only two months after Brenneman's article appeared in the *Herald*, Joseph Stuckey brought the attention of the ministers attending the annual Amish conference of
1866 to this call for union.[45] He had recently been ordained bishop in
the Rock Creek congregation in central Illinois. Stuckey's ideas on the
union of all Mennonites may have been more ambitious than those of
Schmucker and the Brennemans, for in 1868 and again in 1869 he
visited the Mennonite congregations in Lee County, Iowa.[46] At that
time they were organizing what came to be called the General Conference Mennonite Church.

Enthusiasm for a union of Amish Mennonites and Mennonites
continued throughout the year 1866 and reached into the early months
of 1867. The brothers John M. Brenneman and Daniel Brenneman, the

latter of Elkhart, Indiana, and possibly John F. Funk, all Mennonites, apparently thought the time was ripe for action. On the Amish Mennonite side was Isaac Schmucker, who gave the Brennemans every encouragement to work for a merger. Late in November 1866 a delegation of Mennonite ministers—Daniel Brenneman, R. J. Schmidt, and Joseph Blosser—made a circuit of a number of the Mennonite and Amish Mennonite congregations in northern Indiana and southern Michigan. Such ministerial tours were an accepted part of Amish, Amish Mennonite, and Mennonite ecclesiastical procedures. Yet the size of this delegation and the frequent recurring subject of "reunion" of the two bodies indicate that this trip was designed to promote such a merger.

In reporting this trip to the readers of the *Herald of Truth*, Daniel Brenneman was manifestly complimentary to "our Omish Mennonite brethren." Isaac Schmucker's congregation at the Haw Patch, he said, "received us very cordially and showed us more kindness and brotherly love than we felt worthy to receive." Here the delegation chanced to meet Full Deacon John P. King, Amish Mennonite from Champaign County, Ohio, who was included in the discussions which took place that afternoon in the home of Isaac Schmucker. "Among other things discussed," wrote Brenneman,

> was the subject of the reunion of the several branches of the Mennonite Church. No just reason could be adduced why we, as brethren, whose views in point of faith and doctrine rest upon the same foundation, should stand aloof from each other.

The last half of the report reverted entirely to the subject of union, with Brenneman observing that "we seem to be divided by names of distinction only."[47]

The Haw Patch congregation reciprocated quickly. Less than a month after the Mennonite delegation had visited at the Haw Patch, a similar delegation of brothers and sisters from the latter congregation came to fellowship with the Mennonites at Yellow Creek. Jacob Wisler and the visiting Amish Mennonite Isaac Schmucker spoke in German, and Daniel Brenneman in English. In reporting this visit, Deacon George Z. Boller of the Haw Patch proposed to call the Yellow Creek people "brethren and sisters in the Lord." He expressed the prayer "that we might be united in his love forever more and by his grace may become bound in the bonds of a common brotherhood."[48]

This flurry of activity in pursuit of a merger of Mennonites and Amish Mennonites was renewed one month later with the visit of another delegation of Menrionites to the Haw Patch. Brennemans—the brothers John M., Daniel, and George—dominated this delegation, although two other unnamed brethren accompanied them. John M. had been "previously invited" to come to the Haw Patch. The delegation spent two days and two nights there, lodging again with Bishop Schmucker. A part of the delegation stayed on to attend a "devout Omish meeting to the north in the Elkhart Branch Amish Meeting house" (the Forks) in Lagrange County. Said John M. Brenneman, who reported on this trip, "I do not regret it that I have been with the Omish brethren, for I greatly enjoyed myself among them." He indicated that he especially enjoyed his preaching ministry with them, and hoped that the two groups might "eventually become entirely united and form one people."[49]

The Brennemans and J. F. Funk continued to be the principal proponents of an early union with the Amish Mennonites. But after 1866 they may have perceived that the process would take somewhat longer than envisaged in 1865-66. In obvious contrast to the travels of other Mennonites, especially those from Virginia and Lancaster County,[50] these three men continued to visit Amish Mennonite congregations until 1873. Judging by the reports of their travels which they submitted to the *Herald*, however, they did not continue to press for a quick merger in their conversations with their Amish Mennonite hosts.[51]

The role of Editor Funk and the *Herold der Wahrheit* in drawing the Mennonites and Amish Mennonites together can scarcely be exaggerated. Publishing both a German paper, the *Herold der Wahrheit*, and an English paper, the *Herald of Truth*, may have contributed to this end. Yet the Mennonites probably used German and the Pennsylvania German dialect about as consistently as the Amish Mennonites.[52] A survey of the first year of these two papers (1864) indicates that they were essentially (Old) Mennonite periodicals. Until the December issues of 1864, only the aforementioned short note to Editor Funk by John Ringenberg, a few letters from subscribers, and a small proportion of subscribers with Amish names indicate any involvement of Amish or Amish Mennonites with Funk and his papers.

All this changed quickly. In the December 1864 issue of the *Herold der Wahrheit*, Shem Zook submitted a writing of Menno Simons in support of shunning. Full Deacon John P. King also sent a question about the meaning of James 2:10, concerning how one may be guilty of the whole law if offending only in one point.[53] In 1865 a few Amish Mennonite ministers began to report deaths occurring in their congregations to the *Herold der Wahrheit.* Joseph Stuckey became the first change-minded Amish preacher to follow the lead of several Mennonite ministers in reporting their ecclesiastical travels. A similar report followed in March 1866 by J[onas] D. Troyer, and another in May 1866 by Joseph Burkey of Tazewell County, Illinois.[54] Only two articles by change-minded Amish or Amish Mennonites appeared in Funk's two periodicals in 1865.[55] Then in 1866 articles and poems by Amish Mennonites, as well as the previously mentioned travel journals of ministers and obituary items, become commonplace features in the *Herold.*

Already in 1865 expressions of appreciation by Amish Mennonites for the *Herold der Wahrheit* were coming into Funk's office.[56] Funk's prize exhibit in that category must have been a letter some years later from J[oseph] D[etweiler], recently ordained minister in the newly settled Amish Mennonite colony in Knox County, Tennessee. He wrote that he had been reading the *Herold der Wahrheit* for twelve years—since its beginning, or nearly so. In the winter which was just then ending (1876), he had again read the issues for the years 1866-68 and had "found them so inspiring as if [he] had never read them."[57]

Already in 1866 these emerging Amish Mennonites had turned from John Baer's Sons in Lancaster, Pennsylvania, to Funk's "Office of the *Herold der Wahrheit*" in Chicago for the printing of the minutes of the annual Amish conferences.[58] By the early 1870s Funk's two papers had become as much the quasi-official organ of the Amish Mennonite church as they had become earlier for the Mennonites. This is especially indicated therein by the frequent announcements of the annual conferences of the 1870s.[59] By 1894, Daniel Kauffman could say that the *Herald of Truth* is called the "organ of 14 Mennonite and Amish Mennonite Conferences in the United States and Canada."[60]

From the mid-1870s to the mid-1880s or later, little or no progress was made toward the merger of Mennonites and Amish Mennonites, not even in Indiana. Probably the reason for this stalemate was a growing rift among the Mennonites based at Yellow Creek and Elkhart, a three-way division which added, alongside the old church, a revivalistic Mennonite branch led by Preacher Daniel Brenneman and an Old Order one led by Bishop Jacob Wisler. The reluctance of the Virginia and Lancaster County Mennonites to cooperate or mingle with the Amish Mennonites extended through this period.[61]

J. S. Coffman, who came to Elkhart from Virginia in 1879, contributed greatly to this closer cooperation which began in the 1890s. According to J. C. Wenger, Coffman said that "he couldn't help it . . . if the great-grandparents had had a little quarrel (1693). But he thought that to perpetuate the quarrel now would be sin!"[62] Coffman's gracious ways often won reluctant Amish Mennonites to his support, as J. C. Wenger has illustrated so graphically. In 1886, at age 63, Bishop David J. Zook, Amish Mennonite of Mifflin County, Pennsylvania, had moved to Harvey County, Kansas. He likely wanted to be near his son David D. Zook, who was ministering to a small Amish Mennonite congregation a few miles northwest of Newton. For a time this congregation shared the use of a schoolhouse with the "Pennsylvania" congregation of Mennonites located in the same area.[63] While living in the community, the elder Zook evidently accepted bishop oversight of the congregation of Amish Mennonites.[64]

When J. S. Coffman came into the community on one of his evangelistic tours, his fellow Mennonite in the Pennsylvania church, R. J. Heatwole, suggested the home of the elder Zook for his lodging. The younger Zook, however,

> knowing his father's coolness toward the Mennonite Evangelist, tried to stop the fulfillment of the plans, but in vain. Gradually [the elder] Zook warmed up to Coffman, and Sunday morning when the Amish Mennonites observed the communion of the Lord's Supper, Zook invited Coffman to preach. Coffman shared with the audience his understanding of the Prayer Veiling (I Cor. 11). Zook was deeply moved as Coffman waxed warm in his exposition, and Zook's tears flowed freely.[65]

This kind of experience, says Wenger, was "repeated all through the Midwest."

Coffman could find acceptance with Amish Mennonite youth as well as with their elders. When he came to the Partridge (Metamora) Amish Mennonite congregation, the young C. Henry Smith found in him "a kindred spirit," knowledgeable in the same areas in which the young man was studying in high school.[66]

J. S. Coffman preached in Amish Mennonite congregations from Kansas to Oak Grove in Wayne County, Ohio, to Ontario, Canada, mostly in what could be classified as revival meetings. The "meetings" which he held in John K. Yoder's congregation in the spring of 1885, however, were evidently not thought to be protracted, or revival, meetings.[67] Other Mennonite evangelists who preached in Amish Mennonite congregations include John F. Funk, M. S. Steiner, and D. H. Bender. Bender was the son of Old Order Amish parents in Somerset County, Pennsylvania.[68]

Several Amish Mennonites teamed up with Mennonite evangelists in holding protracted meetings. They include bishops D. J. Johns

Daniel J. (1850-1942) and Nancy Johns (1849-1930) and family. Johns was ordained a minister of the Clinton Frame Amish Mennonite congregation in 1882 and bishop in 1887. Picture taken about 1899. (Courtesy of Galen Johns, Goshen, Indiana.)

and Jonathan P. Smucker, the two most active evangelists in the Amish Mennonite church in the last two decades of the century, and their contemporary, Jonathan Kurtz. These three men were all from northern Indiana, as was J. S. Coffman of the Mennonites. Coffman and Johns collaborated repeatedly in holding revival meetings.[69] In that season of revival in Logan and Champaign counties, Ohio (1890), D. J. Johns, John F. Funk, and J. S. Coffman were all involved, followed by Amish Mennonite bishops John K. Yoder and Jacob D. (?) Bender from Ontario.[70]

A great majority of those revival teams, made up of one Amish Mennonite and one Mennonite, held their meetings in communities which were predominantly Amish Mennonite rather than Mennonite. This suggests that the former may have sought the help of the somewhat more experienced Mennonites. Possibly the same explanation also accounts for the fact that, although many revivals in Amish Mennonite congregations were conducted by one or more Mennonite evangelists without the help of Amish Mennonite ministers, the converse rarely occurred.

In the 1890s, Mennonites and Amish Mennonites drew closer together in still other ways. Both came to have representation on the boards relating to the Elkhart Institute and to the Mennonite Evangelizing Board of America. In that same decade, at least in a few instances, Amish Mennonites and Mennonites partook of communion in the same service and ministers from both groups participated in the serving of the emblems.[71] In the Midwest, already in 1874, the Indiana-Michigan Mennonite Conference had extended the privilege of participation in communion to "Amish brethren who are of one mind with us, and are of good standing [in their home congregations]." However, as late as 1903 this same Mennonite conference had cautioned against Mennonite bishops holding communion or baptizing in Amish Mennonite congregations or vice versa. However, it was conceded that such activity might be permissible under unusual circumstances.[72]

With such close cooperation, it is not surprising that in some instances where a few families of each group found themselves living in the same community, the two groups united in a single congregation. The Harvey County, Kansas, Mennonites and Amish Mennonites, meeting as separate congregations but using the same schoolhouse, merged in the early 1890s under Mennonite auspices. In 1888 in McPherson County, adjoining to the north, the Amish Mennonites were meeting in the Liberty schoolhouse. In this Kansas community visiting Bishop Joseph Yoder found "many familiar faces of Amish and Mennonites all in harmony."[73] This congregation became the West Liberty church under Mennonite auspices.

In the latter years of Moses B. Miller, bishop of the dwindling Amish Mennonite congregations in northern Somerset and southern Cambria counties in Pennsylvania, many members joined the Mennonite congregations in the area.[74] In 1888 Mennonite C. P. Steiner and Amish Mennonite David Hostetler visited mixed settlements of the two groups in Adams County and Allen County, Indiana. They advised in both instances that they meet and work together.[75] In 1886, "a little flock, without a minister" in Antrim County, Michigan, reported a membership of twelve Amish persons and ten Mennonites who were "all willing to join hand in hand, and be united as one body in the Lord."[76]

In most of those communities where Mennonites and Amish Mennonites united, the union was under the auspices of the Mennonites rather than of the Amish Mennonites. Still other cases support this generalization. Deacon John Stoltzfus, founder of the Knox

County, Tennessee, Amish Mennonite settlement, died in 1887. The flock was about to disintegrate when Mennonite Minister H. H. Good, formerly of Virginia, but more recently of Lima, Ohio, moved into the settlement. He persuaded a sprinkling of Mennonites from Virginia to settle there also. Only a year after his coming the congregation was reorganized under Good's leadership and eventually joined the Virginia Mennonite Conference.[77] Joseph Yoder, the resident bishop of the Barker Street congregation on the Indiana-Michigan border, moved away in 1886. The congregation languished until Mennonite Preacher Harvey Friesner moved into the community. He brought the orphan congregation under the supervision of the Indiana-Michigan Mennonite conference.[78]

Both Mennonites and Amish Mennonites—and Old Order Amish as well—began to locate in Dickson County, Tennessee, in the early 1890s. The Amish Mennonites were probably in the majority in the colony. Early lay leaders included Amish Mennonites Michael Schlonecker and A. I. Yoder, son of Preacher Christian K. Yoder, both from Logan County, Ohio.[79] However, visits to this settlement by Mennonites Amos Mumaw; H. H. Good from Knox County, Tennessee; Christian Good of Dale Enterprise, Virginia; and J. S. Coffman, coupled with some help from the Indiana-Michigan Mennonite Conference, resulted in the organization of a Mennonite congregation there in 1896. Amish Mennonite A. I. Yoder was ordained to the ministry for this Mennonite congregation.[80] Mennonite success at the expense of the Amish Mennonites in these instances is probably explained by the superior organization of the former. Mennonite district conferences had been functioning for decades while the Amish district conferences were only beginning during the years when these congregations were either forming or in critical transition.

The three Amish Mennonite district conferences formed in 1888-1893. This new structure clearly facilitated the forthcoming organic union between Amish Mennonites and Mennonites. Already in 1889 the Mennonite Conference held in Missouri invited "the old Amish churches of Missouri and Kansas" to meet with them in their "next conference, or any conference that they may designate, to agree upon some plan for a union of the two churches."[81] This was a year before the western Amish Mennonites organized formally—but not before those several ad hoc meetings of the 1880s. Possibly the organization of the separate Western District Amish Mennonite Conference in 1890 temporarily blunted this attempt at merger of the two groups in Kansas and Missouri.

Gradual changes were destined to precede organic union of Mennonites and Amish Mennonites. Upon the formation of the three Amish Mennonite district conferences, the Mennonites soon began to invite the ordained brethren of the Amish Mennonites to their district conferences. The Amish Mennonites reciprocated.[82] This ritual of reciprocal visitation was practiced throughout the 1890s. The visitors not only observed; they were listed without distinction along with delegates from the sponsoring conference and they participated in the deliberations of the conference. Of the four bishops on the attendance list for the Indiana-Michigan Mennonite Conference of 1899, three—D. J. Johns, J. P. Smucker, and Jonathan Kurtz—were Amish Mennonites. The last named served as assistant moderator.[83] In the 1895 Indiana-Michigan Amish Mennonite Conference, Mennonite J. S. Coffman served on the committee "on resolutions and arrangement of questions," along with Amish Mennonites D. D. Miller and D. J. Johns.[84] There may have been some unwritten agreement or understanding on the extent to which visiting delegates might throw their weight into the deliberations, but such has not been detected.

Not all was harmonious between the Amish Mennonites and Mennonites. J. S. Coffman's comment about the sensitivity between the representatives of the two groups on the Elkhart Institute Association has already been mentioned. Only a few years later conditions in the Prairie Street Mennonite Church in Elkhart were at their lowest ebb because of dissension concerning the operation of the Elkhart Institute and the policies of Bishop Funk. In 1900-01 another brush took place between Mennonites and Amish Mennonites at Elkhart. Some members of the Mennonite congregation at Sterling, Illinois, were stockholders in the Elkhart Institute Association. Hearing of the dissension at Prairie Street, they bypassed Funk and the Prairie Street congregation and wrote to the Indiana-Michigan Amish Mennonite Conference. They asked it "to provide a place of worship for members of the Elkhart Institute where they could worship in peace." Funk took umbrage at being thus ignored or bypassed. In response—or perhaps more accurately, in retaliation—Funk refused to share his pulpit at Prairie Street with Amish Mennonite guest ministers.[85]

The Sunday school conference movement of the 1890s was a joint Mennonite and Amish Mennonite venture and served to draw the two groups closer together. In fact, according to John Umble, writing in 1941, "the coming together of both Amish [Mennonites] and Mennonites" in those first general Sunday school conferences of 1892, 1893, and 1894, served the "secret" purpose of bringing "together the leaders of the two branches of the church, Amish Mennonite and Mennonite, and to make them acquainted with each other in the hope of hastening an organic union between the two groups."[86] Following several area Mennonite Sunday school conferences, the first general Sunday school conference was held on October 7 and 8, 1892, at the Clinton Frame Amish Mennonite church five miles east of Goshen.[87] This conference was planned by two Mennonites, M. S. Steiner and J. S. Coffman, and one Amish Mennonite, D. J. Johns.[88]

In the second Sunday school conference, held on October 4-6, 1893, at the Zion Mennonite meetinghouse near Bluffton, Ohio, participants were evenly divided between Mennonites and Amish Mennonites.[89] The third and last general Sunday school conference was held on October 3-5, 1894, at the Forks or Pleasant Valley church in Lagrange County, Indiana. The large concourse of people at this conference could scarcely be accommodated. This resulted in a formal resolution that the general Sunday school conference be replaced by district Sunday school conferences.[90]

While the resulting district Sunday school conferences were sometimes under the auspices of either a Mennonite conference or an Amish Mennonite conference, they seldom lost their joint Mennonite-Amish Mennonite flavor.[91] Yet there were protests from a few lonely voices such as that of A. C. Kolb of Elkhart, Indiana. As late as 1900 he was insisting that the Sunday school conference "must be distinctly Mennonite" with "no mixing in of any other branches." He sensed that the Sunday school conferences were leading the way to union between Mennonites and Amish Mennonites. In response he urged that if there is to be a union "between the Mennonite Church and others," the church conference should take the lead.[92]

Earlier the Mennonites and Amish Mennonites had borrowed from the mainstream Protestant denominations the institution called the Sunday school. In the process they had come in contact with several Protestant leaders and had accepted, or at least been influenced by, some evangelical Protestant theology. Similarly, the joint Mennonite-Amish Mennonite Sunday school conferences of the 1890s, so zealously promoted by M. S. Steiner, J. S. Coffman, D. J. Johns, and others, brought the leaders of the two groups into closer proximity, personally, ecclesiastically, and doctrinally.

The early suggestions of the 1860s for a union of Mennonites and Amish Mennonites have already been noted. In 1871 John F. Funk urged the formation of a "general conference" to which "our Omish brethren and Swiss brethren might also be invited." The next year in another editorial he called 'for a general conference of Mennonites (but this time without separate mention of Amish Mennonites).[93] In 1880 Funk again urged that Amish and Mennonites plan for and strive toward "the time when we shall all be united in Christ." If only "we were determined," he asserted, almost in the naive manner of Solomon K. Beiler,[94] "to give up everything that the gospel prohibits, and do all that it requires, O how easy it would be to break down all the partition walls and unite in one body."[95]

The final and successful thrust for a general conference of Amish Mennonites and Mennonites began in the late 1880s. Simultaneous with a considerable barrage of articles and editorials in the *Herald of Truth* were resolutions of district conferences in support of a general conference. The Mennonites of Indiana and Michigan had discussed the idea of a general conference—without mentioning the Amish Mennonites—in 1882 and again in 1884. When it was considered again in 1888, the "Amish churches" were named.[96] Included in this 1888 action by the Indiana-Michigan Mennonite Conference was a decision to ask other district conferences to express their views concerning a general conference. This Indiana-Michigan Mennonite Conference, which included J. S. Coffman and John F. Funk in its membership, was probably in the forefront of the movement for a general conference. Yet its counterpart, the Indiana-Michigan Amish Mennonite Conference, was not far behind. In 1890 it went on record as expressing "itself decidedly in favor of a General conference."[97]

In the meantime support for a general conference in the pages of the *Herald of Truth* continued. C. P. Steiner would include Russian Mennonites in such a conference. Funk urged action by "state and district conferences."[98] In 1892 M. S. Steiner, in his usual style, submitted a strongly worded article to the *Herald*. He referred to the flurry of activity and the several expressions of support for a union of Mennonites and Amish Mennonites in the 1860s. Then he asked rhetorically: "If a General Conference had been organized 25 years ago," would the divisions which have taken place in the meantime have occurred and "would the Amish and Mennonite churches be more united today?"[99] In 1894 the *Herald of Truth* carried additional support for a general conference from Daniel Kauffman, the future editor of the *Gospel Herald,* and from D. Z. Yoder, son of Bishop John K. Yoder, and brother to C. Z. Yoder.[100]

The immediate chain of events leading up to the first meeting of General Conference was initiated by "the leading men of the Mennonite Publishing Co. [who] sent out a circular letter to our ministers and church workers generally asking their opinions concerning a General Conference." In November 1896 a planning committee representing ten of the sixteen Mennonite and Amish Mennonite district conferences met at the Mennonite meetinghouse in Elkhart, Indiana. Of this committee, eight men were Mennonites and three were Amish Mennonites: D. J. Johns, Joseph Slegel, and John Smith.[101]

About a year later a "Preliminary General Conference Meeting" was held at the Pike Street Mennonite Church, Elida, Ohio. Of the ordained men at that meeting, less than ten of the seventy present were Amish Mennonite. The report of that meeting to the *Herald* said that "some district conferences did not choose delegates, yet all but one of the sixteen conferences were represented."[102] Evidently some of the ministers in attendance came from conference districts which had chosen not to affiliate and appoint delegates to the Preliminary General Conference meeting. A year later (November 2-3, 1898), the first regular meeting of General Conference took place at Wakarusa, Indiana.[103] The second meeting was held in 1900 at Sterling, Illinois.[104]

The names of the constituent district conferences remained unchanged and the largest conference of all, the Lancaster Mennonite Conference, did not join General Conference. Nevertheless, the adoption of this new instrument of Mennonite–Amish Mennonite church polity was a major step in the eventual merger of the two denominations. It may be likened more to an umbrella than to the twine of a closely bound bundle. Perhaps those impatient advocates of an early merger were wrong. When it finally occurred, 1916-27, it was a true union of peoples of like faith rather than merely an organizational merger of two churches.

The Conservative Reaction of the 1890s

Many of the change-minded ministers who had attended the annual Amish conferences of 1862-78 and had later accepted the name *Amish Mennonite*, were gone by the 1890s. Of the three-man leadership team, Bishop Samuel Yoder had died in 1884, and John P. King in 1887. He had moved to Coffee County, Kansas, less than a year before his death. Only Bishop John K. Yoder remained. Of that first generation of Amish Mennonite leaders who were still on the scene in the last decade of the century, a large proportion were expressing alarm—in some cases, great alarm—at the changes which were taking place in the church. Some of those early leaders who were already gone in 1890, such as John P. King and Deacon John Stoltzfus, had expressed considerable concern and were trying desperately to slow down the rate of change before their death.

The feelings of these conservatives of the 1890s are summarized in a letter of 1892. It was written by the aged Bishop Jacob C. Kanagy to his friend and fellow conservative, Gideon Stoltzfus, bishop of the Millwood congregation in eastern Lancaster County. In the 1850s and early 1860s, first as minister and then as bishop, Kanagy had identified with the changed-minded Amish in the West Liberty, Ohio, area and had attended the annual Amish conferences of 1862 and 1865. In 1866 he had moved to Cass County, Missouri, where he assumed leadership in the organization of the Sycamore Grove congregation and served as its bishop for the remainder of his life. In the letter below, Kanagy treats with little respect the very men who served as leaders in the era of the Quickening. He deplores some of the changes which have been lifted up as wholesome and progressive. Both the spirit and the content of the letter require that it be quoted almost in its entirety.

Friend and fellow Pilgrim on Earth as Were all our fathers for many generations. all passed away and laid in their Silent tombs awaiting the last trump of the Archangel at the morning of the resurrection. We are also burying after to join the innumerable Multitude of Saints now resting from their Labors, Whose Works do follow them. First a friendly Salute in the Lord Amen to you and all kind friends in Love and peace. . . . I have often been Wondering how you are geting along in your Church and [also the] Conestoga Valley [congregation]. We have rather a hard row to labor in Since the Indianna Evangelists have been running the Churches nearly from Atlantic to Pacific Sowing discord broad Cast even [in] Oregon. J. S. Coffmans are the Main runners[.] J[onathan P.] Smoker and others are very busy, Without being invited Crowding in Where they are not Welcome by many[.] they have already formed a new ring and platform With J[ohn] K. Y[oder] Who Stood at the head of the Old ring[.] now his Old ring is Completely broke up after passing resolutions for a number of years[.] now he has them under his feet making a new platform With a Mixed ring[.] Funk and J. S. Coffman and Some of the Russian Mennonites at the head[.] Such little guns as I and you are too puny to be in the 18 inch Caliber Battery. I heard J. Smoker had been East as far as your place trying to get a foot holt[.] if they get a Start they will Crowd in Without being invited, as they have been doing here for Several years now[.] it is impossible to keep Order in the Church Since J. S. C[offman] has his Checker board or figmill in blast. they run the last 2 funerals nearly on their own plan[.] Selected their own Singers and all the hymns all in the English Language[.] I wanted to Select a hymn in german but heatwole the Mennonite Preacher Said they had them all Selected in the English[.] So Old Jake [the writer] had to Submit and let them run their own boat[.] I am trying to keep back the English as much as possible but the Mennonite faction is trying to rule the german out. they can take Some of the Starch out of Old Jake. they Started a young Mans Meeting here before J[oe] H. Beiler left. it is rather Small but they are Still trying to do all they can[.] I fear a few are getting puffed up With Spiritual pride and consequently in danger of falling[.] poor young folks dont know that they are ignorant[.] I dont know what Standing your Church is in but the Churches in the West are like the Laying of Ezra's temple, Old Men Weeping and young men rejoicing. Some Churches of other sects are turned into theaters gambling Shops and places of feasting. the Mennonites are following on their heals[.] Some of the Amish not far behind. While like Peter the night before the Crusifiction following Christ afar off. now here I rais my Warning voice against it. [Here Kanagy inserts some comments about the Seventh Day Adventists.] Yet in the midst of all false predictions let us watch and pray for at the very time We think not he will come, even as a thief in the night[.] the Signs of the times Show his near approach or Coming in the Clouds of heaven[.] I have now passed my 3 Score and ten years Labor and Sorrow indeed, Labored in the vineyard 41 [years], passed the Waters of Strife and Shall never go back. dug the wells of Esek and Sitna (See Genesis 26:19 to 29) And am going to Rehoboth [and] if necessary to beersheba[.] Remember your poor friend in your prayers.

J. C. Kanagy[105]

Almost two years later, in another letter to Gideon Stoltzfus written in the same vein, Kanagy struck out again against "the J. S. Coffman faction" which was

putting in their best licks getting all the revivals they can. . . . they Sometimes hold revivals Several Weeks day and night. there are One Doz[en] Small Squads [congregations] in Kansas needing the aid of Evangelists So called but they dont get much assistance from these Church Visitors [rather] they are very fond of pressing their Way into Larger Churches where they get Well fed 3 times a day, Sometimes Sowing discord to get a party to themselves, like they did here and in Logan Co Ohio after Saying there are too Many factions already.[106]

A sufficient number of letters, quite similar to the above, may be found to indicate that there was a circle of kindred spirits whose concerns were similar to Kanagy's. Included in this group, in addition to bishops Kanagy and Stoltzfus, were Deacon Joshua King of the Maple Grove congregation of Lawrence County, Pennsylvania; Bishop Abraham D. Zook of Mifflin County; and two laymen: Jacob Hooley of Champaign County, Ohio; and John M. Mast of the Conestoga Amish

Mennonite congregation on the northeastern edge of Lancaster County. The latter was father of Bishop John S. Mast of that same congregation. Possibly Bishop Eli Yoder and John Lugbill, both of the Leo congregation in Allen County, Indiana, should be added to this list. Bishop John Werey of Logan County, Ohio, expressed himself in similar vein, although his spirit was not quite as critical and despondent as that of others of the group.[107]

The concern and despair of these men, especially of the two aged ones, Kanagy and Hooley, can scarcely be overstated. In 1896 the latter wrote to Gideon Stoltzfus about a revival that the Mennonites were conducting in the West Liberty, Ohio, area, which "most of our weak mindet omish" attended. One day during the course of those meetings Hooley came back from a short trip to the post office only to find

> their Preacher Hildy & Kauffman [Coffman?] from indiana here busy talking to the weman folks then [they] asket my [me] why I did not come to their meetings I said I had been Reading of jus[t] such men as they were Sneaking from house to house seeking whom they might devour. . . . that Settlet our talk and the[y] left forthwith & I dont think they will bother us again.

Concluded Hooley: "you might as well try to stop a great hurican or storm as to stop the Drift of the People."[108]

Deacon Joshua King complained that his bishop, J. R. Zook, was allowing alarming changes in his congregation. Men "were [wear] caps Buttons shingle hair have top buggies sing base in church the girls were Hoods Coats Fascinators [head scarves]." He added that "them things do not belong to the Amish people." Then, he complained, "When a Deacon tries to keep these things out of the church [they] tell him to shut upp & stay at home."[109] King's addressee, John M. Mast, must have been like-minded, for several years earlier Mast had said that "if we hav to take the fashions of the world into the churches to Build them then we are building the Amish church on sand." Then, referring to Bible study classes, Mast noted that "they say they can learn so much from one another at their Bible classes. John [his recently ordained minister-son] sed god is the one he goes too [*sic*] to learn from."[110]

Bishop John K. Yoder was especially singled out for criticism by the members of this disaffected circle. He had surrendered to the new generation in that historic confrontation in the Oak Grove congregation in 1889. In 1894 Kanagy expressed fears that John Werey's church in Logan County, Ohio, would soon be "like the church in Wayne County, Ohio." John K. Yoder, he continued, "has been leaning towards the ring in Elkhart Ind; they would run the United States and Canada if they could."[111] In 1899 Joshua King said that he had predicted already "when the change was made in Wayne Co Ohio a few years ago" that "it would take all the Amish west of Harisburg[.] My saying came true except [for] a part of the [Kishacoquillas] Valley church."[112] The exception King was referring to was the conservative faction in the split in Mifflin County in 1897 led by Bishop Abraham D. Zook. Jacob Hooley was even more caustic about Bishop Yoder's conduct. From all appearances, said Hooley in 1894, Yoder "will Soon be the Bell Sheep in all the West again."[113]

Although this concerned circle of conservatives was not able to stem the tide of change in the Amish Mennonite church in general, their influence was not without effect. In several instances they were involved in congregational divisions. These conservative leaders—sometimes supported by their congregations—tried to avoid being swept up in the changes which were taking place in the denomination by refusing to join the appropriate Amish Mennonite district conference.

The two easternmost Amish Mennonite congregations, Conestoga and Millwood, were surrounded by the many conservatively inclined churches of the Lancaster Mennonite Conference. They remained relatively unaffected by events in Wayne County, Ohio, and elsewhere in the West. Sunday schools were not introduced until the turn of the century.[114] Conestoga, however, began to make contact with the Eastern Amish Mennonite Conference in the late 1890s. Minister John S. Mast (later bishop) attended for the first time in 1898 and soon came to be used extensively by the conference. In the case of the Millwood congregation, Bishop Gideon Stoltzfus chose not to affiliate with the conference because, as it was later explained, he "had never accepted their platform."[115] Evidently Stoltzfus, who had bishop oversight of the Conestoga church in the 1890s and until 1908, could not or did not choose to prevent the loose affiliation of the latter congregation with the Eastern Amish Mennonite Conference.

In remaining unaffiliated with the eastern district conference, however, Gideon Stoltzfus and the Millwood congregation did not rid themselves entirely of progressive influences within the congregation. Already in the 1880s, Samuel Lantz, Gideon's associate in the ministry at Millwood, was departing from established Amish custom, especially in the way he conducted Sunday morning services. Lantz was about Gideon's age, but ordained in 1878, ten years later than Gideon. Among other deviations, he omitted reading the special chapter in the

Scriptures assigned to each Sunday of the year, spoke from a text, and used a sermon outline. When Lantz was asked to appear before one of the traditional ministers' councils, he did not comply but withdrew from the congregation, along with six or more other families.[116] The role which Gideon played in this division of 1889 is not clear, although as bishop (ordained to that office only the year before) his role could not have been entirely passive.

Neither would Bishop Gideon be moved to the conservative extreme. In the 1890s he stayed aloof when Bishop Abraham D. Zook of Mifflin County and Deacon Joshua King of Lawrence County, Pennsylvania, were insisting that the church be purged from many of the new practices. He said he had experienced the agony of one split (that of the division from the traditional Amish in 1876) and was not about to get involved in another.[117] In spite of a visit Deacon King made to Lancaster County in the spring of 1899, he got only some moral support from the Conestoga church. That primarily came from the layman John M. Mast, brother-in-law to Gideon.[118] In the Millwood congregation, however, King found a kindred spirit in Preacher Daniel Stoltzfus. It appears that for a few years Bishop Gideon Stoltzfus was threatened with the loss of another splinter group under the leadership of Preacher Daniel Stoltzfus. With great patience the bishop weathered this storm.[119]

At least two other Amish Mennonite congregations with conservative leanings, like the Millwood congregation, chose not to affiliate with the Amish Mennonite conferences of their respective areas. The Amish congregation at Croghan, New York, was classified by statistician M. S. Steiner as "Amish Mennonite . . . (Conservative)" in 1905. It remained unaffiliated until 1914, when it joined the Conservative Amish Mennonite Conference.[120]

Another congregation which took this independent course was Townline of Lagrange County, Indiana, established in 1876, and a daughter congregation of nearby Forks. At the time of its founding and for some years following, this congregation was simply the youngest of the half-dozen Amish Mennonite congregations of northern Indiana. Minister Joseph J. Borntrager, although he had previously not been "altogether comfortable" at Forks, did not break his relations with the Amish Mennonites when he participated in the founding of Townline.[121] Amish Mennonites John P. King and Christian K. Yoder of the West Liberty community in Ohio, participated in the organization of the congregation. The bishop of the Amish Mennonite congregation at Barker Street, Michigan, Joseph Yoder, served as nonresident bishop until 1883 or later. Townline was authentically Amish Mennonite in the 1880s.[122]

However, when the Indiana-Michigan Amish Mennonite Conference was formed in 1888, the Townline congregation stood aloof. It was then under the shared bishop oversight of Peter Stuckey of Fulton County, Ohio, and Eli Yoder of Leo (Allen County), Indiana. The latter was not favorably disposed toward the newly formed conference.[123] Of the same disposition also was the most active resident minister at Townline, Jonathan J. Troyer, who was ordained bishop in 1895. Probably it was because of the conservative views of these two leaders that the Townline congregation did not join the conference but remained independent. In 1910-12 it joined in the formation of the Conservative Amish Mennonite Conference.[124]

The Amish Mennonite congregation at Leo, Indiana, likewise chose to remain outside the fold of the Indiana-Michigan Amish Mennonite Conference. Again, this was likely because of the conservative views of Bishop Eli Yoder, who was encouraging the Townline congregation at the same time to take a similar independent course. With the Leo congregation, however, the ultimate outcome was different. In 1905 the congregation affiliated with the conference, although it "had a reputation as one of the most conservative churches in the conference."[125]

Two Pennsylvania congregations eventually suffered divisions led by conservatives. In Lawrence County, Deacon Joshua King, along with a considerable number of his siblings and their families, withdrew from the Maple Grove congregation in 1900. They first met in private homes, but later (1907) moved to Hartville, Stark County, Ohio.[126] There they formed a new congregation and called in Bishop Solomon J. Swartzendruber of the Conservative Amish Mennonite congregation at Pigeon River, Michigan, to ordain Deacon Joshua King as their bishop. Today this group at Hartville remains an independent congregation, neither Old Order Amish, Conservative Mennonite, nor Mennonite. It bears the name Walnut Grove Church, but locally is known as the King Church.[127]

The second Pennsylvania Amish Mennonite community to experience a conservative split consisted of the Belleville and Allensville congregations in Mifflin County. Samuel Yoder had been bishop of the two congregations from 1865 to the time of his death in 1884. His successor, David J. Zook, moved to Kansas in 1886. Then Bishop Michael Yoder, of the Mattawana congregation across the mountain to the south, had his oversight extended to the Kishacoquillas Valley congregations. In 1889, evidently as an understudy to Yoder, Abraham D. Zook was made a bishop. Ordained a minister in 1885, Zook was, or soon became, a member of that informal circle of concerned ministers who wanted to roll back the changes which were taking place in the Amish Mennonite church. The issues at Belleville were "Sunday School, evening church services, education, dress customs, and two-part singing."[128] Trouble may have arisen quickly. Already in 1887 John Yoder, long-time minister in the Belleville congregation, invited Gideon Stoltzfus and J[ohn] P. Mast to a ministers' meeting in the Kishacoquillas Valley, apparently in connection with some problems in the congregation.[129]

Circumstances in the Valley congregations continued to deteriorate. Before the end of the 1890s preachers John Yoder and Sam Peachey returned to the Peachey Old Order Amish congregation.[130] Conditions worsened when the congregations at Belleville and Allensville rejected Bishop Abraham D. Zook's efforts to turn back the tide of change. In 1895 Bishop Zook wrote to another member of the concerned circle, John M. Mast, that "Church matters were in very bad shape since I came home. Mustatch [*sic*] the trouble. the ministers all against me but Deacon Joe Zook had a long time of it but gained the victory at last I think we have it in such shape that they cannot make any more trouble."[131] Back in Champaign County, Ohio, Jacob Hooley heard about the trouble and wrote a letter to Gideon Stoltzfus saying:

> I understand they have a hot time in the Belleville or Zook church & the end of it will be another split then you may as well say farewell to them the time is near at hand when nearly every Body will want to do their own Preaching. it is truly wonderful that so many Sects can be when gods will or law is So Plain that all of us can understand it.[132]

In 1897 a massive effort was made to heal the breach between Bishop Abraham D. Zook and the major part of his flock at Belleville and Allensville. The Eastern Amish Mennonite Conference called "a special conference in Mifflin Co., Pa., near Belleville, beginning on Oct. 7, 1897."[133] D. J. Johns of Goshen, Indiana; Jonathan P. Smucker; and several other visiting bishops came to Belleville to participate in this special conference. Johns served as moderator, and John S. Mast, young minister from Conestoga, preached in the evening. After the conference closed, one of the local ministers declared: "We have chased the devil from the pulpit."[134] The local correspondent reported to the *Herald of Truth* that he had some reason to hope that the efforts put forth "would open the way for a return of peace, love and prosperity."[135] The next spring, however, in spite of this special effort at reconciliation, Bishop Zook and 118 members withdrew and formed the Locust Grove congregation.[136]

By the end of the nineteenth century the Amish Mennonites were everywhere meeting in houses of worship, had virtually abandoned the use of the ban, had joined with the Mennonites in adopting those changes associated with the Quickening or Awakening, and may have moved ahead of the Mennonite Church in adopting "worldly" clothing and hair styles and in cautiously espousing higher education. Slightly more than another quarter century would elapse, however, before the two denominations would become one.

13

Old Order Amish

A New Name for the House Amish

In the annual ministers' conference of 1862 (Klein) Mose Miller announced that if unity was to be restored to the Amish congregations of Holmes and Wayne counties, all would need "to come under the old ordering" (*müssten unter die alte Ordnung kommen*).[1] He was referring to the lifestyle which the Amish had held to for generations. No doubt this emphasis on the "old ordering" is responsible for the name which came to be attached to Amish congregations resisting the "new things," as Mose Miller called those innovations which were creeping into the denomination in the 1850s and 1860s.

For the generation which followed immediately on the heels of the Great Schism, the names applied both to the change-minded Amish and to the conservatives were not fixed. Sometimes they do not indicate to the researcher which faction was intended. The term *Old Amish Mennonite*, for example, was evidently sometimes used as a parallel to *Old Mennonite*. On occasion it was used to designate that group which later, in the decade 1885-95, claimed or reclaimed the name *Amish Mennonite*. That was the original and appropriate name which had been given to, and accepted by, the followers of Jacob Ammann.

From 1865 to about 1885, therefore, the two principal factions of Amish lacked precise and generally accepted appellations. One may be certain that the conservative faction is intended only when the word *Order* is used, as in *Old Order Amish Mennonite*. In the 1890s those congregations which had their roots in the annual conferences of 1862-78 had firmly grasped the name Amish Mennonite. With respect to the conservatives one may safely assume that references in the 1890s to the Old Amish and to the Old Amish Mennonite church both relate to what has come to be called the *Old Order Amish church*.[2] In some Amish communities, however, such as the Conestoga Valley on the Lancaster County–Berks County line, the appellation *House Amish* continued in use well into the twentieth century.

In attempting to list all of the Old Order Amish congregations in existence in North America at the end of the century, three sources have been used. In 1893, Daniel D. Miller, Amish layman who frequently changed locations, submitted an article to the *Herold der Wahrheit* which attempted to identify and locate all Amish congregations in the United States and Canada.[3] The second source used was the *Mennonite Year-Book and Directory, 1905*.[4] The third source was Amish historian David Luthy's tome on defunct Amish congregations.[5] Luthy's work does not attempt to list all the congregations which were functioning at the end of the century. It is useful, however, in identifying some small congregations which were in existence at that time but which were overlooked by the other two sources.

Old Order Amish Congregations in the 1890s

Location	No. of Congregations According to		
	Miller (1893)	Yearbook (1905)	Luthy (1900)*
Pa., Lancaster Co.	6	7	
Pa., Somerset Co.	2		
Md., Garrett Co.	1		
W.Va., Preston Co.	1		1
Pa., Mifflin Co.	3		
Pa., Lawrence Co. (Pulaski)	1	1	
Va., Farquier Co. (Midland)			1
Ohio, Holmes Co.	7	7	
Ohio, Madison Co. (Plain City)		1	
Ohio, Geauga Co.	1	3	
Tenn., Dickson Co.	1		1
Ind., Lagrange-Elkhart Cos.	5	4	
Ind., Marshall Co. (near Nappanee)	1	1	
Ind., Jasper-Newton Cos.	1	1	
Ind., Howard-Miami Cos.	1	1	
Ind., Allen Co.	1		
Ind., Adams Co.	1	1	
Ind., Daviess Co.	1		
Ind., Brown Co. (Cleona)			1

	Miller (1893)	Yearbook (1905)	Luthy (1900)°
Mich., Oscoda Co. (Fairview)		1	
Mich., Newago Co. (White Cloud)		1	1
Ill., Douglas-Moultre Cos. (Arthur)	2	2	
Ill., Fayette Co. (Vandalia)		1	1
Miss., Monroe Co. (Gibson)			1
Minn., Nobles Co. (Wilmot)			1
Minn., Jackson Co.			1
Mo., Audrain-Boone Cos. (Centralia)	1		1
Iowa, Johnson Co.	4	5°°	
Okla., Custer Co. (Thomas)			1
Kan., Ness Co. (Arnold)			1
Kan., McPherson Co. (Monitor)	1		1
Kan., Lyon Co. (Hartford)			1
Kan., Reno Co.	2		
Neb., Seward Co.	1		
Neb., Gosper Co.			1
N.D., Pierce-Rolette Cos. (Island Lake)		1	1
N.D., Foster Co.			1
N.D., Ward Co. (Kenmare)			1
Ore., Clackamas Co. (Needy)			1
Ore., Yamhill Co. (McMinnville)			1
Ont., Canada, Waterloo Co.	5°°°		

° Congregations identified by Luthy include primarily only small, outlying ones, which are now defunct. These are listed here because most of them had escaped the notice of the other two tabulators.

°° The 1905 yearbook (p. 49) mistakenly lists these Johnson County, Iowa, congregations as "Amish Mennonite Churches (Conservative)."

°°° Although the Waterloo County, Ontario, Amish congregations had already built meetinghouses, Miller evidently still considered them to be Old Order Amish. Those who had rejected meetinghouses had withdrawn and by 1891 had formed two authentic Old Order Amish congregations.[6]

Old Order Amish and Amish Mennonites

A glance at the above table will immediately suggest that the Old Order Amish church experienced a diaspora in the last third of the century similar to that of the Amish Mennonites and Mennonites. As they migrated to many parts of the South and West, they often settled in the same localities as the Amish Mennonites and the Mennonites. David Luthy has identified many such instances, including communities at Hartford, Kansas; Carrington and Kenmare, North Dakota; Thomas, Oklahoma; Needy, Oregon; Dickson County, Tennessee; and (in an eastward migration) Norfolk, Virginia.[7] It is not surprising that they settled in the same areas. Amish and Amish Mennonites were often close blood relatives, read the same government and railroad advertisements for cheap western lands, listened to the same land sale promotion agents, and were interested in the same kind of agricultural setting.

Promotional schemes devised by the railroad companies which owned huge strips of land located along their right-of-way went beyond advertisements and sales agents. They provided free transportation to prospective buyers and even to the settlers themselves. In 1892 a carload of fifty-eight Amish people from Middlebury, Indiana, migrated to Reno County, Kansas, in an "elegantly equipped passenger" coach provided by the Rock Island Railroad Company. It took them "to their destination without change of cars or disturbance from other passengers."[8]

The Amish settlement at Arthur, Illinois, requires brief separate attention. It fell between earlier Amish treks to northern Indiana, central Illinois, and Johnson County, Iowa, and the later diaspora to the West. This colony should probably be viewed as the last of a succession of Amish migrations westward from Somerset County, Pennsylvania, and Garrett County, Maryland. The first such was to Tuscarawas and Holmes counties in Ohio (about 1810 and following). The second was to Lagrange and Elkhart counties in Indiana (1840s). The third was to Johnson County, Iowa (late 1840s and 1850s). The fourth and last migration in this sequence was to Arthur, Illinois, in the mid-1860s.

In 1864 Bishop Joel Beachy of Grantsville, Maryland, and Moses Yoder of Summit Mills on the Pennsylvania side of the border went prospecting in the West for a favorable location for a settlement. After touring parts of Wisconsin and Missouri, they selected western Douglas County, in the vicinity of Arthur, Illinois. Although Beachy bought a half section of land in Douglas County, he himself never moved there. The settlement grew rapidly so that in 1888 it was divided into two districts. After the turn of the century each district was divided again.[9]

From its beginning the Arthur settlement remained consistently conservative. The original settlers were from the conservative southern end of the Somerset County-Garrett County Amish congregations and carried their views with them to Illinois. The new congregation did not fellowship with the earlier Amish settlements in McLean and surrounding counties to the north. They never chose to be represented in the annual conferences of 1862-78. In 1865 Bishop Joseph Keim moved into the community from Johnson County, Iowa, where his views had resulted in conflict between him and Bishop Jacob Swartzendruber. Keim was even more conservative than his senior bishop. He was succeeded in 1873 by Jonas J. Kauffman, who moved to Oregon in 1880.[10]

The rending which accompanied the schism between the liberals and the conservatives in the various Amish congregations in the 1850s, 1860s, and 1870s was often sharp and alienating. Yet sometimes it had a soft underbelly. Shunning between the two parties was not always put into force. Tradition did not and does not even yet require it in all instances of a congregational split in which ministers are involved on both sides. Also, so many families were separated when schism took place that it made the application of shunning unusually difficult and onerous.

In the absence of evidence to the contrary, it is doubtful whether shunning was practiced in many instances of congregational or intercongregational divisions in these decades. When the Amish congregations of eastern Lancaster County divided in 1876-77, shunning between the two factions was not initiated.[11] Evidently the same arrangement eventually obtained in Johnson County, Iowa, after the division there of the early 1880s. In that case, however, some of the Old Order Amish wanted to continue to shun those who left the church even after they were "taken in by the Werey [Amish Mennonite] congregation."[12]

Surviving shreds of cooperation between Old Order Amish and Amish Mennonites deserve mention. Exchange or sharing of ministerial duties between the ministers of these two groups was to have been discontinued at the moment of schism. Such sharing was of the essence of spiritual fellowshipping and the ultimate expression of unity. Even here, however, oral tradition records an exception. Some time after the split in the 1850s in the Howard-Miami congregation near Kokomo, Indiana, Bishop John Schmucker, who had remained with the conservatives, is said to have "conducted communion services for them [the liberal faction] at a time when they were without a minister."[13]

At the turn of the century in the mixed settlement in southeastern

Virginia, some mingling of Old Order Amish and Amish Mennonites in worship services occurred when traveling Amish Mennonite ministers came into the community.[14] In 1891 Ministers Peter Zimmerman and Jacob Roth from Cass County, Missouri, preached at the house of Old Order Amish Bishop Jonas Kauffman at Woodburn, Oregon.[15] A few of the Amish settlements planted during the period of the diaspora had some difficulty deciding whether they should identify with the Old Order Amish or with the Amish Mennonites. Such were those at Wilmot, Nobles County, Minnesota, and at Centralia, Missouri. That circumstance probably contributed to their disintegration.[16]

The three Graber brothers of Allen County, Indiana, were unusually slow in making a clean break with the liberals. Nevertheless, they evidently never considered identifying with the Amish Mennonites. They continued sporadically to attend the annual Amish conferences through 1872. At about this time two of them, Jacob (who recently had moved to Daviess County, Indiana) and Peter, attended the funeral of Christian Frey, their cousin, in Fulton County, Ohio. Jacob evidently stayed over and preached the first sermon in the new Amish Mennonite meetinghouse. However, he would not stand on the raised pulpit to preach, an innovation which he considered more significant and less justifiable than that of the meetinghouse itself.[17] Other indications of fraternization between Old Order Amish and Amish Mennonites may be found, particularly by those from the two factions who had been friends before the schism.[18]

The Moses Hartz Affair[19]

The Conestoga Amish congregation in the vicinity of Morgantown, straddling the border between Berks County and Lancaster County, Pennsylvania, experienced its own miniversion of the Great Schism in 1877. Yet, as schisms go, the consequences were unusually tranquil. In the first generation after the division, cooperation between the two factions has been described as almost cozy. Not only was shunning avoided by both groups, but each group attended special meetings arranged by the other. The young people of the two congregations socialized[20] and intermarried. Even church letters or certificates of membership were granted to persons transferring membership from Amish Mennonite to Old Order and vice versa.[21]

Not all the Old Order Amish ministers, however, remained comfortable with this fraternization. In the fall of 1887 these discontents drew up and signed a letter of dissent. "We do not consider it proper," they wrote that members who have been baptized in our congregations are [later] taken up [received into membership] in the meetinghouse [Amish Mennonite] denomination, perhaps only to have more freedom or for other [equally] bad reasons.

We believe that when a member is banned with the Word of the Lord, so it [he] is also banned in heaven, according to the Savior's teaching, and how may such ban be lifted again without making a forthright confession or declaration of repentance (*ohne eine aufrichte Busse zu thun*)? And when a person comes to a true repentance he wants and desires to make peace again and be taken up [restored] by the congregation where he had been cut off. Then the ban may again be lifted according to the command of the Lord, and if it takes place otherwise it will not bring forth good fruit.[22]

This ministerial epistle was signed by Deacon Christian Beiler, ministers David Beiler and Eli Zook (Zug), and bishops Henry Stoltzfus and Christian King (Kinig).

With such a difference of opinion among the ministry concerning the shunning of those going over to the Amish Mennonites, the Hartz affair became a debacle waiting to happen. It occurred in 1894 when Old Order Amishman Moses Hartz, Jr., left his congregation while under discipline and joined the Mennonites. In contrast to joining the Amish Mennonites, joining the Mennonite church was an offense which called for the shunning of the offender. This the Conestoga Old Order Amish congregation proceeded to do. But Moses' father, Moses Hartz, Sr.—a preacher in that same Old Order Amish congregation—and his wife rejected the counsel of the church and refused to shun their son. Facing congregational censure and eventual shunning, they attempted to escape by applying for membership in the Conestoga Amish Mennonite church.

Two years of negotiation took place between the Old Order Amish ministry and the Amish Mennonites (the latter did not want to offend the Old Order Amish). Finally Moses Hartz, Sr., and wife were admitted to membership in the Conestoga Amish Mennonite church. Not satisfied with the circumstances under which the Hartzes had moved from Old Order Amish to Amish Mennonite, the Old Order Amish ministers in Lancaster County proceeded to shun them. Furthermore, the generation-old practice of allowing members in good standing in one church to transfer their membership to the other church without penalty was discontinued. Leaving the Old Order Amish to join the Amish Mennonites was punished thereafter by shunning.

The Hartz affair was really more complex than the above summary suggests. A more careful and meticulous telling follows for those to whom this crisis has special significance.

In 1888 Bishop John P. Mast, owner of the Morgantown Roller Mill, died. The mill came into the possession of David Hartz, son of Moses. For a few years David employed his brother, Moses, Jr., in the operation of the mill, but with the coming of the depression of the early 1890s, David found it necessary to dismiss his brother. Having learned much about the milling industry, Moses, Jr., turned his back on the traditional Amish vocations. He found employment as a traveling agent with a company headquartered in Chambersburg, Pennsylvania, which made milling equipment.[23] His choice of occupation may have raised the eyebrows of the members of the Old Order Amish congregation of which he was a member. More serious was his departure from Amish practice in the matter of clothing and his nonattendance at church services. He needed outside pockets in his coat for his tools, and buttons to make access to them more convenient. His occupation and the location of the headquarters of his company took him away from the church services of his home congregation much of the time.

The Conestoga Old Order Amish congregation felt that Moses, Jr., was not manifesting "the signs of a fruitful member," and repeatedly admonished him to mend his ways.[24] Rather than submitting to this kind of pressure, Moses, Jr., applied for admission to the Conestoga Amish Mennonite church. He was refused, not because he wore pockets and buttons, but because the Amish Mennonites did not approve of his occupation. This consideration had been peripheral, if even that, in the treatment given him by the Old Order Amish congregation.[25] Had he been accepted by the Amish Mennonites, he probably would never have been shunned by the Old Order. As indicated earlier, shunning between the two groups had never been practiced from the time of the division.

Rejected by the Amish Mennonites, Moses, Jr., went over to a nearby Mennonite congregation, where he was accepted into membership. This was a step traditionally worthy of banning and shunning by the Old Order Amish. Moses, Jr., was no exception, in spite of his father's persistent defense of his son. On April 21, 1895, the son was banned. This disciplinary action required shunning by the members of his home congregation, including his parents, siblings, and all Old Order Amish everywhere.

However, Moses Hartz, Sr., and his wife refused to join in the shunning of their son. Moses was an Old Order Amish minister who had remained with the conservative remnant of the Conestoga Amish congregation in the schism of 1876-77 and participated in the banning of others. The Amish said he was *"sehr halstarg [sic]* (very stubborn)."[26] Immediately after the younger Moses was banned, his parents took steps to join the Conestoga Amish Mennonite congregation, normally a simple procedure. But Christian U. Stoltzfus and John S. Mast, ministers of the Conestoga Amish Mennonite group, stalled. They sensed the unusually delicate nature of the situation and earnestly desired to maintain the cordial relations which obtained between the two groups. Moses, Sr., along with his wife, accepted this temporary expedient and went back to the Old Order. He even preached for them for a few months. Then he declared openly that he would terminate the arrangement before the fall 1895 communion service.

Preacher Moses and wife were now guilty of two charges for which the Ordnung required discipline or punishment: failure to observe shunning against their son and failure to attend Old Order church services. On February 23, 1896, or perhaps some days preceding that date, Moses, Sr., was brought before the congregation in a council meeting. As usual, a neighboring bishop (Henry Stoltzfus) and two neighboring ministers (Benjamin Lantz and Benjamin Fisher) were present to assist Benjamin Stoltzfus, the local bishop. Minister Moses Hartz, according to most reports, was the soul of graciousness, but in the matter of his son's excommunication proved to be not wholly docile. At a crucial moment in the meeting he was asked if he would accept whatever discipline the congregation would lay on him. Moses' response indicated his mistrust of the congregation and the assembly of ministers. He really could not make such a promise; just suppose they would vote to send him back to Germany, he said, with a touch of irony. Moses was then asked to leave the meeting while the congregation deliberated on what action should be taken.

Young Amos J. Stoltzfus, who had only recently been taken into the church, was sitting at a window in the room in which the congregational council was being conducted. As he looked out of that window he soon realized that Preacher Hartz did not intend to wait for the verdict of the congregation. He saw the elderly man leaving for his home, "stepping along at seventy-five years of age just as briskly as when he had walked away from the same house sixty years before when he had come there as an orphan asking for a job and had been [momentarily] turned down. He now walked up through the field past the red school house and on to his home."[27] The congregation voted to take Moses' ministry away from him, but Moses had not waited to receive the verdict.

With the application of Moses Hartz, Sr., and his wife to be taken into the Conestoga Amish Mennonite church still pending, the ministers of that congregation found themselves in an increasingly embarrassing situation. Clearly they and the laity of the congregation were ready to accept Moses and wife as members, but knew that such a step would produce hard feelings with the Old Order congregation. A conference with Bishop Benjamin Stoltzfus of the Old Order confirmed this. No, Moses was not "guilty of Eney Bad sins" (as John M. Mast recorded the conversation), but the structure of Old Order Amish church discipline required that he join in the shunning of his son.[28]

The next scene in this episode shifts to the Conestoga Amish Mennonite church and its sister congregation, the Millwood church, about twelve miles southward. Both congregations had taken the change-oriented track in 1876-77, and both had broken with the conservative bishop Christian Ummel within a period of a few months. From that time on bishop oversight of the two congregations was single. Until 1888 John P. Mast of Conestoga presided over both churches, and at his death Gideon Stoltzfus of the Millwood congregation replaced him. In 1894, Gideon's nephew, John S. Mast, had been ordained to the ministry at Conestoga. When the ministers and members of these two congregations counseled together concerning Preacher Moses' application for membership in the Conestoga church, the latter voted unanimously for approval. But Millwood, under the more immediate influence of Gideon, was evenly divided on the question. With such divided counsel it seemed impossible that Moses Hartz and his wife could be admitted to membership at Conestoga.

Clearly the Millwood church and its resident bishop, Gideon Stoltzfus, were opposing the united will of the Conestoga church. Consequently, when Gideon came over to Conestoga on April 19, 1896, he found the congregation unwilling to participate in a communion service under his leadership. Gideon was a forceful leader and evidently more concerned about the effects that the admission of the Hartzes into membership with the Amish Mennonites would have on the Old Order congregations than were the Conestoga people. Yet he was also concerned about his strained relations with the church at Conestoga over which he had responsibilities as a nonresident bishop. It was probably under these circumstances that Gideon made some conciliatory remarks to several members of the Conestoga congregation concerning the admission of the Hartzes: "he had it not to say as it was not his home of [sic] church. he wod not inter fear if we were sattesfide. he would not stop the brotherhood."[29]

Bishop Gideon Stoltzfus had made these statements on a Sunday afternoon in an informal discussion in which no other ministers may have been present. In any case they were not given as directives to the Conestoga ministers. Therefore, in view of traditional Amish and Amish Mennonite church polity, ministers Christian U. Stoltzfus and John S. Mast were probably exceeding their authority when, on June 14, 1896, they received the Hartzes into membership in the Conestoga Amish Mennonite church. To this action the Old Order congregation responded by excommunicating Moses Hartz, Sr. (to be followed by shunning).[30] Bishop Gideon Stoltzfus' response was also negative. He considered the action of the Conestoga ministers and congregation as insubordinate conduct. When the time arrived for fall communion services, he refused to proceed with that ordinance and in effect annulled the action. The admission of the Hartzes to membership in the congregation had to be reconsidered.

Outside help was required to resolve the differences between the two Amish Mennonite congregations and to decide on the fate of the Hartzes. In mid-April, 1897, bishops Fred Mast of Holmes County, Ohio, and Christian Stuckey of Fulton County, Ohio, came to Lancaster County. Three days in conference resulted in (1) an admission by the Conestoga congregation that a mistake had been made in taking in the Hartzes without the presence of a bishop, and (2) a proposal which, hopefully, might allow the Hartzes to retain their membership with the Amish Mennonites while also restoring normal relations with the Old Order Amish.

The Hartzes were given two options. They might return to the Old Order congregation and make peace with them so that they would qualify for a certificate of membership in good standing and could then transfer to the Amish Mennonites in the usual way. Or, the Hartzes might make a confession of failure on bended knees before the Conestoga Amish Mennonite congregation, which would then qualify them for admission (or readmission?) to that church. The aged couple chose the latter option and made their confession in a ceremony heavy with emotion. With this their membership with the Amish Mennonites was confirmed.

Now the scene shifted back to the Old Order Amish congregations. Visiting bishops Stuckey and Mast had succeeded in restoring fellowship between the Millwood and Conestoga Amish Mennonite congregations. It remained to be seen whether the confession made by the Hartzes would satisfy the Old Order Amish congregation and make possible the restoration of the generation-old arrangement of convenience with the latter. When the procedure used with the Hartzes was described to Bishop Benjamin Stoltzfus and his Old Order Amish congregation, they were "pleased" and accepted the solution. A temporary hitch loomed when the neighboring Mill Creek Old Order congregation at first rejected the arrangement. But Bishop Ben Stoltzfus and his congregation were confirmed within a month or two in a general meeting of Lancaster County Old Order ministers, in which Ben "presented his case with much persuasion and prayer."[31] The restoration of peace was then signaled by the observance of communion in the several Old Order congregations of the county. This may have occurred on the regular communion Sunday of the fall of 1897.

It seemed, however, that the Hartz affair would never end. That same fall (1897), at a second Old Order Amish ministers' meeting, the decision of the previous meeting was reversed. The Hartzes must be shunned as long as they refuse to support the action of the church in shunning their son. The sources which are critical of the Old Order Amish in this affair charge that Preacher David Beiler of the Upper Pequea congregation almost single-handedly brought about this decision to put the Hartzes back into the ban.[32] He was son of the patriarch and bishop of the same name and alone had abstained from the aforementioned communion. In view of the ministerial document of 1887, however, it is more plausible to ascribe this adoption of the *streng Meidung* (strict shunning) to all five of those ministers who had composed that minority document.

Bishop Fred Mast, one of the visiting bishops who had come to Lancaster County to resolve the Moses Hartz difficulty, heard that shunning had been resumed against the Hartzes. He wrote to John M. Mast, February 2, 1898, that it appears as though some of the Amish "churches have a law school among themselves, and take the privelige of avoiding Som people as they see fit. . . . What I can learn out of your letter they have cast Brother Moses Hartz back in the old pit and now dought [no doubt] they have set themselves Down to Eat and Drink and bee merry."[33]

Who should receive the blame—or the credit—for the restoration of the ban against the Hartzes may never be determined. More significant is the result. On this question the sources agree that the practice of shunning those who went over to the Amish Mennonites came about as a result of the Moses Hartz affair and in particular as a result of this decision of the Old Amish ministers in the fall of 1897.[34] One document notes an agreement among the Old Order that this shunning was to cease with the death of Moses Hartz, Sr., the offense existing between the two groups thereby being removed.[35] Moses, however, lived another nineteen years. By the time of his death in 1916, other differences between the two groups prevented the restoration of the earlier practice of fraternization. Surprisingly, participation between the Old Order Amish and the Amish Mennonites in Lancaster County in mutual aid or disasters continued until 1923.[36]

A maze of family kinship had evidently contributed to the maintaining of cordial relationships between the Old Order Amish and the Amish Mennonites in the Conestoga community for most of a generation. Amish Mennonite Bishop Gideon Stoltzfus was a brother to Old Order Amish Preacher David Beiler's wife (Maria). Another of his sisters, Rebecca, was the wife of Amish Mennonite layman John M. Mast. Gideon therefore was uncle to Amish Mennonite Preacher John S. Mast. John M. Mast's sister Sarah was married to Old Order Amish Bishop Benjamin Stoltzfus. In 1908 John M. Mast's son, John S., became bishop of the Conestoga Amish Mennonite Church. In 1914 the son of John M.'s sister Sarah, Samuel M. Stoltzfus, became bishop of the Conestoga Old Order congregation. Church loyalties, however, have proved to be stronger than family ties. For the Old Order Amish in Lancaster County, this included faithfulness in shunning those who had left the church in which they were baptized and to which they had made their vows of discipleship.

This streng Meidung, adopted by the Old Order Amish as a result of the Hartz affair, caused considerable discontent which expressed itself continuously in the Pennsylvania congregations. Eventually, in 1909-11, thirty-five families in the Weavertown area of Lancaster County defected from the Old Order Amish church. Later, under the leadership of John A. Stoltzfus, this congregation joined with that of Bishop Moses M. Beachy at Grantsville, Maryland, and other congregations, to form the Beachy Amish Mennonite Fellowship.[37]

The Joni J. Helmuth Affair at Arthur, Illinois, and the Proposal for an Old Order Amish General Conference

At the same time that the Hartz affair was disturbing the peace in the Lancaster County Old Order Amish congregations in the mid-1890s, a similar struggle occurred in the Midwest. Amishman Joni Helmuth and wife, of Moultrie County, Illinois, were banned and shunned by their bishop and congregation for violating the Ordnung of the church. Soon this couple joined a "higher class church," and some members of the congregation wanted to discontinue shunning thereafter. At least one other couple soon followed the first in disobedience, thus compounding the problem. When the two ministers of the congregation refused to follow their bishop's instructions to summon the rebellious couples to a congregational meeting, an impasse resulted.

The entire account of this crisis in Illinois parallels the Hartz affair so closely that its recounting would be redundant. The outcome, however, was different. An uneasy truce was suggested and instituted by visiting bishops. They suggested that the congregation "have patients" (exercise toleration) toward those who refused to shun the defecting couples. Another meeting by visiting bishops was later required when those families which were not shunning the offending couples were themselves offended because the bishop and others were continuing to shun these disobedient couples. The bishops allowed that those who were no longer shunning should have patience with those who were continuing to shun. For a permanent solution, said the visiting bishops, "beings it is [being] worked on to have a general conference," perhaps it can be "decided later on at a general conference."[38]

The idea of a general conference was not unreasonable. Were not the Lancaster Amish and the Amish of southern Somerset County, Pennsylvania, struggling with almost identical questions concerning the application of the ban in these same years? It never happened, however, probably because of the strong Amish commitment to the principle of congregational government.

In spite of the fact that the use of the ban and the practice of shunning have created many problems for the Old Order Amish, they have adhered to Jacob Ammann's position on the practice. This was a principal point of contention in the Amish Division of 1693. The principle of shunning has been difficult to administer and its uniform application throughout the church has not been achieved. But this fact has not relieved the church of carrying out the biblical injunction to "avoid" its unfaithful members. Those several Amish leaders who read and contributed to the *Herold der Wahrheit* did not hesitate to stand their ground in that paper. John (Hansi) Borntreger of Middlebury, Indiana, called attention to Menno Simons' uncompromising position on shunning and asked accusingly whether the Amish were not really the true Mennonites.[39] In the twentieth century, beginning with the defection of the congregations at Weavertown, Pennsylvania, and Grantsville, Maryland, problems associated with the discipline of shunning would continue to occupy the attention of the Old Order Amish.[40]

Meetinghouses Again, and Sunday Schools

In 1881 the Old Order Amish of the Casselman River area which straddled the Pennsylvania-Maryland line in the vicinity of Grantsville, Maryland, built four meetinghouses. Nine years later two congregations of Amish in Johnson County, Iowa, constructed houses of worship. The Amish of Waterloo County, Ontario, likewise built meetinghouses in the decade of the 1880s. This innovation in the Ontario congregations probably stemmed from the same sources and forces as did those aforementioned Amish meetinghouses in the United States. However, in contrast to those congregations south of the border, the congregations in Ontario split over the meetinghouse issue. Furthermore, the meetinghouse Amish in Ontario thereafter moved consistently, although gradually, into the Amish Mennonite camp.[41]

In Johnson County, Iowa, agitation for meetinghouses arose in the late 1880s. From one congregation in the 1850s this settlement had grown to two by 1863. In 1877 each of these two districts were divided again, resulting in the North Sharon and South Sharon congregations, and the Upper Deer Creek and Lower Deer Creek congregations.[42] The pressure for meetinghouses centered in the two latter congregations. Earlier the Deer Creek congregations had taken the lead in introducing Sunday schools, and now in 1890 they were proposing to build meetinghouses.[43] For their modernizing tendencies the members of the Deer Creek congregations were dubbed the *"hoch-müdige Deer Greekers* (the proud Deer Creek people)."[44]

This movement for meetinghouses did not alarm Frederick Swartzendruber, full deacon and acting senior bishop. He observed that "in the entire Bible there is not a word concerning the kind of house in which Christians should worship."[45] Possibly in the same document or elsewhere he wrote further of the meetinghouse controversy: *"Das ist ein Elender Zank* (this is a wretched dispute)."[46] Although Swartzendruber was not opposed to meetinghouses, Christian Miller, bishop of South Sharon congregation, was not so favorably disposed to the idea. The bishops of the two Deer Creek congregations, William K. Miller of Upper Deer Creek and Jacob F. Swartzendruber of Lower Deer Creek, however, were prepared to accept this innovation.[47] In arriving at the decision to proceed with the building of meetinghouses, the four congregations drew up an agreement which included the following provisions:

> 1. This church house shall and dare not be the means of granting us more freedom toward worldliness, and we are minded, and promise to strive for

simplicity and uniformity in all things, and to remain true to the fundamentals of our faith, as well as the rules and regulations of our church.

2. All members are to be held responsible to do their part in laying aside and cleansing everything that is contrary to the rules and regulations of the church, and will assist in bringing under church censure such irregularities in the spirit of Christian love.

3. The church house itself shall be built in a pattern of simplicity and shall be used only for such purposes that the ministers may consider upbuilding to the church.[48]

The elderly bishop Frederick Swartzendruber wrote about "unbiblical divisions" in the *Herold der Wahrheit*, 1892. He was probably defending the arrangement of allowing the Deer Creek congregations to build meetinghouses. Said he, "If we want to follow the example of Abraham, then follow it completely and do not split a congregation, but rather separate in peace from one another before you cause a split; for that is what Abraham and Lot did. They loved each other until death."[49] For about a generation, until 1914–15, the Deer Creek congregations maintained fellowship with the house Amish of Sharon Township and possibly also with some Old Order Amish congregations elsewhere. Meanwhile, the Deer Creek congregations took the liberty of discarding the *Ausbund* for a new collection of songs compiled by a committee composed of S. D. Guengerich, his brother Jacob D., and Christian J. Swartzendruber. The latter, a schoolteacher like S. D., served as chairman.[50] Soon after the 1915 division, the Upper Deer Creek congregation affiliated with the Conservative Amish Mennonite Conference. And in 1921 Lower Deer Creek joined the Western District Amish Mennonite conference.[51]

The construction of four Amish meetinghouses in the Casselman River or Grantsville, Maryland, area actually preceded by a few years their introduction in Ontario and in Johnson County, Iowa. In the last half of the nineteenth century the oversight of the two congregations in the settlement was exercised by Joel Beachy.[52] At the south end of Somerset County, this community straddled the Pennsylvania-Maryland line, and in 1877 it had been divided into two congregations with the state border as the dividing line.[53] Beachy's powerful preaching, gracious personality, and financial benevolence may account in considerable part for the unity and growth of this community.[54]

While Beachy's congregations were prospering, Bishop Moses B. Miller was presiding over the dwindling Amish Mennonite congregations in northern Somerset County, Pennsylvania, and in adjacent

Cambria County. These congregations under Miller's leadership had moved together into the Amish Mennonite fold. However, not until 1875 did they build two meetinghouses. By then these congregations were already in considerable decline.[55] On the other hand, the congregations on the southern border of Somerset County, under Beachy, had taken the conservative fork in the Great Schism. Eventually (about 1895) they took on the Old Order Amish name.

Two years after the Casselman River congregation had been divided at the state line, Bishop Joel Beachy, then sixty-six years of age, ordained Manasses Beachy as bishop of the Pennsylvania congregation. Joel retained oversight of the Maryland congregation for another eight years. In 1881, only six years after their progressive counterparts in the Johnstown area had erected meetinghouses, these Old Order Amish did likewise. Under the skilled leadership of the elderly bishop Joel Beachy, the two congregations proceeded to build four places of worship. Ten years earlier the serving of a noon meal had been discontinued, thus eliminating one practical reason for meeting in homes.

A present resident of the area claims that the custom of serving a meal after the Sunday morning service was discontinued

> because so many non-church people came from Coal Run and . . . Summit Mills for the meal only. They invaded the house and over-ran everything, some of them climbing in through the windows. They even broke the arm of Josiah Yoder [when they pushed him off of the porch]. . . . Following this incident the church leaders said *"Das ist genug!"* (this is enough) and discontinued the custom in this area.[56]

Then too, both congregations had become too large to be accommodated in private homes and members were absenting themselves from services in order to avoid overcrowding. Meetinghouses provided an answer to this problem, although a geographical division of each congregation would have provided another solution.[57]

Although Joel Beachy may have been reluctant personally to make the change to meetinghouses, he nevertheless accepted the will of the majority of the congregation. He probably thereby avoided a cleavage and provided the kind of administration required for implementing that decision. Some members were neutral and willing to abide by the majority decision. Of those who had a definite preference, two-thirds wanted meetinghouses and one-third opposed them. With this divided counsel a church split would have been a definite possibility had it not been for Bishop Beachy's leadership.[58]

Getting the tacit or expressed approval of other congregations

throughout North America for building and worshiping in meetinghouses may have been as difficult as arriving at a local decision to build.
Extant pieces of correspondence with Amish leaders in northern Indiana indicate that the congregations there were quite uneasy about
the Casselman River developments.

From Middlebury, Indiana, John (Hansi) Borntreger, wrote that
the congregations in his area did not want nor intend to build meetinghouses. Alluding to that unforgotten schism of the 1850s in northern
Indiana, he warned that he "knew of none [who built meetinghouses]
which hold to the old Ordnung." Not only had the houses of worship
been constructed "according to the world-mode with a pulpit," but this
was followed with new songs and fast tunes, along with much accommodation to the lust of the eyes. Borntreger likened the desire for
meetinghouses to the desire of the Israelites for a king so they could
"be like all the other heathen."[59] Borntreger's concern about pulpits
which raised the preacher above the laity may have made an impression on Joel Beachy. The meetinghouses built in 1881 in the Casselman
River congregations contained no such furniture.[60]

Building these meetinghouses may actually have resulted in some
temporary suspension of fellowship with other congregations. An unusually frank "Church News" item appeared in the *Herald of Truth* in
1884. It said that the Amish churches of Lancaster County, Pennsylvania, and Holmes County, Ohio, had broken fellowship with the Casselman River congregations because the latter had built houses of worship.[61] This report may have been incorrect. If fellowship was broken, it
was soon restored, and the Amish who worshiped in meetinghouses
continued in fellowship with the house Amish elsewhere.[62] However,
even today Lancaster County ministers insist that services be held in
private homes or barns when preaching in Somerset County Amish
congregations.[63]

Only a little more than a decade after the meetinghouses were
built, differences arose among the four Casselman River congregations.
D. H. Bender, reared in an Amish home, had gone over to the Mennonites for baptism and in the 1890s taught for a time in the Normal
School at nearby Springs, Pennsylvania. Some of the Amish young men
attended this school, a considerable departure from the traditional
Amish lifestyle. These young men were evidently also cutting their hair
rather short and parting it. Other innovations supported by the more
changed-minded were Sunday schools and singing classes. The same
questions concerning banning and shunning which were plaguing the
Conestoga congregations in Lancaster County at this time were also

alive in the Casselman River area. The Pennsylvania-Maryland state line roughly divided the two groups, the Pennsylvania-side congregations being the more conservative.[64]

In 1894, for the first time, each side proceeded with communion without making peace with the other side. The Pennsylvania ministry invited those on the Maryland side who were dissatisfied to cross over and observe communion with them. The Maryland ministry responded in kind. Soon after this break in relations, Bishop Manasses Beachy on the Pennsylvania side became too ill to officiate at communion. The more conservative Pennsylvania congregations refused to let the somewhat more change-minded Joel J. Miller come over from Maryland to administer this ordinance. The next year, after Beachy's death, bishops from Indiana and Virginia came to ordain Moses D. Yoder as bishop to succeed him, without any participation by the ministers or bishop from the neighboring Maryland congregations. By this action the division became final.[65]

Obviously, banning and shunning could not logically be imposed by the Pennsylvania Amish on those across the state line who had never been members in a Pennsylvania congregation. Nevertheless, after the division was in progress in the community, the Pennsylvania Amish followed tradition and shunned those who had only recently transferred their membership from a Pennsylvania congregation to one in Maryland.[66] In the 1920s the Pennsylvania-side congregations experienced another cleavage. Bishop Moses M. Beachy decided he could not conscientiously continue to enforce the streng Meidung which his congregation had adopted in 1895. He is regarded as founder of the Beachy Amish Mennonite Fellowship in 1927.[67]

Sunday school as a teaching institution of the church has never received the general approval of the Old Order Amish. However, a few scattered communities were conducting such schools already in the nineteenth century. Mention has been made of the Sunday schools which the Amish operated in the 1870s in Johnson County, Iowa, before the Great Schism had reached that area. The Old Order Amish, as well as the Amish Mennonites, continued these schools after that disruptive experience. In the late 1880s, in the newly established Amish settlement of East Center, southwest of Hutchinson, Kansas, Daniel E. Mast led a movement to organize a Sunday school. Before the end of the century it was accepted by the congregation. Mast had tried unsuccessfully to start a Sunday school in Holmes County, Ohio, before he moved to Kansas in 1886.[68]

Still another attempt in the 1890s to start a Sunday school was made in the Old Order Amish congregation in Clinton Township, Elkhart County, Indiana. When the promoter, Minister David J. Hochstetler, found the opposition to a Sunday school too great (and also for other reasons), he moved to Brown County, Indiana (1897). There he became leader of a short-lived congregation. However, the Sunday school movement in Clinton Township did not die with the removal of Hochstetler. Under the leadership of laymen Noah Bender and Emanuel Miller, Sunday school was restored. When Samuel D. Hochstetler, son of David J., returned to Clinton Township in 1911 as a minister, he found a permanently established Sunday school in operation.[69] The East Center congregation in Kansas and Samuel D. Hostetler's church district in Clinton Township (he was ordained a bishop in 1923) followed similar courses over the decades. Both finally moved over into the Beachy Amish Mennonite Fellowship in the 1950s.

Ordnung Again

On November 21, 1871, the young Amish congregation in Daviess County, Indiana, possibly in the process of organizing, drew up the "Rules and Order of the Congregation." While many of the regulations contained in this statement have already been considered, the document as a whole, as it appears below, deserves attention as a carefully worded description of the lifestyle generally expected of a member of an Amish congregation in 1871.

Rules and Order of the Congregation

1. Bundling is strictly forbidden.
2. It is not permitted to go to elections or to hold government office.
3. We are not permitted in the gospel to use the power of government to protect ourselves.
4. If a brother or sister commits a sin against another, the rule of Christ (Matthew 18) is to be used and followed.
5. Those who are poor shall not undertake anything or incur any debts that they cannot carry out, except with the counsel of the congregation.
6. No brother or sister shall introduce or begin anything in the congregation that is not already there, without the counsel of the congregation.
7. No member of the brotherhood shall lend money into the world without asking the congregation whether a member needs it.
8. All money loaned to the poor of the congregation shall be loaned without interest.
9. Concerning clothing, we expect to hold to the rules and order of the

Mennonites and not go along with the world in fine array and pride, from one fashion to another, for the world will pass away with its lusts, as John says.

10. The use of tobacco during the church service is not permitted.

11. If holidays are observed, they shall not be observed for carnal pleasure but for the glory of God.

12. If a brother or sister marries outside the church, according to God's Word they cannot be received back into the congregation until he or she brings the spouse and both are received, or they separate from each other.

13. It is not allowed to go to a show or fair, where the spirit of the world has dominion.[70]

This codification of local rules and regulations may be considered an interpretation and an extension of the Ordnung as generally practiced churchwide by the Amish. It is unusual in its clarity, in its careful expression of general principles with relatively few specific restrictions, in its concise proscription of any unauthorized innovation, and in its obvious assumption that the economic resources of each member were to be shared with the poor of the brotherhood as need arose. Those few taboos which are mentioned no doubt reflect the special concerns of the congregation in 1871. Perhaps the members were anxious to prevent the importation into this new congregation of practices considered obnoxious in the communities from which they had come.

Innovations, it will be noted, were not condemned per se. The restriction was that no one should "introduce . . . anything in the congregation" without counseling with the whole group. Innovations could not be introduced at the whim of an individual or family. Nevertheless, the Ordnung was regarded as the guardian of a traditional lifestyle. Only the "high-minded keep pressing for innovation," said John (Hansi) Borntreger.[71] Even to this day the extreme reluctance of the Old Order Amish to adopt new machinery —and much less household conveniences and automobiles—is well known. "Daring worldly vehicles," said Daniel Stutzman, "we should leave for the world. What else could Jesus have meant when he said, 'Do not drive at top speed *(fahret nicht hoch her)*,' Luke 12:29?"[72]

The Daviess County congregation agreed with Jacob Swartzendruber and the Johnson County, Iowa, Amish settlement, in the stricture against bundling. That it was the first rule probably reflects the determination of the Daviess County congregation, especially of the leaders, to prevent the introduction of the practice into the new community. For the Old Order Amish church elsewhere, this ancient custom remained in a number of Amish communities, a circumstance not at all to the liking of Bishop David A. Troyer (Treyer).[73] Actually, according to John A. Hostetler, the most traditional of the Old Order Amish, with their "very rigid sex codes have been least opposed" to bundling.[74] As indicated in a booklet recently published by the Old Order Amish, *Ein Riss in der Mauer: Treatise on Courtship*, the practice has continued into the twentieth century and even to the present time.[75]

In similar manner the Amish wrestled against "oyster suppers, Surprise-parties, Turkey-roasts, Birthday Suppers, *Spiel*parties (play parties) and . . . *Hochzeits-gepränge* (wedding pageantry), and all needless feasts." They opposed the lustful songs and drinking songs often sung at some parties, and the "ugly and shameful joking and unthinkable promiscuous sitting."[76] David Stutzman asserted that the "*Spiel*parties" were "no more Christian than a regular dance" and should be called dances.[77] He said the devil had brought the "play parties" into the church. According to Hostetler, these activities continue among the young people of some Amish communities to this day.[78]

Regulations against expressions of pride in clothing (*Kleiderpracht*) and other kinds of personal adornment became increasingly the major emphasis of the Old Amish Ordnung. However, the rule of the Daviess County congregation relating thereto is phrased as a general principle. J. D. Guengerich's article on the attire of a Christian provides an unusually clear presentation and perceptive analysis of the Amish position on personal adornment and deserves special attention. Said Guengerich:

> Our clothes are . . . a reminder sign of our fallen condition. But I do not want to be understood that clothing alone will assure us of heaven. Yet I believe that adornment and vanity in clothing can thrust us into the pit of hell. Think of the rich man's fate. Where is there a man who eagerly adorns himself with clothing ornaments and who also does not live gloriously and in pleasure[?]

Then, resuming the theme of his first sentence, Guengerich proceeded:

> The first transgression [of Adam and Eve], was to me a trifling matter, the breaking off of the fruit from the tree of the knowledge of good and evil. The necessity of clothing is now a result of this transgression, a constant

Old Order Amish garb of about 1890 is illustrated in this picture of John Weierich, Shipshewana, Indiana. (Courtesy Reta Smoker, Goshen, Indiana.)

visible reminder. Now if we do not respect this [fact] rightly, then it happens that that which should be to our benefit, becomes the second transgression.

Just as we can "eat and drink damnation" to ourselves by using the Lord's Supper as an occasion for gluttony and even drunkenness, Guengerich continued, just so may we pervert God's intended use of clothing. This we do by adorning our fallen bodies with "the newest fashion." As men become slaves of alcohol, so women become slaves of fashion. As men ruin their health "by the misuse of eating and drinking," so do women by wearing "improper clothing . . . so long as the goddess of fashion will have it so."[79] In an 1895 article, J. D.'s brother, Samuel D. Guengerich, declared that "the whole tenor of the scriptures points to plainness, simplicity, and uniformity, not only in attire, but in everything else."[80] In injecting the term, *uniformity,* Samuel gave evidence that he was in tune with the change in emphasis so noticeable in Mennonite and Amish Mennonite writings on attire at the end of the nineteenth century.

Old Order Amish Writers

Only a small group of Old Order Amish men in the last quarter of the nineteenth century laid aside enough of their humility to write, either for the benefit of their own generation or of their posterity. Of these, Bishop David A. Troyer of Holmes County, Ohio, was one of the most able. He was typically Amish in his beliefs and lifestyle, whereas most of the other Old Order Amish who attempted to write were not impeccably Amish in these respects. Troyer's pamphlet-sized "Impartial Account" of the schism of 1860-61 in Holmes County is an invaluable source for that event.[81]

Typically Amish again, Troyer's only book, *Hinterlassene Schriften*,[82] was published posthumously, although one or two of the essays contained in it had been printed previously, probably before his death. As indicated elsewhere, Troyer remained steadfastly Amish in his opposition to any kind of participation in political affairs and to the missionary movement of his day. He supported a strict application of shunning and banning, and insisted on the importance of one's obedience to God and the church. Troyer was also one of a handful of Amish writers who contributed articles to the *Herold der Wahrheit*.[83]

Preacher John (Hansi) Borntreger of Middlebury, Indiana, is best known for his invaluable account of the schism of 1854-57 in northern Indiana.[84] His writings are almost as typically Amish as those of Troyer. Four of his articles appeared in the *Herold der Wahrheit*.[85]

Another writer was Full Deacon Frederick Swartzendruber of Sharon Township, Johnson County, Iowa, son of Bishop Jacob Swartzendruber and maternal grandfather of Sanford C. Yoder. He was somewhat less typically Amish: he did not resist the building of meetinghouses by the Deer Creek congregations, and he favored missionary work.[86] Otherwise, however, he remained in the Amish tradition. He followed his father's footsteps and other Amish reformers in resisting such entrenched Amish customs as bundling, "play parties," and sumptuous wedding feasts.[87] If the initials, "F. S." may be relied upon as indicating Frederick Swartzendruber as author, then no less than fourteen articles in the *Herold der Wahrheit* may be identified as his work.[88] Several of his articles deal with the functions of a deacon, particularly as to whether or how often a deacon may be permitted to preach, a subject for which he himself was the object.[89] Frederick's son, Jacob F., also wrote for the *Herold*.[90]

The writings of Samuel D. Guengerich of Johnson County, Iowa, deserve special attention. He was an Amish layman married to the daughter of Bishop Joel Beachy of Grantsville, Maryland. In 1864 he received a teacher's certificate from the Millersville, Pennsylvania, Normal School and then taught in Iowa public schools for a number of years.[91] Already in the 1870s he was promoting Sunday schools and two decades later became one of the principal organizers and supporters of an Amish parochial school which continued to function until at least 1912. In 1897 he published a forty-page booklet in support of such German schools.[92]

Guengerich's most remarkable undertaking may have been his publication of the youth periodical, the *Christliche Jugenfreund*. It was the first such publication for young people "published anywhere in the Mennonite world."[93] The magazine provided questions and answers to be used in German Sunday schools and also carried religious articles on a mostly adult level by such men as Christian J. Swartzendruber, Jacob D. Guengerich, D[aniel] E. Mast, and the editor himself. Judging by the letters from youthful readers, this paper had more acceptance from the Amish Mennonites than from the Old Order Amish. The venture failed after three years (1878-80) and the paper was then turned over to the Mennonite Publishing Company at Elkhart, Indiana.[94]

For at least several years Guengerich was area "agent" for Funk's publications in Johnson County, Iowa.[95] In the 1890s he engaged in correspondence with members of the Iowa state legislature. This resulted in a state law which provided exemptions from jury duty to those who objected to serving on religious grounds. By the end of the century he was supporting missionary-related projects.[96] Guengerich was obviously not a typical Old Order Amishman, nor was his home congregation, Lower Deer Creek, typically such, for reasons indicated earlier.[97] Nevertheless, he must be given some attention as an Amish writer. During the decades when he did much of his writing, he was a member of an Old Order Amish congregation in fellowship with at least some other congregations of that denomination.

Daniel E. Mast (1848-1930) of Hutchinson, Kansas, was mentioned above as a contributor to the *Christliche Jugenfreund*. He did most of his extensive writing in the twentieth century after he had been ordained to the ministry at age 65 or 66. His six articles appearing in the *Jugenfreund* consisted of gentle exhortations, the retelling of biblical stories such as the incident of Jesus remaining at the temple at age twelve, or the parable of the prodigal son.

The Doctrine of Assurance in Old Order Amish Writings

Earlier references have been made to Samuel Guengerich's valuable manuscript accounts on the Amish settlements in Iowa.[98] His article on the attire of Christians was printed in the *Herald of Truth*. Especially noteworthy is Guengerich's essay in the *Herold der Wahrheit* on "Jesus, the Victor Over Death." Typically Amish in its emphasis on Christ as the Redeemer and this life as "a seedtime for eternity," a preparation for the Last Judgment, it is unusually articulate and emotionally charged. Not typically Amish are Guengerich's final paragraphs. He declares that "as truly as Christ has arisen from the dead, so truly are all those who believe on him free from their sins, so truly do they themselves have forgiveness and eternal life."[99] The new soteriology which was finding acceptance among the Mennonites and Amish Mennonites[100] was not without its influence on the Old Order Amish. Some of them were reading the *Herold der Wahrheit* and probably other Protestant literature as well.

The doctrine of "present assurance," or assurance of salvation conditioned on one's continued personal commitment to Christ, eventually came to be generally accepted by the Mennonite Church and the Amish Mennonites. As noted earlier, in the fall of 1885 Funk had permitted fourteen articles to be printed in the *Herold der Wahrheit* in support of the doctrine of the more extreme version of assurance, that of eternal security. To these articles two Old Order Amish bishops responded, David A. Troyer and Frederick Swartzendruber. Troyer's response was in defense of the Amish doctrine that only "he who endures to the end shall be saved." Yet he took issue primarily with the doctrine of eternal security without openly attacking the principle of present or conditional assurance. Troyer admitted that the newborn Christian "has . . . eternal life," as stated in John 5:24. "But he does not yet possess it; it is only set aside for him . . . and promised by Him who cannot lie."[101] Swartzendruber's response was in similar vein.[102]

Perhaps the doctrine of assurance was gaining more ground among the Amish in the last decades of the nineteenth century than has been realized. John (Hansi) Borntreger wrote in 1892 that, according to his "understanding, salvation . . . has reference to this present life, for one may be saved [or blessed] already here on earth (Matt. 5:3-11)." However, Borntreger hastened to add that one "must strive earnestly to be a true servant of his Lord in the observance of the commandments, for he knows that he must labor and work to receive the promised reward."[103]

In any case, the doctrine of salvation as expounded by S. D. Guengerich and John (Hansi) Borntreger differed not at all from that which was coming into general acceptance among the Amish Mennonites. Likely Old Order Amish leaders who did not read the *Herold der Wahrheit* nor much of any other Protestant literature, and wrote little or nothing for publication, were less inclined to give an ear to the new soteriology. Certainly the belief that one may be sure of one's salvation at any time before he or she stands before God in the Last Judgment has not gained general acceptance among the Old Order Amish.[104]

At the end of the nineteenth century the Old Order Amish church was alive and growing rapidly. Resisting acculturation with the larger society around it, however, was testing the spiritual strength and the corporate ingenuity of the entire body. Continual review was required to decide what innovations in community and personal lifestyle to accept, tolerate, or reject. The proper use of the disciplinary instruments of banning and shunning remained an unresolved issue. The twentieth century would see a continuation of these struggles to discern obedience to Christ.

Abbreviations in Notes

AMC—Archives of the Mennonite Church, located on the campus of Goshen College, Goshen, Indiana.

ME—*Mennonite Encyclopedia*, vols. 1-5 (Scottdale, Pennsylvania: The Mennonite Publishing House, 1955-59, 1990).

MHL—Mennonite Historical Library, Goshen College, Goshen, Indiana.

MQR—*Mennonite Quarterly Review* (Goshen, Indiana).

Stoltzfus Documents—Tennessee John Stoltzfus: Amish Church-Related Documents and Family Letters of the Nineteenth Century, ed. Paton Yoder, Lancaster, Pa.: Lancaster Mennonite Historical Society, 1987.

Verhandlungen—Printed minutes of the churchwide Amish ministers' meetings, 1862-78, held yearly in various Amish communities from Pennsylvania to Iowa. The titles given to these respective yearly minutes varied somewhat. That given to the 1862 minutes was *Verhandlungen der Diener-Versammlung der Deutschen Taufer oder Amischen Mennoniten gehalten in Wayne County, Ohio, in Juny 1862* (Lancaster Pa.: Johan Bär's Söhnen, 1862). In 1866 and following years the printing of the *Verhandlungen* was transferred to the office of the *Herold der Wahrheit*, except in 1868, when the original printer was used once more. A complete set of these minutes may be found in the MHL.

Notes

CHAPTER 1: The Amish in America

1. Silas J. Smucker, *Christian Schmucker, Stalwart Pioneer* (Goshen, Ind.: by the author, 1986), pp. 13-15.

2. Paul Schowalter, "Pioneer Nicholas Stoltzfus," *Mennonite Research Journal*, 4 (Apr. 1963): 1, 22; Paton Yoder, *Eine Wurzel: Tennessee John Stoltzfus* (Lititz, Pa.: Sutter House, 1979), p. 3.

3. John A. Hostetler, *Amish Society*, 3d ed. (Baltimore: The Johns Hopkins University Press, 1980), pp. 56-59; J. C. Wenger, "The Amish," *An Introduction to Mennonite History*, ed. Cornelius J. Dyck (Scottdale, Pa.: Herald Press, 1967), p. 182.

4. Hostetler, *Amish Society*, p. 65, note 34.

5. Joseph F. Beiler in the Foreword to Hugh F. Gingerich and Rachel W. Kreider, *Amish and Amish Mennonite Genealogies* (Gordonville, Pa.: Pequea Publishers, 1986), p. xiii. Beiler estimates that less than 40% of the children of this first wave of Amish immigrants "grew up to remain Amish or to raise an Amish family." Of this second generation, those which did remain Amish were more successful in raising their children to be Amish; for the third generation the rate was still higher.

6. During the French and Indian War, the Indian raid of 1757 on the Jacob Hostetler family of the Northkill Amish settlement in Berks County, northwest of Reading, may constitute one of those instances in which the exception confirms the rule. As a result of this raid, the Amish settlers in that vicinity abandoned their holdings. Similar circumstances obtained in the Tuscararwas County-Holmes County Amish settlement in Ohio during the War of 1812, although tradition is not clear as to whether an Indian raid actually took place or whether there was only the "scare" of such a raid (Hilda Troyer, *Troyer, Treier, Treyer Family Tree Outlined and "Our" John Troyer's 68 Feet Under the Table* (n.p., by the author, 1974), pp. 15-16.

7. For a more extensive treatment of the demography of the Amish population in America before 1800 see Richard K. MacMaster, *Land, Piety, Peoplehood: The Establishment of Mennonite Communities in America, 1683-1790* (Scottdale, Pa.: Herald Press, 1985), pp. 70-71. See also C. Henry Smith, *The Mennonite Immigration to Pennsylvania in the Eighteenth Century* (Norristown, Pa.: 1929), 243-44.

8. An excellent account of the Amish division of the 1690s may be found in Calvin G. Bachman, *The Old Order Amish of Lancaster County*, vol. 44 of the *Proceedings of the Pennsylvania German Society* (Morristown, Pa.: 1942), pp. 35-50. A well-reasoned account of the division, sympathetic to Ammann, including a summary of some findings of Leroy Beachy, may be found in Elmer S. Yoder, *The Beachy Amish Mennonite Fellowship Churches* (Hartville, Ohio: Diakonia Ministries, 1987), pp. 43-59. See also Milton Gascho, "The Amish Division of 1693-1697 in Switzerland and Alsace," *MQR*, 11 (Oct. 1937): 235-66; and *The Letters of the Amish Division of 1693-1711*, trans. and ed. John B. Mast (Oregon City, Ore.: Christian J. Schlabach, 1950).

9. A pastoral letter of about 1720 to the preachers and elders of the congregation at Markirk, written by Uli Ammann, suggests a considerable degree of patience and some toleration in the administration of Amish church affairs (*Mennonite Historical Bulletin*, 38 [Oct. 1977]: 2-3).

10. J. F. B., "Ordnung," *MQR*, 56 (Oct. 1982): 382-84.

11. Hostetler, *Amish Society*, p. 64.

12. Joseph F. Beiler, "Revolutionary War Records," *The Diary*, 7 (Mar. 1975): 71.

13. The late Amos Fisher, Amish historian, has attributed much of the attrition which took place in the Amish church before 1800 to defections to the Dunkards, or Church of the Brethren, and to the movement led by Mennonite Bishop Martin Boehm which eventuated in the formation of the United Brethren church ("The History of the First Amish Communities in America," in Gingerich and Kreider, *Amish Genealogies*, p. xix).

14. Hostetler, *Amish Society*, p. 71.

CHAPTER 2: Era of Consolidation, 1800-50

1. David Beiler, *Eine Vermahnung oder Andenken* (n.p. [1928]), p. 3. This exhortation or memoir has been translated by John Umble in "Memoirs of an Amish Bishop," *MQR*, 22 (Apr. 1948): 101-15. The comments on simplicity and submission to church discipline may be found in Umble's translation on pages 101-02.

2. John Stoltzfus, "Short Account of the Life, Doctrine, and Example of Our Old Ministers" (*Stoltzfus Documents*, doc. no. 22). This man moved to Tennessee in 1872 and is not to be confused with "Groffdale" John Stoltzfus or Bishop John K. Stoltzfus.

3. Identified in *Golden Memories of Amos J. Stoltzfus*, comp. Christian P. Stoltzfus ([Gordonville, Pa.]: by the author, 1984), pp. 181-83, as a letter written in 1893 by Daniel D. Miller and translated from the German by Leander Keim.

4. John A. Hostetler, *Amish Society*, 3d ed. (Baltimore: Johns Hopkins University Press, 1980), p. 64.

5. These schisms took place in Butler County, Ohio, in 1835 (W. H. Grubb, *History of the Mennonites of Butler County, Ohio* [Trenton, Ohio: by the author, 1916], p.13); in Lewis County, N.Y., in the late 1840s (David Luthy, "The Amish in Lewis County, New York," *Family Life* [May 1983]: 21-25); and in Mifflin County, Pa., in 1849 (Samuel W. Peachey, *Amish of Kishacoquillas Valley, Mifflin County, Pa.* [Scottdale, Pa.: by the author, 1930], pp. 32-33).

6. The Discipline of 1809 may be found in "Some Early American Amish Mennonite Disciplines," trans. and ed. Harold S. Bender, *MQR*, 8 (Apr. 1934): 91-93. A facsimile of Bishop Jacob Swartzendruber's copy of this discipline may be found in *MQR*, 20 (July 1946): following page 239.

7. David Beiler, *Vermahnung*, pp. 7-8 (translated in Umble, "Memoirs," p. 103).

8. An account of this meeting, along with some follow-up meetings, attributed to the pen of Bishop Christian Yoder, Senior, has been translated by Harvey J. Miller in "Proceedings of Amish Ministers' Conferences, 1826-31," *MQR*, 33 (Apr. 1959): 134-42 (quotations taken from p. 135).

9. Discipline of 1837 in Bender, "Early . . . Disciplines," p. 94. John Stoltzfus confirmed that newly imposed at this time was the requirement that the penitent requesting restoration to fellowship in the church bring his or her spouse along. See John Stoltzfus, "Short Account."

10. Christian Z. Mast, "The First Church Controversy Among the Amish in America," *Mennonite Historical Bulletin*, 15 (July 1954): 1.

11. Account of Bishop Christian Yoder, Senior, of Somerset County, Pa., of the ministers' meetings of 1830 and 1831, held in Wayne County, Ohio, in Miller, "Ministers' Conferences," pp. 136-40. This account may also be found in Beiler's *Vermahnung*, pp. 18-28 (quotations on pages 20-21 and 26-27), and in Umble's translation of the same ("Memoirs," pp. 110-11, 113). See also Shem Zook, *Eine wahre Darstellung von dem, welches uns das Evangelium in der Reinhart lehrt, so wie auch ein unparteiischer Bericht von den Haupt-Umstanden, welche sich unterschiedlichen Gemeinden ereigneten, woraus die unchristlichen Spaltungen entstanden sind* (Mattawana, Mifflin Co., Pa.: by the author, 1880), p. 11. In his "Short Account" (1862), John Stoltzfus called attention to, and seemingly approved of, the established policy of requiring that applicants for membership in an Amish congregation coming from any other denomination be rebaptized.

12. Hostetler, *Amish Society*, p. 64.

13. John Umble, "Catalog of an Amish Bishop's 'Library,' " *MQR*, 20 (July 1946): 233-34, 238, including notes 5 and 6.

14. *Ein Riss in der Maurer* (Sugarcreek, Ohio: published in the 1970s), p. 22. The title refers to the persistent custom of bundling. It seems likely that George Jutzi, Amish minister in the Richville congregation southwest of Canton, Ohio, was referring to the custom of bundling when he wrote sometime in the 1840s about an unidentified something which originally had been a "forbidden pleasure." It had become so much a custom in his day that it had the approval of the Amish community, and perhaps was even considered as an expression of "Christian Ordnung" *(Ermahnungen von George Jutzi in Stark County, Ohio, an seine Hinterbliebenen, nebst einem Anhange über die Entstehung der Amischen Gemeinde von Sam. Zook* [Somerset, Pa.: Alexander Stutzman, 1853], p. 72).

15. Discipline of 1837, in Bender, "Early . . . Disciplines," p. 95.

16. John Stoltzfus, uncle of "Tennessee" John Stoltzfus, to John Beiler and Christian Zug, both of the latter of Mifflin County, Pa., Mar. 29, 1832 (*Stoltzfus Documents*, doc. no. 1).

17. Swartzendruber's abhorence of the practice of bundling emerges repeatedly in a letter which he sent to the annual ministers' meeting of 1865 held in Wayne County, Ohio ("An Amish Minister's Conference Epistle of 1865," trans. and ed. Harold S. Bender, *MQR*, 20 [July 1946]: 222-29). See also Melvin Gingerich, *The Mennonites in Iowa* (Iowa City, Iowa: State Historical Society of Iowa, 1939), p. 244.

18. David Luthy, interviewed by the author, July 31, 1987.

19. Miller, "Ministers' Conferences," p. 135; also found in Beiler, *Vermahnung*, p. 18, and translated in Umble, "Memoirs," p. 109.

20. Beiler, *Vermahnung*, p. 8, and translated in Umble, "Memoirs," pp. 103-04. This violation of church Ordnung in the late 1850s is alluded to in Christian Stoltzfus to John Stoltzfus, May 20, 1861 (*Stoltzfus Documents*, doc. no. 18); and in John and Ana Neuhauser to Peter Litwiller, May 11, 1858 (Hist. mss. 1-10, box 1/9, AMC).

21. Sketches of the lives of Jacob and Samuel Yoder may be found in Paton Yoder, *A Yoder Family History: Jacob, Samuel, Jonathan* (Goshen, Ind.: by the author, 1980), pp. 1-28.

22. Discipline of 1837, in Bender, "Early . . . Disciplines," pp. 94-95.

23. Beiler, *Vermahnung*, pp. 3-6, translated in Umble, "Memoirs," pp. 101-02. Beiler was writing this in 1861-62.

24. Concerning the westward movement of the Amish in America, see C. Henry Smith, *The Mennonites of America* (Goshen, Ind.: by the author, 1909), pp. 214-24.

25. Gingerich, *Mennonites in Iowa*, pp. 95, 104, 123.

26. David Luthy, "The Amish in Butler County, Ohio," *Family Life*, Apr. 1982: 21-25.

27. For a case study of an immigrant father and elder who sought escape from the militaristic governments of Western Europe, see the study of Elder Christian Engel by Steven Estes, "Love God and Your Neighbor: The Attitudes of Elder Christian Engel Toward War, Peace, and Revolution" (ms. in library of Associated Mennonite Biblical Seminaries, Elkhart, Ind.).

28. James E. Landing, "The Old Order Amish Settlement at Nappanee, Indiana: Oldest in Indiana," *Mennonite Historical Bulletin*, 30 (Oct. 1969): 5. Concerning the general pattern of westward movement and settlement of the Amish, see J. C. Wenger, "The Mennonites Come to North America," *An Introduction to Mennonite History*, ed. Cornelius J. Dyck (Scottdale, Pa.: Herald Press, 1967), pp. 146, 149-54; Willard Smith, *Mennonites in Illinois* (Scottdale, Pa.: Herald Press, 1983), pp. 57-59; and Orland Gingerich, *The Amish of Canada* (Waterloo, Ont.: Conrad Press, 1972), pp. 28-29, 34-39.

29. Communication from Ivan J. Miller, Grantsville, Md., Feb. 1988.

30. Gingerich, *Mennonites in Iowa*, pp. 57ff.

31. Yoder, *Family History*, p. 18.

32. In some recent research, the results of which have not yet been published, Steven Estes has identified twenty Amish families who came to the Rock Creek settlement in Illinois in the years 1847-51 from states to the east.

33. J. S. Hartzler, "Bishop Isaac Schmucker (1810-1893)," *Gospel Herald*, 22 (June 27, 1929): 267; Obituary of Isaac Schmucker, *Herald of Truth*, 30 (Dec. 1, 1893): 373.

34. W. H. Grubb, *Mennonites of Butler County, Ohio*, p. 13; Steven Estes, *A Goodly Heritage, A History of the North Danvers Mennonite Church* (Danvers, Ill.: North Danvers Mennonite Church, 1982), pp. 30-31.

35. See Hostetler, *Amish Society*, p. 65.

36. Beiler, *Vermahnung*, p. 8, translated in Umble, "Memoirs," p. 103.

37. John Stoltzfus, *Von der Vater Zeit, bis auf die jetzige Zeit* (Millwood, near Gap, Pa.: ca. 1880), p. 2, translated by N. B. and reprinted in Paton Yoder, *Eine Wurzel: Tennessee John Stoltzfus* (Lititz, Pa.: Sutter House, 1979), p. 164.

CHAPTER 3: The Amish Congregation
and the Structure of the Ministry

1. Shem Zook to John Stoltzfus, June 24, 1863 (*Stoltzfus Documents*, doc. no. 28).

2. David J. Zook to John Stoltzfus, Nov. 6, 1864 (*Stoltzfus Documents*, doc. no. 43).

3. *Verhandlungen, 1864*, pp. 12-13.

4. Refraining from participation in the Lord's Supper as a way of protesting against the conduct of other members of the congregation was a common practice. On Apr. 16, 1865, in the Sharon Township congregation of Johnson County, Iowa, 66 took communion and 60 refrained. Three years later, in the same congregation, 64 participated and 57 refrained. In the neighboring Deer Creek congregation in 1865, 38 took communion and 48 refrained (Melvin Gingerich, *Mennonites in Iowa* [Iowa City, Iowa: State Historical Society of Iowa, 1939], pp. 125-26).

The circumstances obtaining in the Buffalo Valley congregation are recounted in John Umble, "Amish Mennonites of Union County, Pennsylvania, I. Social and Religious Life," *MQR*, 7 (Apr. 1933): 71-96. Christian Stoltzfus was deacon there from its initial organization in 1839 until the collapse of its congregational structure in 1883.

5. Christian Stoltzfus to John Stoltzfus, Apr. 10, 1860 (*Stoltzfus Documents*, doc. no. 13). For other letters by Christian Stoltzfus telling of conditions in the Buffalo Valley congregation see ibid., docs. no. 2, 18, 24, 26, and 67.

6. John Umble, interview with his aunt Elizabeth Stoltzfus, Oct. 2, 1932, recorded on a note card, box 14/13, John S. Umble Papers, AMC. See also Umble, "Union County," p. 91.

7. Christian Stoltzfus to John Stoltzfus, Oct. 20, 1868 (*Stoltzfus Documents*, doc. no. 54). See also John Stoltzfus to Abraham Peachey, Nov. 8, 1868 (ibid., doc. no. 55).

8. Henry Fisher and wife to Henry U. and Malinda Stoltzfus, Apr. 23, 1877 (*Stoltzfus Documents*, doc. no. 64).

9. The Christian Z. Mast Papers and photocopies comprising the Lydia Mast Collection may be found in the LMHL. Many of the letters of the Lydia Mast Collection appear in translation in *Stoltzfus Documents*. Photocopies of the Long Christian Zook Papers are located in AMC.

10. See Elam R. Stoltzfus "The Amish Mennonites of Buffalo Valley: An Historical Sketch, 1836-88" (unpublished ms. in AMC, 1963) for a description of prolonged visits of young people to Buffalo Valley from other Amish settlements in central and eastern Pennsylvania. For the Pennsylvania-Iowa treks, see Gingerich, *Mennonites in Iowa*, p. 247.

11. For evidence of such family visiting see David Hooley to John Stoltzfus, July 19, 1860, and Jacob Hooley to Gideon Stoltzfus, July 13, 1896 (*Stoltzfus Documents*, docs. no. 73 and 120, respectively).

12. C. Z. Mast, "The First Church Controversy Among the Amish in America," *Mennonite Historical Bulletin*, 15 (July 1954): 1.

13. See the account of this controversy provided by Bishop Christian Yoder, Sr., in Harvey J. Miller, "Proceedings of the Amish Ministers' Conferences, 1826-31," *MQR*, 33 (Apr. 1959): 134-41. Yoder's two trips to Ohio are mentioned on pp. 134-35. This account is also appended to David Beiler, *Vermahnung oder Andenken* (n.p. [1928]), pp. 15-28.

14. Miller, "Ministers' Conferences," pp. 134-41.

15. In "New Light on the Amish Division, 1847-62," a manuscript prepared for publication but evidently never published, John Umble attempted to put together an account of this meeting of 1849 at Berlin based on the two sides of the extant half sheet. A photocopy of this half-sheet, along with a typescript copy of Umble's article, may be found in the Samuel Mast Papers, AMC.

16. Bishop David Beiler to Bishop Christian Ummel and Deacon John Stoltzfus, Mar. 21, 1859 (*Stoltzfus Documents*, doc. no. 8).

17. For a fuller description of these four ministerial offices, see Paton Yoder, "The Structure of the Amish Ministry in the Nineteenth Century," *MQR*, 61 (July 1987), pp. 280-97.

18. The question of whether full deacons should be allowed to preach and, if so, how often, is a striking example of this concern for a strict delineation of the duties for each ministerial office (Paton Yoder, "The Preaching Deacon Controversy Among Nineteenth Century American Amish," *Pennsylvania Mennonite Heritage*, 8 [Jan. 1985]: 2-9).

19. This statement of duties is from an old minister's manual which had been in the possession of Bishop Jacob S. Gerig of the Oak Grove congregation of Wayne County, Ohio, and was copied by John Umble. It appears in the German, followed by the English translation, in John Umble, "Amish Ordination Charges," *MQR*, 13 (Oct. 1939): 233-50. The duties of deacons are enumerated on pp. 235 and 237. Hereafter this document will be referred to as the Gerig Manual.

20. See Hans Nafziger's manual, written in 1781, as published by John D. Hostetler, *Ein alter Brief Copia oder Abschrift eines Briefs, welcher von Dienern und Aeltesten der Gemeinde zu Holland auf ihr Begehren und Ansuchen ist zugeschicht worden den 26ten März, von Hanss Nafziger in Esingen bei Landau in Oberland* (Elkhart, Ind.: Mennonitische Verlagshandlung for Joh. D. Hochstetler, 1916), p. 23.

21. The specification of eight years as the proper length of the probationary period for a deacon is mentioned in a pastoral letter of Aug. 24, 1862, entitled "Von einen völligen Diener zu einen andern völligen Diener (From One Full Minister to Another Full Minister)" (evidently written by Solomon Beiler of Mifflin County, Pa., translated in *Stoltzfus Documents*, doc. no. 25), p. 9.

22. Umble, "Ordination Charges," p. 241.

23. Minister's manual attributed to Joseph Unzicker, "An Amish Minister's Manual," ed. and trans. John Umble, *MQR*, 15 (Apr. 1941): 104-05 (quotation on p. 105, with its translation on p. 110).

24. This statement represents a measure of consensus expressed at the annual ministers' meeting of 1864 (*Verhandlungen, 1864*, p. 15).

25. John Umble, "Union County," pp. 73-74.

26. [Amos L. Fisher?], "Introduction," *Ein Diener Register von Diener Deaconien und Bischof in Lancaster County und umliegende Gemeinde* (Gordonville, Pa.: Pequea Publishers, 1983), p. 7.

27. Umble, "Ordination Charges," p. 250. John C. Yoder was ordained deacon in 1852 and advanced to full deacon in 1861 in Lagrange County, Ind. He died in 1906 (Hans Borntreger, *Eine Geschichte der ersten Ansiedelung der Amischen Mennoniten und die Gründung ihrer ersten Gemeinde im Staate Indiana nebst einer kurzen Erklarung über die Spaltung die in dieser Gemeinde geschehen ist* [Elkhart Ind.: Mennonite Publishing Company, 1907], pp. 9, 13, 18).

28. For two instances in which Eli S. Miller carried out functions pertaining to the office of bishop—those of ordaining a minister and of administering communion—see

Abraham Mast's Walnut Creek Record Book (Holmes County, Ohio) for the years 1860-98, entries for Oct. 17, 1891, and May 14, 1893 (photocopy in AMC).

29. Gingerich, *Mennonites in Iowa*, p. 181 and note 132 on p. 388. John Umble, interview with S. C. Yoder, June 12, 1933, quotes Yoder as saying that "his mother's father [Frederick Swartzendruber] was a full deacon and . . . people always thought that as such he did not quite have full authority, but he did preach some" (Umble Collection, box 14/13, AMC).

30. A news item in the *Herold der Wahrheit*, 11 (Dec. 1874): 201, records that "Deacon John Stoltzfus was . . . promoted [erhöhet] in his office."

31. This incorrect statement by Umble of the circumstances under which a deacon was ordained a full deacon may be found in his "Early Sunday Schools at West Liberty, Ohio," *MQR*, 4 (Jan. 1930): 13; and again in his "Union County," pp. 73-74. In *Mennonites in Iowa*, p. 181, Gingerich repeats this misstatement.

32. Three letters of Frederick Swartzendruber of Johnson County, Iowa, undated but written in about 1889, to Old Order Bishop John L. Miller, of Elkhart County, Ind. (Heritage Historical Library, Aylmer, Ont.), indicate that the office of full deacon itself was in some question at that time.

33. Nafziger's manual, *Ein alter Brief*, pp. 21-22.

34. The "Gemeinde Buch," the 1750-1896 record book of the Montbéliard congregation in Alsace, used the French form, *predicateur*, consistently throughout the time span, when denoting the office of minister. A typescript of this ms. may be found in the MHL.

35. Erismann's journal, a "Kurtze [sic] Lebensbeschreibung und Tagebuch," is located in the AMC. For the Mast letters see Abraham Mast to John K. Yodter (Yoder), Nov. 6, 1878, John K. Yoder Correspondence, AMC. Mast used the term again in 1891 in his Walnut Creek Record Book, p. 20.

36. Cornelius Krahn, "The Office of Elder in Anabaptist-Mennonite History," *MQR*, 30 (Apr. 1956): 120-27; Harold S. Bender, "The Office of Bishop in Anabaptist-Mennonite History," *MQR*, 30 (Apr. 1956): 128-32.

37. The difference between the Amish office of *Ältester* and that of the Mennonites is uniquely illustrated by an exchange of notes appearing in the pages of the *Herald of Truth* for July and Sept., 1865. In July (p. 48) a reader made inquiry about the duties of a deacon. In September (pp. 69-70), Elias Yoder of McLean County, Ill., attempted an answer, but spoke of the duties, not of a deacon, but of an elder, even using the term *bishop's office* at one point. The confusion is easily explained by referring to the German version of this exchange of notes as they appeared in the *Herold der Wahrheit*. For the word *deacon* in the English version, the German version in the *Herold* for July (p. 48) used *Ältester*. But to the Amish reader, Elias Yoder, this word signified elder or bishop, and his response (*Herold der Wahrheit*, 2 [Sept. 1865]: 69) was made with that understanding. Evidently the editor of these two papers did not notice, or perhaps chose to ignore, this misunderstanding. This significant confusion of terms was called to my attention by Mennonite historian Steven Estes.

38. Montbéliard "Gemeinde Buch," pp. 73 and 77 of typescript.

39. Nafziger manual, *Ein alter Brief*, p. 22.

40. Anonymous ms. "Concerning the Matter that Pertains to the Ordination of Samuel Yoder as Full Minister" (*Stoltzfus Documents*, doc. no. 35). See also *Verhandlungen, 1864*, pp. 7, 8, 10; and Christian Ummel, *et al.*, to Solomon K. Beiler, Sept. 7, 1864 (*Stoltzfus Documents*, doc. no. 41). Obviously further research might change the year in which the Amish began to use the term *Bischof*, but quite certainly the choice of the year 1864 cannot be greatly amiss.

41. Concerning the incident of the button affair, see David Luthy, *The Amish in America: Settlements That Failed, 1840-1960* (Aylmer, Ont.: Pathway Publishers, 1985), p. 427.

42. The duties of an elder or full minister are delineated in the Nafziger, the Unzicker, and the Gerig manuals.

43. These excerpts from Jacob Swartzendruber's letter are from Gingerich, *Mennonites in Iowa*, p. 129.

44. S. D. Guengerich, "A Brief History of the Amish Settlement in Johnson County, Iowa," *MQR* 3 (Oct. 1929): 246; David Luthy, "Three Somerset County Settlements," *Family Life* (Jan. 1982): 19; "An Amish Bishop's Conference Epistle of 1865," ed. and trans. Harold S. Bender, *MQR*, 20 (July 1946): 222.

45. J. S. Hartzler, "Fifty Mennonite Leaders: Bishop Isaac Schmucker," *Gospel Herald*, 22 (June 27, 1929): 267-68.

46. Among the several boxes of the John S. Umble Collection, AMC, especially in box 18, may be found typescript translations of Amish sermons, formularies, and parts of minister's manuals. The origin of some of these are indicated, but many are not identified. According to a note from Umble, apparently to the director of the Archives (John S. Umble Collection, box 18/1), it appears that most of these typescripts are translations of papers originally collected by Christian Lehmann and presented to H. S. Bender in 1948 by H. Volmer. Not all of them were necessarily written by Lehmann. Comments by Umble in "An Early Amish Formulary," *MQR*, 34 (Jan. 1960): 57, support these deductions. Unfortunately, finding the originals of these translations in the MHL or in the AMC has thus far been an unsuccessful ordeal, making corroboration of these translations impossible for the present. These anonymous sermons and formularies will be identified by the heading given to the document by the translator, followed by "Sermons and Formularies (Lehmann)," its location in the John S. Umble Collection, and the page number of the translator's typescript copy of the document under discussion. Accordingly, this note should read: Part of a minister's manual "Concerning the Selecting and Ordaining of Ministers," in "Sermons and Formularies (Lehmann)" (box 18/16, John S. Umble Collection), p. 4. Since it is an established fact that Amish sermons were traditionally extemporaneous and not recorded, J[ohn] S. O[yer]'s search for an explanation for the existence of such sermon manuscripts ("Introduction" to [Joseph Klopfenstein], "An Amish Sermon," *MQR*, 58 [July 1984]: 296-317) may be useful.

47. Ezekiel 3:17, which was much quoted by Amish ministers, speaks of a prophet as a spiritual watchman. For illustrations of the incessant exhortations to ministers that they be "auf der Hut und auf der Wacht" (on guard and on the watch) and/or be careful the "Trumpete [zu] blasen" (to blow the trumpets), see *Verhandlungen, 1872*, pp. 16, 30; *1873*, pp. 22-23; *1875*, pp. 10-11, 22, 25, 30, 37; *1876*, pp. 4, 7, 18; Joseph Stuckey to the *Herold der Wahrheit*, 2 (Sept. 1865): 67; and [Christian Peterschmitt], [*Gottesdienst*], (n.p., [1871]), p. 14. A cataloger's note at MHL concerning this book reads: "Apparently published without title page or caption title, ascribed to Christian Peterschmitt of the Hang congregation, Alsace, by H. Volmar in conversation with H. S. Bender prior to May, 1949."

48. *Verhandlungen, 1875*, p. 36.

49. George Jutzi, *Ermahnungen von George Jutzi in Stark County, Ohio, an seine Hinterbliebenen nebst einem Anhang über die Entstehung der amischen Gemeinde, von Sam. Zook* (Somerset, Pa.: Alexander Stutzman, 1853), p. 4.

50. David A. Treyer [Troyer], *Ein unparteiischer Bericht von den Hauptumständen welche sich ereigneten in den sogenannten Alt-Amischen Gemeinden in Ohio, vom Jahr 1850 bis ungefähr 1861, wodurch endlich eine vollkommene Spaltung entstand* (n.p., n.d.), p. 5.

51. Borntreger, *Geschichte*, p. 13.

52. Use of this term as an expression of opprobrium is illustrated in an exchange of letters between John Stoltzfus and Bishop Elias Riehl, of the Buffalo Valley congregation, dated Jan. 17 and Jan. 20, 1860 (*Stoltzfus Documents*, docs. no. 11 and 12, respectively).

53. Umble, "Union County," p. 87.

54. David A. Treyer [Troyer], *Hinterlassene Schriften von David A. Treyer von Holmes County, Ohio, unter welchem sind auch mehrer Erbauliche und Geistreiche Gedichte*, 2d ed. (Arthur, Ill.: L. A. Miller, 1925), section containing "A Presentation or Clarification Concerning the Office of Preacher," pp. 126, 130, and 133. The pledge to

accept the ministry if the lot should fall on him was reaffirmed by the bridegroom at the time of his marriage. This is indicated at the close of an undated ms. of thirteen pages containing a marriage sermon and a guide to the marriage ceremony, in the D. B. Swartzendruber Collection (box 2/7, AMC).

55. *Verhandlungen, 1866*, p. 8. As late as 1897 the Eastern District Amish Mennonite Conference ruled that if a minister refused to serve in his office "without a just cause," he should be dealt with as a "transgressor" (*Report of the Eastern Amish Mennonite Conference from the Time of Its Organization to the Year 1911*, comp. C. Z. Yoder [Sugar Creek, Ohio: 1911], p. 7). In 1898 the Western District Amish Mennonite Conference ruled that, once chosen and ordained, a minister could not be released from "the office to which he has been called," although, if incapable, "he should not be required to preach, but rather to serve God with the talents which he has received" (*Western District A[mish] M[ennonite] Conference*, comp. S. C. Yoder [Scottdale, Pa.: Mennonite Publishing House, 1912], p. 25).

56. Umble, "Union County," p. 87.

57. C. Henry Smith, *Mennonite Country Boy: The Early Years of C. Henry Smith* (Newton Kansas: Faith and Life Press, 1962), pp. 122-23. Smith added that, for many Amishmen, ordination to the ministry "meant a life of hard study and endless regret for inability to measure up to the task imposed on them."

58. John Umble, interview with David W. Kennel, Nov. 22, 1932, recorded on a note card (box 14/13, Umble Collection). This story without the names of the men involved in the lot appears in Umble, "Union County," p. 88.

59. Christian Stoltzfus to C[hristian] and S[usanna] Zook, Aug. 27, 1883, original in the possession of Harold R. Mast, Leola, Pa.

60. John Umble, "Mennonites in Lyon County, Kan., 1880-1890: A Memoir," *MQR*, 26 (July 1952): 234.

61. Sanford Calvin Yoder, *The Days of My Years* (Scottdale, Pa.: Herald Press, 1959), p. 25; S. D. Guengerich, "A Brief History of the Origin and Development of the So-called Amish Mennonite Congregation of Johnson Co. Iowa . . ." pp. 24-26 (30-page typescript copy in MHL).

62. Luthy, *Amish in America*, p. 411.

63. Eli Gingerich, Middlebury, Ind., to Paton Yoder, Dec. 12, 1983; E. J. Borntreger in the Foreword to Treyer, *Hinterlassene Schriften*, p. 3.

64. David A. Treyer [Troyer], "Wer aber beharret bis an's Ende, der wird selig," *Herold der Wahrheit*, 23 (Jan. 15, 1886): 17-18. In the text the modern spelling *Troyer* has been used.

65. Quotations taken from David A. Treyer, *Hinterlassene Schriften*, section on the "Office of Preacher," pp. 126-33.

66. This formulary may be found in the D. B. Swartzendruber Collection (box 2/7).

67. *Verhandlungen, 1864*, p. 15.

68. *Verhandlungen, 1868*, pp. 13-14.

69. *Verhandlungen, 1874*, p. 9.

70. The choice of a minister by the "most votes" rule is indicated in almost all of the minister's manuals coming from Europe, including the Nafziger and Unzicker manuals. However, there is an Amish formulary used in ordination services which may have come from Europe, in "Sermons and Formularies (Lehmann)." It calls for the use of the lot in the selection of a minister (box 18/11, Umble Collection).

71. Montbéliard "Gemeinde Buch," p. 79 of typescript.

72. J. F. Beiler, "Lewis County, New York," *The Diary*, 6 (Sept., Nov., Dec. 1974): (December installment) 282.

73. John Stoltzfus, "Short Account" (*Stoltzfus Documents*, doc. no. 22).

74. Paul Peachey, "Anabaptism and Church Organization, *MQR*, 30 (July 1956): 214, 217, and 219.

CHAPTER 4: Nineteenth-Century Amish Beliefs and Lifestyle
1. Christian Stoltzfus to John Stoltzfus, May 20, 1861 (*Stoltzfus Documents*, doc. no. 18).
2. For an illustration of the kind of respect given to the Dordrecht Confession of Faith, see the reference made to it in an anonymous document "Concerning the Matter that Pertains to the Ordination of Samuel Yoder as Bishop," which certainly is a record of a meeting on Apr. 20, 1864, at Pequea in Lancaster County, Pa., of the Amish ministers of eastern Pennsylvania (*Stoltzfus Documents*, doc. no. 35).
3. *Verhandlungen, 1864*, p. 19.
4. *Verhandlungen, 1872*, p. 8.
5. "Report of Preliminary General Conference Meeting," *Herald of Truth*, 34 (Dec. 15, 1897): 371-72.
6. "Brief Summary of the Eighteen Articles Which are to be Explained to Children [young people] who are uniting with the Church," in "Sermons and Formularies (Lehmann)" (box 18/15, John S. Umble Collection). On pages 5-13 of these instructions to candidates for baptism may be found a running commentary on each of the eighteen articles of the Dordrecht statement. See note 46 of chapter 3 for further identification of this source. Page numbers in this and subsequent references to "Sermons and Formularies (Lehmann)" refer to the translator's typescript copy of the document under discussion.
7. J. C. Wenger, "The Amish," *An Introduction to Mennonite History*, ed. Cornelius J. Dyck (Scottdale, Pa.: Herald Press, 1967), p. 184.

The careful reader may want to compare nineteenth-century Amish theology, particularly in the area of soteriology, with that of the Mennonites in the same period by referring to J. Denny Weaver's analytical paper on "The Quickening of Soteriology: Atonement from Christian Burkholder to Daniel Kauffman," *MQR*, 61 (Jan. 1987): 5-45. Weaver has not been intimidated by Robert Friedmann's observation that Anabaptist beliefs are not very susceptible to analysis by the instruments and procedures of systematic theology.

A readily available copy in English of the Dordrecht Confession of Faith may be found in *Mennonite Confession of Faith* (Crockett, Ky.: Rod and Staff, first printed in 1965, followed by later printings), pp. 28-89. This document may also be found in *Mennonite Confesson of Faith: Adopted April 21st, 1632, at Dordrecht, The Netherlands*, ed. and tr. Irvin B. Horst (Lancaster, Pa.: Lancaster Mennonite Historical Society, 1988); and in Thieleman J. van Braght, *Martyrs Mirror*, tr. Joseph F. Sohm (Scottdale, Pa.: Herald Press, 1938, 1990), pp. 38-44. For a brief historical treatment of this confession, see Irvin B. Horst, "The Dordrecht Confession of Faith: 350 Years," *Pennsylvania Mennonite Heritage*, 5 (July 1982): 2-8.
8. Norman Kraus, "American Mennonites and the Bible, 1750-1950," *MQR*, 41 (Oct. 1967): 316-17.
9. Shem Zook, "Geschichte der Amischen Gemeinde," *Herold der Wahrheit*, 2 (Dec. 1865): 102.
10. David Beiler, *Das Wahre Christenthum, Eine christliche Betrachtung nach den Lehren der Heiligen Schrift* (Lancaster, Pa.: Johann Bär's Söhnen, 1888), pp. 167-68.
11. [Christian Peterschmitt], [*Gottesdienst*], [ca. 1871], p. 3. See note 47 of chapter 3 for information concerning this anonymous book.
12. Beiler, *Wahre Christenthum*, p. 168.
13. *Verhandlungen, 1862*, p. 3.
14. David A. Treyer [Troyer], *Ein Unparteiischer Bericht von den Hauptumstanden welche sich ereigneten in den sogenannten Alt-Amischen Gemeinden in Ohio, vom Jahr 1850 bis ungefähr 1861, wodurch endlich eine volkommene Spaltung entstand* [n.p., n.d.], pp. 2-3. Some have ascribed the authorship of this booklet to Frederick Hege, bishop of the Martin's Creek congregation in Holmes County, Ohio, rather than to Troyer because the document is followed by the words: "*Abgeschrieben* [copied] . . . David A. Treyer [Troyer]." However, this writer finds otherwise, for the

writer of this booklet, by internal evidence, was almost certainly present at the 1865 ministers' meeting of the traditionalists in Holmes County, Ohio, on June 1 and also at the churchwide annual ministers' meeting in neighboring Wayne County immediately following, which was attended by change-minded ministers as well as conservatives. Troyer attended these meetings, whereas Hege did not.

15. For examples of Amish references to Old Testament "types and shadows," see sermon in the Hans Tschantz Papers, p. 12b, LMHL, photocopy in AMC; John P. King, "Der Thurm und der Tempel," *Herold der Wahrheit*, 13 (Oct., Nov. 1876): 179-81, 194-95; Christian Stoltzfus to John Stoltzfus, Apr. 10, 1860, and Solomon Beiler to John Stoltzfus, Sept. 6, 1864 (*Stoltzfus Documents*, docs. no. 13 and 40, respectively); George Jutzi, *Ermahnungen von George Jutzi in Stark County, Ohio, an seine Hinterbliebenen, nebst einem Anhang über die Entstehung der amischen Gemeinde von Sam. Zook* (Somerset, Pa.: Alexander Stutzman, 1853), p. 23; "Funeral Sermons" in "Sermons and Formularies (Lehmann)" (box 18/13 and 18/14, Umble Collection).

16. *Verhandlungen, 1868*, p. 11.

17. *Verhandlungen, 1876*, pp. 13-16.

18. David A. Treyer [Troyer], *Hinterlassene Schriften von David A. Treyer von Holmes County, Ohio, Unter welchem sind auch mehrere Erbauliche und Geistreiche Gedichte*, 2d ed. (Arthur, Ill.: L. A. Miller, 1925), p. 17. Tobit 4:21 was used as a text for a short article by J. Stoltzfus, "Kindliche Vertrauen auf Gott," *Herold der Wahrheit*, 2 (Nov. 1865): 90.

19. John Umble, "An Amish Minister's Manual," *MQR*, 15 (Apr. 1941): 101, 108.

20. Umble, "Minister's Manual," 101, 108; "Niederschrift um 1800 von Amische Gemeinde Ordnung in der Alsace," *The Diary*, 15 (Sept. 1983): 9-10. Currently the Old Order Amish of southern Somerset County, Pennsylvania, do not use the book of Tobit in the wedding service.

21. For an account of the origins and the various editions of the *Martyrs Mirror* see Gerald Studer, "A History of the *Martyrs Mirror*," *MQR*, 22 (July 1948): 163-179.

22. The full title of the *Fundament Book* in English translation is, *A Foundation and Plain Instruction of the Saving Doctrine of Our Lord Jesus Christ* (n.p., 1539). For an Introduction to this book see C[ornelius] K[rahn], "Foundation," *ME*, 2: 358. The *Enchiridion* was published in 1564. For an Introduction to this book see Krahn, "Enchiridion oft Hantboecxken," *ME*, 2: 213.

23. For an Introduction to the *Ausbund* see R. F[olk], "Ausbund," in *ME*, 1: 191-92, and Edward Yoder, "Oldest Mennonite Hymnbook," *Mennonite Historical Bulletin*, 3 (Dec. 1942): 2-3.

24. David Luthy interviewed by the author, July 31, 1987. The *Ernsthafte Christenpflicht* is described briefly by R[obert] F[riedmann], *ME*, 2: 244-45. See also Robert Friedmann, *Mennonite Piety Through the Centuries* (Goshen Ind.: Mennonite Historical Society, 1949), pp. 195-96; and David Luthy, "A History of the *Ernsthafte Christenpflicht*," *Family Life* (Feb. 1981): 19-23.

25. The full title of this volume was *Neu vermehrtes geistliches Lust-Gärtlein frommer Seelen, das ist heilsame Anweisung und Regeln zu einem gottseligen Leben: wie auch shöne Gebethe und Gesange täglich und auf alle Festtage im Jahr, in allerley Anliegen zu gebrauchen, samt einem nothwendigen Bericht von dem Gebrach des heiligen Abendmahls.*

26. Robert Friedmann, *Mennonite Piety*, p. 208.

27. Robert Friedmann, "Geistliches Lustgärtlein," *ME*, 2: 447.

28. The full title of Lapp's booklet was *Ein erbauliches unpartheyisches kleines Hand-Büchlein, oder Heilsame Anweisungen zu einer Gottseligen Leben; für alle gottsuchende Seelen, die ihn fürchten, wie sie ihre Gedanken, Worte und Werke führen sollen auf dieser Welt; wie auch einige kurze und nützliche Trost- und Lehr-Sprüche aus der heiligen Schrift, für Junge und Alte zur Aufmunterung und nützlich zu lesen* (Johann Bär und Söhnen, Lancaster [Pa]: 1854). The compiler, M. L., was Deacon Michael Lapp, as determined by Amos B. Hoover ("The Hand-Buechlein of 1854," *Mennonite Historical Bulletin*, 38 [Jan. 1977]: 7).

29. This section of the *Geistliches Lustgärtlein* appeared serially in *Der Christliche Jugenfreund* on the front page of the Jan., Feb., Apr., May, and June issues, 1 (1878), under the title, *"Anweisungen und Regeln wie ein jeder Mensch sich eines frommen und Gott wohlgefälligen Lebens befleissigen sollte,"* without any recognition of its source.

30. *Verhandlungen, 1866,* p. 4.

31. "After the First Prayer," in "Sermons and Formularies (Lehmann)" (box 18/2, Umble Collection), pp. 3, 17-18.

32. Jutzi, *Ermahnungen,* pp. 20-21.

33. Booklet of Three Sermons, Sermon no. 2, in "Sermons and Formularies (Lehmann)" (box 18/8, Umble Collection), p. 3.

34. Harvey J. Miller, "Proceedings of Amish Ministers' Conferences 1826-31," *MQR,* 33 (Apr. 1959): 141.

35. Treyer, *Hinterlassene Schriften,* p. 69.

36. Melvin Gingerich, *The Mennonites in Iowa* (Iowa City, Iowa: State Historical Society of Iowa, 1939), p. 173.

37. "After the First Prayer," in "Sermons and Formularies (Lehmann)" (box 18/2, Umble Collection), pp. 3-8.

38. Admonition given by Christian Schlegel at the annual ministers' meeting of 1872, *Verhandlungen, 1872,* p. 10. See also Beiler, *Wahre Christenthum,* p. 142.

39. Beiler, *Wahre Christenthum,* pp. 138, 140.

40. David Beiler's *Wahre Christenthum* is literally crammed with admonitions to obedience and biblical examples of obedience and disobedience; see especially pp. 55-56, 148-49. The quotation referring to Saul's disobedience may be found on p. 120.

41. Peter Lehman (1829-1896) "Notebook of Sermons" (Peter Lehman Collection, AMC), p. 34.

42. See, for example, Abner Yoder's Foreword to Jutzi, *Ermahnungen,* p. ix. Abner Yoder (1814-1883) was an Amish bishop first in Somerset Co., Pa., and then in Johnson Co., Iowa.

43. Jutzi, *Ermahnungen,* p. 91.

44. R[obert] F[riedmann], "George Jutzi," *ME,* 3: 133.

45. Robert Friedmann, "The Doctrine of Original Sin as Held by the Anabaptists of the Sixteenth Century," *MQR,* 33 (July 1959): 206-10.

46. Jutzi, *Ermahnungen,* p. 92. For another description of man's sinfulness see Beiler, *Wahre Christenthum,* pp. 293-94.

47. Jonas D. Troyer, "Leget ab alle Bosheit," *Herold der Wahrheit,* 3 (July 1866): 55.

48. Treyer, *Hinterlassene Schriften,* pp. 13-14; see also p. 42.

49. See Miller, "Ministers' Conferences," p. 141, for the baptismal vow taken by applicants for baptism.

50. Leonard Verduin, "Menno Simons' Theology Reviewed," *MQR,* 24 (Jan. 1950): 62-64. See also Friedmann, *Anabaptism,* pp. 65-67.

51. Christian Stoltzfus to John Stoltzfus, March 15, 1869 (*Stoltzfus Documents,* doc. no. 59).

52. Robert Friedmann, *The Theology of Anabaptism: An Interpretation* (Scottdale, Pa.: Herald Press, 1973), pp. 42-43.

53. John A. Hostetler, "Amish Preaching" (ms. in MHL, 1947), p. 4.

54. Beiler's chapter on the new birth is entitled "Eine Betrachtung über Johannes 3," *Wahre Christenthum,* pp. 215-73.

55. This statement was made in a position paper, anonymous but obviously written by Bishop Solomon Beiler, with the heading, "Von einer völligen Diener zu einer andern völligen Diener (From One Full Minister to Another Full Minister)" (*Stoltzfus Documents,* doc. no. 25, dated Aug. 24, 1862), p. 6.

56. "After the First Prayer," in "Sermons and Formularies (Lehmann)" (box 18/2, Umble Collection), p. 9. References to the new birth in Amish writings abound. See Christian Troyer to Hannes Mast, Mar. 3, 1812, original in the possession of Harold R.

Mast, Leola, Pa.; Jutzi, *Ermahnungen*, pp. 40-41; exhortation of Joseph Stuckey, *Verhandlungen, 1871*, pp. 11-12; and of Elias Riehl, *Verhandlungen, 1872*, pp.13-14; [*Gottesdienst*], p. 64; and John Stoltzfus to Joseph Detweiler, et al., July 7, 1877 (*Stoltzfus Documents*, doc. no. 65).

57. For examples of service manuals outlining the yearly calendar of Amish biweekly services and listing the principal Scriptures to be read, see John Umble, "Amish Service Manuals," *MQR*, 15 (Jan. 1941): 29-32.

58. Beiler, *Wahre Christenthum*, p. 159.

59. Jutzi, *Ermahnungen*, pp. 57-58.

60. Beiler, *Wahre Christenthum*, pp. 153-54.

61. For a description of the *Ordnungs Gemeinde* as it functioned in the Buffalo Valley congregation of Union County, Pa., see John S. Umble, "The Amish Mennonites of Union County, Pennsylvania: I. Social and Religious Life," *MQR*, 7 (Apr. 1933): 90-91. A comparable description of the Ordnungs Gemeinde as it was conducted in the Iowa congregations may be found in Gingerich, *Mennonites in Iowa*, p. 193.

62. Sermon, " Von der Taufe," Christian Esch (1818-1882) Papers, AMC.

63. Lilian Kennel, *History of the Wilmot Amish Mennonite Congregation* (Baden, Ont.: Steinmann Mennonite Church, 1984), p. 10.

64. [*Gottesdienst*], p. 57. A similar enumeration of sins which must be eradicated may be found in Beiler, *Wahre Christenthum*, p. 39.

65. Sandra Cronk, "*Gelassenheit*: The Rites of the Redemptive Process in Old Order Amish and Old Order Mennonite Communities," *MQR*, 55 (Jan. 1981): 7-8.

66. John A. Hostetler, *Amish Society*, 3d edition (Baltimore: The Johns Hopkins University Press, 1980), p. 298, says that *Gelassenheit* has "many meanings: resignation, calmness of mind, composure, staidness, conquest of selfishness, long-suffering, collectedness, silence of the soul, tranquillity, inner surrender, yieldedness, equanimity, and detachment."

67. Beiler, *Wahre Christenthum*, pp. 39, 129, 133; Christian Stoltzfus to John Stoltzfus, Dec. 25, 1862 (*Stoltzfus Documents*, doc. no. 26).

68. See *verlassen* as used in Peter Lehman "Notebook of Sermons," p. 1, and *heruntergelassen* as used by Jacob Graber, *Verhandlungen, 1872*, p. 29.

69. John Stoltzfus to Gideon and Susanna Stoltzfus, Jan. 19, 1881 (*Stoltzfus Documents*, doc. no. 66).

70. See, for example, Treyer, *Hinterlassene Schriften*, p. 17.

71. *Verhandlungen, 1870*, p. 4.

72. The well-known Mennonite Bishop J. M. Brenneman (1816-1895) said that "without humility no saving grace is promised and without this same humility no one can be a child of God nor His heir" (J. M. Brenneman, "Hoffart und Demut einander gegenübergestellt," *Herold der Wahrheit*, 3 [Aug. 1866]: 61).

73. Beiler, *Wahre Christenthum*, p. 209.

74. J[onas] D. Troyer, "Schicket Euch in die Zeit," *Herold der Wahrheit*, 3 (Mar. 1866): 23.

75. This simile was used by Bishop Peter Litwiller of Ontario, Canada, in his communion sermon, Hist. mss. 1-10, box 1/21, AMC, and may be found also in "Sermon for Communion Service," in "Sermons and Formularies (Lehmann)" (box 18/18, Umble Collection), pp. 3-4. Robert Friedmann, *Anabaptism*, pp. 140-43, has noted that this simile was drawn from the Didache or "The Teaching of the Twelve Disciples," a document dating back to the end of the first or the beginning of the second century A.D., and introduced into Anabaptist writings in the sixteenth century by Hans Hut.

76. Deacon John Stoltzfus to John K. Stoltzfus, Sept. 12, 1875 (*Stoltzfus Documents*, doc. no. 63).

77. Treyer, *Hinterlassene Schriften*, p. 11.

78. Shem Zook to John Stoltzfus, Feb. 12, 1863 (*Stoltzfus Documents*, doc. no. 27).

79. For examples of such churchly letters expressing humility, see the exchange of letters between John Stoltzfus and Solomon Beiler, Nov. 30, 1859, and Dec. 8, 1859, and

John Stoltzfus to Elias Riehl, Jan. 17, 1860 (*Stoltzfus Documents*, docs. no. 9, 10, and 11, respectively).

80. David Beiler to Moses Miller, Oct. 14, 1851 (*Stoltzfus Documents*, doc. no. 4).

81. John Stoltzfus to Daniel Miller, Jan. 10, 1861 (*Stoltzfus Documents*, doc. no. 76).

82. Joseph C. Liechty, "Humility: The Foundation of Mennonite Religious Outlook in the 1860s," *MQR*, 54 (Jan. 1980): 14.

CHAPTER 5: The Amish View of Christ and His Church

1. "Der Anfang [The Beginning]" in "Sermons and Formularies (Lehmann)" (box 18/6, Umble Collection; see chapter 3, note 46, for identification of this source), p. 1: page numbers in this and subsequent references to "Sermons and Formularies (Lehmann)" refer to the translator's typescript copy of the document under discussion. Menno Simons' original version of this monologue may be found in *The Complete Writings of Menno Simons*, trans. Leonard Verduin, and ed. John Christian Wenger (Scottdale, Pa.: Herald Press, 1956), p. 147. I am indebted to J. C. Wenger for discovering the origin of this discourse.

2. As J. Denny Weaver, "A Believers' Church Christology," *MQR*, 57 (Apr. 1983): 112-31, points out, the Christology of the several early Anabaptists writers was really not homogeneous, although that of Dirk Philips and Menno Simons was largely so.

3. David Beiler, *Das Wahre Christenthum, eine Christliche Betrachtung nach den Lehren der Heiligen Schrift* (Lancaster, Pa.: Johann Bär's Söhnen, 1888), p. 271.

4. This selection from the Dordrecht Confession of Faith is a part of the second paragraph of article 4 as translated by J. C. Wenger in his *Glimpses of Mennonite History and Doctrine* (Scottdale, Pa.: Herald Press, 1949), p. 217.

5. Beiler, *Wahre Christenthum*, p. 12; see also p. 245.

6. Sermon, p. 4, Hans Tschantz Papers, AMC.

7. Leonard Verduin, "Menno Simons' Theology Reviewed," *MQR*, 24 (Jan. 1950): p. 64.

8. William E. Keeney, *The Development of Dutch Anabaptist Thought and Practice from 1539-1564* (The Netherlands, 1968), p. 93.

9. "After the First Prayer," in "Sermons and Formularies (Lehmann)" (box 18/2, Umble Collection), p. 5.

10. John Stoltzfus, "The Word of God," a printed leaflet (*Stoltzfus Documents*, doc. no. 71).

11. Admonition by Christian Slegel (*Verhandlungen, 1875*, pp. 15-16).

12. [Christian Peterschmitt], [*Gottesdienst*], p. 16. See chapter 3, note 47, for a fuller identification of this source.

13. There are abundant references in Amish writings to Christ as the Passover Lamb, or the Pascal Lamb, or the spotless Lamb of God who, as the perfect sacrifice, shed his blood for all persons. See George Jutzi, *Ermahnungen von George Jutzi in Stark County, Ohio, an seine Hinterbliebenen nebst einem Anhange über die Entstehung der amischen Gemeinde von Sam. Zook* (Somerset, Somerset Co., Pa.: Alexander Stutzman, 1853), pp. 18, 31; [*Gottesdienst*], p. 3; Beiler, *Wahre Christenthum*, pp. 15, 51-52, 110, and especially 135-36.

14. "After the First Prayer," in "Sermons and Formularies (Lehmann)" (box 18/2, Umble Collection), p. 8. For comments relating to the theme of atonement, made in connection with the Lord's Supper, see "Remarks Immediately Preceding the Partaking of the Bread and the Wine," in "Sermons and Formularies (Lehmann)" (box 18/6, Umble Collection), p. 15; and [*Gottesdienst*], p. 58.

15. John Umble, "Amish Mennonites of Union County, Pennsylvania: I. Social and Religious Life," *MQR*, 7 (Apr. 1933): p. 93. One of the members of Gideon Stoltzfus' Lower Pequea congregation in eastern Lancaster County (a majority faction of which formed the Millwood Amish Mennonite congregation in 1877 under the leadership of Gideon) said that he "could listen to him for hours. He makes it so plain that one can

almost hear the blood dropping to the ground" (Sarah Marie Kauffman, "Gideon Stoltzfus" [ms. in MHL], pp. 2-3).

16. Jutzi, *Ermahnungen*, pp. 94-100. See also David A. Treyer [Troyer], *Hinterlassene Schriften von David A. Treyer von Holmes County, Ohio, unter welchem sind auch mehrere Erbauliche und Geistreiche Gedichte*, 2d ed. (Arthur, Ill.: L. A. Miller, 1925), p. 36, for yet another expression of the atonement theme.

17. Beiler, *Wahre Christenthum*, p. 249.

18. John Stoltzfus to John K. Stoltzfus, Sept 12, 1875 (*Stoltzfus Documents*, doc. no. 63). On the same theme, see also John Stoltzfus' leaflet, "The Word of God" (*Stoltzfus Documents*, doc. no. 71).

19. Beiler, *Wahre Christenthum*, p. 57; see also p. 183; and Peter Lehman "Notebook of Sermons" (Peter Lehman Collection, AMC), p. 1.

20. In Christian Stoltzfus to John Stoltzfus, Mar. 15, 1869 (*Stoltzfus Documents*, doc. no. 59), the writer speaks twice of Christ as "the Great Prophet." See also [*Gottesdienst*], p. 15.

21. Beiler, *Wahre Christenthum*, p. 181.

22. Beiler, *Wahre Christenthum*, p. 256.

23. "A Talk to the Children," in "Sermons and Formularies (Lehmann)" (Umble Collection), p. 9.

24. Beiler, *Wahre Christenthum*, p. 293.

25. "Graveside Remarks," in "Sermons and Formularies (Lehmann)" (box 18/13, Umble Collection), p. 3.

26. [*Gottesdienst*], p. 8; Beiler, *Wahre Christenthum*, p. 252.

27. Jutzi, *Ermahnungen*, p. 46.

28. Christian Stoltzfus to John Stoltzfus, Apr. 10, 1860 (*Stoltzfus Documents*, doc. no. 13).

29. Beiler, *Wahre Christenthum*, pp. 65, 228, and 233. See also Joseph Gascho, "Die Hoffart und der Geiz," *Herold der Wahrheit*, 12 (July 1875): 115; and "For Communion Service," in "Sermons and Formularies (Lehmann)" (box 18/18, Umble Collection), p. 4.

30. Gascho, "Hoffart," p. 115. See also Jutzi, *Ermahnungen*, p. 92, and Beiler, *Wahre Christenthum*, p. 294. Concerning the innocence of children, see "Graveside Funeral Service for a Child," in "Sermons and Formularies (Lehmann)" (box 18/15, Umble Collection), p. 4; and Beiler, *Wahre Christenthum*, p. 260.

31. In insisting that one must walk in obedience to Christ in order to lay a valid claim to his atonement, the Amish were again following early Anabaptist doctrine. In 1527, Jakob Kautz, Palatine Anabaptist, wrote in his "Seven Theses" that "Jesus Christ of Nazareth did not suffer for us and has not satisfied [for our sins] in any other way but this: that we have to stand in his footsteps and have to walk the way that he has blazed for us first, and that we obey the commandments of the Father and the Son. . . . He who speaks differently of Christ makes an idol of Christ" (Robert Friedmann, *The Theology of Anabaptism: An Interpretation* [Scottdale, Pa.: Herald Press, 1973], p. 85).

32. "For the Communion Service," in "Sermons and Formularies (Lehmann)" (box 18/18, Umble Collection), p. 4.

33. In a discussion involving a variety of questions concerning water baptism at the annual ministers' meeting of 1863, Bishop Abner Yoder defended the baptism of sick persons, evidently of those who had shown some evidence of repentance but were not in physical condition to receive prebaptismal instruction. He thus implied that the practice was not in general favor in the Amish church (*Verhandlungen, 1863*, p. 6).

34. David A. Treyer [Troyer], "Wer aber beharret bis an's Ende, der wird selig," *Herold der Wahrheit*, 23 (Jan. 15, 1886): 17.

35. Jutzi, *Ermahnungen*, pp. 28-29.

36. Beiler, *Wahre Christenthum*, pp. 142-44; see also pp. 197 and 263. On p. 19 Beiler talks about a "confident expectation," so that one can say: "Death where is your sting? Hell where is your victory?"

37. Jutzi, *Ermahnungen*, p. 22.

38. Treyer, *Hinterlassene Schriften*, p. 72.

39. Christian Stoltzfus to John Stoltzfus, Mar. 15, 1869 (*Stoltzfus Documents*, doc. no. 59).

40. Christian Stoltzfus to Christian and Susanna Zook, Nov. 27, 1882, original in the possession of Elmer Stoltzfus, Goshen, Ind.

41. Ivan Miller, "Errors in Amish Theology" (ms. in MHL, 1958); Joseph W. Yoder, *Amish Traditions* (Huntingdon, Pa.: The Yoder Publishing Co., 1950), preface, p. v. In the mid-1880s, three sons of "Tennessee" John Stoltzfus defected to the Plymouth Brethren, where they found an assurance of salvation in the doctrine of the eternal security of the believer. They had not found this in the Amish church (Paton Yoder, *Eine Wurzel; Tennessee John Stoltzfus* [Lititz, Pa.: Sutter House, 1979], pp. 97-99).

42. References to or brief descriptions of the judgment day may be found in the *Verhandlungen, 1871*, p. 10 (admonition by John Egly) and p. 15 (admonition by John Gunden); John Stoltzfus, "For the Watchman" (*Stoltzfus Documents*, doc. no. 70); Jutzi, *Ermahnungen*, pp. 47, 59; and Beiler, *Christenthum*, p. 73. Treyer, *Hinterlassene Schriften*, pp. 137-49, presents a longer "Exposition concerning the prophecy of Malachi where he writes of the great and terrible Day of the Lord." The Day of the Lord is really an age, says Troyer. It began with the coming of Christ as Savior and will end with his coming as judge of all the earth on the judgment day. In the same volume, pp. 119-20, Troyer relates the experience of the ten virgins (Matt. 25:1-13) to the last judgment.

43. Peter Schrack, "Ein Ruf an die hoffärtigen Sünder," *Herold der Wahrheit*, 13 (Jan. 1876): 7.

44. Beiler, *Wahre Christenthum*, p. 265. Note also similar statements in "Funeral Sermon," in "Sermons and Formularies (Lehmann)" (box 18/15, Umble Collection), pp. 1-2; and Treyer, *Hinterlassene Schriften*, p. 36.

45. "Der Anfang," in "Sermons and Formularies (Lehmann)" (box 18/4, Umble Collection), p. 3.

46. Abner Yoder [1814-1883] in the Foreword to Jutzi, *Ermahnungen*, pp. vi-viii. John A. Hostetler, "Amish Preaching" (ms. in MHL), p. 13, tells of attending an Old Order Amish baptismal service in 1948 and hearing the bishop say that "the apostles were sent out to preach the Word; a minister is to care for the flock."

47. Treyer, *Hinterlassene Schriften*, pp. 156-60.

48. Beiler, *Wahre Christenthum*, p. 84. See also Deacon John Stoltzfus to Gideon and Susanna Stoltzfus, Jan. 19, 1881 (*Stoltzfus Documents*, doc. no. 66).

49. D[avid] Stutzman, *Der schmale Verleugnungsweg: Eine kurze Christliche Vermahnung an meine Kinder* (Millersburg, Ohio: by the author, 1917), p. 9. Some uncertainty exists as to whether Stutzman's given name was David or Daniel.

50. *Verhandlungen, 1866*, p. 12.

51. *Verhandlungen, 1871*, p. 18.

52. *Verhandlungen, 1871*, pp. 23-27; *1873*, pp. 38-45; *1875*, pp. 43-49.

53. James O. Lehman, "Conflicting Loyalties of the Christian Citizen: Lancaster Mennonites in the Early Civil War Era," and "Duties of the Mennonite Citizen: Controversy in the Lancaster Press Late in the Civil War," *Pennsylvania Mennonite Heritage*, 7 (Apr. 1984): 2-15, and 7 (July 1984): 5-21, respectively. In a book-length manuscript, a copy of which has been loaned to the MHL, Lehman has recently expanded his Civil War research to include the Mennonites (and Amish) elsewhere in Pennsylvania and to some extent in Ohio and Indiana. In making these generalizations about the Amish in the Civil War, I have drawn considerably from his manuscript, "Mennonites in the North Face the Crises of the Civil War."

54. In 1864 John (Hansi) Borntreger of Lagrange County, Indiana, made three payments totaling $42.12 into a church fund for hiring substitutes, and on Sept. 4 he attended "the war meeting to raise money to buy recruits" (Joseph Stoll, "An Amishman's Diary—1864 [Notes from the Diary of John E. 'Hans' Borntreger]," *Family Life* [Sept. 1969], p. 38). At about the same time Samuel L. Kauffman and Shem Riehl of Lancaster

County, Pennsylvania, paid their fines for not taking up arms; see John Stoltzfus to James B. Fry, Feb. 17, 1864 (*Stoltzfus Documents*, doc. no. 77). See also Steven Estes, *Living Stones: A History of the Metamora Mennonite Church* (Metamora, Ill.: Metamora Mennonite Church, 1984), pp. 85-88, and Gingerich, *Mennonites in Iowa*, p. 130. For a general description of Amish and Mennonite participation and nonparticipation in the Civil War, see Guy F. Hershberger, "Mennonites in the Civil War," *MQR*, 18 (July 1944): 131-44.

55. "An Amish Bishop's Conference Epistle of 1865," trans. and ed. Harold S. Bender, *MQR*, 20 (July 1946): 225.

56. Paton Yoder, *Eine Wurzel, Tennessee John Stoltzfus* (Lititz, Pa.: Sutter house, 1979), p. 34.

57. *Verhandlungen, 1863*, p. 14.

58. *Verhandlungen, 1863*, p. 16.

59. *Verhandlungen, 1864*, p. 11.

60. *Verhandlungen, 1868*, pp. 6-10.

61. *Verhandlungen, 1868*, pp. 7-8.

62. For David Beiler's concern about the increasing affluence which he detected in Amish family and community life, see his *Vermahnung oder Andenken* (n.p., [1928], published posthumously), pp. 3-6, and his *Wahre Christenthum*, pp. 82-83. Beiler's response to the increasing resort to the use of the civil courts by Amishmen desiring to protect or recover their possessions is recorded in his *Wahre Christenthum*, pp. 115, 124, 128, 152-53, and 157.

63. *Vermahnung*, p. 9.

64. Treyer, *Hinterlassene Schriften*, pp. 58-59.

65. David A. Treyer [Troyer], "Eine Erklärung in Bezug auf die weltliche Obrigkeit," a 9-page addendum to his *Ein unparteiischer Bericht von den Hauptumstanden welche sich ereigneten in den sogenannten Alt-Amischen Gemeinden in Ohio, von Jahr 1850 bis ungefähr 1861, wodurch endlich eine vollkommene Spaltung entstand* (n.p., n.d.), pp. 8-16.

66. *Verhandlungen, 1863*, p. 14-15; and *1864*, p. 14. See also John Stoltzfus, "Short Account of the Life, Doctrine, and Example of Our Old Ministers" (*Stoltzfus Documents*, doc. no. 22).

67. Describing what is evidently primarily contemporary or near-contemporary Amish practice, John A. Hostetler, *Amish Society*, 3d ed. (Baltimore: The Johns Hopkins University Press, 1980), p. 253, states that voting in public elections is rather widespread and "in the past some Amish people have served as school directors and supervisors of roads." See also Lehman, "Mennonites in the North Face the Crises of the Civil War."

68. This claim was made by J. E. Borntreger, an Old Order Amish minister of Middlebury, Ind., "Ueber die Meidung," *Herold der Wahrheit*, 29 (Mar. 1892): 82.

69. Richard K. MacMaster, *Land, Piety, Peoplehood: The Establishment of Mennonite Communities in America, 1683-1790* (Scottdale, Pa.: Herald Press, 1985), pp. 165, 177, 182.

CHAPTER 6: "Keeping House": Banning and Shunning

1. *Descendants of Christian Fisher and Other Amish-Mennonite Pioneer Families*, ed. Janice A. Egeland (Baltimore, Md.: Moore Clinic, Johns Hopkins Hospital, 1972), Family no. 1421.

2. John Umble, "Amish Mennonites of Union County, Pennsylvania: I. Social and Religious Life," *MQR*, 7 (Apr. 1933): 89-90.

3. Christian Stoltzfus to sons Eli and Ben, Oct. 28, 1882. See also Christian Stoltzfus to son Ben, Mar. 14, 1883. Both letters are in the possession of Elmer Stoltzfus, Goshen, Ind.

4. The first annual ministers' meeting in 1862 ruled resolutely on this question (*Verhandlungen, 1862*, pp. 10-12).

5. Robert Friedmann, *The Theology of Anabaptism: An Interpretation* (Scottdale, Pa.: Herald Press, 1973), p. 126.

6. David A. Treyer [Troyer]', *Hinterlassene Schriften von David A. Treyer von Holmes County, Ohio, unter welchem sind auch mehrere Erbauliche und Geistreiche Gedichte*, 2d. ed. (Arthur, Ill.: L. A. Miller, 1925), p. 56.

7. J. F. B., "Ordnung," *MQR*, 56 (Oct. 1982): 382-84. For excellent formal treatments of Ordnung as a basic Amish concept, see John A. Hostetler, *Amish Society*, 3d. ed. (Baltimore: The Johns Hopkins University Press, 1980), pp. 84-86; Theron Schlabach, *Peace, Faith, Nation: Mennonites and Amish in Nineteenth-Century America* (Scottdale, Pa.: Herald Press, 1988), pp. 207-10; and Donald B. Kraybill, *The Riddle of Amish Culture* (Baltimore: The Johns Hopkins University Press, 1989), pp. 235-49.

8. David Beiler, *Das Wahre Christenthum, Eine Christliche Betrachtung nach den Lehren der Heiligen Schrift* (Lancaster, Pa.: Johann Bär's Söhnen, 1888), p. 199; Christian Stoltzfus to John Stoltzfus, Oct. 20, 1868 (*Stoltzfus Documents*, doc. no. 54).

9. That the church should enforce biblical commandments is universally assumed in the several Amish disciplines of the nineteenth century. See David Beiler's chapter, "Vom aus das Rath stellen," *Wahre Christenthum*, pp. 165-79.

10. Concerning Conrad's excommunication, compare Malinda Stoltzfus' Travel Diary of 1866 (entries for May 30 and 31) with Shem Zook's letter to John Stoltzfus, July 6, 1866 (*Stoltzfus Documents*, docs. no. 78 and 51, respectively).

11. The legalistic approach to disciplining and particularly to the use of witnesses is illustrated by a question which was asked and answered in the annual ministers' meeting of 1865: "A brother brings a complaint to another brother against a third brother, but denies it later. But he has told the same thing to a fourth person on another occasion. May the fourth person be used as a witness in such a case? It was decided and voted that such a fourth person is a valid witness in such circumstance" (*Verhandlungen, 1865*, p. 6).

12. *Verhandlungen, 1868*, p. 10. While Bishop Yoder made this comment in connection with those who were slow to shun persons who had been excommunicated, the point remains that a tardy compliance with the Ordnung required disciplinary action.

13. Erv Schlabach, "A History of the Walnut Creek Mennonite Church," in *A Century and a Half with the Mennonites at Walnut Creek* (Strasburg, Ohio: [Walnut Creek Mennonite Church], 1978), pp. 12-14. Versions of the Henry Yoder story vary. However, Schlabach's account does not do violence to traditional Amish disciplinary procedure.

14. See Umble, "Union County," p. 91, for an example of the use of the congregational *Ordnungs Gemeinde* to satisfy personal grudges.

15. Dietrich Philip [sic], *Enchiridion or Handbook of the Christian Doctrine and Religion*, trans. A. B. Kolb (Elkhart, Ind.: Mennonite Publishing Co., 1910), p. 237.

16. David Beiler, *Wahre Christenthum*, pp. 127, 198.

17. Peter Lehman "Notebook of Sermons," p. 35, as translated by John Umble, Peter Lehman Collection, AMC.

18. *Verhandlungen, 1865*, p. 3. The annual ministers' meeting of 1865 was largely preoccupied with the problem of personal adornment. See also Beiler, *Wahre Christenthum*, p. 155. Concerns expressed about any and all forms of embellishment may be found everywhere in Amish writings relating to church affairs. Expressions which specifically link adornment with pride may be found in a six-page discourse on "Hochmut" (pride) in Treyer, *Hinterlassene Schriften*, pp. 45-50; in article 9 of the Discipline of 1809 and article 2 of the Discipline of 1837 ("Some Early American Amish Mennonite Disciplines," ed. and trans. Harold S. Bender, *MQR*, 8 [Apr. 1934]: 92 and 94, respectively); and in a letter from Peter Litwiller and other Ontario ministers to the ministers' meeting of 1863 (*Verhandlungen, 1863*, p. 13).

19. The Discipline of 1865, the position paper drawn up by the more conservative wing of the Amish church, may be found in *Begebenheiten in der Amische Gemeinde von 1850 biss 1898* (Millersburg Ohio: John Y. Schlabach, [1963]), pp. 69-71, and in Bender, "Early Amish . . . Disciplines," pp. 95-98.

20. J. F. B., "Ordnung," pp. 382-84. With respect to the concern of Amish leaders about this new affluence, see David Beiler, *Eine Vermahnung oder Andenken* (n.p., [1928]), pp. 3-6; and John Stoltzfus, "Short Account of the Life, Doctrine, and Example of Our Old Ministers" (*Stoltzfus Documents*, doc. no. 22).

21. In 1872 a committee appointed by the annual Amish ministers' meeting to investigate conditions in Joseph Stuckey's church at Danvers, Ill., included in their report a recommendation that the ministers "work toward some kind of mark of recognition *(Kennzeichen)*" in clothing (*Verhandlungen, 1872*, p. 8). See also Steven R. Estes, *Living Stones: A History of the Metamora Mennonite Church* (Metamora, Ill.: Metamora Mennonite Church, 1984), p. 67. In 1895 Old Order Amishman S. D. Guengerich, "Simplicity and Uniformity of Attire," *Herald of Truth*, 32 (July 1, 1895), p. 205, argued that "the whole tenor of the Scriptures points to plainness, simplicity, and *uniformity*, not only in attire, but in everything else" (emphasis added).

22. *Verhandlungen, 1865*, p. 5.

23. *Verhandlungen, 1868*, p. 9. The annual ministers' meeting of 1865 asserted that if one persisted in absenting oneself from the communion table or in conforming to the world in clothing and hairstyle, it became a sin worthy of excommunication (*Verhandlungen, 1865*, pp. 4-5). See also, Beiler, *Wahre Christenthum*, p. 198.

24. Three levels of discipline are mentioned in the Amish Discipline of 1809, article 5. These are (1) "confession to the church," (2) "full (*hoechst*) confession" and (3) "excommunication from the church" (Bender, "Early Amish . . . Disciplines," p. 92). This 1809 Discipline does not precisely describe current Amish practice.

25. Jacob Ammann's insistence on shunning persons who had been placed in the ban is well described by John A. Hostetler, *Amish Society*, 3d ed. (Baltimore: The Johns Hopkins University Press, 1980), pp. 33-37. See Elmer S. Yoder, *The Beachy Amish Mennonite Fellowship Churches* (Hartville, Ohio: Diakonia Ministries, 1987), pp. 43-59, for an Amish-oriented interpretation of the history of shunning.

26. This term is used constantly in connection with shunning. A brief but well-expressed explanation of the term may be found in Beiler, *Wahre Christenthum*, pp. 191-92.

27. John Stoltzfus to Henry U. and Malinda Stoltzfus, Mar. 11, 1872 (*Stoltzfus Documents*, doc. no. 96). See also Paton Yoder, *Eine Wurzel: Tennessee John Stoltzfus* (Lititz, Pa.: Sutter House, 1979), pp. 58-60.

28. "Der Anfang," in "Sermons and Formularies (Lehmann)" (box 18/4, John S. Umble Collection; for identification of this source, see note 46 of chapter 3), p. 2; Discipline of 1809 in Bender, "Early Amish . . . Disciplines," p. 92; comments in the annual ministers' meetings, by Andreas Rupp in 1862, by Bishop John K. Yoder in 1868, and by John P. King in 1872: in *Verhandlungen, 1862*, p. 10; *1868*, pp. 9-10; and *1872*, p. 11, respectively.

29. Harvey J. Miller, "Proceedings of Amish Ministers' Conferences, 1826-31," *MQR*, 33 (Apr. 1959): 135.

30. Comments of Bishop Abner Yoder in the annual ministers' meeting of 1862, *Verhandlungen, 1862*, p. 10.

31. [Christian Peterschmitt], [*Gottesdienst*], (n.p., [ca. 1871]), p. 27. For information on this anonymous volume, see note 47 of chapter 3. See also "After the First Prayer," in "Sermons and Formularies (Lehmann)" (box 18/2, Umble Collection), p. 16.

32. Peter Lehman "Notebook of Sermons," pp. 26-27. There is some confusion of page numbering in Lehman's Notebook, to which the researcher should be alerted.

33. Beiler, *Wahre Christenthum*, pp. 192-93.

34. *Verhandlungen, 1867*, p.10.

35. John Umble, "Union County," p. 92.

36. Beiler, *Wahre Christenthum*, pp. 104-05. See also "Instructions to Candidates for Baptism," in "Sermons and Formularies (Lehmann)" (box 18/15, Umble Collection), p. 12.

37. [*Gottesdienst*], p. 27.
38. *Verhandlungen, 1872*, p. 11.
39. "An Early Amish Formulary," trans. and ed. John Umble, *MQR*, 34 (Jan. 1960): 59.
40. Bender, "Early Amish . . . Disciplines," p. 92.
41. Miller, "Ministers' Conferences," p. 135.
42. *Verhandlungen, 1864*, p. 7.
43. Comments of Jacob Graber and Bishop John K. Yoder at the 1864 annual ministers' meeting, *Verhandlungen, 1864*, pp. 13 and 17, respectively; see also p. 15.
44. John Stoltzfus, "Short Account" (*Stoltzfus Documents*, doc. no. 22).
45. Bender, "Early Amish . . . Disciplines," p. 94.
46. Beiler, *Wahre Christenthum*, pp. 96-97.
47. Melvin Gingerich, *Mennonites in Iowa* (Iowa City, Iowa: State Historical Society of Iowa, 1939), p. 178.
48. Bender, "Early Amish . . . Disciplines," p. 95.
49. Indications that bundling was and continued to be a problem in the Amish church may be found in chronologically consecutive letters and other documents of the nineteenth century: Bishop John Stoltzfus to Bishop John Beiler and Christian Zook, Mar. 29, 1832 (*Stoltzfus Documents*, doc. no. 1); the Discipline of 1837, Bender, "Early Amish . . . Disciplines," p. 95; George Jutzi, *Ermahnungen von George Jutzi in Stark County, Ohio, an seine Hinterbliebenen nebst einem Anhang über die Entstehung der amischen Gemeinde von Sam. Zook* (Somerset, Pa.: Alexander Stutzman, 1853), pp. 5-6, 74-76; "An Amish Bishop's Conference Epistle of 1865," trans. and ed. Harold S. Bender, *MQR*, 20 (July 1946): 226-28; Treyer, *Hinterlassene Schriften* (written in the 1880s and 1890s), pp. 64-65; D[avid] Stutzman, *Der schmale Verleugnungsweg: Eine kurze Christliche Vermahnung an meine Kinder* (Millersburg, Ohio: by the author, 1917), p. 157; and *Ein Riss in der Mauer (Treatise on Courtship)*, (Sugarcreek, Ohio: Schlabach Printers, [1980]).
50. Ezra Yoder to John K. Yoder, Mar. 11, 1867 (John K. Yoder Correspondence, AMC). See also James O. Lehman, *Creative Congregationalism: A History of the Oak Grove Mennonite Church in Wayne County, Ohio* (Smithville, Ohio: Oak Grove Mennonite Church, 1978), pp. 86-87.
51. "Suggested Remarks to Be Made to Formerly Banned Persons on Their Reinstatement," in "Sermons and Formularies (Lehmann)" (box 18/11, Umble Collection).
52. This is a translation of a formulary found in the D. B. Swartzendruber Collection (box 2/7, AMC). A similar form may be found in Miller, "Ministers' Conferences," p. 141.

CHAPTER 7: The Coming of the Great Schism, 1848-62

1. Hans E. Borntreger, *Eine Geschichte der ersten Ansiedelung der Amischen Mennoniten und die Gründung ihrer ersten Gemeinde im Staate Indiana, nebst einer kurzen Erklärung über die Spaltung die in dieser Gemeinde geschehen ist* (Elkhart, Ind.: Mennonite Publishing Company, 1907), pp. 8-9.
2. Shem Zook, *Eine wahre Darstellung von dem, welches uns das Evangelium in der Reinheit lehrt, so wie auch ein unparteiischer Bericht von den Haupt-Umständen, welche sich in unterschiedlichen Gemeinden ereigneten, woraus endlich die unchristlichen Spaltungen entstanden sind* (Mattawana, Mifflin Co., Pa.: by the author, 1880), pp. 11-12; translated in John A. Hostetler, "Memoirs of Shem Zook (1798-1884)," *MQR*, 38 (July 1964): 291; Samuel W. Peachey, *Amish of Kishacoquillas Valley* (Belleville, Pa.: by the author, 1930), pp. 27-33; John A. Hostetler, "Life and Times of Samuel Yoder," *MQR*, 22 (Oct. 1948): 228.
3. A number of letters relating to the church troubles in the Wooster congregation have been translated by John Umble. The translations are located in several boxes of the John S. Umble Collection and in the Samuel Mast Collection, both in

the AMC. The service in the spring of 1848 involving baptism in water is described in a letter which Umble thinks was written by Frederich Hege to a person named John Stoltzfus of Lancaster County, Pa. (dated May 31, 1848; Samuel Mast Papers), although the latter was certainly Bishop John K. Stoltzfus rather than Tennessee John Stoltzfus, as Umble mistakenly assumed. The latter was a deacon at that time. In a paper prepared for publication, "New Light on the Amish Division, 1847-62" (box 14/9, Umble Collection), but evidently never published, Umble put together his version of the events of 1847-62 in the Amish congregations of Holmes and Wayne counties, from which I have drawn occasionally.

4. In a manner similar to Hans Borntreger's *Geschichte*, David A. Treyer [Troyer], *Ein unparteiischer Bericht von den Hauptumständen, welche sich ereigneten in den sogenannten Alt-Amischen Gemeinden in Ohio, vom Jahr 1850 bis ungefähr 1861, vodurch endlich eine vollkommene Spaltung entstand* (n.p., n.d.), has described the schism in the Amish congregations of Wayne and Holmes counties, Ohio, as it unfolded from 1850 to 1861. His version of the Jacob D. Yoder affair, in which he was at times a participant and sometimes a bystander, may be found on pp. 1-6. Troyer's account states that Yoder was ordained in "about the year 1850." But if Yoder is to be associated with the beginnings of the controversy in the Wooster congregation over baptism (as Troyer states), it makes more sense to accept Umble's date of 1847 ("New Light on the Amish Division," p. 8). The first baptism in a stream in Wayne County clearly took place in 1848.

5. See statement by Levi Miller in *Stoltzfus Documents*, doc. no. 7, excerpt no. V.

6. David Beiler, *Das Wahre Christenthum: Eine Christliche Betrachtung nach den Lehren der Heiligen Schrift* (Lancaster, Pa.: Johann Bär's Söhnen, 1888), p. 69.

7. [Hege] to John Stoltzfus, May 31, 1848 (see note 3).

8. Photocopies of both sides of this half-sheet may be found in the Samuel Mast Papers, AMC.

9. *Herald of Truth*, 19 (Nov. 1, 1882): 330.

10. Borntreger, *Geschichte*, p. 9.

11. Obituary of Isaac Schmucker, *Herald of Truth*, 30 (Dec. 1, 1893): 373; J. S. Hartzler, "Fifty Mennonite Leaders: Bishop Isaac Schmucker (1810-1893)," *Gospel Herald*, 22 (June 27, 1929): 267.

12. J. C. Wenger, *The Story of the Forks Mennonite Church* (Middlebury, Ind.: Forks Church, 1982), p. 20.

13. Borntreger, *Geschichte*, pp. 10-11.

14. Borntreger, *Geschichte*, p. 12.

15. Interview, Paton Yoder with Daniel Bontrager, Goshen, Ind., Aug. 2, 1984.

16. Joseph Stoll, "An Amishman's Diary—1864 (Notes from the Diary of John E. 'Hans' Borntreger)," *Family Life* (Sept. 1969): 38.

17. Jonas D. Troyer to John K. Yoder, July 11, 1860, John K. Yoder Correspondence, AMC. Although the principal concern of this letter relates to Jacob D. Yoder, bishop of the Wooster congregation in Wayne County, Ohio, who had left his congregation in disgrace and had gone to Indiana, yet it is my firm opinion that Troyer's comments about a schism in his congregation as quoted in the text relate to the division of 1854-57.

18. James E. Landing, "The Old Order Amish Settlement at Nappanee, Indiana: Oldest in Indiana," *Mennonite Historical Bulletin*, 30 (Oct. 1969): 5; Eldon Schrock, *100th Anniversary Edition of the History and a Pictorial Directory of the First Mennonite Church, Nappanee, Indiana* (n.p., 1975), p. 4.

19. Glenn L. Troyer, et al., *Mennonite Church History of Howard and Miami Counties, Indiana* (Scottdale, Pa.: Mennonite Publishing House, 1916), pp. 88-89.

20. William C. Ringenberg, "Development and Division in the Mennonite Community in Allen County, Indiana," *MQR*, 50 (Apr. 1976): 124.

21. Herbert E. Zook, "A History of the Maple Grove Mennonite Church" (ms. in MHL, 1972), p. 3.

22. *Des blutigen Schauplatzes der Taufs-Gesinnten oder wehrlosen Christen* (Philadelphia: Shem Zook, 1849).

23. The frontispiece of some of the copies of the Ephrata edition of 1748-49 shows Christ being baptized by immersion, in contrast to the baptismal scene appearing in Shem Zook's edition.

24. This statement concerning baptism in flowing water may be found in Zook's edition of the *Martyrs Mirror*, part 1, p. 40. Additionally, in part 1, p. 25, of this edition may be found an account of two young women who were baptized similarly. These two references to baptism in "running water" may be found in the 1814 (German) edition of the *Martyrs Mirror*, printed at Lancaster, Pa., by Joseph Ehrenfried, on pages 40 and 26, respectively, of part 1; this edition was in common use among nineteenth-century Amish. David Luthy called these passages to my attention.

25. In the decades of the 1870s and the 1880s Funk's *Herald of Truth* carried a large number of articles on baptism with such titles as, "Did Menno Immerse," "The Mode of Baptism Practiced by the Early Mennonites" (a three-issue series by John S. Coffman), "The Bible Mode of Baptism," "Baptism Not Immersion," and "Scriptural Mode of Baptism" (an eleven-issue series). In an editorial Funk justified such articles, saying that he was compelled to speak out for "the error was so widespread . . . that our own people . . . were beginning . . . to doubt" (*Herald of Truth*, 13 [Mar. 1876]: 40).

26. "Jacob Krehbiel, 'A Few Words About the Mennonites in America,' " trans. and ed. Harold S. Bender, *MQR*, 6 (Jan. 1932): 56-57. Much later, May 6, 1868, Mennonite Jost Schelly wrote to Mennonites Joseph Bixler and Jacob Kolb about baptizing *im Wasser mit Wasser* (Hist mss. 1-10, AMC).

27. Further research is required to determine the source of the idea of stream baptism and the extent of this controversy among the Mennonites. Since it made its appearance among them already in the 1830s, it is entirely plausible that in the following decade it spread from the Mennonites to their Amish neighbors. Both spoke the same Pennsylvania German dialect. The ways and the extent to which the Amish and the Mennonites influenced each other await further investigation. The occasional instances of intermarriage between the two denominations must not be ignored. For example, note the marriage in Lee County, Iowa, of Mennonite John C. Krehbiel to Amishwoman Catharine Raber (Melvin Gingerich, *Mennonites in Iowa* [Iowa City, Iowa: State Historical Society of Iowa, 1939], pp. 68-69); see also ibid., p. 56. J. C. Wenger is of the opinion that the Mennonites of Lancaster County adopted the semiyearly pattern of the observance of the Lord's Supper from the Amish (interview with the author, June 8, 1987).

28. David Luthy, "German Printings of the Martyr's Mirror," *Family Life*, Aug./Sept. 1976, p. 19.

29. Shem Zook, "Glaubens-Bekenntnis der Taufgesinnten in Greechenland," *Herold der Wahrheit*, 2 (June 1865): 45-46.

30. The story of the Thessalonians was included in that edition of the *Ausbund* which was printed at Germantaun [*sic*] in 1785, pp. 97-103 of a 103-page supplement, under the title: "Ein schönes neues geistliches Lied aus einer Historie gezogen von denen dreyen Christen wo aus Thessalonich in die Pfaltz kommen sind. Dieses Lied ist gemacht worden in Jahr Anno Domini 1540. . . ." Evidently not knowing of Zook's article of 1865, Robert Friedmann presented this Thessalonian confession of faith as a hitherto unpublished document in "Christian Sectarians in Thessalonica and Their Relationship to the Anabaptists," *MQR* 29 (Jan. 1955): 54-69.

31. Zook, *Wahre Darstellung*.

32. Zook, *Wahre Darstellung*, 12-13. This booklet has been translated in John A. Hostetler, "Memoirs of Shem Zook (1798-1884); A Biography," *MQR*, 38 (July 1964): 287-299, 303. In translating excerpts from *Eine Wahre Darstellung*, I have frequently referred to Hostetler's article and translation. See also Peachey, *Kishacoquillas Valley*, pp. 27-36, for background information concerning the Amish of Mifflin County in this period.

33. This report may be found in translation in *Stoltzfus Documents*, doc. no. 5. The copy of the report from which this translation was taken consists of an entry in a church

memo book kept by an unidentified Amish minister. This ledger is in the possession of the Pequea Bruderschaft Library, Gordonville, Pa.

34. David Beiler to Moses Miller, Oct. 14, 1851 (*Stoltzfus Documents*, doc. no. 4). Although this letter is signed by eleven Lancaster County ministers, it is written in the first person. A postscript signed only by Beiler implies that he had written the letter previous to a meeting of the Lancaster County ministers. He waited to send it until after the meeting so that they could present a united front on the question of baptism in water.

35. Beiler's chapter on baptism in his *Wahre Christenthum*, pp. 32-86, is entitled "Eine Verhandlung von der Taufe"; see especially pp. 39-43 and 70-71. See also Beiler's *Eine Vermahnung oder Andenken* (n.p., [1928]), completed in 1862, pp. 9-10.

36. In 1860 Shem Zook wrote in one of his many letters to Deacon John Stoltzfus that if Bishop David Beiler "would have permitted those who requested it to be baptized that way [in a stream], a lot of dissatisfaction would have been avoided because many look to him" (*Stoltzfus Documents*, doc. no. 14).

37. Zook, *Wahre Darstellung*, p. 13.

38. Zook, *Wahre Darstellung*, pp. 13-14.

39. "Excerpts from Eight Churchly Letters Relating to Baptism in Water" (*Stoltzfus Documents*, doc. no. 7, excerpt no. VIII).

40. Although Zook indicated that Jonas Troyer was from Holmes County, Ohio, quite certainly he was referring to the Jonas D. Troyer who had moved from Ohio to Elkhart County, Ind., in 1854.

41. Zook, *Wahre Darstellung*, p. 17.

42. It cannot be proved that bishops Miller and Troyer made this compilation during or after their visit to Mifflin County in Nov. 1857. What is certain is that these passages were excerpted and compiled in about 1857 and were concerned with "the administering of water baptism, as well as other affairs and deliberations that took place in the Kishacoquillas congregations . . . relative to baptism in water [introductory statement to the composition]." A translation of this document may be found in *Stoltzfus Documents*, doc. no. 7. Manuscript copies of this compilation may be found in the Lydia Mast Collection (LMHL), and in the Jacob Frederick Swartzendruber Copy Book (Daniel B. Swartzendruber Collection, AMC), pp. 94-102. Curiously, a copy was printed in the *Herold der Wahrheit*, 12 (May 1875): 68-69, "by request." This appears to be one of the few instances in which any one of the major issues of the Great Schism in the Amish denomination was addressed openly in that paper or in its counterpart, the *Herald of Truth*. In view of Shem Zook's interest in the subject and practice of stream baptism, one may suspect that he was the one who persuaded the editor of the *Herold*, evidently with some trepidation, to print this document.

43. In the annual ministers' meeting of 1862, Levi Miller, conservative bishop from Holmes County, Ohio, said that the issue of baptism in water would not constitute a hindrance to the restoration of unity in the Holmes County-Wayne County area if other differences could be reconciled (*Verhandlungen, 1862*, p. 4). Years later, in his account of this same split in central Ohio, David A. Troyer (Treyer) also asserted that baptism in itself would not have caused the division (*Unparteiischer Bericht*, p. 6.). One would encounter more difficulty in making this same claim, however, for the schism in Mifflin County, Pa.

44. Zook, *Wahre Darstellung*, p. 18.

45. Christian Stoltzfus to John Stoltzfus, May 20, 1861 (*Stoltzfus Documents*, doc. no. 18).

46. The controversy over the role of Full Deacon Samuel Yoder in Solomon Beiler's congregation has come to light only recently with the discovery of a cache of letters and other documents, until 1987 in the possession of Lydia Mast of rural Atglen, Pa., now deceased. Over twenty of the papers concerned with this controversy are reproduced in translation in the *Stoltzfus Documents*. Many of these documents are identified more specifically in certain notes which follow below.

47. Hostetler, "Samuel Yoder," p. 227.

48. Deacon John Stoltzfus to Solomon Beiler, Nov. 30, 1859, and Beiler's reply, Dec. 8, 1859; also Deacon Christian Stoltzfus to John Stoltzfus, May 20, 1861 (*Stoltzfus Documents*, doc. nos. 9, 10, and 18, respectively).

49. Deacon Christian Stoltzfus to Deacon John Stoltzfus, Dec. 12, 1860 (*Stoltzfus Documents*, doc. no. 15). See also Shem Zook to Deacon John Stoltzfus, Feb. 7, 1861 (ibid., doc. no. 16).

50. "From One Full Minister to Another Full Minister" (*Stoltzfus Documents*, doc. no. 25), p. 1. See also Deacon John Stoltzfus to Elias Riehl, Jan. 17, 1860, and Riehl's reply, Jan. 20, 1860 (ibid., doc. nos. 11 and 12, respectively).

51. John Yoder to Deacon John Stoltzfus, Apr. 1, 1864 (*Stoltzfus Documents*, doc. no. 34).

52. Hostetler, "Samuel Yoder," p. 231.

53. For bits of information concerning the alignment of parties in the Buffalo Valley congregation, see John Umble, "The Amish Mennonites of Union County, Pennsylvania: I. Social and Religious Life," *MQR*, 7 (Apr. 1933): 74, 78, and 91.

54. Deacon Christian Stoltzfus to Deacon John Stoltzfus, Apr. 10, 1860, and May 20, 1861 (*Stoltzfus Documents*, docs. nos. 13 and 18, respectively).

55. Deacon Christian Stoltzfus to Deacon John Stoltzfus, Dec. 25, 1862 (*Stoltzfus Documents*, doc. no. 26).

56. In reconstructing the events relating to the Great Schism in Wayne, Stark, and Holmes counties, I have drawn freely from James O. Lehman, *Creative Congregationalism: A History of the Oak Grove Mennonite Church in Wayne County, Ohio* (Smithville, Ohio: 1978), pp. 40-50; John Umble, "The Oak Grove-Pleasant Hill Amish Mennonite Church in Wayne County, Ohio, in the Nineteenth Century (1815-1900)," *MQR*, 31 (July 1957): 164-65 and 172-73; David A. Treyer [Troyer], *Unparteiischer Bericht*, pp. 1-5; and Umble's ms., "New Light." Troyer was a participant in many of the events which he describes. Correspondence between the participants in the painful events of the 1850s may be found in the Samuel Mast Papers and the John K. Yoder Correspondence, AMC. In some instances I have relied primarily on John Umble's translations of the originals.

57. Letters no. 9, 10, and 11 (so numbered in Umble's translations) of July 28, Aug. 7, and Oct. 10, 1853, written by laymen, jointly with some ministers, to those who were critical of Bishop Yoder or who were to be placed under the ban, Samuel Mast Papers; and a similar letter of Mar. 15, 1857, John K. Yoder Correspondence.

58. Letter of Oct. 7, 1853, Samuel Mast Papers, published in translation in *Mennonite Historical Bulletin*, 27 (July 1966): 5.

59. Christian Brandt to Christian Graber, Nov. 15, 1855, "A Christian Brandt Letter," *Mennonite Historical Bulletin*, 26 (July 1965): 6.

60. Sometime in the mid-1850s Bishop Levi Miller had said that baptism in water was "more in keeping with the Word and with the example of Jesus Christ than the old custom" of baptizing in the house, but concluded by observing that "to me the difference is quite insignificant" (*Stoltzfus Documents*, doc. no. 7, excerpt no. V).

61. Treyer, *Unparteiischer Bericht*, p. 6.

62. Treyer, *Unparteiischer Bericht*, p. 3.

63. John K. Yoder Correspondence, AMC.

64. Umble, "Oak Grove," p. 165; Lehman, *Creative Congregationalism*, pp. 47-49. Curiously and perhaps significantly, the accusation against Bishop Yoder of "rather grave social misconduct" is not confirmed by his chief critic, David A. Troyer (*Unparteiischer Bericht*), who accuses him of almost every other kind of misconduct. Conceivably, some of his accusers found it convenient to heap this accusation upon an already discredited man.

65. Fourteen ministers and laymen of the Wooster congregation, presumably to the Clinton Township congregation in Indiana, Feb. 10, 1861, John K. Yoder Correspondence.

66. Jonas D. Troyer, presumably but rather obviously to John K. Yoder, July 11,

1860; and Jonas D. Troyer and John Smiley to Christian Brandt and John K. Yoder, Apr. 10, 1861; in John K. Yoder Correspondence.

67. Treyer, *Unparteiischer Bericht*, p. 2.

68. Treyer, *Unparteiischer Bericht*, p. 5.

69. Treyer, *Unparteiischer Bericht*, p. 4.

70. *Verhandlungen, 1862*, pp. 4-7.

71. Amos L. Fisher, "History of the First Amish Communities in America," in Hugh F. Gingerich and Rachel W. Kreider, *Amish and Amish Mennonite Genealogies* (Gordonville, Pa.: Pequea Publishers, 1986), p. xxiii.

72. Steven R. Estes, *A Goodly Heritage: A History of the North Danvers Mennonite Church* (Danvers, Ill.: North Danvers Mennonite Church, 1982), p. 30.

73. Orland R. Grieser and Ervin Beck, Jr., *Out of the Wilderness: History of the Central Mennonite Church, 1835-1960* (Grand Rapids, Mich.: 1960), pp. 74-75.

74. The Stark County division is recounted in a letter of Peter Schmucker of Stark County, Ohio, apparently to his daughter Verena or Fannie Lengacher of Allen County, Ind., Mar. 5, 1862, Heritage Historical Library, Aylmer, Ontario. I am indebted to Joseph Stoll and Lloyd Conrad for bringing this letter to my attention. The Mary (or Marie) Eicher affair is told in some detail in Joseph Stoll, "An Early Amish Lawsuit, 1861," *Family Life* (Aug./Sept. 1987): 23-28.

75. Melvin Gingerich, *Mennonites in Iowa*, pp. 59-60, 66, 102-05. See also S. D. Guengerich, "A Brief History of the Origin and Development of the So-called Amish Mennonite Congregation of Johnson Co Iowa Also Giving a Short History of Their Early Settlements in the State of Iowa," p. 30 of typescript, MHL.

76. Beiler, *Vermahnung*, pp. 6-7.

CHAPTER 8: The Diener Versammlungen, 1862-65

1. David Beiler, *Eine Vermahnung oder Andenken* (n.p., [1928]), p. 11. Beiler's analysis of the causes of the Great Schism (pp. 9-13) presents the conservative interpretation thereof as of 1861-62.

2. See the "Compilation Made in 1857 of Excerpts from Eight Letters Relating to Baptism in Water" (*Stoltzfus Documents*, doc. no. 7).

3. Shem Zook to Deacon John Stoltzfus, Feb. 7, 1861 (*Stoltzfus Documents*, doc. no. 16).

4. "From One Full Minister to Another Full Minister" (*Stoltzfus Documents*, doc. no. 25, Aug. 24, 1862).

5. Deacon Christian Stoltzfus to Deacon John Stoltzfus, May 20, 1861 (*Stoltzfus Documents*, doc. no. 18).

6. Shem Zook to Deacon John Stoltzfus, Sept. 23, 1871, and again on Oct. 11, 1871 (*Stoltzfus Documents*, docs. no. 60 and 61).

7. Bishop David Beiler, et al., to Bishop Moses Miller, Oct. 14, 1851 (*Stoltzfus Documents*, doc. no. 4); Solomon Beiler's position paper, "From One Full Minister to Another Full Minister," Aug. 24, 1862 (*Stoltzfus Documents*, doc. no 25), p. 10; Henry Egli to Peter Litwiller, Dec. 30, 1864, Hist. mss. 1-10, box 1/19, AMC.

8. See Acts 4:4, 31-32. This passage of Scripture is quoted in Solomon Beiler's position paper or letter of Aug. 24, 1862 (*Stoltzfus Documents*, doc. no. 25), p. 3, and referred to repeatedly in the following pages of this 10-page document.

9. Joseph C. Liechty, "Humility: The Foundation of Mennonite Religious Outlook in the 1860s," *MQR*, 54 (Jan. 1980): 17.

10. This interpretation of the Beiler-Peachey controversy is implied by John A. Hostetler, "Memoirs of Shem Zook (1798-1884): A Biography," *MQR*, 38 (July 1964): 286.

11. David Beiler, et al., to Bishop Moses Miller, Oct. 14, 1851 (*Stoltzfus Documents*, doc. no. 4).

12. Christian Brandt to Christian Graber, Nov. 15, 1855, *Mennonite Historical Bulletin*, 26 (July 1965): 6.

13. This lengthy proposal for a churchwide ministers' meeting may be found in *Stoltzfus Documents*, doc. no. 17. Deacon Stoltzfus' reference to "our articles of faith" is meant to refer to the Dordrecht Confession of Faith, which was drawn up 229 years previously, rather than 238 years, as stated in the document.

14. Shem Zook to John Stoltzfus, Nov. 7, 1861 (*Stoltzfus Documents*, doc. no. 19).

15. Deacon John Stoltzfus attended the annual conferences of 1862, 1863, 1867, and 1868. In 1864, when he found he would not be able to attend, Stoltzfus sent a note which was read to the conference assembled near Goshen, Ind. He wished the assembled delegates success and God's blessing (*Verhandlungen, 1864*, p. 11).

16. The many letters constituting the correspondence between Shem Zook and John Stoltzfus and between Christian Stoltzfus and John Stoltzfus may be found in *Stoltzfus Documents*.

17. *Verhandlungen, 1862*, p. 4.

18. [Joseph F. Beiler], "Millwood Church History," *The Diary*, 9 (Jan. 1977): 24.

19. Solomon Beiler wanted to make a few changes in the Ordnung of the Amish church, yet his thinking was more rigid than that of most of the change-minded ministers. His ten lengthy pages "From One Full Minister to Another Full Minister" resound with near-conceited assumptions that his interpretation of the Scriptures was the only possible interpretation and that where the Scriptures spoke to him he would not budge (*Stoltzfus Documents*, doc. no. 25).

20. John Stoltzfus' open letter of March 8, 1861 (see note 13), used the word *Conferenz*, as did the minutes already of the 1864 meeting (*Verhandlungen, 1864*, pp. 5-6). I therefore feel it is quite proper to use this term in referring to the ministers' meetings of 1862-78. The minutes of later ministers' meetings refer to the Conferenz repeatedly (*Verhandlungen, 1873*, pp. 3, 16, 25; *1876*, pp. 16, 20; and *1878*, pp. 5-8). See also Shem Zook to Deacon John Stoltzfus, July 23, 1868 (*Stoltzfus Documents*, doc. no. 53).

21. John Stoltzfus to his wife, Catharine, June 10, 1862 (*Stoltzfus Documents*, doc. no. 23).

22. *Verhandlungen, 1862*, pp. 15-16; *1863*, pp. 17-18; and *1864*, p. 19.

23. The printed minutes (*Verhandlungen*) of 1862 appear to be signed by Solomon K. Beiler, Samuel Yoder, Enoch Zook, and John Hertzler. On closer scrutiny it will be discovered that these signatures are in reality attached to an appendage to the minutes which constitutes an invitation to the second conference to be held in 1863 in Mifflin County, Pa. The fact that the four signatures are those of the ministry in Beiler's congregation supports this conclusion. Even more conclusive is the report which Bishop Elias Riehl of Union County, Pa., gave to his hometown paper on his return from the conference, stating that Shem Zook was the conference's secretary (*Union County Star and Lewisburg Chronicle*, June 17, 1862). This newspaper report is appended to doc. no. 24 in *Stoltzfus Documents*.

24. *Verhandlungen, 1862*, p. 4.

25. *Verhandlungen, 1862*, p. 3.

26. *Verhandlungen, 1862*, pp. 3-4.

27. *Verhandlungen, 1863*, p. 3. James Nelson Gingerich, "Ordinance or Ordering: *Ordnung* and Amish Ministers Meetings, 1862-1878," *MQR*, 60 (Apr. 1986): 191, suggests that Abner Yoder was proposing that the ministers' meetings be open only to ordained brethren. However, the restricting noun is *der Brüderschaft*, which should be translated "the brotherhood" rather than "the ministry." Nowhere in the records is there any indication that Amish laypersons were excluded from the conferences or that it was thought advisable to exclude them.

28. *Verhandlungen, 1864*, pp. 5, 7. For the way in which this new procedure was carried out, see pp. 10 and 16.

29. Gingerich, "Ordinance or Ordering," p. 197.

30. *Verhandlungen, 1862*, p. 4.

CHAPTER 9: Point of No Return, 1965

1. James Nelson Gingerich, "Ordinance or Ordering: *Ordnung* and Amish Ministers Meetings, 1862-1878," *MQR*, 60 (Apr. 1986): 190-95.

2. This Short Account bore the date June 4, 1862, just six days before the opening of the conference of 1862 (*Stoltzfus Documents*, doc. no. 22). John Stoltzfus may have referred to this document in a letter to his wife on June 10: "My writing was read today before the assembled congregation" (*Stoltzfus Documents*, doc. no. 23).

3. *Verhandlungen, 1864*, pp. 3-4.

4. *Verhandlungen, 1866*, p. 4.

5. *Verhandlungen, 1863*, p. 14.

6. Gingerich, "Ordinance or Ordering," pp. 196-97.

7. The identity of the "Elkhart congregation" has been mistaken by some historians. That it did not refer to the Amish settlement in Clinton Township, Elkhart County, as assumed by some, is clearly indicated by two separate entries in the minutes of the 1862 conference (*Verhandlungen, 1862*, pp. 5-6). In that record Joseph Miller represents the Elkhart congregation. This man served as bishop for the conservatives in the Newbury Township, Lagrange County, congregation from the time of the division (1854-57) until his death in 1877 (Hans [John] E. Borntreger, *Eine Geschichte der ersten Ansiedelung der Amischen Mennoniten und die Gründung ehrer ersten Gemeinde im Staate Indiana nebst einer kurzen Erklärung über die Spaltung die in dieser Gemeinde geschehen ist* [Elkhart, Ind.: by the author, 1907], pp. 9, 15). One must therefore conclude that the body referred to as the Elkhart congregation was the one located in Newbury Township, so named because it was situated in the area of the "forks" of the Little Elkhart River. Three entries in the minutes of the 1864 conference (*Verhandlungen, 1864*, pp. 4, 8-9) confirm my conclusion that the Elkhart congregation is not to be confused with the congregation in Clinton Township. Those notes refer to the difficulties *between* the Elkhart and the Clinton congregations. Clearly these two congregations were not one and the same.

8. *Verhandlungen, 1862*, pp. 4-5.

9. *Verhandlungen, 1862*, pp. 4-5.

10. A possible exception should be noted. The conference of 1863 discussed briefly a letter from the congregation in Lee County, Iowa, concerning "outward behavior" which was answered with scriptural quotations relating to personal adornment (*Verhandlungen, 1863*, pp. 9-10).

11. Conditions in this Butler County, Ohio, congregation received lengthy consideration in the 1862 ministers' meeting (*Verhandlungen, 1862*, pp. 7-8, 12-15).

12. *Verhandlungen, 1862*, pp. 8-10.

13. *Verhandlungen, 1862*, p. 15.

14. David Beiler, *Eine Vermahnung oder Andenken* (n.p., [1928]), pp. 12-13. A translation may be found in "Memoirs of an Amish Bishop," ed. and trans. John Umble, *MQR*, 22 (Apr. 1948): 106-07.

15. Concerning Abner Yoder's assignment, made by the conference in 1871, see *Verhandlungen, 1871*, p. 13. The report which followed may be found in *Verhandlungen, 1872*, pp. 6-8.

16. *Verhandlungen, 1863*, pp. 4-5.

17. Already in 1859, soon after Samuel Yoder had been advanced to full deacon, the word of his preaching activities had reached Lancaster County and David Beiler had heard that he was taking "his turn with the rest of [the] . . . ministers in the office of the Word [preaching]"; see Deacon John Stoltzfus to Solomon Beiler, Nov. 30, 1859 (*Stoltzfus Documents*, doc. no. 9). Solomon Beiler's quick and sharp reply to Deacon Stoltzfus' letter reveals great sensitivity to this accusation, suggesting that this complaint about his preaching deacon had already been comimg to his attention for some time; see Solomon K. Beiler to John Stoltzfus, Dec. 8, 1859 (*Stoltzfus Documents*, doc. no. 10).

18. Discussion in the 1863 conference concerning the duties of full deacons is recorded in *Verhandlungen, 1863*, pp. 7-8.

19. The dispute about deacons who preach is mentioned repeatedly in John Stoltzfus' correspondence of the early 1860s (*Stoltzfus Documents*, docs. no. 11, 12, 14, 15, 16 and 22). For a lengthier treatment of the question of allowing deacons to preach as it related to Full Deacon Samuel Yoder, see Paton Yoder, "The Preaching Deacon Controversy Among Nineteenth Century American Amish," *Pennsylvania Mennonite Heritage*, 8 (Jan. 1985): 2-9.

20. *Verhandlungen, 1863*, p. 17.

21. Shem Zook to Deacon John Stoltzfus, June 24, 1863, and David J. Zug to John Stoltzfus, Nov. 6, 1864 (*Stoltzfus Documents*, docs. no. 28 and 43, respectively).

22. The ministers' meeting at Pequea is mentioned or alluded to in a large number of documents in the Lydia Mast Collection (LMHL; available in *Stoltzfus Documents*, docs. no. 28, 32, 34, 35, 38, 39, 40, and 41).

23. John Yoder to Deacon John Stoltzfus, Apr. 1, 1864 (*Stoltzfus Documents*, doc. no. 34).

24. Beiler, *Vermahnung*, p. 29. An anonymous document found in the Lydia Mast Collection (LMHL), "Concerning the Matter That Pertains to the Ordination of Samuel Yoder as Bishop" (*Stoltzfus Documents*, doc. no. 35), certainly recorded a part of the conclusions of the Pequea conference. It suggests that the matter of Samuel Yoder's preaching was a principal concern of the meeting.

25. Shem Zook, *Eine Wahre Darstellung von dem welches uns das Evangelium in der Reinhart lehrt, so wie auch ein unparteiischer Bericht von den Haupt-Umstanden, welche sich in unterschiedlichen Gemeinden eriegneten, woraus endlich die unchristlichen Spaltungen entstanden sind* (Mattawana, Mifflin County, Pa.: by the author, 1880), p. 20.

26. John Stoltzfus to David J. Zug, Oct. 13, 1864 (*Stoltzfus Documents*, doc. no. 42).

27. See chapter 3 on the structure of the ministry. The attitude of some of the more conservative Amish brethren relative to ordaining a deacon as a bishop is reflected in John Umble's translation of an anonymous letter (the original of which has not been found) which reads as follows: "If in the year 1864 the seven bishops [at the Pequea ministers' meeting] would have followed the advice of the apostles . . . the Spirit would have shown it to them . . . that it is not fitting, in case of need, to take the ministers to the poor [the deacons] from their office and calling to which the Lord had appointed them and, at the request of the people, ordain a bishop" (box 18/22, Umble Collection, AMC).

28. Solomon Beiler's stubborn opposition to ordaining Samuel Yoder bishop is indicated in Solomon Beiler to Deacon John Stoltzfus, Sept. 6, 1864; Christian Ummel, et al., to Solomon Beiler, Sept. 7, 1864; Shem Zook to John Stoltzfus, Dec. 7, 1864; Shem Zook to John Stoltzfus, Dec. 17, 1864; and Shem Zook to John Stoltzfus, Dec. 26, 1864 (*Stoltzfus Documents*, docs. no. 40, 41, 44, 45, and 46, respectively).

29. Christian Ummel, et al., to Solomon K. Beiler, Sept. 7, 1864 (*Stoltzfus Documents*, doc. no. 41).

30. Solomon Beiler wrote of this state of affairs in his home congregation in a letter, presumably to Deacon John Stoltzfus, July 31, 1864 (*Stoltzfus Documents*, doc. no. 38).

31. *Verhandlungen, 1864*, pp. 8, 10.

32. See note 28, above.

33. Shem Zook to John Stoltzfus, May 8, 1865 (*Stoltzfus Documents*, doc. no. 48). See also Shem Zook to John Stoltzfus, Mar. 18, 1865, ibid., doc. no. 47.

34. Shem Zook to John Stoltzfus, Aug. 11, 1865 (*Stoltzfus Documents*, doc. no. 49).

35. Shem Zook to John Stoltzfus, July 6, 1866 (*Stoltzfus Documents*, doc. no. 51).

36. Shem Zook to John Stoltzfus, Nov. 14, 1868 (*Stoltzfus Documents*, doc. no. 56).

37. *Verhandlungen, 1862*, p. 10.

38. *Verhandlungen, 1863*, pp. 16-17.

39. *Verhandlungen, 1864*, p. 7.

40. *Verhandlungen, 1863*, p. 9.

41. *Verhandlungen, 1864*, p. 12.

42. *Verhandlungen, 1862,* pp. 10-11.

43. *Verhandlungen, 1864,* pp. 9-10.

44. *Verhandlungen, 1870,* pp. 19-24.

45. *Verhandlungen, 1864,* p. 9.

46. Discussions in conference relating to voting and office holding may be found in *Verhandlungen, 1863,* pp. 14-15; and *1864,* p. 11.

47. *Verhandlungen, 1863,* pp. 8-9.

48. *Verhandlungen, 1863,* pp. 15, 17.

49. *Minutes of the Indiana-Michigan Mennonite Conference, 1864-1929,* comp. Ira S. Johns, J. S. Hartzler, and Amos O. Hostetler (Scottdale, Pa.: Mennonite Publishing House [ca. 1929]), p. 305.

50. *Verhandlungen, 1864,* p. 4.

51. See note 7, above.

52. Borntreger, *Geschichte,* pp. 11-13.

53. J. C. Wenger, *The Story of the Forks Mennonite Church* (Middlebury, Ind.: Forks Church, 1982), pp. 20, 22.

54. A list of ministers who registered for the 1864 conference, along with their addresses, may be found in *Verhandlungen, 1864,* pp. 20-23.

55. *Verhandlungen, 1864,* p. 3.

56. *Verhandlungen, 1864,* p. 4.

57. *Verhandlungen, 1864,* p. 8.

58. *Verhandlungen, 1864,* p. 4.

59. *Verhandlungen, 1865,* p. 5.

60. I have translated this document from *Begebenheiten in der Amische Gemeinde von 1850 biss 1898* (Millersburg, Ohio: John Y. Schlabach [ca. 1963]), pp. 69-71. Harold S. Bender, using an unidentified manuscript copy which differs only in minor details from the above has provided an English translation in "Some Early American Amish Disciplines," trans. and ed. Harold S. Bender, *MQR,* 8 (Apr. 1934): 95-98.

61. Gingerich, "Ordinance or Ordering," pp. 190-91.

62. David A. Treyer [Troyer], *Ein Unparteiischer Bericht von den Hauptumständen, welche sich ereigneten in den sogenannten Alt-Amischen Gemeinden in Ohio, vom Jahr 1850 bis ungefähr 1861, wodurch endlich eine vollkomme Spaltung entstand* (n.p., n.d.), p. 7.

63. *Verhandlungen, 1865,* p. 5.

64. There was considerable opposition in Lancaster County to the annual conferences but also some freedom of choice as to attendance thereat by individual ministers. See [Deacon?] Daniel Mast to Deacon John Stoltzfus, May 8, 1864 (*Stoltzfus Documents,* doc. no. 36). This latitude, it appears, was not provided after 1868.

65. Evidently twentieth-century Old Order Amish also feel that the conference of 1865 in Wayne County marks the parting of the ways for the conservatives and the liberals. That booklet, *Begebenheiten* (see note 60), published in 1963 or thereabouts under Old Order Amish auspices, includes the *Verhandlungen* of 1862, 1863, and 1864. Instead of continuing with the *Verhandlungen* of 1865, however, the Amish compilers of this little volume chose to conclude this part of the book by inserting the resolutions of the conservative Holmes County meeting of June 1, 1865. This indicates that they did not consider as authentic Amish ministers' meetings the fourth (1865) of those annual conferences and the twelve conferences which followed.

CHAPTER 10: The Annual Conferences of 1866-78

1. A list of ministers who attended each annual conference and registered their names was appended to the minutes each year.

2. *Verhandlungen, 1868,* p. 24.

3. *Martin's Creek* [Ohio] *Mennonite Church Centennial Book* (n.p.; n.d.), p. 11.

4. Arletha Zehr Bender, *A History of the Mennonites in Croghan and Lowville (Lewis County) New York,* (n.p., n.d.), part 2 (pages unnumbered); Perry A. Klopfenstein,

Marching to Zion: A History of the Apostolic Christian Church of America (Fort Scott, Kan.: 1984), pp. 11-16.

5. Steven R. Estes, *Living Stones: A History of the Metamora Mennonite Church* (Metamora Ill.: Metamora Mennonite Church, 1984), p. 80; Steven R. Estes, *A Goodly Heritage: A History of the North Danvers Mennonite Church* (Danvers, Ill.: North Danvers Mennonite Church, 1982), p. 24; Willard Smith, *Mennonites in Illinois* (Scottdale, Pa.: Herald Press, 1983), pp. 66, 166.

6. William C. Ringenberg, "Development and Division in the Mennonite Community in Allen County, Indiana," *MQR*, 50 (Apr. 1976): 126.

7. Klopfenstein, *Marching to Zion*, p. 88; Benjamin Eicher, "Letter from Iowa," *Herald of Truth*, 5 (May 1868): 73; Melvin Gingerich, *Mennonites in Iowa*, (Iowa City, Iowa: State Historical Society of Iowa, 1939), p. 62.

8. Amos L. Fisher has studied the genealogical data presented in Hugh F. Gingerich and Rachel W. Kreider, *Amish and Amish Mennonite Genealogies* (Gordonville, Pa.: Pequea Publishers, 1986). In his introductory essay ("History of the First Amish Communities in America," p. xix) to that volume, he concluded that "probably no other one denomination has made such serious inroads into the membership of the early Amish church as has that of the Dunkards." Much of this process continued into and throughout the nineteenth century. For example, of the Amish in the northern end of Somerset County, Pa., in the nineteenth century, Fisher observes (p. xxi) that the "Dunkards gained many converts," and that many families "joined Mennonite, Dunkard, Lutheran and Reformed Churches."

9. For correspondence relative to settlements in Michigan and Minnesota, see *Herald of Truth*, 20 (Nov. 1, 1883): 330; 30 (Aug. 15, 1893): 258; 31 (Feb. 1 and Nov. 1, 1894): 42 and 321 respectively; and 34 (Aug. 15, 1897): 249.

10. For information concerning these three settlements in Tennessee, see Paton Yoder, *Eine Wurzel; Tennessee John Stoltzfus* (Lititz, Pa.: Sutter House, 1979), pp. 88-100 and 124-27; and John Christian Wenger, *The Mennonites in Indiana and Michigan* (Scottdale, Pa.: Herald Press, 1961), pp. 131 and 202.

11. Steven Dale Reschly, "From *Amisch* Mennoniten to Amish *Mennonites*: A Clarion Call in Wright County, Iowa, 1892-1910" (ms. submitted in partial fulfillment for the Master of Arts degree at the University of Northern Iowa, 1987), especially pp. 47-89. Sanford C. Yoder has described the experiences of his youth in Wright County in *The Days of My Years* (Scottdale, Pa.: Herald Press, 1959), pp. 33ff.

12. John Umble, "Mennonites in Lyon County, Kansas, 1880-1890: A Memoir," *MQR*, 26 (July 1952): 232-53; David Luthy, *The Amish in America: Settlements That Failed* (Aylmer, Ont.: Pathway Publishers, 1986), pp. 125-28.

13. For examples of the many letters from outlying Amish Mennonite congregations to the *Herald of Truth*, see C. F. Detweiler, "From East Tennessee," 10 (Oct. 1873): 170; Charles E. Kuntze, "From Missouri," 4 (June 1867): 90; "Church News" concerning the congregation in Holt County, Neb., 22 (Mar. 1, 1885): 73; Frederick Funk letter concerning the congregation in Sherman County, Kan., 25 (Nov. 15, 1888): 345; announcement on the editorial page concerning the same congregation, 27 (Jan. 15, 1890): 24; report from Arapahoe, Neb., in "Correspondence," 29 (Jan. 15, 1892): 25. Reports of visitation trips to remote congregations taken by bishops from established Amish Mennonite communities also abound in the *Herald of Truth*: report of a tour taken by Bishop Joseph Burkey of Tiskilwa, Ill., to scattered congregations in Kansas, 24 (Mar. 1, 1887): 74; report of Joseph Yoder's trip to Missouri and Kansas, 25 (Feb. 15, 1888): 75-76; and J. P. Smucker's trip to the West Coast in "Returned Home," 26 (Dec. 1, 1889): 362-63.

14. David Luthy, "Three Somerset County Amish Settlements," *Family Life* (Feb. 1982), p. 27; Fisher, "First Amish Communities," p. xxi.

15. Alvin J. Beachy, "The Amish Settlement in Somerset County, Pennsylvania," *MQR*, 28 (Oct. 1954): 269-90; David Luthy, "Somerset County," (Jan. 1982), pp. 17-18; and (Feb. 1982), pp. 26-27.

16. John S. Umble, "The Amish Mennonites of Union County, Pennsylvania: II. A History of the Settlement," *MQR*, 7 (July 1933): 182-86; David Luthy, *Amish in America*, pp. 427-28. Most of the Christian Stoltzfus clan moved away from the settlement in Lyon County, Kan., in the early 1890s, although the final disintegration of that settlement did not take place until after the turn of the century.

17. David Luthy, *Amish in America*, pp. 432-33. Lamenting the essential demise of the Tuscarora Valley and the Buffalo Valley congregations, a correspondent from Mifflin County wrote to the *Herald of Truth* (29 [Dec. 1, 1892]: 362-63): "Twenty-five years ago, ministers came to [share ministerial duties with] us from the adjoining counties of Juniata and Union. Now the churches in those counties which fellowshiped [with] us . . . are without ministers. One is broken up entirely, the other much reduced in number and without a minister."

18. Steven R. Estes, *A Goodly Heritage*, pp. 69-70.

19. In the conference of 1868 Shem Zook actually took part briefly in the discussion about reporting a thief to a local law enforcement agency. Later in that conference he reported on his progress in getting free passes on the railroad for the ministers (*Verhandlungen, 1868*, pp. 7, 12). Zook probably supervised the printing of the minutes for most of the conferences through that of 1868 and raised the needed money for this purpose; see Shem Zook to Deacon John Stoltzfus, July 18, 1864; May 8, 1865; July 23, 1868; and Nov. 16, 1868 (*Stoltzfus Documents*, docs. no. 37, 48, 53, and 57, respectively).

20. Christian Erismann, "Kurtze [*sic*] Lebensbeschreibung und Tagebuch" (ms. in AMC), p. 37.

21. Joseph Stuckey, "A Visit to the Churches in Iowa," *Herald of Truth*, 3 (July 1866): 56.

22. Reprint from the *Mount Pleasant Free Press*, May 28, 1874, in Melvin Gingerich, "Amish Ministers' Meeting, 1874," *Mennonite Historical Bulletin*, 3 (Dec. 1942): 1.

23. "The Mennonites," reprint from the *Pekin Times Press*, May 1875, in *Tazewell County Genealogical Society Newsletter*, 5 (Apr. 1893): 42 (photocopy in the Illinois Mennonite Historical and Genealogical Society Library).

24. This estimate is taken from an anonymous document (p. 2) found in the family Bible of Christian Stuckey. The ms. is headed "Religious Intelligence; The Amish in Conference." This heading and the style of writing used suggest strongly that it was written by a reporter for a local newspaper. The conference in question was "the Sixteenth Annual Conference" of the Amish Mennonites held "near Eureka." Clearly the reporter is describing that final Amish Mennonite general conference of 1878 held at Eureka, Woodford County, Ill. The Bible in which this ms. is located resides in the Illinois Mennonite Historical and Genealogical Society Library, Metamora, Ill. In succeeding notes this writing will be referred to as "The Amish in Conference." I am deeply indebted to Steven Estes for bringing this recently discovered document to my attention.

25. "The Amish in Conference"; see note 24. In 1875 the conference was held at Hopedale, Ill., in a "mammoth red barn, with a speaker's stand erected near the middle," according to "The Mennonites" (note 23).

26. Editorial in the *Herald of Truth*, 7 (July 1870): 104.

27. The late Martin E. Ressler of Quarryville, Pa., research specialist on Mennonite and Amish hymnals, has supplied this information (Martin E. Ressler to Paton Yoder, Aug., 1983). The first edition of this book is dated 1860, but the edition used in these conferences was either that of 1864, 1867, or 1870, all three of which have identical page numbering, and were printed at Lancaster, Pa., by John Bär's Sons.

28. *Verhandlungen, 1868*, pp. 11, 13.

29. *Verhandlungen, 1871*, pp. 12-13.

30. *Verhandlungen, 1873*, pp. 29-34.

31. *Verhandlungen, 1875*, pp. 27-40.

32. These rules of order were reinserted in the minutes of the conferences of 1868, 1870, and 1873-76. They are affirmed without insertion in the minutes of 1869. The minutes of 1871, 1872, and 1878 contain no reference to these rules.

33. *Verhandlungen, 1866,* pp. 4-5.

34. *Verhandlungen, 1864,* p. 8.

35. *Verhandlungen, 1867,* p. 4.

36. *Verhandlungen, 1863,* p. 14.

37. Bishops Jonas D. Troyer and Isaac Schmucker made an apology to the conference of 1864 for ordaining a full deacon without requiring the customary probationary period (as called for by a ruling of 1862). It therefore seems probable that these men were the guilty parties in question (*Verhandlungen, 1862,* p. 9; and *1864,* pp. 5-6).

38. James N. Gingerich, "Ordinance or Ordering: *Ordnung* and Amish Ministers Meetings, 1862-78," *MQR,* 60 (Apr. 1986): 194-95.

39. *Verhandlungen, 1872,* p. 28.

40. *Verhandlungen, 1875,* pp. 19-20.

41. *Verhandlungen, 1876,* p. 16.

42. *Verhandlungen, 1870,* pp. 18-19.

43. Shem Zook's letter to Deacon John Stoltzfus, July 6, 1866 (*Stoltzfus Documents,* doc. no. 51), suggests a possible additional instance of the use of sanctions by the conference. He wrote that in the conference of the preceding May "the ministers from one congregation were set back." This may have been the Gridley, Ill., congregation or, more likely, the troublesome splinter group in Fulton County, Ohio, under Jacob Rupp's leadership. In any case it appears that the conference took to itself the power of denying delegate status to certain ministers who were bona fide representatives of a congregation to the conference.

44. *Verhandlungen, 1871,* pp. 5-6.

45. This information was reported to Shem Zook by Bishop Jonathan Yoder; see Shem Zook to Deacon John Stoltzfus, Nov. 14, 1868 (*Stoltzfus Documents,* doc. no. 56).

46. *Verhandlungen, 1874,* p. 7; and *1878,* pp. 5-6.

47. *Verhandlungen, 1870,* pp. 19-24.

48. Discussions and personal admonitions encouraging voluntary intercongregational and especially interregional visitation by ministers may be found in *Verhandlungen, 1873,* pp. 11 and 27-28; and *1874,* pp. 12-13.

49. Autobiography of Henry Egli, pp. 1-3, as translated by Mrs. Emma Steury. The original of this autobiography is apparently lost. A photocopy of Mrs. Steury's longhand translation resides in the AMC, along with a typescript copy. The page numbers above and later refer to the typescript copy. See also Stan Nussbaum, *You Must Be Born Again: A History of the Evangelical Mennonite Church* (Fort Wayne, Ind.: [Evangelical Mennonite Church], 1980), pp. 2-3 and 8.

50. Ringenberg, "Allen County, Indiana," p. 125.

51. Henry Egli to Peter Litwiller, Dec. 30, 1864, *Mennonite Historical Bulletin,* 23 (July 1962). The original resides in Hist mss. 1-10, box 1/19, AMC.

52. Egli's Autobiography, p. 10.

53. Nussbaum, *Evangelical Mennonite Church,* p. 8.

54. J. S. Hartzler and Daniel Kauffman, *Mennonite Church History,* (Scottdale, Pa.: Mennonite Book and Tract Society, 1905), p. 147.

55. *Verhandlungen, 1863,* pp. 5-8.

56. Orlando R. Grieser and Ervin Beck, Jr., *Out of the Wilderness; History of the Central Mennonite Church, 1835-1960* (Grand Rapids, Mich.: Dean-Hicks Co., 1960), pp. 65-67.

57. *Verhandlungen, 1864,* p. 4.

58. The conference minutes of 1865 make no mention of Rupp's petition. The minutes of 1866, however, record that Jacob Rupp had submitted such a paper the preceding year and that an investigating committee had then been appointed (*Verhandlungen, 1866,* pp. 6-7).

59. Compare *Verhandlungen, 1866*, p. 6, with Joseph Stuckey, "A Visit to the Churches in Iowa, *Herald of Truth*, 3 (July 1866): 56-57. I am indebted to Steven Estes for this explanation concerning the "congregation in Livingston Co., Ill." Several references, mostly favorable, to the "Eikleys" [the Egli Amish Mennonites] at Gridley, Ill., may be found in Christian Erismann's "Tagebuch," entries for December 19, 1867, Dec. 4, 1870, and Dec. 29, 1872.

60. *Verhandlungen, 1870*, p. 17. The questions are posed on pp. 12 and 15.

61. These articles by Henry Egli in the *Herold der Wahrheit* include the following:
a. "Die Eingezogenheit der Christen," 10 (Nov. 1873): 178.
b. "Essen und Trinken das Fleisch und Blute Christi," 14 (Nov. 1877): 167-68.
c. "Vom Friedensreich Jesu Christi," 14 (Dec. 1877): 183-85.
d. "Ein neu Gebot," 15 (Feb. 1878): 19-20.
e. "Säen und Ernten," 15 (Dec. 1878): 201-02.
f. "Die Sanstmüthigen," 16 (Mar. 1879): 85.
g. "Die Pfingsten," 16 (June 1879): 101.
h. "Jesu der wahre Helfer," 16 (Sept. 1879): 166.
i. "Der seligmachende Glaube," 27 (June 1890): 161-62.

62. See Henry Egli to John K. Yoder, Feb. 6, 1866, and Mar. 19, 1880; also John K. Yoder to Henry Egli, Apr. 7, 1880; in John K. Yoder Correspondence, AMC. Also see Henry Egli to John K. Yoder, Apr. 16, 1880, Hist. mss. 1-10, box 2/2, AMC.

63. Ruth Litwiller and Viola Gerig, *History of the Salem Evangelical Mennonite Church of Gridley, Illinois*, (n.p., n.d.), p. 7.

64. Grieser, *Out of the Wilderness*, p. 67.

65. Nussbaum, *Evangelical Mennonite Church*, pp. 43, 47.

66. The *Mount Pleasant Iowa Free Press*, May 24, 1874 (note 22). See also Samuel Floyd Pannabecker, *Faith in Ferment: A History of the Central District Conference* (Newton, Kan.: Faith and Life Press, 1968), p. 23.

67. Already in 1870 Eicher had attended the sessions of the General Conference of Mennonites at West Point, Iowa (Pannabecker, *Faith in Ferment*, p. 23). Within a year or two after the conference of 1874 at Wayland, Eicher was called to Cass County, Missouri, to help a group of about 50 persons who were in the process of withdrawing from Bishop Jacob C. Kanagy's congregation (*Sycamore Grove Centennial, 1866-1966* [Iowa Falls, Iowa: 1966], p.14). Kanagy blamed Eicher for this division and later wrote bitterly that Eicher "split this church the first time. . . . The members are [in 1894] scattered into the four winds after having a Law Suit among themselves" (J. C. Kanagy, presumably to Gideon Stoltzfus, Jan. [?] 6, 1894, in the Lydia Mast Collection, LMHL).

68. For extended accounts of Eicher's and Roulet's congregations, see Gingerich, *Mennonites in Iowa*, pp. 103-04, 106, 109, and 293 (Eicher), and 64-65 and 289-90 (Roulet); and Pannabecker, *Faith in Ferment*, pp. 23-25 and 85.

69. For the later history of the Butler County congregations, see W. H. Grubb, *History of the Mennonites in Butler County, Ohio* (Trenton, Ohio: by the author, 1916), pp.15-18; and Doris L. Page and Marie Johns, *The Amish Mennonite Settlement in Butler County, Ohio* (Oxford, Ohio: by the authors, 1983), pp. 32-35.

70. Gingerich, *Mennonites in Iowa*, p. 109.

71. An excellent extended account of the Stuckey division may be found in Estes, *A Goodly Heritage*, pp. 57-86.

72. *Verhandlungen, 1866*, p. 13.

73. *Verhandlungen, 1871*, p. 12.

74. *Verhandlungen, 1872*, pp. 7-8.

75. *Verhandlungen, 1870*, p. 18.

76. *Verhandlungen, 1865*, pp. 3-4.

77. *Verhandlungen, 1872*, pp. 7-10.

78. *Verhandlungen, 1872*, p. 14.

79. Several poems by Joseph Yoder of McLean County, Ill., had appeared in the *Herold der Wahrheit* during 1865; see his "Der Pharisaer und der Zölner," 2 (May 1865):

34; his "Heil," 2 (Nov. 1865): 91; and his "Seid ihr aber ohne Züchtigung, so seid ihr Bastarde, und nicht Kinder," in the same issue, p. 93.

80. This poem appears both in the German and in translation in Estes, *A Goodly Heritage*, pp. 291-300.

81. *Verhandlungen, 1872*, p. 21.

82. Estes, *A Goodly Heritage*, pp. 80-81; Smith, *Mennonites in Illinois*, p. 88.

83. Estes, *Living Stones*, p. 68.

84. Isaac Schmucker to J. K. Yoder, May 31, 1876; Elias Riehl to J. K. Yoder, June 21, 1876; and Isaac Schmucker to J. D. Yoder, Aug 1, 1876; in John K. Yoder Correspondence, AMC.

85. *Verhandlungen, 1870*, pp. 9-12.

86. Smith, *Mennonites in Illinois*, p. 88.

87. Estes, *A Goodly Heritage*, p. 90.

88. John P. King, "A Visit to Illinois," *Herald of Truth*, 9 (Dec. 1872): 188.

89. One of these traveling ministers, John P. King, submitted a log of this trip to the *Herald of Truth*, 9 (Dec. 1872): 188-89, mentioning the services at "Stuckey's new Meeting-house." A similar report of this tour by John K. Yoder, possibly also prepared for publication in the *Herald of Truth* but never appearing therein, may be found in the Christian Z. Yoder Collection (Hist. mss. 1-88, box 1, AMC). In "A Journey to Illinois," *Herald of Truth*, 9 (Dec. 1872): 189-90, Benjamin Eicher reported that he was present at that meeting on Oct. 10 in Stuckey's meetinghouse. Like King and Yoder, he made no mention of any confrontation of the eastern ministers with Stuckey.

90. Willard Smith (*Mennonites in Illinois*, p. 89) has recently corrected Pannabecker's mistranslation (*Faith in Ferment*, p. 35) of the term, *Die Einigkeit*, as it appeared in the *Verhandlungen, 1873*, p. 26. Stuckey told John K. Yoder that he, Stuckey, "ihn [Joseph Yoder] als Bruder hält, und auch mit zur Einigkeit gegangen sei." He was saying that he observed communion with Joseph and not that he was in full agreement with him in doctrine. *Die Einigkeit* was a term commonly used by the Amish when speaking of the Lord's Supper. Illustrations of this use may be found in Shem Zook to Deacon John Stoltzfus, Nov. 16, 1868 (*Stoltzfus Documents*, doc. no. 57); and in *Verhandlungen, 1872*, pp. 11-12. In the latter instance laypersons from Leo, Ind., asked the conference for "ministers and brethren to serve us and administer communion (*die Einigkeit auszutheilen*)."

91. *Verhandlungen, 1873*, pp. 25-26.

92. Estes, *A Goodly Heritage*, p. 94; C. Henry Smith, *The Mennonites of America* (Goshen Ind.: by the author, 1909), p. 251; William B. Weaver, *History of the Central Conference Mennonite Church* (Danvers, Ill.: by the author, 1926), pp. 95-97; Smith, *Mennonites in Illinois*, p. 91.

93. Smith, *Mennonites in Illinois*, p. 89; Weaver, *Central Conference*, p. 97.

94. Estes, *A Goodly Heritage*, pp. 85-86.

95. Pannabecker, *Faith in Ferment*, p. 140.

96. Smith, *Mennonites in Illinois*, p.90.

97. *Verhandlungen, 1873*, p. 26.

98. Jonathan P. Smucker's "Church Acount Book," entries for 1877, 1878, 1881, and 1899, Jonathan Smucker Collection (Hist mss. 1-219, AMC); *Herald of Truth*, 19 (July 1, 1882): 201; ibid. 21 (Oct. 1, 1884): 297; ibid 27 (July 1, 1890): 202; Henry Ringenberg to Menno C. Smucker, May 3, 1885, letter in the possession of Silas Smucker, Goshen, Ind.

99. Jonathan P. Schmucker, "Church Acount Book," page 2.

100. G. Z. Boller to the *Herald of Truth*, 19 (June 15, 1882): 185.

101. "Church News," *Herald of Truth*, 19 (July 1, 1882): 201.

102. News note from Danvers, Ill., *Herald of Truth*, 21 (Oct. 1, 1884): 297.

103. Notices in *Herald of Truth*, 22 (June 1, 1885): 168; and 23 (June 15, 1886): 185.

104. "Correspondence," *Herald of Truth*, 26 (Dec. 1, 1889): 361. See also

Pannabecker, *Faith in Ferment*, p. 36. A news item in the *Christlicher Bundesbote*, 8 (Nov. 14, 1889): 5, dates Yoder's visit to Danvers as Nov. 1-3. One is almost forced to conclude that Yoder made two visits to Danvers, the first being interrupted by the death of Yoder's grandson in Wayne County, Ohio.

105. Hartzler and Kauffman, *Mennonite Church History*, pp. 306-07.

106. James O. Lehman, *Creative Congregationalism: A History of the Oak Grove Mennonite Church in Wayne County, Ohio* (Smithville, Ohio: Oak Grove Mennonite Church, 1978), pp. 104-12. My account of Bishop John K. Yoder's visit to Stuckey's church in 1889 attaches considerably more significance to the event than does Lehman's.

107. Cordial relations continued between Stuckey and many of the congregations and ministers of the larger Amish Mennonite church described in this and the preceeding paragraphs. The *Herald of Truth* and the *Herold der Wahrheit* published entries about and from Stuckey. Samuel L. Pannabecker's observation therefore seems incorrect, that "following 1872 his [Stuckey's] reports to the *Herold der Wahrheit* decrease and practically disappear," and that "his travels [thereafter] are more in the direction of Iowa and Nebraska than Indiana and Ohio" (*Faith in Ferment*, p. 36).

108. Hartzler and Kauffman, *Mennonite Church History*, p. 149.

109. Pannabecker, *Faith in Ferment*, pp. 143-46, 155-59.

110. Pannabecker, *Faith in Ferment*, pp. 37-42.

111. Gingerich, *Mennonites in Iowa*, pp. 130-31.

112. *Verhandlungen, 1866*, pp. 9-10; and *1867*, pp. 5, 7.

113. John Umble, "Early Sunday Schools at West Liberty, Ohio," *MQR*, 4 (Jan. 1930): 17-22.

114. *Verhandlungen, 1862*, pp. 8-9; *1863*, pp. 7-8; *1864*, 5-7.

115. *Verhandlungen, 1867*, p. 9; and *1868*, pp. 11, 13.

116. Joseph Stuckey, "From Illinois," *Herald of Truth*, 5 (Sept. 1868): 137.

117. *Verhandlungen, 1875*, p. 23; and *1876*, p.16.

118. *Verhandlungen, 1878*, pp. 10-11.

119. *Verhandlungen, 1872*, p. 31.

120. This announcement, signed by Schmucker and his co-workers, appeared in the *Herold der Wahrheit*, 9 (Dec. 1872): 182-83; it did not appear in the *Herald of Truth*.

121. "General Conference," *Herald of Truth*, 10 (Jan. 1873): 10.

122. John P. King to John K. Yoder, Sept. 25, 1876; and John K. Yoder to John P. King, Sept. 30, 1876; in John K. Yoder Correspondence, AMC.

123. See note 24, above.

124. *Verhandlungen, 1878*, pp. 3-5.

125. *Verhandlungen, 1878*, p. 8.

126. "The Amish in Conference," see note 24.

127. *Verhandlungen, 1878*, pp. 12-13.

128. *Herald of Truth*, 15 (Aug. 1878): 136.

129. A letter signed by four ministers from Logan and Champaign counties—Christian K. Yoder, John P. King, Moses Stutzman, and Christian Z. King—to John K. Yoder, April 22, 1878 (John K. Yoder Correspondence, AMC) reads like a call of desperation for Yoder's presence and help in investigating "how J. P. King stands in the congregation."

130. Hartzler and Kauffman, *Mennonite Church History*, p. 146.

131. *Mennonite Yearbook and Directory, 1905*, comp. J. S. Shoemaker, M. S. Steiner, and Aaron Loucks (n.p.: Mennonite Board of Charitable Homes and Missions, 1905), pp. 39, 43-44.

132. Hartzler and Kauffman, *Mennonite Church History*, p. 146.

133. Constant Reader, "A General Conference," *Herald of Truth*, 36 (Feb. 15, 1899): 51-52, with italics and parenthetical statements as they appear in the original article.

CHAPTER 11: Amish Mennonites

1. H[arold] S. B[ender], "Amish Mennonites," *ME*, 1: 93-98.

2. The many announcements in the *Herald of Truth* usually spoke of those affiliated with the conference as *Amish* (or *Omish*) *Mennonites*, but occasionally referred to them or to the conference as *Amish*, or Amish brethren (*Herald of Truth*, 11 [Apr., 1874]: 72; 12 [Sept. 1875]: 152; 14 [Mar. 1877]: 41; 15 [Mar. and Aug. 1878]: 46 and 136; 19 [June 15, 1882]: 185; 26 [July 15, 1889]: 216; 29 [April 15, 1892]: 120; and 34 [July 1897]: 218). The same group was occasionally referred to as the *Old Amish Mennonites* (*Herald of Truth*, 19 [June 1, 1882]: 170; 27 [Jan. 15, 1890]: 25). Christian Erismann, "Kurtze [*sic*] Lebensbeschreibung und Tagebuch" (ms. in AMC), entries for sometime in 1866 and Dec. 4, 1870, referred to the same group as *alt Amonischen Mennoniten* (Old Amish Mennonites), and in another entry (May 19, 1876) as *unsere alt Amischen Brüder* (our old Amish brethren). He spoke of the annual Amish Mennonite conference of 1866 as the conference of *Alt Amischen Mennoniten* (Old Amish Mennonites; entry for week of May 12-18, 1866). In the *Herold der Wahrheit*, 27 (Jan. 15, 1890): 25, John P. Schmitt wrote of a meeting in the "Old Amish Mennonite" meetinghouse. A similar use of *Old Amish Mennonites*, referring to the Amish Mennonite congregation at Hubbard, Ore., may be found in "Church News," *Herald of Truth*, 19 (June 1, 1882): 170. Daniel F. Driver, "Conference in Missouri," *Herald of Truth*, 26 (Nov. 1, 1889): 331, spoke of the close similarities between the "old Mennonite and the Amish Mennonite churches of Missouri and Kansas." He consequently invited the "old Amish churches" of those states to meet with the Mennonites in their next conference, thus using the names *Amish Mennonite* and *Old Amish* interchangeably.

3. *Mennonite Yearbook and Directory, 1905*, comp. J. S. Shoemaker, M. S. Steiner, and Aaron Loucks (n.p.: Mennonite Board of Charitable Homes and Missions, 1905), p. 49; David Luthy, "The Amish in Lewis County, New York," *Family Life* (May 1983): 24.

4. Deacon Christian Stoltzfus to Deacon John Stoltzfus, Oct. 20, 1868 (*Stoltzfus Documents*, doc. no. 54).

5. Deacon John Stoltzfus to Bishop Abraham Peachey, Nov. 8, 1868 (*Stoltzfus Documents*, doc. no. 55).

6. Bishop Christian Ummel, Daniel Mast, David Mast, David [F.] Stoltzfus, and Deacon John Stoltzfus, to Bishop Solomon K. Beiler, Sept. 7, 1864 (*Stoltzfus Documents*, doc. no. 41).

7. Shem Zook to Deacon John Stoltzfus, Mar. 15, 1869 (*Stoltzfus Documents*, doc. no. 58). See also Shem Zook to Deacon John Stoltzfus, Nov. 16, 1868 (*Stoltzfus Documents*, doc. no. 57).

8. John Stoltzfus, sojourning in Pennsylvania, to his congregation in Knox County, Tenn., July 2, 1877 (*Stoltzfus Documents*, doc. no. 65).

9. Ms. written by John M. Mast concerning the division of 1877 in the Conestoga Amish congregation and including also the Moses Hartz affair of the 1890s (box 11, Christian Z. Mast Collection, LMHL). The conservative Bishop John K. Stoltzfus, mentioned in Mast's account, was deeply concerned about this division, as indicated by a letter which he wrote while the split was in progress (*Golden Memories of Amos J. Stoltzfus*, comp. Christian P. Stoltzfus [Gordonville, Pa.: Pequea Publishers, 1984], pp. 183-85).

10. In large part the story of the division in the Conestoga and Lower Pequea congregations has been taken from J. Lemar and Lois Ann Mast, *As Long as Wood Grows and Water Flows: A History of the Conestoga Mennonite Church* (Morgantown, Pa.: Conestoga Mennonite Church, 1982), pp. 53-57; and Paton Yoder, *Eine Wurzel: Tennessee John Stoltzfus* (Lititz, Pa.: Sutter House, 1979), pp. 82-87.

11. A well-balanced account of the division in the Lower Pequea congregation may be found in [Joseph F. Beiler], "Millwood Church History," *The Diary*, 9 (Jan. 1977): 24, 20.

12. Stoltzfus, *Golden Memories*, p. 136.

13. Melvin Gingerich, *Mennonites in Iowa* (Iowa City, Iowa: State Historical

Society of Iowa, 1939), p. 133. I have relied freely on this source for specific details in relating the progress of the schism of the 1880s in Johnson County, Iowa. A near-primary useful source for the history of the Amish Mennonites of Johnson County, from which Gingerich drew, is "S[amuel] D. Guengerich, A Brief History of the Origin and Development of the So-called Amish Mennonite Congregation of Johnson Co., Iowa, Also Giving a Short History of Their Early Settlements in the State of Iowa." A typescript copy of this ms. is located in the MHL.

14. *Verhandlungen, 1866*, p. 10; and *1867*, p. 5.

15. *Verhandlungen, 1871*, p. 13; and *1872*, pp. 6-8.

16. Gingerich, *Mennonites in Iowa*, p. 134.

17. Sanford Calvin Yoder, *The Days of My Years* (Scottdale, Pa.: Herald Press, 1959), pp. 25-26.

18. S. D. Guengerich, "Brief History," p. 24.

19. Werey's imminent move to Johnson County, Iowa, was announced in the *Herald of Truth*, 21 (Mar. 1, 1884): 72.

20. C[hristian W[erey] to the Noah Troyers, Feb. 15, 1879, in L. Glen Guengerich, *Our Goodly Heritage* (Kalona, Iowa, 1984), p.49.

21. Gingerich, *Mennonites in Iowa*, pp. 136-37, 318.

22. Orland Gingerich, *The Amish of Canada* (Waterloo, Ont.: Conrad Press, 1972), pp. 68-70, 75-80. See also Lilian Kennel, *History of the Wilmot Amish Mennonite Congregation* (Baden, Ont.: Steinmann Mennonite Church, 1984), pp.7, 11, 14-17.

23. J. S. Hartzler and Daniel Kauffman, *Mennonite Church History* (Scottdale, Pa.: Mennonite Book and Tract Society, 1905), pp. 250-51.

24. Hartzler and Kauffman, *Mennonite Church History*, pp. 306-07; M[elvin] G[ingerich], "Western District Amish Mennonite Conference," *ME*, 4: 932-33; *Herald of Truth*, 24 (Dec. 15, 1887): 377; *Western District A*[mish] *M*[ennonite] *Conference*, comp. S. C. Yoder (Scottdale, Pa.: Mennonite Publishing House, 1912), pp. 9-10. A report of the 1890 conference appeared in the *Herald of Truth*, 27 (July 1, 1890): 204.

25. "Church News," *Herald of Truth*, 25 (May 1, 1888): 137; J[ohn] S. U[mble], "Indiana-Michigan Mennonite Conference," *ME*, 3: 29; *Minutes of the Indiana-Michigan Mennonite Conference, 1864-1929*, comp. Ira S. Johns, J. S. Hartzler, and Amos O. Hostetler (Scottdale Pa.: Mennonite Publishing House [ca. 1929]), p. 140.

26. "Report of the Proceedings of the District Conference of Amish Ministers in Wayne County, Ohio, March 22, 23, 1883," *Herold der Wahrheit*, 20 (Apr. 1883): 121-22. Jonathan P. Smucker, bishop of the Amish Mennonite congregation at Nappanee, Ind., read this "Report" and wrote to his son Menno that he thought "but little of" such regulations, or "at least some of them." "Time will tell," he added, "what the result of their Conference will be; yes it will show for itself" (J. P. Smucker to his son Menno, July 22, 1883, AMC.)

27. Sarah A. Bontrager to the *Herald of Truth*, 25 (May 1, 1888): 138.

28. H[arold] S. B[ender], "Eastern Amish Mennonite Conference," *ME*, 2: 130.

29. *Report of the Eastern Amish Mennonite Conference from the Time of Its Organization [1893] to the Year 1911*, comp. C. Z. Yoder (Sugar Creek, Ohio, 1911), pp. 1, 3, 5, 7, 9, 11-12, 14.

30. *Western A. M. Conference*, pp. 10, 16-17, 19-20, 24, 26, 28.

31. Hartzler and Kauffman, *Mennonite Church History*, p. 308.

32. *Indiana-Michigan Conference*, p. 143.

33. *Indiana-Michigan Conference*, p. 147.

34. *Indiana-Michigan Conference*, p. 152.

35. *Indiana-Michigan Conference*, pp. 60, 63.

36. "From One Full Minister to Another Full Minister" (*Stoltzfus Documents*, doc. no. 25, Aug. 24, 1862), p. 2.

37. S. D. Guengerich, "Brief History," p. 28.

38. Hans [John] E. Borntreger, *Eine Geschichte der ersten Ansiedelung der Amischen Mennoniten und die Gründung ihrer erste Gemeinde im Staate Indiana, nebst*

einer kurzen Erklärung über die Spaltung die in dieser Gemeinde geschehen ist (Elkhart, Ind.: Mennonite Publishing Co., 1907), p. 11.

39. David A. Treyer [Troyer], *Ein unparteiischer Bericht von dem Hauptumständen, welche sich ereigneten in den sogenannten Alt-Amischen Gemeinden in Ohio, vom Jahr 1850 bis ungefähr 1861, wodurch endlich eine vollkommene Spaltung entstand* (n.p., n.d.), p. 5.

40. Christian Erismann, "Tagebuch," entries for Dec. 25, 1865; Feb. 4, 1866; July 19, 1868; and Feb. 7, 1869.

41. An excellent account of the transition "From the Old Order to the New—The Final Step" in the Oak Grove congregation of Wayne County, Ohio, including a reluctant consent by Bishop John K. Yoder to the wearing of buttons and the shingling of hair for the men, may be found in James O. Lehman, *Creative Congregationalism: A History of the Oak Grove Mennonite Church in Wayne County, Ohio* (Smithville, Ohio: Oak Grove Mennonite Church, 1978), pp. 104-12. See Melvin Gingerich, "Sebastian Gerig (1838-1924): His Life and Times," *MQR*, 35 (Oct. 1961): 302, for an account of the discontinuance of the hooks-and-eyes requirement in the Sugar Creek congregation at Wayland, Iowa.

42. Having one's picture taken was denounced in the annual conferences as late as 1876. At the Metamora church photographs were forbidden but children's pictures were taken as early as 1864 (Steven R. Estes, *Living Stones: A History of the Metamora Mennonite Church* [Metamora, Ill.: Metamora Mennonite Church, 1984], p. 164). Photographs were specifically condemned by the Eastern Amish Mennonite Conference as late as 1899 (*Eastern Amish Mennonite Conference*, p. 12). The many extant photographs of Amish Mennonite people taken in the last quarter of the nineteenth century, along with private letters and memoirs, provide indisputable evidence that having one's picture taken was common practice among these people. In 1893 the use of musical instruments was condemned by the Western District Conference (*Western A. M. Conference*, p. 16). The congregation at Metamora in central Illinois continued to oppose the use of musical instruments although young men were allowed mouth organs.

43. This picture, with Gingerich's comments, may be found on the front page of the *Mennonite Historical Bulletin*, 26 (July 1965). See also the picture of the Jacob W. Kauffman family (ca. 1895-98) on the front page of the *Mennonite Historical Bulletin*, 28 (Jan. 1967). Jacob W. Kaufman was the grandson of "rich" Isaac Kaufman.

44. The term *Kennzeichen* is used in *Verhandlungen, 1872*, p. 8. See also C. Henry Smith, *Mennonite Country Boy: The Early Years of C. Henry Smith* (Newton, Kan.: Faith and Life Press, 1962), p. 132. See Melvin Gingerich, *Mennonite Attire Through Four Centuries* (Breinigsville, Pa.: The Pennsylvania German Society, 1970), p. 6, for a discussion of the change in rationale at the end of the nineteenth century for the wearing of plain clothing.

45. *Western A. M. Conference*, p. 27. In 1881 marriage with "a valued member of the Presbyterian Church" was allowed by the Metamora congregation (Estes, *Living Stones*, p. 164). See also *Indiana-Michigan Conference*, p. 151 (1892).

46. Entire document may be found near the end of chapter 9.

47. JFB, "Ordnung," *MQR*, 56 (Oct. 1982): 382-84.

48. Notation made by David Luthy (1983) on the first draft of my paper on the *Diener Versammlungen* of 1862-78.

49. *Indiana-Michigan Conference*, p. 144.

50. The principle that a minor deviation from the Ordnung becomes a gross sin, that of disobedience and rebellion, expressed repeatedly in the annual conferences (e.g., John K. Yoder's exposition of Matt. 18:15-17, *Verhandlungen, 1868*, pp. 9-10), remained a basic tenet of the Amish Mennonite church to the end of the century and beyond.

51. A Brother of the Amish Mennonite Church, "Matth. 18:15-17," *Herold der Wahrheit*, 4 (Mar. 1867): 36-37.

52. *Indiana-Michigan Conference*, p. 165 (1896). See also *Western A. M. Conference*, pp. 11, 16-17, and 29 (1891, 1893, and 1900).

53. *Indiana-Michigan Conference*, p. 67.

54. In 1902 someone asked (*Western A. M. Conference*, p. 32) whether shunning should be observed only "in the spiritual sense, or also in the daily repast." The inquirer was simply referred to article 17 of the Dordrecht Confession of Faith, which forthrightly described shunning as social ostracism. Two years later in the same setting (*Western A. M. Conference*, p. 36), the purpose of shunning was discussed as though the practice remained an essential instrument of congregational discipline.

55. *Verhandlungen, 1872*, p. 11.

56. *Verhandlungen, 1874*, p. 8.

57. "A Question" from "A Brother," requesting the "true meaning of I Cor. 5:9, 10, 11," *Herald of Truth*, 1 (Oct. 1864): 67.

58. P. S., "An answer to the Question on I Cor. 5:9, 10, 11," *Herald of Truth*, 1 (Dec. 1864): 81.

59. Letter signed, "I am also your Brother," *Herald of Truth*, 2 (Feb. 1865): 10-12. This same article appeared in the *Herold der Wahrheit*, 2 (Feb. 1865): 10-12, and was followed on page 12 by "Noch Eine andere Antwort über I Cor. 5:9, 10, 11." On the conservative side S. Z. (Shem Zook ?) submitted some writing by Menno Simons on shunning (*Herold der Wahrheit*, 1 (Dec. 1864): 79).

60. J. F. F., "A Question asked and answered," *Herald of Truth*, 2 (Mar. 1865): 22. Just two years later Funk entered an article by "A Pilgrim," which this time took the hard line by submitting a writing of Menno Simons on "The Duty of Shunning the Company of impenitent Members who have fallen into Sin" (*Herold der Wahrheit*, 4 [June 1867]: 81-82).

61. Lehman, *Creative Congregationalism*, pp. 86-87. Some of the correspondence between Ezra Yoder and his bishop uncle may be found in the John K. Yoder Correspondence, AMC. In Our Family Register, p. 67, a family history in manuscript form, J. Harvey Yoder and Alta Yoder Bauman have included a biography of Ezra Yoder. This ms. is in the possession of Alta Yoder Bauman, Lancaster, Pa.

62. John Umble, "The Oak Grove-Pleasant Hill Amish Mennonite Church in Wayne County, Ohio, in the Nineteenth Century (1815-1900)," *MQR*, 31 (July 1957): 172.

63. Jonathan P. Smucker, "Church Acount Book," entry for the year 1888 (Jonathan Smucker Collection, AMC).

64. Mast and Mast, *Conestoga Mennonite Church* p. 241.

65. See *Indiana-Michigan Conference*, pp. 9 (1864), 13-14 (1868), 26 (1876), and a report on the Mennonite conference held in 1883 at the Mt. Zion church in Morgan County, Mo. (*Herald of Truth*, 20 [Nov. 1, 1883]: 329), for the Mennonite position on shunning.

66. J. K. Zook, "Avoiding Expelled Members," *Herald of Truth*, 22 (Feb. 1, 1885): 37-38.

67. J. H., "Ist unsere Gemeine heute in gutem Zustande?" *Herold der Wahrheit*, 24 (Dec. 1, 1887): 353-54. This article did not appear in the *Herald of Truth*. Funk, however, again allowed the proponents of strict shunning to respond. The following month he printed an article by J. F. Swartzendruber which wholly defended Menno Simons' and Dirk Philips' position (*Herold der Wahrheit*, 25 [Jan. 15, 1888]: 17-18). One of the last articles which Funk accepted in favor of strict shunning was that of J[ohn] Gascho, Amish Mennonite from Ontario, Canada, "Ueber die Meidung," *Herold der Wahrheit*, 29 (Jan. 15, 1892): 20.

68. In the Metamora congregation, Metamora, Ill., and certainly among the Stuckey Amish, shunning had been discontinued by 1885 (Steven R. Estes, *Living Stones*, p. 164).

69. Hartzler and Kauffman, *Mennonite Church History*, p. 308.

70. John Umble, "The Background and Origin of the Ohio and Eastern Mennonite Conference," *MQR*, 38 (Jan. 1964): 60. According to Hartzler and Kauffman, *Mennonite Church History*, pp. 307-08, the western district of Amish Mennonites, in one of its ad

hoc conferences of the 1880s, decided that the practice of shunning expelled members should "be left open to the individual conscience of each member." However, no conference minutes or reports to that effect have been found.

71. John A. Hostetler, "The Life and Times of Samuel Yoder (1824-1884)," *MQR*, 22 (Oct. 1948): 238. See also "Church News," *Herald of Truth*, 19 (Oct. 1, 1882): 297. Some congregations and bishops, however, continued to be careful to observe baptism "in water" (in a stream), as well as "with water" (pouring). Note reports in the *Herald of Truth* of baptismal services at Walnut Creek, Ohio (26 [Oct. 15, 1889]: 313; and 27 [Sept. 1, 1890]: 266); and of services at Martin's Creek, Ohio (28 [Oct. 1, 1891]: 298).

72. Yoder, *The Days of My Years*, p. 27.

73. *"Text,"* a transliteration from the English, appears in the minutes of the 1876 annual conference (*Verhandlungen, 1876*, p. 27).

74. *Verhandlungen, 1873*, pp. 19-20; *Western A. M. Conference*, pp. 25-26 (1898), 27 (1899).

75. *Western A. M. Conference*, p. 16 (1893); *Eastern Amish Mennonite Conference*, pp. 5 (1893) and 11 (1898).

76. After the Civil War members of the Metamora congregation in Illinois voted freely in political elections (C. Henry Smith, *Mennonite Country Boy*, pp. 101-02).

77. Harvey Wish, *Society and Thought in Modern America* (New York, N.Y.: David McKay Company, 1962), p. 126.

78. *Verhandlungen, 1866*, pp. 10-11.

79. *Verhandlungen, 1873*, pp. 12-13, 15-16.

80. *Verhandlungen, 1873*, p. 15.

81. Lehman, *Creative Congregationalism*, pp. 74-76.

82. Abraham Mast, Church Record Book of the Walnut Creek congregation, Holmes County, Ohio, entries for Apr. 22, 1888; Apr. 2, 1891; May 6, 1888; June 17, 1888; Apr. 19, 1889; and June 3, 1889, respectively, photocopy in AMC.

83. *Indiana-Michigan Conference*, p. 153; *Western A. M. Conference*, pp. 10, 14; *Eastern Amish Mennonite Conference*, pp. 2, 4-5, 7-8, 13.

84. Steven R. Estes, *Living Stones*, p. 165.

85. C. Henry Smith, *Mennonite Country Boy*, p. 135.

86. Reported to me by my father, Silvanus Yoder.

87. Lehman, *Creative Congregationalism*, p. 76. The layman referred to was my grandfather, Jonathan S. Yoder.

88. *Herald of Truth*, 10 (June 1873): 104.

89. Thomas J. Meyers, "Amish Origins and Persistence: the Case of Agricultural Innovation" (ms. in MHL, 1983), pp. 18-20.

90. In the decades before the Great Schism, Amishman Frederick Swartzendruber of Johnson County, Iowa, maternal grandfather of S. C. Yoder, was usually the first one in the community to get a "new machine or devise" which had come on the market. "He owned the first McCormick reaper in the community. The same was true of the table rake, the Marsh Harvester, the self-binder, the hayrake, the corn planter, and the checkrow. The barn and grove were filled with these cast-off machines which had been set aside when new and better ones became available. The horsepower, treadmill, and portable steam engine, as well as the early types of threshing machinery, among which was the chaff piler, were also included in his equipment." Windmills encountered some resistance in the church, but soon Frederick got himself one of these also (Yoder, *Days of My Years*, pp 9-10).

91. Deacon John Stoltzfus to Henry U. and Malinda Stoltzfus, Dec. 16, 1881 (*Stoltzfus Documents*, doc. no. 106).

92. John Stoltzfus volunteered this information on the margin of a copy of his short Family History which he sent to Levi King. A photocopy is in my possession.

93. Melvin Gingerich, "Sebastian Gerig," pp. 307-08.

94. Willard Smith, *Mennonites in Illinois* (Scottdale, Pa.: Herald Press, 1983), pp. 67, 76. See also Estes, *Living Stones*, p. 35.

95. This statement from Sirach 27:2 was quoted by Deacon John Stoltzfus in the annual conference of 1868 (*Verhandlungen, 1868,* p. 11).

96. *Verhandlungen, 1868,* pp. 9-11; *1875,* pp. 12-13. In the 1893 meeting of the Eastern District it was declared not to be "upbuilding . . . for ministers or lay members to traffic in live stock" (*Eastern Amish Mennonite Conference,* p. 3).

97. *Verhandlungen, 1875,* pp. 9-10, 20; *1876,* p. 10.

98. *Verhandlungen, 1875,* p. 9. In 1893 the Western District Conference delegates agreed that owning "stock in corporations or stock companies . . . is inadvisable" because participation in lawsuits and use of force may be involved (*Western A. M. Conference,* p. 16).

99. Mast and Mast, *Conestoga Mennonite Church,* pp. 63-64.

100. John A. Hostetler, "Memoirs of Shem Zook (1798-1880): A Biography," *MQR,* 38 (July 1964): 283.

101. James Norman Kauffman, "My Autobiography," *Mennonite Historical Bulletin,* 28 (Jan. 1967): 2.

102. This picture has been preserved and until 1987 was in the possession of a descendant, the late Frank Yoder, of Davidsville, Pa. Recently it was given to the Conemaugh Township Area Museum of Davidsville.

103. *The Daily Tribune-Johnstown,* Oct. 18, 1886.

104. Erismann, "Tagebuch," p. 134.

105. Smith, *Mennonites in Illinois,* p. 79; Erismann, "Tagebuch," pp. 46, 89, 95.

106. Lehman, *Creative Congregationalism,* pp. 129-31. See also Silvanus Yoder, "Pioneer Mennonite Students at Ada, Ohio," *Mennonite Historical Bulletin,* 3 (Mar. 1942): 1, and (June 1942): 3.

107. Smith, *Mennonites in Illinois,* pp. 249-55.

108. C. Henry Smith, "History of the Institute," *Elkhart Institute Memorial* (n.p., Elkhart Institute Alumni Association, [ca. 1905]), p. 7.

109. Bryan Kehr, "John F. Funk and the Elkhart Institute," *Mennonite Historical Bulletin,* 46 (Oct. 1985): pp. 2, 6.

110. *Western A. M. Conference,* p. 19 (1895).

111. *Indiana-Michigan Conference,* p. 175 (1899). See also *Eastern Amish Mennonite Conference* p. 2 (1893).

112. John S. Umble, *Goshen College, 1894-1954: A Venture in Christian Higher Education* (Goshen, Ind.: Goshen College, 1955), p. 8.

CHAPTER 12: Toward Union with the Mennonite Church

1. "Correspondence" from Joseph Stuckey, *Herald of Truth,* 28 (Feb. 15, 1891): 57.

2. This term is borrowed from the writings of Theron Schlabach; see, for example, his "Reveille for *die Stillen im Lande:* A Stir Among Mennonites in the late Nineteenth Century," *MQR,* 51 (July 1977): 220, and his *Gospel Versus Gospel: Mission and the Mennonite Church, 1863-1944* (Scottdale, Pa.: Herald Press, 1980), p. 31.

3. *Verhandlungen, 1876,* p. 7.

4. J[acob] Hooley to [Gideon Stoltzfus], Mar. 9, 1896 (Lydia Mast Collection, LMHL). Although the addressee is not indicated in the letter, the original, in the possession of the heirs of Lydia Mast, resides in an envelope addressed to Gideon Stoltzfus, son of Deacon John Stoltzfus. Jacob Hooley of Kennard, Champaign County, Ohio, evidently a layman, was a first cousin to Catharine Hooley Stoltzfus, wife of "Tennessee" John Stoltzfus and Gideon's mother (Hugh F. Gingerich and Rachel W. Kreider, *Amish and Amish Mennonite Genealogies* [Gordonville, Pa.: Pequea Publishers, 1986], pp. 118-19).

5. Jacob Hooley to Gideon Stoltzfus, June 27, 1897 (Lydia Mast Collection, LMHL).

6. J. Denny Weaver, "The Quickening of Soteriology: Atonement from Christian Burkholder to Daniel Kauffman," *MQR,* 61 (Jan. 1987): 43-44.

7. Many articles and sermons illustrate that the first generation of Amish Mennonites held onto the traditional emphasis on obedience. For example, Benjamin Slegel of Gridley, Ill., wrote "Trostesworte für gottsuchende Seelen" (Comfort for God-seeking Souls), *Herold der Wahrheit*, 4 (May 1867): 75, written shortly before or about the time he joined the Egli Amish. In the same periodical see also articles by John P. King: "Wachen und schlafen," 10 (Apr. 1873): 55-56; "Das lebendige Opfer," 12 (June 1875): 83-84; and "Was Er euch saget, das thut," 12 (Aug. 1875): 130-32; and by Jonas D. Troyer, "Leget ab alle Bosheit," 3 (July 1866): 55.

8. Deacon John Stoltzfus to Gideon and Susanna Stoltzfus, July 27, 1885 (*Stoltzfus Documents*, doc. no. 69).

9. Joseph Yoder in "Correspondence," *Herald of Truth*, 20 (Dec. 15, 1883): 379.

10. *Western District A[mish] M[ennonite] Conference*, comp. S. C. Yoder (Scottdale, Pa.: Mennonite Publishing House, 1912), pp. 14 (session of 1892) and 24 (1898); *Minutes of the Indiana-Michigan Mennonite Conference*, comp. Ira S. Johns, J. S. Hartzler, and Amos O. Hostetler (Scottdale, Pa.: Mennonite Publishing House [ca. 1929]), p. 152 (session of 1892); p. 170 (1898); *Report of the Eastern Amish Mennonite Conference from the Time of its Organization* [1893] *to the Year 1911*, comp. C. Z. Yoder (Sugar Creek, Ohio, 1911), p. 9 (session of 1898); p. 12 (1899); p. 17 (1901). Although the phrase, "salvation of our souls" (*das Heil unserer Seele*) may be found much earlier than the 1890s (*Verhandlungen, 1875*, pp. 7-8), the term *Heil* sometimes should be translated "welfare" or "well-being," rather than "salvation." Furthermore, in the above reference the speaker was indicating concern about the welfare of "our souls," and not the souls of the unchurched.

11. Theron Schlabach, *Gospel Versus Gospel*, pp. 19-82.

12. Samuel Floyd Pannabecker, *Open Doors: The History of the General Conference Mennonite Church* (Newton, Kan.: Faith and Life Press, 1975), pp. 62, 71, 76-77. Eicher and Roulet were interested in missionary outreach already in the 1860s (Eicher, "Unsere Pflichten gegen unsere Mit-menschen," *Herold der Wahrheit*, 2 [Oct. 1865]: 86; and "Visits of the Apostles to the Churches," *Herald of Truth*, 4 [Apr. 1867]: 61; Phillippe Roulet, "Die Missions Sache," *Herold der Wahrheit*, 5 [June 1868]: 91); Steven R. Estes, *A Goodly Heritage: A History of the North Danvers Mennonite Church* (Danvers, Ill.: North Danvers Mennonite Church, 1982), p. 114.

13. Schlabach, *Gospel Versus Gospel*, p. 39.

14. "Report of the Annual Meeting of the Mennonite Evangelizing Committee, Held at the Salem Meeting House, Elkhart County, Indiana, Wednesday, January 20, 1892," *Herald of Truth*, 29 (Feb. 1, 1892): 43.

15. *Western A. M. Conference*, p. 12 (1891); and p. 24 (1898).

16. "Correspondence," *Herald of Truth*, 29 (Mar. 15, 1892): 88.

17. *Herald of Truth*, 25 (Aug. 15, 1888): 249.

18. *Western A. M. Conference* (1892), p. 14.

19. *A B C und Buchstabir-Büchlein* (New York, N.Y.: Amerikanischen Traktat-Gesellschaft, n.d.), p. 62. A copy of this booklet in the author's possession was "presented to Nancy A. Bontrager by the Sunday school, 1878."

20. This is J. Denny Weaver's definition of salvation as perceived by "prequickened" Mennonites and Amish Mennonites in "The Quickening," pp. 6-7.

21. Articles on assurance included John Fast, "Die Gewissheit der Seligkeit," *Herold der Wahrheit*, 19 (Feb. 15, 1882): 58; "Assurance; or the Certainty of Salvation," *Herald of Truth*, 19 (May 15, 1882): 145-46; and "Können wir es wissen?" *Herold der Wahrheit*, 25 (Oct. 1, 1888): 289-90.

22. For a fuller treatment of those articles on eternal security in the *Herold der Wahrheit*, see Paton Yoder, "The *Herold der Wahrheit* on Eternal Security," *Mennonite Historical Bulletin*, 47 (Apr. 1986): 2-4.

23. John P. Schmitt, reporting on the preaching of visiting Minister Joseph Gasho (*sic*), *Herald of Truth*, 22 (Feb. 14, 1885): 57.

24. C. Z. Mast, "The Life of Samuel Lantz," *Mennonite Historical Bulletin*, 15 (Jan. 1954): 5.

25. Weaver, "The Quickening," pp. 43-44.

26. Christian Erismann, "Kurtze [*sic*] Lebensbeschreibung und Tagebuch" (ms. in AMC), entries made in about 1860 (pp. 23 and 24); entries for Apr. 10, 1869 (p. 88); April 18 and 25, 1869 (p. 89); May 31, 1869 (p. 93); June 6, 1869 (p. 94); and, perhaps a week later (p. 96). Similar influences from the outside must have prompted Mrs. Joel (Elizabeth) Riehl—whose private Sunday school in her home in Buffalo Valley, Pa., preceded the organization of a congregational school—to observe that "other religions appear to have much more enthusiasm in their worship services than [we have] in ours, for they gather themselves week-long every evening to hold worship services" (Elizabeth Riehl to John K. and Lydia Yoder, Feb. 14, 1874, John K. Yoder Correspondence, AMC).

27. Jacob Hooley to Gideon Stoltzfus, Mar. 9, 1896 (see note 4).

28. Joshua King, presumably to John M. Mast, Morgantown, Pa., Nov. 19, 1899 (John M. Mast box, Christian Z. Mast Collection, LMHL).

29. Theron Schlabach, "Reveille," p. 220.

30. Marlene Kropf and Lois Janzen Preheim, "God's Constant Love," *Adult Bible Study Guide*, 51: no. 3 (Mar., Apr., May 1987; Scottdale, Pa.: Mennonite Publishing House, 1987), p. 12.

31. Weaver, "The Quickening," p. 44.

32. This role has been attributed to Bishop Yoder by James O. Lehman, in *Creative Congregationalism: A History of the Oak Grove Mennonite Church in Wayne County, Ohio* (Smithville, Ohio: Oak Grove Mennonite Church, 1978), p. 105.

33. "Correspondence," *Herald of Truth*, 27 (June 15, 1890): 186.

34. Lehman, *Creative Congregationalism*, p. 117.

35. *Herald of Truth*, 27 (Apr. 15 and May 15, 1890): 123 and 154, respectively.

36. See reports of revival meetings in Waterloo County, Ont.; Harvey County, Kan.; and Smithville, Ohio, in "Correspondence," *Herald of Truth*, 29 (Mar. 1, 1892): 73. J. S. Coffman's meetings in the spring of 1892 at Strasburg, Waterloo County, Ont., resulted in 100 decisions (*Herald of Truth*, 29 [Apr. 1, 1892]: 106). See also a report from Cass County, Mo., in "Correspondence," *Herald of Truth*, 29 (Aug. 1, 1892): 233.

37. Elmer Borntrager, "Borntragers of Bloomfield, Montana," *Mennonite Historical Bulletin*, 46 (Apr. 1985): 4-5.

38. Samuel W. Peachey, *Amish of Kishacoquillas Valley, Mifflin County, Pa.* (Scottdale, Pa.: by the author, 1930), p. 37; A. D. Zook, bishop in the Amish Mennonite church, at Allensville, Mifflin County, Pa., to John M. Mast, Nov. 21, 1895 (Christian Z. Mast Collection, LMHL). According to this letter John Yoder's ministry was taken away from him because he began to express dissatisfaction with many things and became a troublemaker, whereupon he joined the Peachey Old Order Amish congregation.

39. John Ringenberg to the *Herold der Wahrheit*, 1 (July 1864): 43.

40. Eldon Schrock, *100th Anniversary Edition of the History and a Pictorial Directory of the First Mennonite Church, Nappanee, Indiana* (n.p., 1975), p. 4.

41. Obituary of Mrs. John (Barbara) Ringenberg, *Herald of Truth*, 6 (Mar. 1869): 47.

42. *Herald of Truth*, 1 (Nov. 1864): 72.

43. John M. Brenneman, "Unity Among the Brethren," *Herald of Truth*, 3 (Mar. 1866): 17.

44. Isaac Schmucker, "Habt einerlei Sinn unter einander," *Herold der Wahrheit*, 3 (May 1866): 39-40.

45. *Verhandlungen, 1866*, p. 13.

46. Joseph Stuckey, "A Journey to Iowa," *Herald of Truth*, 5 (Aug. 1868): 121; Joseph Stuckey, "A Visit," ibid., 6 (July 1869): 105.

47. Daniel Brenneman, "A Visit—Thoughts and Suggestions in Relation to a Reunion," *Herald of Truth*, 4 (Jan. 1867): 11-12. Jacob Hahn of Clarence Center, N.Y., a fourth member of the delegation, may have been an Amish Mennonite.

48. *Herold der Wahrheit*, 4 (Feb. 1867): 25.

49. J. M. Brenneman, "A Journey to Indiana," *Herald of Truth*, 4 (Mar. 1867): 41.

50. I have found only one instance in the 1860s of exploratory conversations between the Amish Mennonites and the Mennonites of Pennsylvania and Virginia. It took place in 1867, when Jonathan K. Hartzler, Amish Mennonite of Belleville, Pa., visited the Mennonite congregations of the Shenandoah Valley in Virginia. The initiative in that case was taken by an Amish Mennonite. Said Hartzler after this visit, "Are we not really in the sight of God, one people?" (Jonathan K. Hartzler, "A Visit to the Shenandoah Valley," *Herald of Truth*, 4 [July 1867]: 106).

51. Daniel Brenneman, "A Visit to DeKalb and Noble County, Ind.," and J. M. Brenneman, "A Visit to Michigan," *Herald of Truth*, 4 (Dec. 1867): 185 and 187, respectively; John F. Funk, "A Visit to Noble and Whitney County, Ind.," ibid., 5 (Sept. 1868): 137; J. M. Brenneman, "A Visit," ibid., 5 (Nov. 1868): 172; Joseph Summers, "A Visit to DeKalb Co., Ind.," ibid., 6 (Jan. 1869): 10; J. M. Brenneman, "A Visit to Pennsylvania," ibid., 6 (July 1869): 105; Daniel Brenneman, "A Visit," ibid., 7 (June 1870): 89. See also Editor Funk's comments appended to Deacon John Stoltzfus' article on "The Amish Mennonites." Funk wrote of some inconsequential differences between Amish Mennonites and Mennonites which he hoped would soon become "entirely obliterated, and the distinction of names blotted out" (*Herald of Truth*, 10 [Feb. 1873]: 36).

52. Contrary to common opinion, although some issues were quite similar, the *Herold der Wahrheit* and the *Herald of Truth* were by no means the same paper in two different languages. In particular, the menu of articles appearing in each quite often differed.

53. *Herold der Wahrheit*, 1 (Dec. 1864): 79 and 84.

54. Joseph Stuckey, "A Journey to Iowa," *Herold der Wahrheit*, 2 (Dec. 1865): 101-02; J. D. Troyer's report on a trip to Logan County, Ohio, ibid., 3 (Mar. 1866): 20; Joseph Burkey, "Ein Besuch," ibid., 3 (May 1866): 42.

55. Shem Zook, "Glaubens-Bekenntniss der Taufgesinnten in Greichenland," *Herold der Wahrheit*, 2 (June 1865): 45-46; and Benjamin Eicher, "Unsere Pflichten gegen unsere Mit-Menschen," ibid., 2 (Oct. 1865): 86.

56. J[ohn] R[ingenberg], "Ein Brief von Elkhart Co., Ind.," *Herold der Wahrheit*, 2 (March 1865): 21; and Jonathan Zug to the *Herold der Wahrheit*, 2 (Nov. 1865): 94.

57. J[oseph] D[etweiler] to the *Herold der Wahrheit*, 13 (Mar. 1876): 57.

58. An exception should be noted; in 1868 the minutes of the annual conference were once more and for the last time printed by Johann Bär's Söhnen.

59. An indication of the position accorded Funk's periodicals by the Amish Mennonites may be found in the minutes of the annual conference of 1874; since no place for the next conference had been determined, it was indicated that, once a place had been found, it could then "be announced in the *Herold der Wahrheit*" (*Verhandlungen, 1874*, p. 14).

60. Daniel Kauffman, "Should There Be a General Conference of Mennonites?" *Herald of Truth*, 31 (Feb. 1, 1894): 35. Evidently in making this statement Kauffman was quoting someone else. He was clearly affirming, however, the one whom he was quoting.

61. Throughout this period of stalemate, Isaac Schmucker and the Haw Patch congregation maintained contact and continued to cooperate with the Mennonites at Elkhart. In 1880 John F. Funk preached at the first services held in the new meetinghouse at the Haw Patch (*Herald of Truth*, 17 [Feb. 1880]: 30). In 1884 J. S. Coffman held revival meetings there, resulting in seventeen applicants for baptism (ibid., 21 [Mar. 1884]: 73).

62. J. C. Wenger, *The Yellow Creek Mennonites: The Original Mennonite Congregations of Western Elkhart County* (Goshen, Ind.: Yellow Creek Mennonite Church, 1985), p. 204.

63. Lois Ann Zook, *Only a Twig: A Branch of the Zugs/Zooks from Pennsylvania* (Strasburg, Pa.: by the author, 1979), p. 47. In 1891 R. J. Heatwole (reporting on the joint Sunday school then in operation) referred to David [D.] Zook as "our young Amish

minister" (*Herald of Truth*, 28 [Apr. 15, 1891]: 122). The two congregations made common use of a schoolhouse, as indicated in David Luthy, *The Amish in America: Settlements That Failed, 1840-1960* (Aylmer, Ont.: Pathway Publishers, 1986), p. 133.

64. David J. Zook had charge of this small Amish Mennonite congregation until it merged with the Pennsylvania Mennonite church northwest of Newton. This merger probably took place in 1893, when the elder Zook moved back to Mifflin County, although it may have taken place as early as 1890 (Trennis King, *History of the Maple Grove Mennonite Church* [Belleville, Pa., ca. 1974], p. 42).

65. Wenger, *Yellow Creek*, p. 204.

66. C. Henry Smith, *Mennonite Country Boy: The Early Years of C. Henry Smith* (Newton, Kan.: Faith and Life Press, 1962), pp. 109-10.

67. Coffman's meetings at Oak Grove, held in 1885, preceded by almost five years that congregation's crisis of 1889, in which "series of meetings days or evenings" were first approved (Lehman, *Creative Congregationalism*, p. 111).

68. See J. S. Hartzler and Daniel Kauffman, *Mennonite Church History* (Scottdale, Pa.: Mennonite Book and Tract Society, 1905), pp. 268-69, for a general statement concerning the cooperation between Amish Mennonites and Mennonites in many areas of ecclesiastical activity, especially in cooperative evangelistic efforts.

69. For examples of cooperative meetings held by Coffman and Johns, note their visit to Cass County, Mo., in 1887 (J. S. Coffman, "Notes on My Trip," *Herald of Truth*, 24 [Apr. 15, 1887]: 120) and their shorter visit to the Howard County-Miami County congregation in 1888 (ibid., 25 [Nov. 15, 1888]: 345).

70. *Herald of Truth*, 27 (Apr. 15, 1890): 123; ibid., 27 (May 15, 1890): 154-55; ibid., 27 (Oct. 15, 1890): 314. James O. Lehman should be credited with alerting me to this unusual revival season in the area of West Liberty, Ohio.

71. "Correspondence" from Howard and Miami counties, *Herald of Truth*, 32 (Nov. 15, 1895): 345. In 1895, when David D. Zook of Harvey County, Kan., visited his boyhood home in Mifflin County, Pa., he and the small congregation to which he had been preaching in Kansas had recently joined the Mennonites of the Pennsylvania congregation (see note 64, above). Nevertheless he participated "in the services and also partook with us the bread and wine" in the Amish Mennonite church at Belleville ("Correspondence" from Mifflin County, ibid., 32 [Dec. 1, 1895]: 361). David signed his name in 1895 as one of "the preachers of the Harvey County, Kansas, congregation," along with six other Mennonite ministers (*Herold der Wahrheit*, 32 [May 1, 1895]: 138), providing firm evidence that he had joined the Mennonites by that date.

72. *Indiana-Michigan Conference*, pp. 22 (1874) and 83 (1903).

73. Joseph Yoder, "A Journey to Missouri, Illinois, and Kansas," *Herald of Truth*, 25 (Feb. 15, 1888): 58.

74. S. G. Shetler, "Bishop Moses B. Miller," *Gospel Herald*, 22 (Aug. 1, 1929): 380. See also Alvin J. Beachy, "The Amish Settlement in Somerset County, Pennsylvania," *MQR*, 28 (Oct. 1954): 269-72; and David Luthy, "Three Somerset County Amish Settlements," *Family Life* (Jan. 1982): 20-21 and (Feb. 1982): 26-27.

75. C. P. Steiner, "A Visit," *Herald of Truth*, 25 (Mar. 1, 1888): 74.

76. News item signed by J. D. Troyer, *Herald of Truth*, 23 (Mar. 1, 1886): 73-74.

77. An account of the reorganized congregation in Knox County may be found in Paton Yoder, *Eine Wurzel: Tennessee John Stoltzfus* (Lititz, Pa.: Sutter House, 1979), pp. 124-27. See also H. H. Good to the *Herald of Truth*, 26 (May 1, 1889): 139; and J. M. Shenk, "A Trip to Tennessee," ibid., 28 (May 1, 1891): 139.

78. Although a few Mennonites were evidently living in the Barker Street area during the era of Joseph Yoder and may have been using the same schoolhouse for separate services, they evidently had no resident minister ("Church News," *Herald of Truth*, 20 [Dec. 1, 1883]: 361). Joseph Yoder's move from Barker Street to Goshen, Ind., is indicated in the *Herald of Truth*, 23 (Nov. 1, 1886): 328. In 1891 the correspondent from Barker Street wrote to the *Herald* that "although this little community of believers is partly of old Mennonite and partly of Amish Mennonite extraction, the members work

together harmoniously for the cause of Christ," although the congregation is "still without a resident minister" (ibid., 28 [Sept. 15, 1891]: 283). By July 1 of the next year, Mennonite minister Harvey Friesner had become the pastor at Barker Street under Mennonite auspices (ibid., 29 [July 1, 1892]: 202). A "neat little meetinghouse" was built in 1893 (ibid., 31 [Feb. 15, 1894]: 57).

79. Composition of the settlement in Dickson County, Tenn., may be loosely determined by references to this colony in the *Herald of Truth* as follows: 28 (Feb. 15, 1891): 57; 29 (Mar. 1, 1892): 74; 30 (Apr. 1, 1893): 116; 32 (Mar. 15, 1895): 81; 32 (Apr. 1, 1895): 107; and 32 (Sept.1, 1895): 267. These references also indicate when traveling ministers visited this area. See also John C. Wenger, *The Mennonites in Indiana and Michigan*, (Scottdale, Pa.: Herald Press, 1961), p. 131.

80. "Correspondence from Dickson Co., Tenn.," *Herald of Truth*, 33 (Mar. 15, 1896): 89. Later, in 1911, after having been ordained a Mennonite bishop in Texas, A. I. Yoder was called back to Logan County, Ohio, to serve as bishop of the South Union Amish Mennonite congregation (John Sylvanus Umble, *Ohio Mennonite Sunday Schools* [Goshen, Ind.: The Mennonite Historical Society, 1941], p. 117).

81. "Conference in Missouri," *Herald of Truth*, 26 (Nov. 1, 1889): 331.

82. Invitations in the 1890s, of the Amish Mennonites to Mennonites to attend the former's conferences, as announced in the *Herald of Truth*, and vice versa, abound throughout the 1890s.

83. *Indiana-Michigan Conference*, p. 69.

84. *Indiana-Michigan Conference*, p. 162.

85. Bryan Kehr, "John F. Funk and the Elkhart Institute," *Mennonite Historical Bulletin*, 46 (Oct. 1985), p. 6. The congregation at Sterling, Illinois, was Mennonite, rather than Amish Mennonite, as Kerr mistakenly indicates.

86. Umble, *Ohio Mennonite Sunday Schools*, p. 399.

87. The "Proceedings" of this conference may be found in the *Herald of Truth*, 29 (Nov. 1 and 15, 1892): 326-27 and 340-42. Another news note on this conference is located in the "Correspondence" section of the *Herald of Truth*, 29 (Oct. 15, 1892): 314.

88. Roy H. Umble, "Mennonite Preaching: 1864-1944" (doctoral thesis, ms. in MHL, 1949), p. 206; *Indiana-Michigan Conference*, p. 305.

89. "Proceedings of the Second Annual S. S. Conference," *Herald of Truth*, 30 (Nov. 1 and 15, and Dec. 1, 1893): 338, 354-55, and 369-70, respectively.

90. "Proceedings of the Mennonite General Sunday School Conference held at the Pleasant Valley [Forks] M[eeting] H[ouse] in Lagrange Co., Ind., Oct. 3, 4, 5," *Herald of Truth*, 31 (Nov. 1 and 15, and Dec. 1, 1894): 330-32, 346-47, and 362-64, respectively.

91. The Sunday school conference movement in the Amish Mennonite and Mennonite churches throughout North America is ably described in Umble, *Ohio Mennonite Sunday Schools*, pp. 393-408.

92. A. C. Kolb, "What Does the S. S. Conference Do for the Church?" *Herald of Truth*, 37 (Sept. 1, 1900): 260-61. To Kolb's sectarian position John Horsch responded quickly and critically with an article in his own privately published paper, *Mennonitische Vierteljahrschrift* (Oct. 1900): 6-8, entitled "Eine Spaltung zu verhüten."

93. *Herald of Truth*, 8 (Aug. 1871): 122; and ibid., 9 (Sept. 1872): 138.

94. See Solomon K. Beiler's open letter "From One Full Minister to Another Full Minister" (*Stoltzfus Documents*, doc. no. 25).

95. Editorial, *Herald of Truth*, 17 (Feb. 1880): 30.

96. *Indiana-Michigan Conference*, pp. 32, 34, 39.

97. *Indiana-Michigan Conference*, p. 146.

98. C. P. Steiner, "A Visit in Logan and Champaign Counties, Ohio," *Herald of Truth*, 26 (Sept. 15, 1889): 283; Editorial, ibid., 26 (Oct. 1, 1889): 297. See also Editorial, "A General Conference," ibid., 27 (Feb. 15, 1890): 58.

99. M. S. Steiner, "The Solving and Resolving of Problems," *Herald of Truth*, 29 (Sept. 1, 1892): 257.

100. Daniel Kauffman, "Should There Be a General Conference of Mennonites?"

Herald of Truth, 31 (Feb. 1, 1894): 35-36; D. Z. Yoder, "A General Conference," ibid., 31 (Mar. 1, 1894): 76.

101. Report of the "General Conference Committee," *Herald of Truth*, 33 (Dec. 15, 1896): 373-74; Daniel Kauffman, "Our General Conference," ibid., 37 (Oct. 1, 1900): 291-92; LeRoy Kennel, "Origin and History of Mennonite General Conference" (ms. in MHL, 1953), p. 7.

102. "Report of Preliminary General Conference Meeting," *Herald of Truth*, 34 (Dec. 15, 1897): 371-72.

103. "Minutes of General Conference," *Herald of Truth*, 35 (Dec. 1, 1898): 363-64.

104. "Proceedings of the Second Mennonite General Conference," *Herald of Truth*, 37 (Dec. 1, 1900): 362-66.

105. Jacob C. Kanagy to [Gideon Stoltzfus], Apr. 10, 1892 (Lydia Mast Collection, LMHL).

106. J. C. Kanagy to [Gideon Stoltzfus], Jan.[?] 6, 1894 (Lydia Mast Collection, LMHL).

107. John Werey to John M. Mast, Feb. 11, 1896 (box 11, Christian Z. Mast Collection, LMHL).

108. J[acob] Hooley to [Gideon Stoltzfus], Mar. 9, 1896 (see note 4).

109. Joshua King to John M. Mast, Nov. 19, 1899 (box 11, Christian Z. Mast Collection, LMHL).

110. John M. Mast to David Zook, Jan. 28, 1895 (box 11, Christian Z. Mast Collection, LMHL).

111. J. C. Kanagy to [Gideon Stoltzfus], Jan. 6, 1894.

112. Joshua King to John M. Mast, Dec. 3, 1899 (box 11, Christian Z. Mast Collection, LMHL).

113. J[acob] H[ooley], to Gideon Stoltzfus, June 18, 1894 (Lydia Mast Collection, LMHL).

114. J. Lemar and Lois Ann Mast, *As Long as Wood Grows and Water Flows: A History of the Conestoga Mennonite Church* (Morgantown, Pa.: Conestoga Mennonite Church, 1982), p. 111; Otto J. Miller, *History of the Millwood Mennonite Church District* ([Lancaster, Pa.]: Historical Society of Lancaster Mennonite Conference, 1960), p. 9.

115. This statement is attributed to Bishop John A. Kennel of the Millwood congregation (Miller, *Millwood Mennonite Church*, p.16).

116. C. Z. Mast, "Samuel Lantz," p. 5; Grant M. Stoltzfus, *Mennonites of the Ohio and Eastern Conference from the Colonial Period in Pennsylvania to 1968* (Scottdale, Pa.: Herald Press, 1969), p. 148.

117. C. Z. Mast to Elmer Stoltzfus, Feb. 24, 1972 (original in the possession of the addressee, Goshen, Ind.).

118. Joshua King's correspondence with John M. Mast has been identified in earlier notes. That Deacon Joshua King visited Lancaster County in 1899 is indicated in a letter which he wrote on Nov. 19, 1899, to John M. Mast sometime after his return to Lawrence County (box 10, Christian Z. Mast Collection, LMHL).

119. Much of the story of the disturbance caused by Daniel Stoltzfus may be abstracted from three letters in the Christian Z. Mast Collection (box 10, LMHL) written by Samuel L. Kauffman, layman in the Millwood congregation, to his brother-in-law, John M. Mast, layman in the Conestoga congregation, bearing the dates Sept. 21, 1898; Dec. 5, 1898; and Mar. 26, 1899. Both of these laymen were married to sisters of Bishop Stoltzfus.

120. David Luthy, "The Amish in Lewis County, New York," *Family Life* (May 1983): 24; Ivan J. Miller, *History of the Conservative Mennonite Conference, 1910-1985* (Grantsville, Md.: by the author, 1985), pp. 176-180.

121. J. C. Wenger, *The Story of the Forks Mennonite Church* (Middlebury, Ind.: Forks Church, 1982), p. 23.

122. Eli D. Miller, *1876-1976: Townline Conservative Mennonite Church, Shipshewana, Indiana: A Brief Sketch and History of 100 Years* (Middlebury, Ind.: 1976),

pp. 8-9. The first bishop of Townline 'was Joseph Yoder, not John Yoder as indicated by Miller.

123. In the spring of 1900 Joshua King visited in northern Indiana and conferred with the ministry of the Townline congregation and found that Bishop "J[onathan] J Troyer & his help mates & Brother [Eli] Yoder & [John] Lugbill of Allen Co. Ind are not in favor of working with the Conference as they [*sic*] are conducted" (Joshua King to [John M. Mast], Apr. 12, 1900, in the Christian Z. Mast Collection, LMHL).

124. Eli D. Miller in interview with Paton Yoder, Sept. 6, 1984; Miller, *Townline*, p. 9. An historical survey of the Townline congregation may be found in Ivan J. Miller, *Conservative Mennonite Conference*, pp. 96-102.

125. William C. Ringenberg, "Development and Division in the Mennonite Community in Allen County, Indiana," *MQR*, 50 (Apr. 1976): 124; *Indiana-Michigan Conference*, pp. 320-21.

126. Herbert E. Zook, "A History of the Maple Grove [Lawrence Co., Pa.] Mennonite Church" (typescript ms. in MHL), p. 4. A considerable understanding of the reasons for this schism and some information on the steps leading up to it may be gained from letters written by Joshua King to John M. Mast in the years 1899 and 1900, and from formal statements drawn up by participants in the division, all of which may be found in the Christian Z. Mast Collection (box 11, LMHL).

127. Elmer Yoder and Paton Yoder, *The Hartville Amish and Mennonite Story, 1905-1980* (Hartville, Ohio: Stark County Mennonite and Amish Historical Society, 1980), pp. 9, 15, 24.

128. Zook, *Only a Twig*, p. 47.

129. John Yoder to Gideon Stoltzfus, Mar. 8, 1887 (Lydia Mast Collection, LMHL).

130. A[braham] D. Zook to John M. Mast, Nov. 21, 1895 (box 11, Christian Z. Mast Collection, LMHL).

131. A[braham] D. Zook to [John M. Mast], May 20, 1895 (box 11, Christian Z. Mast Collection, LMHL).

132. Jacob Hooley to Gideon Stoltzfus, June 27, 1897 (see note 4).

133. "Conferences," *Herald of Truth*, 34 (Sept. 1, 1897): 266.

134. C. Z. Mast to Elmer Stoltzfus, Feb. 24, 1972 (see note 117).

135. "Correspondence," *Herald of Truth*, 34 (Nov. 15, 1897): 345.

136. See Miller, *Conservative Mennonite Conference*, pp. 231-37, for a concise history of the Locust Grove congregation.

CHAPTER 13: Old Order Amish

1. *Verhandlungen, 1862*, p. 5.

2. For example, in 1890 the members of the Upper Deer Creek congregation in Johnson County, Iowa, drew up some special regulations and spoke of their church as the *Alt Amishen [sic] Gemeinde*, known as the Upper Deer Creek congregation (William Swartzendruber, et al., *Upper Deer Creek Conservative Mennonite Church Centennial Anniversary* [Wellman, Iowa, ca. 1977], p. 12).

3. Daniel D. Miller, "Die altamischen Mennoniten-Gemeinden," *Herold der Wahrheit*, 30 (Feb. 1, 1893): 34-35. A thumbnail sketch of the life of Daniel D. Miller may be found in David Luthy, *The Amish in America: Settlements That Failed* (Aylmer, Ont.: Pathway Publishers, 1986), p. 384.

4. *Mennonite Year-Book and Directory, 1905*, comp. J. S. Shoemaker, M. S. Steiner, and Aaron Loucks (n.p.: Mennonite Board of Charitable Homes and Missions, 1905), pp. 51-52.

5. Luthy, *Amish in America*.

6. Orland Gingerich, *The Amish of Canada* (Waterloo, Ont.: Conrad Press, 1972), p. 79.

7. Luthy, *Amish in America*, pp. 125-26, 328, 332, 376, 393, 449, 476.

8. "Correspondence," *Herald of Truth*, 29 (Mar. 15, 1892): 88.

9. Alvin J. Beachy, "The Amish Settlement in Somerset County, Pennsylvania,"

MQR, 28 (Oct. 1954): 291-93; David Luthy, "Three Somerset County Amish Settlements," *Family Life* (Jan. 1982): 18; Jane Anne Ping, *Where Past Meets Present: A History of the Arthur Amish* (Arthur, Ill.: 1975), pp. 30-31.

10. Melvin Gingerich, *Mennonites in Iowa* (Iowa City, Iowa: State Historical Society of Iowa, 1939), pp. 124-25; Ping, *Arthur Amish*, pp. 33-34.

11. J. Lemar and Lois Ann Mast, *As Long As Wood Grows and Water Flows: A History of the Conestoga Mennonite Church* (Morgantown, Pa.: Conestoga Mennonite Church, 1982), p. 58; Otto J. Miller, *History of the Millwood Mennonite Church District* ([Lancaster, Pa.]: The Historical Society of Lancaster Mennonite Conference, 1960), p. 5.

12. In 1887 Full Deacon Frederick Swartzendruber of the Johnson County, Iowa, Old Order Amish, wrote to Bishop Christian Peachey in Mifflin County, Pa., humbly inquiring of the latter about what to do with those who were going over to the Amish Mennonites in Werey's congregation at the Union church. He referred to the schism of the 1860s in Mifflin County, which Peachey had lived through. Then he observed that "you beloved brethren are better experienced in the Word and also in such evil circumstances" than the Iowa congregations (Frederick Swartzendruber to Christian Pietschie, July 6, 1887, in box 2/12 of the D. B. Swartzendruber Collection, AMC). The Heritage Historical Library, Aylmer, Ont., holds what is almost surely a copy of a copy of Christian Peachey's letter in reply to Frederick Swartzendruber's inquiry, signed by Peachey and others, but undated. The tone of this reply was ambivalent, but may have given Swartzendruber sufficient latitude to decide not to shun those who became members of Werey's congregation, a policy which evidently was eventually adopted (Gingerich, *Mennonites in Iowa*, p. 177).

13. Paul M. King, *The Old Order Amish of the Howard Miami Community* ([Kokomo, Ind.]: Kokomo Chamber of Commerce, 1967), p. 4.

14. Luthy, *Amish in America*, p. 476.

15. "Correspondence," *Herald of Truth*, 28 (Jan. 1, 1891): 10.

16. Luthy, *Amish in America*, pp. 213, 250.

17. Orland R. Grieser and Ervin Beck, Jr., *Out of the Wilderness: History of the Central Mennonite Church, 1835-1960* (Grand Rapids, Mich.: 1960), pp. 73-74. For additional identification of Jacob Graber see O[ra] A. Graber, *The Graber Immigrants: Ancestors—Descendants—Connections, 1650-1984*, (Bronson, Mich.: by the author, 1984), p. 77.

18. In 1880 the elderly Deacon Christian Stoltzfus, of Union County, Pa., wrote of his intentions to return to Lancaster County "to See My old friends at [the Old Order Amish congregational] Meating in Lower Millcrick. I have not been in there meating for a long time. I wish to see the peoble and dear friends which I hav not seen a goodmeny years, but I Doe not wish to take part in there meating no more then the[y] doe want me" (Deacon Christian Stoltzfus to C. and S. Zook, Aug. 2, 1880, in the Lydia Mast Collection, LMHL).

19. The retelling of the famous or infamous Moses Hartz affair (1892-97) requires a mini-bibliographical essay. Two accounts were written by eyewitnesses. Representing the Amish Mennonite interpretation is the detailed account by John M. Mast, my great uncle, which may be found in several stages of revision in the Christian Z. Mast Collection (box 11/10, LMHL). What appears to be Mast's final (handwritten) revision has been photocopied by his grandson, Harold R. Mast, and stapled together in 13 unnumbered pages entitled "Writings by John M. Mast Concerning the Conestoga Amish Church Including the Hartz Schism," and deposited with Mast's original document, as indicated above. The account of Amos J. Stoltzfus (1872-1947), who witnessed parts of the affair as a young member of the congregation, represents the Old Order Amish viewpoint. His account eventually appeared as a 4-page printed statement entitled "Ein bericht wie es begeben hat das der bahn twichen [sic] die Hausgemein und die Kirchgemein gekommen ist in der Conestoga valley, Lancaster County, Pennsylvania," a copy of which may be found in the Pequea Bruderschaft Library, Gordonville, Pa.

In 1983 Christian P. Stoltzfus, grandson of Amos J. Stoltzfus, reconstructed the Hartz affair, relying on the above sources; he also used what he recalled of the "many times" in which his grandfather "spoke openly" about it ("The Old Shepherd in the Conestoga Valley," ms. of 10 pages, in AMC). In 1912 J. D. Guengerich attempted to write an account of the Hartz affair, evidently using primarily Mast's account, in an 8-page printout entitled "Statement of Church Affairs from an Old Manuscript." A copy of this account may be found in the LMHL. See also Mast and Mast, *Conestoga Mennonite Church*, pp. 83-87; and *Moses Hartz Family History, 1819-1965*, comp. Amos and Susan Hartz (Elverson, Pa.: by the authors, 1965), pp. 6-7 and 28.

20. *Golden Memories of Amos J. Stoltzfus*, comp. Christian P. Stoltzfus ([Gordonville, Pa.]: by the author, 1984), p. 156.

21. Mast and Mast, *Conestoga Mennonite Church*, pp. 58, 83.

22. The source of this quotation is a copy made in 1980 by Joseph Stoll of an old writing found among the papers of Noah M. Yoder, Elk Lick, Pa. The document is headed "ABSCHRIFT VON DEM DIENER in LANCASTER CO. PA.," followed by "Ronks Lancaster Co. Pa. Oct 11, 1887." The copy may be found in the Heritage Historical Library, Aylmer, Ont., Canada.

23. Mast and Mast, *Conestoga Mennonite Church*, p. 84.

24. Amos J. Stoltzfus, "Bericht," p. 1.

25. Christian P. Stoltzfus, "The Old Shepherd," p. 2.

26. Amos J. Stoltzfus, "Bericht," p. 2.

27. Christian P. Stoltzfus, "The Old Shepherd," pp. 5-6.

28. John M. Mast, "Writings," p. 4.

29. John M. Mast, "Writings," p. 7.

30. The several accounts of the Moses Hartz affair disagree as to whether Moses and wife were taken into membership by the Conestoga Amish Mennonite church immediately before or immediately after they were excommunicated by the Old Order Amish.

31. Christian P. Stoltzfus, "The Old Shepherd," p. 4. See also Stoltzfus, *Golden Memories*, pp. 138-39.

32. Preacher David Beiler had strict views concerning the application of the ban and shunning. This is confirmed by a letter written by Beiler's brother-in-law, Samuel L. Kauffman, Dec. 13, 1897, in which he discusses the case of a certain C. Petersheim whose circumstances were somewhat similar to those of Moses Hartz. As in the Hartz case, Beiler was insisting that Petersheim "join their meeting before they can release him of[f] the ban" (Samuel L. Kauffman to John M. Mast, Dec. 13, 1897, in box 11/10, Christian Z. Mast Collection, LMHL).

33. Box 11/10, Christian Z. Mast Collection, LMHL.

34. Amos J. Stoltzfus, "Bericht," p. 4.

35. Christian P. Stoltzfus, "The Old Shepherd," p. 4.

36. Stoltzfus, *Golden Years*, p. 203.

37. Elmer S. Yoder, *The Beachy Amish Mennonite Fellowship Churches* (Hartville, Ohio: Diakonia Ministries, 1987), pp. 103-10.

38. David S. Beachy, "A History of Transaction That Occured in This Church of Moultrie Co., Ill." (Jan. 30, 1932, Perry Beachy Collection, Illinois Mennonite Historical Society Library, Metamora, Ill.).

39. J. E. Borntreger, "Ueber die Meidung," *Herold der Wahrheit*, 29 (Mar. 15, 1892): 82. For other statements by Amish writers on shunning, see F[rederick] Swartzendruber, "Haltet ihn als einen Heiden und Zollner," *Herold der Wahrheit*, 26 (Mar. 1, 1889): 68; J. F. Swartzendruber, "Nochmals über die Meidung," ibid., 29 (Jan. 1, 1892): 4-5; and D[avid] Stutzman, *Der schmale Verleugnungsweg: Eine kurze christliche Vermahnung an meine Kinder* (Millersburg, Ohio: by the author, 1917), pp. 106-08. Although Stutzman's writing falls in the twentieth century, his views are not far removed—if at all—from traditional late nineteenth-century Old Order Amish thought. It should be noted that the cataloger of Stutzman's book at the MHL indicates that D.

Stutzman was Daniel Stutzman; however, Eli Gingerich of Middlebury, Ind., a grandnephew of said Stutzman, says his given name was David.

40. The following statement, given to me by Eli E. Gingerich, minister in the North Barrens district, Middlebury, Ind., describes banning and shunning, and particularly the circumstances under which the ban may be lifted, as practiced in the Amish church in 1987:

"The practice of lifting the ban under certain conditions is upheld by most Amish Churches that fellowship together with the exception of the very conservative ones. There are some groups (Lancaster, Pa. and some others) that hold to the more strict non-lifting of the ban but still fellowship with those that lift the ban. There is a long-standing agreement between them that each will accept and acknowledge the other's policy of shunning or lifting, as the case may be. . . . [If a banned member] goes to a church that practices non-conformity (even though their Ordnung is different from ours) and upholds New Testament ordinances such as non-resistance, non-swearing of oaths, feet washing, the prayer veiling, the non-cutting of women's hair, and does not condone divorce and remarriage, TV and such, and [if] then that church acknowledges and duly lifts *them out of the ban* of the Old Order Church, then such an *Aufnahm* or admission [restoration] is acknowledged. This [is] after a probation period of at least six months, after which that member is expected to bring a church letter or *Zeugnis* that they are in good standing in the new church, and also are not causing trouble in the Old Order Church from which they came. The ban is then lifted and shunning is discontinued, and the matter is left between them and God."

A recently published booklet by "the Committee of 1968," a body of Amish ministers, entitled *Wer will die Leuken verzaunen und die Wege bessern? Ein Untersuchung und kurze Darstellung von Umständen und Begebenheiten in Holmes County, Ohio, durch Adams County, Indiana, nach Seymour, Missouri, von 1922 bis 1974, und Auskunften davon* (n.p., 1978), wrestles openly with the problem of the misuse of the discipline of shunning.

41. For an account of the division in Ontario concerning meetinghouses, see chapter 11.

42. Gingerich, *Mennonites in Iowa*, pp. 126, 133; Swartzendruber, *Upper Deer Creek*, p. 7.

43. The building of these two Amish meetinghouses was announced in the *Herald of Truth*, 27 (Aug. 1, 1890): 233. Concerning Sunday schools in the Deer Creek congregations, see *Herald of Truth*, 19 (July 1, 1882): 201.

44. Sanford Calvin Yoder, *The Days of My Years* (Scottdale, Pa.: Herald Press, 1959), p. 33.

45. Gingerich, *Mennonites in Iowa*, p. 307.

46. Yoder, *Days of My Years*, p. 34.

47. Gingerich, *Mennonites in Iowa*, p. 132; Swartzendruber, *Upper Deer Creek*, pp. 13-14; Centennial Committee, *A Centennial History of the Lower Deer Creek Mennonite Church, 1877-1977* (Kalona, Iowa: Centennial Historical Committee, 1977), p. 11.

48. Swartzendruber, *Upper Deer Creek*, pp. 12-13.

49. F[rederick?] S[wartzendruber?], "Unbiblische Spaltungen," *Herold der Wahrheit*, 29 (Mar. 15, 1892): 86.

50. David Luthy, conversation with the author, July 31, 1987; Gingerich, *Mennonites in Iowa*, pp. 275-76.

51. Gingerich, *Mennonites in Iowa*, pp. 259, 307-16. Edward Yoder, who taught at Hesston College in the 1920s, at Goshen College in the 1930s, and then moved on to the Publishing House at Scottdale, writes of his youth in the Lower Deer congregation in the first decade of the twentieth century and of his moving over to the East Union Amish Mennonite church in 1909 for baptism (Edward Yoder, *Edward, Pilgrimage of a Mind: The Journal of Edward Yoder, 1931-1945*, ed. Ida Yoder [Scottdale, Pa.: Ida and Virgil E. Yoder, 1985], pp. 66, 102, 105).

52. Alta Schrock, "Joel Beachy, Benevolent Amish Patriarch," *The Casselman Chronicle*, 17 (no. 2, 1977): 18.

53. Ivan J. Miller, "Maple Glen, Conservative Mennonite Church," *The Casselman Chronicle*, 17 (no. 1, 1977): 26-27.

54. Alta Schrock, "Joel Beachy," p. 18.

55. Beachy, "Somerset County," p. 283.

56. Alta E. Schrock, "The First and Last Amish Church Dinners," *Casselman Chronicle*, 21 (nos. 1 and 2, 1981): 24. Noah Wengerd, "History of the Old Order Amish of Somerset County, Pa.," (second installment) *The Diary*, 1 (Dec. 1969): 40, has said that the intrusion of the non-Amish coal miners in the Amish church dinners is to be associated with the building of meetinghouses. However, it seems much more logical to accept Alta Schrock's explanation, which associates this intrusion with the discontinuance of church dinners.

57. Beachy, "Somerset County," p. 278; David Luthy, "Somerset County," *Family Life* (Jan. 1982): 18.

58. Miller, "Maple Glen," p. 26.

59. John E. Borntreger to Joel Beachy, Jan. 17, 1881 (Heritage Historical Library, Aylmer, Ont.).

60. Ivan J. Miller, interviewed by the author, Mar. 18, 1984.

61. "Church News," *Herald of Truth*, 21 (Sept. 1, 1884): 264-65.

62. Beachy, "Somerset County," p. 281.

63. David Luthy, interviewed by the author, July 31, 1987.

64. The story of the division of the 1890s in the Grantsville area is well summarized in Ivan J. Miller, *History of the Conservative Mennonite Conference, 1910-1985* (Grantsville, Md.: by the author, 1985), pp. 144-46. See also Beachy, "Somerset County," pp. 279-80; and Wengerd, "Somerset County" (third installment), *The Diary*, 2 (Jan. 1970): 20.

65. Beachy, "Somerset County," pp. 280-81.

66. Beachy, "Somerset County," pp. 282-83.

67. Yoder, *Beachy Amish*, pp. 112-21.

68. Val J. Headings, Jr., "History of the Old Order Amish Mennonite Sunday School at East Center Congregation, Hutchinson, Kansas," *Mennonite Historical Bulletin*, 20 (Apr. 1959): 7. See also L. A. M[iller], "Daniel E. Mast," *ME*, p. 536; and David L. Miller, "Incidents and Observations in the Life and Faith of Daniel E. Mast, 1848-1930" (unpublished ms., a copy of which is in the possession of Daniel Hochstetler, Goshen, Ind.).

69. Elam Hochstetler, son of Samuel D. Hochstetler, and Daniel Hochstetler, grandson, interviewed by the author, Aug. 13, 1987.

70. This entire document as translated by Elizabeth Horsch Bender is taken from the *Mennonite Historical Bulletin*, 36 (Oct. 1975): 4, 6-7. In this version, for Bender's *brotherhood* translation of *Gemein*, I have substituted the word *congregation*. This congregation used *Mennonite*, rather than *Amish*, to indicate its church affiliation, because some of its members, including its leader, Jacob Graber, originated from the Montbéliard congregation in Europe, which commonly identified itself as Mennonite (communication from Joseph Stoll, Apr. 1988).

71. John E. Borntreger to Joel Bitsche, Jan. 17, 1881.

72. Stutzman, *Schmale Verleugnungsweg*, p. 174. This quotation from the Lutheran Bible, last clause of Luke 12:29, differs radically in meaning from the King James Version. Although the scriptural passage referred to may be translated otherwise than indicated, as an idiom it is translated entirely correctly.

73. David A. Treyer [Troyer], *Hinterlassene Schriften von David A. Treyer von Holmes County, Ohio, unter welchem sind auch mehrere Erbauliche und Geistreiche Gedichte*, 2d ed. (Arthur, Ill.: L. A. Miller, 1925), pp. 64-67. In the text the modern spelling *Troyer* has been used.

74. John A. Hostetler, *Amish Society*, 3d edition (Baltimore: The Johns Hopkins University Press, 1980), pp. 150, 364.

75. Anonymous, *Ein Riss in der Mauer: Treatise on Courtship* (Sugarcreek, Ohio: Raber's Bookstore, n.d.).

76. Frederick Swartzendruber, *Eine ernste Betrachtung über die Übertriebenen Mallzeiten und Hochzeiten* (Elkhart, Ind.: by several brethren of the Amish church in Iowa, 1895), p. 4. See also F[rederick?] S[wartzendruber?], "Christliche Nüchternheit und Mässigkeit," *Herold der Wahrheit*, 31 (Jan. 1, 1894): 10-11; "Missbrauch geistiger Gesänge," *Herold der Wahrheit*, 12 (Jan. 1875): 7; and an anonymous communication from Amish, Iowa, in the *Herold der Wahrheit*, 32 (July 1, 1895): a 4-page supplement inserted between pages 196 and 197.

77. Stutzman, *Schmale Verleugnungsweg*, p. 169-70.

78. Hostetler, *Amish Society*, pp. 346-47.

79. J. D. Guengerich, "Ueber Kleidertracht," *Herold der Wahrheit*, 25 (June 1, 1888): 162.

80. S. D. Guengerich, "Simplicity and Uniformity of Attire," *Herald of Truth*, 32 (July 1, 1895): 205.

81. David A. Treyer [Troyer], *Ein Unparteiischer Bericht von den Hauptumständen welche sich ereigneten in den sogenannten Alt-Amischen Gemeinden in Ohio, vom Jahr 1850 bis ungefähr 1861, wodurch endlich eine vollkommene Spaltung entstand* (n.p., n.d.), a 16-page booklet.

82. The first edition (203 pages) of Troyer's *Hinterlassene Schriften* was printed in 1920 by the Mennonite Publishing Co., Elkhart, Ind., and published by his grandchildren.

83. Articles by Troyer in the *Herold der Wahrheit* include "Weitere Erklärung betreffs der Taufe über den Todten," 12 (Dec. 1875): 198; "Wer aber beharret bis an's Ende, der wird selig," 23 (Jan. 15, 1886): 17-18; "Eine Erklärung," 26 (Oct. 15, 1889): 315-16; and "Wehrlosigkeit," 29 (Jan. 15, 1892): 18-19.

84. *Eine Geschichte der ersten Ansiedelung der Amischen Mennoniten und die Gründung ihrer ersten Gemeinde im Staate Indiana, nebst Einer kurzen Erklärung über die Spaltung die in dieser Gemeinde geschehen ist* (Elkhart, Ind.: Mennonite Publishing Company, 1907), 20 pages.

85. Borntreger's articles which appeared in the *Herold der Wahrheit* include "Die Furcht des Herrn ist der Weisheit Anfang," 21 (Feb. 1, 1884): 36; "Gedanken über die Ostern," 25 (Apr. 1, 1888): 97; "Ueber die Meidung," 29 (Mar. 15, 1892): 82-83; and "Ueber Glauben, Werke, und die christliche Liebe," 29 (May 15, 1892): 146-47.

86. Frederick Swartzendruber's support of missions is indicated in his "Mission unter den Heiden," *Herold der Wahrheit*, 31 (July 15, 1894): 209. In this article Swartzendruber called attention to John G. Paton's work among the cannibals of the islands of the South Pacific and to the book which told of his work, available from Funk's publishing company in Elkhart, Ind.

87. See note 76.

88. In addition to those articles referred to elsewhere, possibly the more significant of Frederick Swartzendruber's articles in the *Herold der Wahrheit* are "Der König Saul und die Harfe," 24 (Dec. 15, 1887): 370-71; "Sie gehen verloren," 25 (July 1, 1888): 196; "Haltet ihn als einen Heiden und Zollner," 26 (Mar. 1, 1889): 68; "Hiobs Söhne und Töchter, damals und jetz," 27 (Mar. 15, 1890): 82-83; and "Nicht zum wohlleben berufen, sondern zur Nachfolge Christi," 32 (Apr. 15, 1895): 113-14.

89. Articles by Frederick Swartzendruber in the *Herold der Wahrheit* on the functions of a deacon include "Was ist recht?" 26 (Dec. 1, 1889): 335; "Eine Frage," 28 (Sept. 1, 1891): 267; and "Der Armendienst," 28 (Sept. 15, 1891): 277-78.

90. Jacob F. Swartzendruber submitted the following articles to the *Herold der Wahrheit*: "Machet euch Freunde mit dem ungerechten Mammon," 23 (Feb. 15, 1886): 49-50; "Der knechtliche und der kindliche Geist," 23 (Dec. 1, 1886): 352-53; "Von der Meidung," 25, (Jan. 15, 1888): 17-18; "Nochmals über die Meidung," 29 (Jan. 1, 1892): 4. In 1915, when Bishop Jacob F. Swartzendruber's Upper Deer Creek congregation broke with the Old Order Amish, he and a few others left the congregation and affiliated with the Old Order house Amish of Sharon Township (Gingerich, *Mennonites in Iowa*, pp. 311-12).

91. A. Lloyd Swartzendruber, "Samuel D. Guengerich," *ME*, 2: 608.

92. *Deutsche Gemeinde Schulen, ihren Zweck, Nutzen und Nothwendigkeit zum Glaubens-Unterricht, deutlich dargestellt, nebst einen Plan, solche Schulen zu gründen und zu unterhalten, verfasst von dem Deutschen Schul Verein, in Johnson County, Iowa* (Amish, Iowa: by the author, 1897), 40 pages.

93. H[arold] S. B[ender], "Christlicher Jugenfreund," *ME*, 1: 585; but publisher Guengerich named it "Christliche Jugenfreund."

94. I am indebted to David Luthy for this synopsis. He has examined Guengerich's periodical at considerable length and has provided me with a short description and evaluation of it, from which I have borrowed freely.

95. *Herald of Truth*, 16 (Apr., 1879): 70; ibid., 18 (Dec. 1881): 208.

96. Much of the information concerning Samuel D. Guengerich is based on Gingerich, *Mennonites in Iowa*, pp. 132, 202, 266-68, 276, and 308-09. See also Swartzendruber, "Samuel D. Guengerich," *ME*, 2: 608.

97. In his later years, during the troublous times of 1912-15 in the Deer Creek congregations and the years which followed, Samuel D. Guengerich moved with his congregation as it migrated from Old Order Amish to Conservative Amish Mennonite.

98. One of these accounts was reproduced as "A Brief History of the Amish Settlement in Johnson County, Iowa," *MQR* 3 (Oct. 1929): 243-48.

99. Samuel D. Guengerich, "Jesus der Todes-Ueberwinder," *Herold der Wahrheit*, 26 (Apr. 15, 1889): 113-14.

100. See chapter 12 for the change of emphasis in Amish Mennonite soteriology in the latter decades of the nineteenth century.

101. David A. Treyer [Troyer], "Wer aber beharret bis an's Ende, der wird selig," *Herold der Wahrheit*, 23 (Jan. 15, 1886): 17.

102. Paton Yoder, "The *Herold der Wahrheit* on Eternal Security," *Mennonite Historical Bulletin*, 47 (Apr., 1986): 2-4.

103. J. E. Borntreger, "Ueber Glauben, Werke und die christliche Liebe," *Herold der Wahrheit*, 29 (May 15, 1892): 146-47.

104. Hostetler, *Amish Society*, pp. 78-79.

Index

The Author

Paton Yoder, now retired, has taught American history for forty years—at Westmont College, California; Taylor University, Indiana; Hesston College, Kansas; and Malone College, Ohio. He is a graduate of Goshen College (1935) and received his Ph.D. degree in history from Indiana University in 1941.

More than the above, however, Yoder's own roots qualify him to write this account of the Amish church in the nineteenth century. All of his forebears reach back to the Amish Mennonites and thus to the nineteenth-century Amish. He was nurtured, baptized, and reared in the Clinton Frame Mennonite Church, Goshen, Indiana, at a time when the congregation retained much of its Amish Mennonite ways. His understanding of Amish Mennonite attitudes and patterns of church procedures is virtually firsthand.

To this background is added his daily contacts with his Old Order Amish schoolmates and the many Amish neighbors of his youth. He recalls pleasant experiences over six seasons as a member of a threshing crew consisting in part of Amishmen, operating in predominately Amish neighborhoods.

There is thus an obvious basis for Yoder's sympathetic treatment of the Amish of the nineteenth century and of the Old Order Amish as they took on a separate identity at the end of that century. One of his regrets is that, in joining with the Mennonites and taking on their name, the Amish Mennonites have lost track of their roots.

Yoder is the author of three other books: *Eine Wurzel: Tennesee John Stoltzfus* (1979); *Tennessee John Stoltzfus: Amish Church-Related Documents and Family Letters* (1987); and *Taverns and Travelers: Inns of the Early Midwest* (1969).

Paton and his wife, Hazel Smucker Yoder, are the parents of five grown children and are members of College Mennonite Church, Goshen, Indiana.